Criminal Justice in Scotland

Edited by
PETER DUFF AND NEIL HUTTON
University of Aberdeen and University of Strathclyde

DARTMOUTH
Aldershot • Brookfield USA • Singapore • Sydney

Published by
Dartmouth Publishing Company Ltd
Ashgate Publishing Ltd
Gower House
Croft Road
Aldershot
Hants GU11 3HR
England

Ashgate Publishing Company
Old Post Road
Brookfield
Vermont 05036
USA

British Library Cataloguing in Publication Data
Criminal justice in Scotland
  1. Criminal law - Scotland 2. Criminal justice,
  Administration of - Scotland
  I. Duff, Peter, 1954- II. Hutton, Neil, 1953 -
  345.4'11

Library of Congress Cataloging-in-Publication Data
Criminal justice in Scotland / [edited by] Peter Duff and Neil Hutton.
  p. cm.
  Includes bibliographical references.
  ISBN 1-85521-890-9 (hb). -- ISBN 1-85521-899-2 (pbk.)
  1. Criminal justice, Administration of--Scotland. 2. Crime-
-Scotland. I. Duff, Peter. II. Hutton, Neil. 1953-
HV9960.G72S263 1999
364.9411--dc21   98-44662
                            CIP

ISBN 1 85521 890 9 Hbk
ISBN 1 85521 899 2 Pbk

Printed and bound in Great Britain by MPG Books Ltd, Bodmin, Cornwall

Contents

About the Editors and Contributors

Peter Duff is Professor in Criminal Justice in the Law Department at Aberdeen University. His major research interests are: the criminal jury; public prosecution systems; victims of crime; and comparative criminal procedure. Additionally, he has carried out several empirical studies of the Scottish criminal justice process for the Scottish Office. He has published in a wide range of legal and criminological periodicals and is the author or co-author of books on *Criminal Injuries Compensation, Juries - A 'Hong Kong Perspective*, and *Victims in the Criminal Justice System.*

Neil Hutton has an MA and PhD from the University of Edinburgh. He is currently a senior lecturer in the Law School at the University of Strathclyde. He has published work on a range of socio-legal topics but his recent writing has concentrated on sentencing and punishment. He is a member of the team which has developed the Sentencing Information System for the High Court and is a founding member of the Centre for Sentencing Research at the University of Strathclyde.

Simon Anderson is an Associate Director of the research agency System Three, which he joined in August 1995 to help set up a dedicated Social Research Unit. Among the recent projects he has been responsible for are a large-scale study of crime in rural Scotland, research into police-led initiatives for tackling underage drinking, and a study of police witness duty at court. Simon was previously employed at Edinburgh University, where he worked on the first Edinburgh Crime Survey and a large-scale study of young people and crime, and in the Central Research Unit of The Scottish Office, where he was responsible for the design, management and analysis of the 1993 Scottish Crime Survey.

Stewart Asquith holds the St Kentigern Chair for the Study of the Child and is a member of the Centre for the Child & Society and the Department of Social Policy & Social Work, at the University of Glasgow. He has written widely on children's issues and in particular on juvenile justice from an international perspective - particularly in the context of rapid social change in Central and Eastern Europe. His other main areas of interest are currently the commercial sexual exploitation of children (on which he has written reports for the Council of Europe) and children in situations of armed conflict.

Jon Bannister is a lecturer in Social Policy attached to the Centre for the Child and Society, in the Department of Social Policy and Social Work at the University of Glasgow. Jon previously held an ESRC fellowship in the Department of Urban Studies at the University of Glasgow. Jon has researched and published extensively on the issues of crime generally, the fear of crime and crime prevention. Jon (with Jason Ditton) has recently completed a major Economic and Social Research Council funded investigation entitled 'Fear of Crime: Conceptual Development, Field Testing and Empirical Confirmation'.

Michèle Burman teaches Criminology, Research Methods and Women's Studies in the Department of Sociology at the University of Glasgow, where she is also Director of the Criminology Research Unit. She has a long-standing research interest in women, law, sexuality and the criminal justice system and is the co-author of *Sex Crimes on Trial* and *Police Specialist Units for the Investigation of Crimes of Violence against Women and Children*. Her current research interests are sexual offences and the judicial process, and young women's use of violence.

James Carnie is Senior Research Officer in the Scottish Prison Service (SPS) and is responsible for the management and conduct of SPS's varied research agenda. He previously held research posts at the Universities of Edinburgh and Stirling and has undertaken consultancy work on criminological issues on various occasions for the Scottish Office. He has published widely in the fields of criminal justice and social welfare.

Derek Chiswick has been a consultant forensic psychiatrist for 18 years and is the visiting psychiatrist to HM Prison, Edinburgh. He is responsible for forensic psychiatry services in the City of Edinburgh. He was a member of the Parole Board for Scotland between 1983 and 1988 and its vice chairman from 1984 to 1988. He was one of the two psychiatrist members of the Home Office Advisory Board on Restricted Patients between 1991 and 1997. He is co-editor of *Seminars in Practical Forensic Psychiatry* (Gaskell Publications, 1995).

Clare Connelly is a Lecturer in Private Law at the University of Glasgow. Her research and teaching interests are within the fields of criminal law and sociology, focusing on mentally disordered offenders and battered women who kill violent men. She is currently undertaking research on provisions to deal with mentally disordered offenders, funded by the Scottish Office, and is reading for a Doctorate in the Department of Sociology, University of Glasgow. She is a qualified Solicitor.

Jason Ditton is currently Professor of Criminology and Director of Graduate Studies in the Faculty of Law at the University of Sheffield, and Director of the Scottish Centre for Criminology. He has been researching in Scotland for over 20 years, and has published widely on the use of illegal drugs (mostly concentrating on heroin, cocaine and ecstasy), on crime prevention (the effect of improved street lights and open-street CCTV on crime rates), and on the fear of crime.

Mike Docherty qualified as a social worker in 1985. Following a period with Barnardo's, he worked with Strathclyde Regional Council for over seven years as a social worker and senior social worker, working with children and young people in trouble and adult offenders. He then worked for three years as a lecturer in social work at Glasgow University, with his main areas of interest being social work in the Children's Hearing and Criminal Justice Systems. He is currently the Manager of the West of Scotland Consortium for Education and Training in Social Work.

Nicholas R. Fyfe is an urban geographer at Strathclyde University who has published widely on the inter-relationships between society, space and the criminal justice system. He is co-author of *Crime, Policing and Place: Essays in Environmental Criminology* (Routledge) and editor of *Images of the Street: Planning, Representation and Control in Public Space* (Routledge). He acted as an advisor to the Home Office on community-police consultation arrangements in England and Wales and has conducted research for the Scottish Office on police user surveys and the Strathclyde Police witness protection programme. He is currently working on a book exploring the links between geography, crime and policing.

Christopher Gane is Professor of Scots Law and Head of the Law Department at Aberdeen University. His research interests are domestic criminal law, criminal procedure and international criminal law. He is author, or co-author, of: *A Casebook on Scottish Criminal Law*; *Criminal*

Procedure in Scotland: Cases and Materials; *Sexual Offences*; and *Criminal Procedure Systems in the European Community*. He has published annotations to the Incest and Related Offences (Scotland) Act 1986 and the Criminal Justice (Scotland) Act 1987. He is author of reports on *Homosexuality and Human Rights and Related Matters* and *The Law and Procedure Relating to Offences of Fraud in Scotland*.

David Garland is Professor of Law and Sociology at New York University. He was educated at the Universities of Edinburgh and Sheffield and was Professor of Penology at the University of Edinburgh before moving to New York in 1997. He is the author of the award-winning books *Punishment and Welfare* (Ashgate, 1985) and *Punishment and Modern Society* (Oxford, 1990) and editor of *The Power to Punish* (with Peter Young, Heinemann, 1083) and *A Reader on Punishment* (with Anthony Duff, Oxford, 1994). He is the Editor-in-Chief of *Punishment and Society: The International Journal of Penology*.

Lesley McAra is a lecturer in Criminology in the Centre for Law and Society, University of Edinburgh. Her research interests are in the general areas of the sociology of punishment and the sociology of law and deviance. Her particular interests include: the interface between social work and criminal justice; juvenile justice; gender; crime and criminal justice; and the relationship between offending behaviour and mental health problems. She is currently co-director of an ESRC funded programme of research on youth transitions and crime. Recent publications include two volumes on aspects of social work and criminal justice and co-authorship of a report on community services for mentally disordered offenders.

Gill McIvor is Professor and Director of the Social Work Research Centre (SWRC) at Stirling University. Since joining SWRC in 1986, she has undertaken research into a wide range of social work services to the criminal justice system, including probation, community service and community-based through care. Her current research interests include young people and offending and women offenders in the criminal justice system. Her publications include *Sentenced to Serve: The Operation and Impact of Community Service by Offenders* (Avebury, 1992); *Working with Offenders* (Jessica Kingsley, 1995); and *Bail Services in Scotland* (with Sue Warner, Avebury, 1996).

Jim McManus is currently the Scottish Prisons Complaints Commissioner, on leave of absence from the Law Faculty at Dundee University. In addition to lecturing, researching and writing on penology, he has been a member of the Parole Board for Scotland, a consultant to HMCIP (England and Wales) and a regular contributor to courses at the Scottish Police College. He acts as an expert adviser to the Council of Europe Committee for Prevention of Torture, Inhuman or Degrading Treatment or Punishment. He is the author of *Prisons, Prisoners and the Law* (Greens, 1995).

Sue Moody is a Senior Lecturer in Law at the University of Dundee. She has worked as a researcher in the Scottish Office Central Research Unit undertaking, commissioning and supervising research studies in Scottish criminal justice. Before taking up her present post she was Director of Victim Support Scotland, a voluntary organisation supporting crime victims, and she has continued her involvement in Victim Support locally. She is a member of the Criminal Courts Rules Council, representing victims and witnesses. She is currently undertaking comparative work on victims and criminal justice with colleagues at Leiden University.

Fiona Paterson studied sociology at the Universities of Glasgow and Edinburgh. Her publications have included studies of truancy, bail decision making and social work criminal justice policy. She works in the Scottish Office Central Research Unit where she is Head of Social Work Research.

David J. Smith is Professor of Criminology at the University of Edinburgh. He has conducted pioneering studies of racial discrimination and disadvantage in Britain, inequality between Protestants and Catholics in Northern Ireland, and policing in London. In collaboration with Sir Michael Rutter, he carried out a study of cross-national trends in crime, suicide, depression, eating disorders, and alcohol and drug abuse, published in 1995 as *Psychosocial Disorders in Young People: Time Trends and their Causes*. Ethnicity and crime is another of his current research interests. In the 1980s he carried out a major study of the difference that secondary schools can make to individual development through the adolescent years. With Lesley McAra, he is presently leading a team that is studying youth transitions and crime in Edinburgh, by charting the development of a cohort of 4,500 adolescents and mapping the social geography of the city.

Neil Walker has been Professor in Legal and Constitutional Theory at the University of Aberdeen, Law Department, since 1996. He is the author of a number of works on policing, including studies of the organisation and governance of the police, of European policing and of the relationship between the police and the state. He also writes more generally within constitutional law and theory, with a particular emphasis upon the constitutional implications of the decline of the nation state.

Bryan Williams was appointed Professor of Social Work at Dundee University in 1989, having been on the academic staff there since 1976. Prior to this, he worked as a probation officer, resident social worker, teacher and radiochemist. His research interests lie mainly in the field of social work within criminal justice settings and he has been involved in a number of predominantly government funded evaluations of community penalties. His most recent research is concerned with applications of information technology in criminal justice contexts. He remains active in voluntary sector organisations and has been a member of a number of oficial committees.

Peter Young is Director of the Centre for Law and Society at the University of Edinburgh. He is author or editor of a number of books, including *Major Property Crime in the UK* (1976) and *The Power to Punish* (with D. Garland, 1983) and articles in criminological theory and the sociology of punishment. His most recent book is *Crime and Criminal Justice in Scotland* (1997), the first general account of patterns of crime and social control in Scotland.

Preface

DAVID GARLAND

This fine book, ably orchestrated and edited by Peter Duff and Neil Hutton, is the first publication ever to present such a comprehensive and expansive account of Scotland's criminal justice processes and agencies. Combining detailed description of legal rules and institutional structures with insightful policy analysis and socio-legal reflection, the book is one that will be welcomed by anyone wishing to understand the distinctive characteristics of the Scottish system and its relation to the criminal justice practice of other jurisdictions.

In its conception and execution, the book is guided by today's most important imperatives for the analysis of criminal justice. It concerns itself with practices and outcomes as well as with laws and official policy statements. It views criminal justice not as a closed, coherent 'system' but as a chain of loosely coupled agencies whose inter-relations are problematic and whose practices are subject to external demands and political pressures. It reaches out beyond 'the criminal justice state' to discuss the ways in which citizens and private agencies play a part in preventing and controlling crime. It highlights the variation that characterizes those caught up in the criminal justice process - juveniles, women, racial minorities, victims, the mentally-ill - and describes the distinctive treatment that they receive. It has a sense of history and of the ways in which institutions are shaped by past practices as well as by contemporary problems. It is imbued with a sociological perspective that situates contemporary criminal justice within the broader processes of social, political and cultural action. And finally, it is conscious of the need for a comparative perspective, so that these accounts of Scottish criminal justice can contribute to the development of general theory and the identification of international patterns as well as to specification of Scotland's particularities and institutional arrangements.

One of the enlivening features of the chapters contained here is that they frequently begin with descriptive accounts of how criminal justice works in Scotland and then use these as points of departure for more theoretical discussions that engage issues of general interest in criminology, socio-legal studies or comparative law. The result is a book that discusses the fundamentals of the system with the clarity and comprehensiveness needed for readers unfamiliar with the Scottish jurisdiction, but which also offers enough in the way of original, ambitious and provocative analyses to keep the attention of the expert insider. Readers from outside Scotland will appreciate the succinct accounts of the distinctive systems of prosecution, criminal procedure, juvenile justice and computer-aided sentencing that operate there. Scholars of criminal justice and crime control will be interested to learn of the particular ways in which the international trends towards crime prevention, victims' rights, community policing and the privatisation of criminal justice have taken hold in Scotland. And criminologists everywhere will be intrigued by the crime rate trends suggested by Scottish data over the last few decades and by the possibility that these trends may cast doubt upon claims that there is a causal link between decreasing crime rates and increasing levels of imprisonment. (As it happens, a combination of falling crime rates and unchanged local imprisonment rates is also characteristic of New York City in the period from 1992 to the present, giving further reason to be sceptical of the 'prison works' credo.)

Any attempt to characterize a national system of criminal justice - particularly one concerned not just with institutional scaffolding but also with culture and ethos and the logic of practice that results - must come to grips with the tension between local variation and general pattern. This is of particular importance when the jurisdiction in question is a small one, and differs from the standard reference points for scholarly discussion which, in the English-speaking world, tend still to be the USA and the UK (and all too often 'the UK' really means England and Wales.) In my opinion the editors and contributors have done a fine job of managing this tension, and have succeeded in giving both a nuanced sense of Scotland's distinctiveness and a more structural account of its place in the general scheme of things.

Nils Christie says somewhere that we might think of criminal justice in the same way that we think of other national institutions such as the National Theatre - not just as instruments for controlling crime and punishing offenders but also as cultural institutions that express and exemplify the distinctive mix of values that obtains within the society. In the pages of this book a similar viewpoint can be discerned, though contributors point to the peculiarities of Scotland's political and legislative structures which mean that 'national culture' is often expressed obliquely, by varying and adapting policies that originate in UK government offices in Whitehall, rather than directly through homegrown initiatives. (One of the major arguments for political 'devolution' and for the Scottish Parliament that will be established in the very near future, was that Scotland had need of its own political forum and legislature in which its distinctive voices could be directly expressed and its own policies directly controlled. It will be interesting to see whether this will further widen the gap between Scottish criminal justice and that of the rest of the UK.) There is, for example, a sense that Scotland's civil society and indigenous political culture have resisted the neo-liberalism policies of recent UK governments and remain committed to a welfare state ethos that is expressed in the continuing commitment to social work with offenders or the entrenched welfarism of the Children's Hearing System. Likewise we learn that the particular arrangements, alliances and objectives that characterize Scottish policing, and Scottish prisons, or even the Scottish versions of UK-wide initiatives such as the Safer Cities crime prevention programme, are shaped by local actors and structures and the specific history of their interplay.

At the same time, however, Scotland is a nation locked for nearly three centuries into a political and bureaucratic union with the rest of the UK, integrated into the global networks of economic trade and cultural diffusion, and exposed to the international trends that sweep across the developed world. For at least a century now, representatives of Scottish criminal justice agencies have played a full part in the many international congresses that discuss criminology, criminal justice and law reform, and have encouraged a two-way flow of ideas, research findings, methods and technologies. Since the 1970s there has been a constant stream of researchers and government officials arriving in Scotland to study the Children's Hearing System and the generic social work departments (both of which emerged out of that classic of penal-welfarist philosophy, the Kilbrandon Report of 1964), or else to learn about other path-breaking developments such as the Barlinnie Prison Special Unit, or Scotland's early experiments in mediation and restorative justice. There is also much traffic in the other direction. In recent years the Scottish Prison Service has been drawing upon the experience of American and Canadian experts to help shape its new 'opportunity and responsibility' regime and to build better relations between staff and inmates. And, within months of New York's much-touted success in combating crime and disorder, Strathclyde police were hosting visits by NYPD officers who were debriefed about the details of 'quality of life' policing and the new system of computer-assisted crime management. In criminal justice, as in everything else, Scotland has become thoroughly internationalised.

Not surprisingly then we find in these pages the traces of trends and developments that have been much discussed in other jurisdictions and subjected to extensive analysis by criminal justice scholars elsewhere. The now familiar (and often contradictory) themes of managerialism, the new penology, punitive populism, victims' rights, community notification, and mandatory sentencing all make an appearance here. So too do community policing, inter-agency crime prevention schemes, private prisons, private police - and a thriving commercial security sector, and a new emphasis upon protecting the public - through control oriented community sanctions, CCTV, restricted use of parole and lengthy prison sentences. The book will serve then, not only as a primer on crime and criminal justice in Scotland, but also as a rich resource for scholars interested in comparative criminal justice, and as a new challenge to theorists trying to make sense of the diverse ways in which crime control across the developed world is currently being restructured.

1   Introduction

PETER DUFF AND NEIL HUTTON

This book is intended to serve two main functions. The first and principal aim is simply to provide a description of the whole range of the criminal justice process in Scotland. The second aim is to locate Scottish institutions and practices in broader theoretical and political contexts. The perspective is primarily socio-legal in that the book is more concerned with what happens in reality on a day-to-day basis rather than with the more abstract and distant legal rules which govern the system. Such rules are of course always mediated to a greater or lesser extent by those who are forced to work within them. Until now, no socio-legal text on Scottish criminal justice has existed, although Young (1997) has recently produced an extremely helpful little book packed with useful facts and figures about the process. Nevertheless, Scottish readers, wishing to know more about both the theorisation and broader social and political context of the process of criminal justice, are forced to turn to such recent English texts as Cavadino and Dignan's (1992) *The Penal System* and Sanders and Young's (1994) *Criminal Justice*. Inevitably, these books draw almost exclusively upon English material and discuss English institutions rather than their Scottish equivalents which, while broadly similar, are in many ways quite distinct. It is not that the necessary knowledge of the Scottish criminal justice process is lacking because considerable empirical research has now been done, much of which appears in the series of papers produced by the Scottish Office Central Research Unit. The problem is simply that this and other relevant research has never before been pulled together in one volume. Rather than undertake this task ourselves, we thought it would be both easier and much more likely to produce the required accuracy and comprehensiveness if we, as editors, asked a team of experts to write chapters on all major aspects of the Scottish criminal justice process.

The essays in this book show that Scotland has a distinctive criminal justice culture. This is not to say that Scotland has developed entirely different responses to crime from those adopted elsewhere, but rather to argue that ideas, practices and trends which have their roots in other jurisdictions have been borrowed, adapted and applied with distinctive results by Scottish agencies and institutions. Thus the book can also be read

1

as an example or a case study of the way in which global movements are interpreted and applied in local settings. This is of course a dynamic and interactive process and it is possible that local adaptations in Scotland - such as Children's Hearings (see chapter 14) - will go on to have an impact in other jurisdictions and influence global trends in new directions. The potential audience for this book includes students, practitioners and academics from within Scotland, who wish to know more about the practical workings of their own process of criminal justice, as well as scholars and practitioners from other jurisdictions who have an interest in comparing local practices in Scotland with developments and trends elsewhere.

The introduction falls into two parts. In the first, we have tried to identify a number of the more significant themes which emerge from the essays. There is no attempt to pin down the exact relationships between these themes nor provide an overall explanatory model of recent developments in the Scottish criminal justice process. Time, space - and probably the abilities of the editors - precluded such an ambitious aim. Nor is this first part of the introduction meant to be a summary of the issues raised by the contributors; it is very much the editors' selection and some of the authors might well disagree with our judgement about what constitute the main themes of the book. However, our view is that these issues are raised with sufficient regularity to justify an editorial overview which might help readers less familiar with recent penological theorising to identify some recurring and significant themes and to locate them in a broader context. In the second part of the introduction, we have simply summarised the essays. This is intended not only to give readers an idea of what to expect, primarily in terms of identifying the approach adopted by each author and indicating the topics to be discussed, but also to identify where the issues raised by contributors touch upon the more general themes raised by the book as a whole.

Recurring Themes

Criminal Justice in Scotland: System or Process?

Most of the contributors would agree that it is inappropriate to describe criminal justice in Scotland as a system. We have used the term process throughout. What is wrong with the use of 'system'? The term implies a strong element of rational co-ordination amongst the agencies involved and, as the essays show, this is absent in Scotland. As in the rest of the United Kingdom, there is no Ministry or Department of Justice. Instead, the Crown Office is responsible for prosecution, the eight Chief Constables for policing, the judiciary for sentencing, the local authority social work departments for community based disposals, the Scottish Prison Service for imprisonment, and so on. This multiplicity of agencies means, for instance, that: there is a lack of coherence in plans to meet the needs of victims (see chapters 9, 16 and 18 respectively); there is wide geographical variation in provision for mentally disordered offenders (see chapter 15); prisons simply have to deal with as many or as few offenders as are sent to them by the courts and thus have little control over the demand for their limited resources (see chapter 13); and social workers and judges do not share the same picture of the types of case where a community based disposal may be regarded as appropriate (see chapter 12). As Gane argues (see chapter 4), criminal justice in Scotland is closer to the Anglo-American tradition of linked - or 'co-ordinate' - institutions than to the continental European traditional of centralised - or 'hierarchical' - direction. At an institutional level, then, criminal justice in Scotland is not a system but a process involving the interaction of a number of relatively autonomous institutions (Adler and Longhurst, 1994). Another indicator of the non-systemic nature of criminal justice is the absence of what might be called a 'shared ideology'. There is no mission statement for criminal justice, no shared aims and objectives between agencies and no centralised direction. Thus, the various institutions have no shared rationale for their work beyond perhaps a rather vague and unspoken assumption that they share the aim of controlling crime. The book shows that different agencies have adopted a variety of approaches to defining their role, setting objectives, measuring their effectiveness and presenting the results of their work to the public. As Shapland (1988) has argued, the 'system' actually comprises a series of separate agencies, each with their own agenda, which uneasily co-exist, as did the mediaeval barons who had considerable autonomy within their own fiefdoms.

Discretion and Accountability

As a result of the loose way in which the Scottish criminal justice process is organised, and the relative autonomy of the various agencies, a great deal of discretionary decision-making takes place. This is in contrast to the hierarchically organised and centrally directed criminal justice systems of continental Europe which are at pains to regulate closely the activities and decision-making of their bureaucrats (Damaška, 1986). For instance, the Scottish procurator fiscal has almost total freedom to decide whether or not to prosecute an alleged offender, whereas the public prosecutor on the continent is frequently under a legal obligation to prosecute in every case where there is sufficient evidence (see chapters 5 and 7). Similarly, Scottish judges have a very wide discretion in sentencing because very little constrains their freedom to select both the type and severity of sanction they think appropriate in any particular case (see chapter 10). Further, the absence of centralised direction allows the development of quite distinctive local criminal justice cultures based on the working practices of local agencies which enjoy a considerable degree of autonomy in their decision making (see chapter 8). The fact that the process is decentralised and fragmented can also provide opportunities for initiatives and inter-agency co-operation at the local level (see chapters 4 and 12).

The existence of discretion, particularly when it is relatively unfettered, raises questions of accountability and consistency. One of the major criticisms of judicial discretion is that it leads to disparities in sentencing and hence injustice (see chapter 10). How then can the exercise of discretion be shaped or controlled? A key issue is who monitors, supervises, guides or controls the exercise of discretion and how this is done? Can 'bad' decisions or policies be challenged and if so by whom and how? In his chapter on the prosecution system, Duff discusses these issues in the context of the wide discretion granted to the procurator fiscal (see chapter 7). In similar vein, Walker (see chapter 6) discusses the broader problem of rendering a large and powerful agency like the police accountable for its actions, and discusses the complex and not altogether satisfactory nature of the present arrangements.

Managerialism and Privatisation

In common with global trends, some agencies such as the police (see chapters 6 and 19), the Scottish Prison Service (see chapter 13) and the social work departments (see chapter 12) have adopted managerialist strategies within their organisations, partly in response to demands for increased accountability and partly as a result of increased budgetary pressures. These bodies have devised for themselves performance indicators and procedures for measuring the achievement of these. However, such instruments frequently measure 'output' rather than 'outcomes', in that some of the explicitly instrumental goals of fighting crime and stopping re-offending have been replaced by goals which measure how the institutions use their resources - for instance, measuring the number of emergency calls processed rather than the number of offenders arrested as a result or the overall effect on the crime rate (Garland, 1996). Other institutions have remained relatively immune to managerialist ideology. In the case of sentencing, for example, although individual cases of apparent inconsistency have captured the headlines from time to time, there has been no sustained public critique of judicial discretion nor much in the way of attempts to introduce more centralised direction or assessment of performance (see chapter 10).

Alongside managerialism, and related to it, there has also been a trend towards the increased privatisation of functions previously carried out by state agencies, the classic example being the introduction of private prisons. As Fyfe and Bannister show (see chapter 19), privatisation has taken place both to reduce costs and to divert some of the responsibility for crime control away from the state. Carnie's chapter illustrates the way in which the Safer Cities Programme attempted to involve the broader community in crime prevention (see chapter 4). In these, and other such developments, we can see the government and criminal justice agencies attempting to shift part of the responsibility for controlling crime away from state institutions and on to the community, a strategy of 'responsibilisation'. As Fyfe and Bannister argue, the related notions of privatisation and responsibilisation open up questions about the nature and location of the public-private divide in the criminal justice process and, more generally, in civic society as a whole.

Justice or Welfare or 'New Penology'?

Many commentators have identified a shift in penal ideologies over the past 20 years from welfare to justice or to a 'new' managerialist penology (see chapter 20). Broadly speaking, the claim is that criminal justice has given up the general aim of controlling crime by rehabilitating offenders, thus turning them away from a life of crime, and now seeks to punish offenders, by attempting to sentence them to their 'just deserts' or simply to 'manage' them by trying to minimise the disruption they might cause. The contributions to this volume suggest that there is little evidence for the existence of this type of shift in Scotland. While, as in other jurisdictions, there has long existed a tension in Scottish criminal justice between the ideologies of welfare and punishment, there does not appear to have been any significant change in the balance between them over the last decade in Scotland.   Indeed, the clash between these two aims makes a major contribution to the continuing lack of a coherent philosophy underlying sentencing (see chapter 10) and the very mixed nature of the prison population (see chapter 13).

McAra, in particular, argues that welfare remains at the heart of the Scottish process in a number of different locations including practice in social work and in the prison service and in the Childrens' Hearings system (see chapter 20). This claim finds support in chapters 12, 13 and 14 in this volume (by, respectively, McIvor and Williams, McManus, and Asquith and Docherty) which demonstrate and also explicitly advocate adherence to a welfare ideology. Thus, in McAra's view, although other ideologies have had effects in different areas of the criminal justice process, the welfare rationale has never disappeared and continues to exert a strong influence. In particular, she argues that 'managerialist' ideas have been co-opted in order to advance welfare aims, a claim which McIvor's and Williams' contribution strongly supports. Similarly, Hutton demonstrates that the 'just deserts' approach, which has been the basis of recent sentencing reforms in many jurisdictions, has had little impact on sentencing in Scotland (see chapter 10).

Populism and Politics

The way the 'crime problem' is conceptualised in Scotland is similar to other places. The pattern of recorded crime has followed a similar trend in Scotland to that in many other western jurisdictions, showing a steep rise from the 1960s which has flattened out over the last few years (see chapters 2 and 3). However, the fact that crime rates are no longer rising does not yet appear to have registered with the general public, much of the media or many politicians. The prison population has risen steadily throughout this period, continuing to increase in spite of the recent end of sharp increases in recorded crime (see chapter 13). There seems however to be no link between crime rates and imprisonment rates (see chapter 2). The apparent failure of punishment, throughout the western world, to have any influence upon crime has resulted in what Bottoms (1995) has described as 'populist punitiveness'. This refers to the response from the public and tabloid press that the answer to rising crime is more and harsher punishment, a response which many politicians have echoed both in 'sound bites' and in policies. There is limited evidence of populist punitiveness in Scotland (see, respectively, chapters 3, 14 and 20), although the Scottish prison population has continued to rise.

Nevertheless, one of the dilemmas facing criminal justice agencies in Scotland, as elsewhere, is how to respond to the perceived problem of their ineffectiveness, in terms of preventing crime, catching criminals and punishing offenders. This ineffectiveness has led to what Garland (1996) has described as the decline of the claim of 'state sovereignty' in crime control, and is one of the reasons for the 'responsibilisation' strategy described above. This problem has become particularly acute at a time when there is increasing pressure on many agencies to demonstrate their effectiveness and to provide evidence of the value they provide for the expenditure of public money, a factor underlying the growth of managerialism. In many jurisdictions, the issue of ineffectiveness is seen as leading to a potential loss of public confidence in the institutions of criminal justice, a confidence which can be bolstered or restored through populist punitiveness. Many of the chapters in the book touch on these topics and show the varied responses to these public moods by the agencies responsible for the criminal justice process in Scotland.

Globalised Trends and 'Transformation'

Some of the contributions caution against characterising a complex range of changes in different criminal justice agencies in different jurisdictions as an apparently simple and global uni-directional shift. As noted above, McAra (see chapter 20), in particular, is critical of such generalisations, in particular the argument that the criminal justice process is presently undergoing a 'transformation', rejecting the notion that 'welfarism' is disappearing fast, and putting forward the case that more attention should be paid to local cultures and political conditions. Hutton, too, indicates that 'just deserts' theory has yet to make significant inroads into Scotland (see chapter 10). In a rather different way, Young is also critical of meta-theoretical explanations in contemporary penology (see chapter 11). He argues that explanatory theories based on single factors such as the exemplar of the prison, or Foucault's concept of discipline, are flawed because they fail to take account of the fact that the fine has consistently been the standard response to offending, not only in Scotland, but in most other western jurisdictions. Since the fine is neither disciplinary nor rehabilitative, nor strictly desert based, it does not fit any of the globalised meta-theories which are popular with academic commentators. Young describes the fine as a kind of 'auto-punishment', but this is not intended as an alternative meta-theory explaining punishment but rather as a useful heuristic device to help our understanding of how punishment is related to particular social and political conditions.

Perhaps one of the messages from this book is the importance of looking at how global trends operate in particular local conditions. This is not to deny the value of trying to identify broad trends in criminal justice but rather to note the limited explanatory or predictive power of such theorising. Nor is it to argue for the uniqueness of each criminal justice culture, as the book shows clearly that much of what happens in Scotland had its origins elsewhere and is shared with many other jurisdictions.

Devolution

The new Scottish parliament will take over responsibilities for most aspects of criminal justice currently administered by the Scottish Office. Although Scotland has always had a separate criminal justice process, the legislation which shapes its development has come from Westminster and has frequently paid insufficient attention to distinct Scottish practices. In particular, during the last years of the outgoing Conservative administration, the populist punitiveness which has characterised reforms of the criminal justice process in England and Wales threatened to spill over into Scotland, most notably in the recent Crime and Punishment (Scotland) Act 1997. Clearly, the existence of a Scottish parliament offers opportunities to develop further the distinctive Scottish approach which McAra summarises in the final chapter of this book. Other contributors also emphasise the possibilities presented by a Scottish parliament. Walker, for example, specifically addresses the opportunity to re-think the existing arrangements for police accountability (see chapter 6) and Asquith and Docherty (see chapter 14) discuss a possible way forward for juvenile justice, which they advocate should be based on the welfarism which is now deeply embedded in the Scottish approach rather than the punitiveness which has recently become so influential south of the border.

The Essays

The book begins with two chapters by Smith and Young (chapter 2) and by Anderson (chapter 3) which examine the available information about trends in crime and punishment in Scotland. Smith and Young argue that the evidence from Scotland does not appear to fit the theories put forward by Farrington and his colleagues which suggest that the levelling off of crime which has occurred in Scotland, as in the USA and in England and Wales, may be explained by increases in the likelihood of punishment. Anderson's chapter takes issue with those who argue that crime statistics are measurements of an 'objective reality' of crime and also with those who argue that crime statistics are no more than 'indices of the activities of the organisations which produce them'. He uses Scottish crime data to demonstrate both that the figures tell us something useful and real about crime in Scotland and that the way in which the information is classified and gathered plays an important part in the way in which we conceive of 'the crime problem'. His argument is that we can use information about crime to change the way we conceive of 'the crime problem' and thus open up new ways of managing crime. In chapter 4, Gane argues that the Scottish criminal justice process is closer to that of the adversarial common law jurisdictions than the civilian systems of continental Europe. He highlights the lack of a coherent and centrally managed criminal justice system and the consequent wide use of discretion, issues which are subsequently picked up by many other contributors. Following this, Carnie provides a detailed description of how the fashionable idea of inter-agency, community based crime prevention was taken up in Scotland. In particular, he shows how, under the nationally run 'Safer Cities' initiative, different local political cultures produced quite distinctive approaches to crime prevention.

The next nine chapters roughly follow the chronological stages of the criminal justice process in Scotland from policing, through prosecution and the courts, to the wide range of disposals used in Scotland. In chapter 6, Walker examines policing in Scotland from a broad, historical perspective. He shows how Scottish police forces have adopted some of the global ideology of managerialism but yet retain a distinct national character and argues that the current arrangements for accountability present problems which could be addressed by the forthcoming Scottish parliament. In chapter 7, Duff argues that there are also problems with the procedures for holding prosecutors accountable for their decision making while allowing them to retain sufficient independence from political influence. He provides a comprehensive review of research into the exercise of prosecutorial discretion in Scotland and also describes the gradual move towards the use of diversion which the exercise of that discretion allows. The chapter by Paterson, like the chapter by Carnie, provides a very detailed example of how local criminal justice cultures, constructed by different agencies operating with wide discretion, can produce quite different approaches to bail decision-making (see chapter 8). One result of this is that it is extremely difficult to make meaningful comparisons between figures on bail for different areas because the figures in each area do not have the same meaning. This is a example of the general point made by Anderson, about the statistics produced by the criminal justice process. In chapter 9, Connelly describes the structure of the criminal courts in Scotland and points out that, in practice, court proceedings are not as adversarial as theory suggests and popular culture implies, a point also made by Gane and Duff (see chapters 4 and 7). She also describes some of the conflicts between lay and professional approaches to criminal justice which arise through the use of lay justices in the District Court and juries in the Sheriff and High courts.

The following four chapters deal with sentencing and punishment in Scotland. The chapter by Hutton (chapter 10) reviews the powers of the courts and the range of disposals available and the following chapters deal with fines, community based disposals and imprisonment. Hutton argues that sentencers in Scotland have considerable independence and discretion. The limited research which has been carried out on sentencing is reviewed along with some recent developments in providing support for sentencers. In chapter 11, Young briefly describes the extensive use of the fine in Scotland and argues that the neglect of this sanction by many theorists, particularly those indebted to Foucault, has led to an overemphasis on the idea of discipline and the institution of the prison in attempts to understand the nature of modern punishment. As noted above, he begins to develop a theory of the fine as a form of 'auto-punishment'. McIvor and Williams (chapter 12) provide a very detailed account of the slow but steady growth in the use of community sanctions in Scotland and the development of several variants of such sentences. They describe the tension between the original welfare orientation of these sanctions and more recent managerialist developments which have emphasised their control element. While there has been some success in using these sanctions as an alternative to custody, they have also been used as alternatives to fines and although the use of community sanctions has increased in recent years, so has the use of imprisonment. They conclude that while practitioners in Scotland now have a better idea of 'what works' and for whom, there remains a difficulty in sustaining public (and judicial) confidence in community sanctions as appropriate disposals. In chapter 13, McManus then provides a brief but comprehensive history of imprisonment in Scotland. Although the Scottish Prison Service has developed clear objectives and implemented management strategies to achieve these, it is hampered by the absence of any control or influence over the numbers or nature of the offenders it receives from the courts, leading McManus to argue that there is a pressing need for improved co-ordination between the sentencers who allocate punishment and agencies like the Scottish Prison Service which provide punishment. In particular, he argues that there is the potential to remove a considerable proportion of short term prisoners, prisoners on remand and fine defaulters from the prison system, which would free resources for more constructive rehabilitative work by prison staff with the remaining inmates. McManus also describes how political concerns, rather than informed rational debate, have shaped recent policy on parole.

The role of political factors is also taken up by Asquith and Docherty in their chapter on juvenile justice in Scotland (chapter 14). They argue that while research evidence consistently shows the value of a preventive approach to deal with juvenile offending, politicians have continued to feel the need to use the language of punishment and control. Despite the increase in populist punitiveness, the Childrens' Hearings System, which deals with the great majority of offenders under the age of 16 in Scotland, has survived. This system was introduced nearly 30 years ago and is based on a welfare approach where the best interests of the child are paramount and punishment is not a consideration. In chapter 15, Chiswick provides a detailed guide to the labyrinthine legislation governing the many pathways through which the mentally disordered offender can receive assessment and treatment. He observes that there is no national policy for the provision of services to such offenders, although moves are afoot to create a more coherent and uniform approach. A particular difficulty is that local responses are largely dependent on the availability of psychiatric facilities in the area.

The next three chapters each deal with an important aspect of criminal justice in Scotland: gender, ethnic minorities and victims. Burman pulls together a wide range of information about women in the criminal justice process in Scotland (see chapter 16). While there have been some significant policy developments, such as improvements in the criminal justice response to domestic violence, 'shield legislation' for sexual offence cases, and a recently announced investigation into how to reduce the level of womens' imprisonment, the overall picture remains of a criminal justice process designed to deal with male offending. There remain significant problems with women's imprisonment and a lack of consideration for women victims in the criminal justice system. In chapter 17, Ditton explains that race is an under-researched aspect of criminal justice in Scotland. The British Crime Survey shows that in England and Wales ethnic minority populations are more likely to be victimised and more likely to fear victimisation than the white population. Scotland has a proportionately smaller and less diverse ethnic minority population than exists south of the border and Ditton reports the results of recent research which attempted to survey this population. In contrast with England and Wales, the research found few differences between respondents in the white sample and respondents in the ethnic minority sample. In chapter 18, Moody argues that the development of services for victims in Scotland is following international trends but that the pace of change has been slow. She also argues that victims should be more involved in the criminal justice process but recognises that the movement is susceptible to being used by politicians to serve their own political ambitions rather than to further the needs of victims. The fragmented and unsystematic nature of criminal justice in Scotland also makes it more difficult to advance the interests of victims.

The final two chapters place Scottish criminal justice in a broader context. Fyfe and Bannister (chapter 19) describe how the global trend of privatisation - in the two forms of a brand of managerialism which seeks to implement a social market approach to the public sector and a policy of active citizenship - has shaped contemporary public policing in Scotland. The chapter also discusses the roles that the private security industry and the development of Closed Circuit Television (CCTV) have played in shifting the boundaries of public and private space.

In the final chapter, McAra reviews recent developments in Scottish criminal justice in the light of some influential recent theorising about penal 'transformations' in the western world (see chapter 20). She concludes that penal change in Scotland does not fit neatly into any of the suggested explanatory schemes. Instead, she claims that penal welfarism has dominated official policy discourse in Scotland over the last 25 years and that the growth of managerialism is being used to facilitate rehabilitation rather than to replace welfarism, particularly in prisons, social work criminal justice services and the juvenile justice system. She also argues that the persistence of rehabilitative and reintegrative values at the centre of the penal process in Scotland can be explained by a distinctive civic culture based on a strong democratic tradition, the dominance of socialist and communitarian principles in local government and the existence of a network of elite decision makers protected from UK-wide political influences by the domestic policy making powers of the Scottish Office and, finally of course, the existence of a separate Scottish legal system.

Conclusion

Taken as a whole the book demonstrates both the distinctiveness of Scottish criminal justice and how Scottish procedures have been influenced by global trends. Clearly the forthcoming Scottish parliament offers opportunities to build on this distinctiveness and perhaps even to develop more rational, constructive and cost-effective approaches to criminal justice - maybe influenced by the many suggestions offered by the contributors to this book. In conclusion, it is perhaps worth re-emphasising two points which emerge from the contributions. The first is that, whatever the reasons, Scotland seems to have avoided the worst excesses of the populist punitiveness which has affected other jurisdictions, particularly the USA and England and Wales. A future government will nevertheless need to ensure that public confidence in criminal justice institutions in Scotland is sustained. There is an opportunity to base this on a cogent and empirically based programme of reform which will have some chance of success rather than on a combination of populist sound-bites and tough looking measures that are not supported by any evidence nor properly thought through. Second, and to return to the starting point of this introduction, many contributors have pointed to the unsystematic nature of criminal justice in Scotland. Most ask for better communication or co-ordination between the various agencies and institutions. One way of achieving this would be to establish a Ministry of Justice; another would be to take advantage of the fact that Scotland is a small jurisdiction and take steps to improve the existing informal networks of communication. There is no space here to develop this debate but it seems clear from the contributions to this volume that there is considerable scope for improved co-operation.

We should like to record our thanks to Fiona Leverick for the enthusiastic and excellent job she did in preparing the manuscript for publication.

2 Crime Trends in Scotland Since 1950

DAVID J. SMITH AND PETER YOUNG

Introduction

There have been striking increases in recorded crime since 1950 in all developed countries except Japan. There are essentially three patterns. In Japan, recorded crime was at much the same level in 1950 as in many European countries, but thereafter it remained level, or declined slightly. In North America, crime rose strongly between 1950 and 1975, but property crime, and maybe also violent crime, levelled off from 1980 onwards. In most European countries, crime increased strongly and continuously over the entire post-war period, although there are indications of a levelling off from the early 1990s onwards in England and Wales, and some other countries in Europe.

In this chapter we consider which of these patterns applies to Scotland, and we ask whether Scotland may be a crucial test of one theory that has been put forward to explain post-war crime trends. This is the theory that crime grew in the post-war period because of a decline in the effectiveness of the criminal justice system in catching and punishing offenders; and that it levelled off in the USA around 1980 because of an increase in the proportion of offenders who were caught and punished by imprisonment. More detailed research must be done before strong conclusions can be drawn from the Scottish case, but on the face of the evidence it seems that crime levelled off in Scotland without any increase in the likelihood or severity of punishment.

The significance of the Scottish case does not only lie in the statistics, and the dimension they add to cross-national comparisons. It is equally important that the declining level of punitiveness in Scotland is the expression of a broad trend in policy which contrasts in the most striking way with an opposite movement of policy in the US. This chapter aims to put on the agenda the question of whether Scottish criminal justice policy has proved to be successful.

The first section reviews problems of definition and measurement, and the limitations of the two main data sources - the recorded crime statistics, and the Scottish Crime Survey. The following sections summarise the available information on trends in crime in Scotland from 1950 to 1995 from the recorded crime statistics and the crime surveys, and compare crime rates and trends between Scotland and its closest neighbour, England and Wales. The final section briefly reviews possible explanations for post-war crime trends, and asks how the Scottish case can help to choose between them.

Definition and Measurement

The central problem in discussing crime trends is that crime is not an uncontested social fact: instead, it arises from moral judgements, from a legal code, and from a multitude of decisions taken by officials and citizens about whether to invoke the legal process on a particular occasion. The two main sources of information used in this chapter - statistics of police-recorded crime, and victimisation surveys - provide contrasting and complementary descriptions; yet each has substantial weaknesses, and paints the picture from a particular viewpoint. The statistics of recorded crime are a by-product of the administrative process for dealing with matters reported to the authorities as crimes or possible crimes. Consequently, they leave out obviously criminal acts, and incidents which might have been considered criminal had the question been raised, where these were not reported to the police. They also leave out incidents which the police decided, whether for good or bad reasons, not to record as crimes. Essentially these statistics describe the pool of incidents that form the starting point for the formal law enforcement process. As such, they leave out every kind of behaviour that citizens or officials decide to control by more informal means, or ignore. Equally important, they reflect the priorities, activities, and control strategies of law enforcement officers. For example, recorded offences of breach of the peace, drunkenness, and possession of controlled drugs largely reflect the level of police resources, the pattern of police activity, decisions taken by police officers about whether and if so how to control a situation, and higher-level police decisions about priorities.

An interpretation of recorded crime statistics must therefore take account of a number of problems and limitations. First, the data are crucially dependent on legal definitions and the related systems of crime classification; where these change, the time series is interrupted, and where these vary between one country and another, comparison becomes difficult. In Scotland, the system of crime classification was revised in 1978, right in the middle of the period reviewed in this chapter. The detailed problems of interpretation that arise from this change will be discussed in later sections. At the same time, the criminal law and procedure of Scotland is, of course, distinct from that of England. These differences are enough to cause substantial problems when attempting to make exact comparisons between recorded crime in the two countries. Second, the amount of crime recorded may change quite quickly because of administrative changes affecting the capacity to record it. In 1975, the police in Scotland underwent a major reorganisation. The number of forces was reduced to eight, and one result of this was the introduction of standardised recording practices, which caused a 'sharp increase in the statistics of crime when compared to previous years' according to the annual statistical report (Scottish Office, 1975a, p.5). Third, as noted above, the statistics are partly a reflection of law enforcement policy and activity. This particularly affects the mostly minor offences, such as breach of the peace and drunkenness, that arise from widely defined police powers which give them discretion to control situations. However, enforcement practice also changes in response to profound yet diffuse changes in public sensibility. Obvious examples in recent years are changes in the police response to child abuse, domestic violence, and rape. For a variety of reasons, therefore, changes in policing may lead to changes in the quantity of recorded crime. Fourth, incidents which (unlike for example breach of the peace) are not generated by police enforcement decisions mostly come to the notice of the police through a member of the public; therefore, changes in the proportion of incidents that are reported to the police can have a major effect on the amount of crime recorded.

Victim surveys provide a complementary description of the extent and pattern of crime. The method followed is to ask a representative sample of adults whether each of a number of things has happened to them over a reference period of twelve months. The incidents are mostly described in simple language, sometimes without reference to the word describing the corresponding criminal offence. These surveys therefore count incidents that appear to have been criminal offences from the victims' descriptions, although not enough detailed questions are asked to establish that there was a criminal offence in every case.

There have so far been four national crime surveys in Scotland, in 1982, 1988, 1993, and 1996. The first two surveys were part of the British Crime Survey, which was co-ordinated by the Home Office, whereas the last two were designed and co-ordinated by the Central Research Unit of the Scottish Office. The two earlier surveys were confined to central and southern Scotland, whereas the two later ones covered the whole of mainland Scotland together with the larger islands. The sample size for each survey in Scotland was around 5,000.

Victim surveys reveal a great deal of crime that is not shown in recorded crime statistics. Offences that can be strictly compared between the Scottish Crime Survey and the recorded crime statistics are vandalism, housebreaking, theft of motor vehicle, theft of bicycle, assault, and robbery. The estimated number of these incidents based on the 1996 Scottish Crime Survey is 2.7 times the number shown in the recorded crime statistics. The crime survey results are nevertheless subject to important limitations. They can only include crimes against individual adults (aged 16+) and their households. They do not include crimes against public or private organisations (such as shoplifting, or break-ins and thefts from commercial premises), crimes against the public in general (such as pollution of the atmosphere), victimless crimes (such as possession of drugs, or prostitutes soliciting), offences generated by enforcement activity (such as speeding, or obstructing a police officer in the execution of his duty) or, most important, crimes against children. Within the field that they do cover, victim surveys provide a more complete description than recorded crime statistics. Even so, many incidents that might in principle be recorded as crimes are not mentioned in victim surveys, because the respondent did not notice or care about or recall them, or did not want to think of them as crime, or did not want to tell anyone about them. This is particularly true of sexual offences, and of violence between people who know each other well. Thus, for example, the number of domestic assaults reported by the British Crime Survey in England and Wales rose by 79 per cent between 1981 and 1991 (Mayhew *et al.*, 1993), probably partly or wholly because of an increasing recognition of the importance and seriousness of this type of offence and more explicit efforts of the police to deal with it (Smith, D., 1995, p.393). Finally, victim surveys are subject to inevitable sampling limitations and biases. The sampling methods exclude people living in institutions such as prisons and mental hospitals, and those without a fixed address. Even where they are not excluded, people living unconventional lives will tend to be under-represented.

The results of victim surveys over time show fairly similar trends to the statistics of recorded crime both in England and Wales and in Scotland. The main difference is that the curves shown by victim survey statistics are flatter and smoother. Between 1981 and 1991, for those crime categories that can be precisely compared, recorded crime in England and Wales nearly doubled, whereas crime measured by the British Crime Survey rose by 50 per cent (Mayhew *et al.*, 1993, p.24). Crime survey respondents are asked whether each incident of victimisation was reported to the police. In England and Wales these results have shown an increase over time in the proportion of certain crimes (vandalism and violence in particular) that are reported to the police, and this increase in reporting accounts for much of the divergence between the trends shown by the survey and the statistics of recorded crime. On the one hand, these comparisons have shown that rises in recorded crime are partly a reflection of an increasing tendency for people to deal with unwanted behaviour by referring it to the criminal justice system. On the other hand, they suggest that trends in survey-estimated and police-recorded crime tend to go in the same direction, because changes in the proportion of incidents reported to the police are gradual, and do not run counter to the underlying trend in crime. On balance, therefore, it seems likely that recorded crime statistics for periods before 1981 (for which no survey data are available) are informative about changes in the level of crime, even if they tend to exaggerate them.

Trends in Recorded Crime 1950-95

In Scotland, unlike England, national statistics are published on minor infractions recorded by the police (known as 'offences') as well as more serious ones (known as 'crimes'). Figures 2.1 and 2.2 (all figures are displayed at the end of this chapter) show the distribution of crimes and offences recorded in 1995. Theft and housebreaking predominated among the crimes, while vandalism was also common. Although this is not shown separately in Figure 2.1, much of the large quantity of theft was of or from motor vehicles. Violent and sexual crimes were far less common than property crimes. Among the offences (Figure 2.2), the majority were connected with driving and parking, but substantial numbers of offences of breach of the peace and petty assault were also recorded.

In considering time trends, it is best to concentrate on crimes rather than offences. For the most part, offences are infractions that arise out of the process of law enforcement (for example, a person who resists the authority of a police officer may be charged with breach of the peace) or usually come to light as a result of proactive police work (as in the case of drunkenness and most driving offences). By contrast, most crimes are reported to the police by victims, the main exceptions being possession of drugs, and crimes against public justice (which includes, for example, resisting arrest). It follows that time trends in offences will mainly reflect the level and pattern of police activity, whereas time trends in crimes will largely reflect the quantity of incidents reported by members of the public. Time trends in crimes are therefore a more useful reflection of societal changes in unlawful behaviour than trends in offences.

Figure 2.3 shows trends between 1950 and 1995 in offences classified into three broad categories.[1] The picture is dominated by driving and parking offences, which rose by a factor of 4.5 over the period.[2] Offences of breach of the peace and petty assault, although smaller in number, rose by a factor of 6.3 over the period, to reach 112,692 in 1995. A majority of these (59 per cent in 1995) were breach of the peace.[3] Both of these offences grew at about the same rate in the first and second halves of the 45-year period. By contrast, there was little change over the entire period in the number of offences of drunkenness recorded.

Figures 2.4 to 2.6 show trends between 1950 and 1995 in nine selected categories of crime.[4] There were substantial increases in violent crimes and sexual assault (Figure 2.4) in most years from 1950 to 1992, followed by a major drop in violent crimes but not sexual assaults in 1993. The pattern since 1993 for these crimes is inconsistent, but it seems possible that the long period of increases has come to an end. The trends in recorded crimes of housebreaking and theft (Figure 2.5) are influenced by a change of definition in 1972; before then, theft from a lockfast place was counted as housebreaking, but from 1972 it was counted as theft. This transfer accounts for the sharp rise in theft and the dip in housebreaking in 1972. Recorded thefts rose consistently from 1954 to 1971; in most years from 1972 to 1991 they rose still more sharply, although there were two dips, and some fluctuations; from 1991 to 1995, however, thefts fell quite steeply. This rather complex pattern of strong and sustained increase in thefts is important, because these crimes are so large in number (43 per cent of all recorded crimes in 1995 were thefts). The pattern of increase in housebreaking was similar to that of theft up to 1971, but thereafter (and even allowing for the change in definitions) housebreaking increased much more slowly than theft. Like theft, it dropped sharply after 1991. Figure 2.6 shows a pattern of strong increase in recorded vandalism starting in 1956, with only one major interruption between 1983 and 1988, up to a peak in 1992, when the long period of increases may have come to an end. Fire-raising increased in a particularly spectacular way, although from a very low base, but then declined after 1991. The increases in fraud were much less striking than those in vandalism and fire-raising, and they levelled off much earlier, from 1987.

These striking increases in recorded crime in Scotland are not dissimilar to those in other European countries. They are lower than those in England and Wales. An exact comparison is not possible, because of major differences in crime classification, but for the purpose of making a rough estimate, notifiable crimes in England and Wales may be compared with crimes in Scotland. The increase in notifiable crimes in England and Wales between 1950 and 1993 was by a factor of ten, compared with a 7.3 times increase in Scotland. Comparison for a specific offence such as robbery is more exact. Over the same period (1950 to 1993) recorded robberies increased by a factor of 48 in England and Wales, compared with 16 times in Scotland.[5]

The factor by which recorded crime has increased is a useful way of summarising the trends. Figure 2.7 shows the factor by which each category of crime increased between 1950 and 1971, and between 1972 and 1995. We chose 1971/72 as the break point, because there was a major change in the classification of crimes then,[6] but in any case the two periods are of roughly equal length. For all nine crimes, with the exception of fraud, the increase was greater in the first 21 years than in the following 23. In particular, the rate of increase slowed very markedly in the cases of serious assault, robbery, other violence and handling of offensive weapons, and housebreaking. However, in the case of theft, which accounts for a substantial proportion of all recorded crimes, the rate of increase slowed only slightly. Figure 2.7 also shows that the rate of increase varied considerably between categories of crime. Fire-raising rose by a factor of 15 (from a very low base) in the 21 years from 1950; over the same period, there were also particularly sharp increases in serious assault, robbery, and other violence and handling.

The annual number of homicides[7] in Scotland rose from around 30 in the early 1950s to 133 in 1995, although it dropped to 118 in 1996 (Scottish

Office, 1997e). Because this crime is rare, there are bound to be random fluctuations from one year to the next, but allowing for that, the increase in homicide has been continuous over the post-war period, although it was particularly strong between the mid 1950s and mid 1960s. More recently, there was a sudden increase from 85 homicide cases in 1991 to 131 in 1992, but this was followed by drop in the two succeeding years. The fourfold increase in homicide in Scotland over the post-war period compares with a twofold increase in England and Wales (Home Office, 1997, table 4.1). There are also considerable differences between other European countries. In some, such as Austria, Denmark, France, West Germany, and Greece, intentional homicide has remained fairly level during the post-war period; whereas in others, such as Hungary, Norway, Scotland, Sweden, Spain, and to a lesser extent the Netherlands, there have been considerable increases (Smith, D., 1995, p.405).[8]

Crime Trends 1981-95

We have seen that the statistics of recorded crime show smaller increases in most categories for the period 1972-95 than for the earlier period 1950-71, and that there is evidence of a levelling off or drop in recorded crime from around 1992. For the period 1981-95 there are also crime survey data on trends, which can be closely compared with recorded crime statistics. These comparisons must be based on the 'comparable subset' of crimes that are covered by both the recorded crime statistics and the crime survey, and where exactly the same definitions can be used. These directly comparable crimes are vandalism, housebreaking, theft of a motor vehicle, theft of a bicycle, robbery, and assault. Figure 2.8 shows trends in these crimes from 1981 to 1995 as measured by the crime survey and the statistics of recorded crime; it also shows the trend in crimes reported to the police, according to survey respondents. The results are indexed, so that the 1981 figure is always 100, and the figures for later years are relative to that: for example, an indexed figure of 200 would mean that crime had doubled since 1981.

Figure 2.8 shows that recorded crime (within the comparable subset) rose by about 50 per cent between 1981 and 1992, but then fell slightly between 1992 and 1995. However, crime as measured by the survey remained roughly level, and had if anything fallen slightly by 1995. The explanation for the divergence between the two trends is an increase in the proportion of incidents that were reported to the police. This is shown by the trend for survey incidents reported to the police, which is similar to that for police-recorded crime. Figure 2.9 again shows the two main trend lines from Figure 2.8 (survey crime and recorded crime in Scotland) alongside the comparable trend lines for England and Wales. The rise in recorded crime over this period (1981-95) was considerably greater in England and Wales than in Scotland, although the shape of the curve was the same, with a drop towards 1995. In England and Wales, survey crime rose continuously over the whole period, to reach a figure 80 per cent higher in 1995 than in 1981, even though it levelled off between 1993 and 1995; in Scotland, by contrast, survey crime remained roughly level throughout.

Figures 2.10 to 2.12 show separate trends for three broad categories of crime within the comparable subset: acquisitive crimes, vandalism, and violence. In Scotland, the survey results show little change in vandalism or violent crime over the period. They show an increase in acquisitive crime between 1981 and 1993, followed by a sudden drop, bringing the count by 1995 back to the 1981 figure. The comparable recorded crime figures for Scotland show a considerable increase both in vandalism and in violent crime, but the survey results suggest that this was largely because of an increase in the proportion of incidents reported to the police. For all three categories of crime, there were considerably greater increases in England and Wales than in Scotland, whether the survey estimate or police statistics are used as the basis for the comparison.

Comparison Between Scotland and England and Wales

In the early 1980s, Home Office researchers made detailed comparisons between the extent and pattern of crime in England and Wales and Scotland on the basis of reaggregated recorded crime statistics (Smith, L., 1983) and the newly established national crime survey (Mayhew and Smith, 1985). The comparisons of recorded crime aimed to overcome the problems caused by different crime classifications in the two countries by reaggregating the Scottish statistics to fit the English classification. The results showed that for five offence categories, Scotland had a higher rate of recorded crime per head of population than England and Wales. Only for violence against the person was the rate lower in Scotland than in England and Wales (see Table 2.1 in the text below). Over the period from 1969 to 1981, Smith also found a stronger upward trend in these recorded crimes in Scotland than in

England and Wales, although, as set out in this chapter, this contrast does not apply to the post-war period as a whole.

Table 2.1   Rates per 10,000 population of recorded crimes in Scotland and notifiable offences in England and Wales, 1981

	England & Wales	Scotland
Violence against the person	20	15
Sexual offences	4	4
Burglary	147	185
Robbery	4	8
Theft and handling of stolen goods	325	389
Fraud and forgery	22	42
Criminal damage	78	120

Source: Mayhew and Smith (1985).

On the basis of the first British Crime Survey, Mayhew and Smith (1985) compared estimated crime rates in Scotland and England and Wales for seven household and six personal offences. For ten of these offences, there was no significant difference between the two countries. The three exceptions were woundings and thefts, which were more prevalent in England, and thefts of motor vehicles, which were more prevalent in Scotland. However, this latter difference only appeared when the rates were calculated on the base of vehicle owners; there was no difference between the rate of vehicle thefts based on all households in Scotland compared with England and Wales. The implication was that a similar incidence of vehicle thefts (in relation to the population) in Scotland was concentrated on a smaller number of targets, because vehicle ownership was lower. In broad terms, therefore, the difference in recorded crime between Scotland and England and Wales was not borne out by the findings of the British Crime Survey. Mayhew and Smith (1985) suggested that the divergence could be explained by two factors: looser counting rules in Scotland, leading to inflation of the recorded crime statistics; and a higher proportion of incidents reported to the police in Scotland than in England and Wales (37 per cent compared with 31 per cent, a difference that was statistically significant at the 95 per cent level of confidence).

As set out in the previous section, since 1981, increases in recorded crime have been much less marked in Scotland than in England and Wales; and crime as estimated by the survey method has remained level in Scotland, whereas it has increased substantially in England and Wales. We have not attempted a detailed comparison between the recorded crime rates in the two countries in 1995 (on the model of L. Smith's for 1981) because it is preferable to compare the survey-based victimisation rates. The crime surveys carried out in the two countries use closely comparable methods and definitions, whereas differences in counting rules and crime categories underlying the recorded crime statistics remain.[9] Figure 2.13 compares the survey-based rates of victimisation for the two countries in 1995. It should be noted that the estimates here apply to the whole of Scotland, whereas those shown in earlier figures apply to central and southern Scotland only. It can be seen that by 1995 the rate of victimisation for every offence category was substantially higher in England and Wales than in Scotland.

An accurate comparison between rates of recorded crime in the two countries would show them to be closer together in 1995 than the rates of victimisation. That is because a higher proportion of incidents are reported to the police in Scotland than in England and Wales. In both countries, reporting rates rose considerably between 1981 and 1992, but if anything the gap in reporting rates between the two countries widened. Hence the recorded crime statistics over-state the level of crime in Scotland compared with England and Wales.

Explaining Crime Trends

For most of the many explanations that have been put forward to explain the post-war rise in crime (Smith, D., 1995), the Scottish case does not constitute a crucial test. For example, increased opportunity associated with economic growth, decline in informal social controls, changes in family structure and functioning, and changes in the nature of adolescence, are all factors that may apply to Scotland, as to other developed countries. However, an important debate has developed in the 1990s about the role of the criminal justice system in shaping divergent crime trends in different countries. In three articles, Farrington and Langan (1992), Farrington and Wikström (1993), and Farrington, Langan and Wikström (1994) have compared crime trends in the 1980s and early 1990s in England, the US, and Sweden. Using crime survey estimates as well as recorded crime statistics they showed that increasing crime in England and Sweden was accompanied by a decline in the likelihood that an offender would be punished, and, more specifically, sent to prison; whereas level crime in the US was accompanied by an increasing likelihood that an offender would be punished and imprisoned. Failing to find an alternative explanation for the divergence in crime trends, they suggested that changes in the likelihood of punishment, given an offence, *may* be the explanation. This argument, which has been hotly contested by other writers (e.g. Currie, 1996) is particularly relevant to policy debate in the US, where rates of imprisonment have increased to unprecedented levels in recent years, and now stand at a level five times that in the UK. The question at issue is whether America's imprisonment binge has worked.

We have seen in earlier sections that in Scotland, as in the US, rising crime levelled off in the early 1980s. Here we consider, in a preliminary way, whether this might be explained by an increase in the likelihood of punishment. There are, in any case, great difficulties in interpreting a negative association between punishment and crime, such that more punishment is associated with less crime, and less punishment with more crime (Nagin, 1998; von Hirsch *et al.*, forthcoming). That is because of the difficulty of specifying the direction of causation. More punishment (especially an increasing likelihood that someone who offends will be punished) might tend to reduce the amount of crime through mechanisms of deterrence or incapacitation, or both. On the other hand, a reduction in the amount of crime for other reasons (say strengthened social bonds and informal social controls) might tend to increase the likelihood that offenders will be punished, because the same criminal justice resources would be available to tackle a smaller number of offenders. Because both interpretations are initially plausible, it is difficult to demonstrate that there is, in fact, a causal relationship running from the likelihood of punishment to the amount of crime, although various strategies can be used to try to eliminate the possibility that causation runs in the opposite direction (Levitt, 1996; Nagin, 1998; von Hirsch *et al.*, forthcoming).

On the other hand, it is perfectly possible, in principle, to falsify the hypothesis. If there is a country or region where crime has risen, then levelled off or fallen, and where this change in the trend was not accompanied by an increase in the likelihood that offenders were punished, then that weakens the inference that an increase in the likelihood of punishment was the decisive factor in halting a rise in crime elsewhere. Whether or not it fatally weakens the inference depends on whether there were special factors at work in the new case that provide an alternative explanation for the end of the rise in crime, and which did not apply to the original case. The question is whether Scotland may provide a crucial example of this kind.

Farrington and Langan (1992) and Farrington and Wikström (1994) made detailed calculations from various sources of data to show how many offenders reach each stage of criminal justice process in the US, England, and Sweden. We have not yet been able to repeat these calculations for Scotland, but from the raw data on the number of persons charged and the prison population, it seems unlikely that the end of the post-war rise in crime was heralded by an increase in the likelihood that offenders would be punished. The total number of persons charged with crimes and offences in 1974 was 224,947. Between 1974 and 1982, the number of charges dropped slightly to 215,718, at a time when recorded crime was rising strongly. At this point, according to the newly established crime survey, the post-war rise in crime levelled off, but the number of charges continued to fall each year, to reach 158,119 in 1994. Thus, the end of the rise in crime seems to have been preceded by a decline in the number of prosecutions, which then continued for 20 years, whereas survey crime remained level (although recorded crime continued to rise to some extent).

Of course, the above comparisons are crude, because all charges have been lumped together. However, it is also the case that charges for most specific crimes, including the more serious ones, declined or remained roughly level before and during the period when the rise in crime levelled off. For example, except for a sudden rise in 1982, charges for serious assault hovered around 1,100 to 1,200 between 1974 and 1994. A notable exception is that charges of robbery increased substantially from 348 in 1974 to 701 in 1982, although the earlier part of this rise coincided with a precipitous increase in the number of reported robberies. More detailed research will be needed to support firmer conclusions, but the indications from the raw data are that the arresting of the rise in crime was preceded and accompanied by a decline in the likelihood that offenders would be punished.

Trends in the prison population and receptions to prison tend to support this conclusion, too. Figure 2.14 shows that the average daily prison population in Scotland fluctuated around the 5,000 mark between 1970 and 1990, when it began to rise quite steeply. It was in the middle of this period that the post-war rise in crime came to an end. Figure 2.15 shows that there was a considerable rise in receptions to prison between 1980 and 1985, followed by a slower decline up to 1991. The rise was too late to account for the end of the post-war rise in crime, and the later fall was not accompanied by a resumption in the growth of crime.

These broad statistical trends in the level of punitiveness in Scotland are in line with changes of policy noted by other commentators (Tombs and Moody, 1993). There has been a notable development of policies to divert offenders from prosecution from the 1960s onwards. Most important among these was the establishment of a unique system of juvenile justice, the Children's Hearing System, which diverts young offenders from the courts except in the case of very serious offences, such as robbery, rape, or murder (see chapter 14). This system, which has been described as 'a radical institution' (Young, 1996, p.136), seeks to act in the best interests of the young person, and deals with young offenders by means of compulsory measures of care rather than penal sanctions. Arising out of the recommendations of the Kilbrandon Committee, which reported in 1964, and established by the Social Work (Scotland) Act of 1968, the Children's Hearing System came into operation in 1971. There was also a large increase in the diversion of adult offenders from prosecution before and during the period when crime levelled off in Scotland. Tombs and Moody (1993) stated that the proportion of offences reported to the fiscal in which formal court proceedings were not instituted rose from around 7-12 per cent during the 1970s, to 19 per cent in 1981, 39 per cent in 1986, and almost half in 1991. A major impetus to these developments was the reports of the Stewart Committee (1980; 1983) which recommended an extension of the fixed penalty system, and increased use of discretion to take no action (see chapter 7). Increasing pressure on relatively fixed resources caused by rising crime may also have been an important factor, according to Tombs and Moody (1993). Thus, at a time when US policy was moving decisively and fast towards greater punitiveness and much higher imprisonment rates, Scottish policy was moving firmly in the opposite direction. In both countries, rising crime levelled off.

Conclusion

The findings set out in this chapter suggest that Scotland may be a particularly interesting example for the study of crime trends. It is an example that will reward study because of the large fund of data provided by regular crime surveys starting in 1982, in combination with the detailed statistics of recorded crime, and because of the potential for close comparisons with England and Wales. These comparisons can be telling, because Scotland shares so much with its neighbour, yet shows contrasting trends in crime in recent years.

We have argued that Scotland may be the crucial example in discussion of the link between the quantity of crime and the quantity of punishment. The US has pursued a policy of vastly increasing the use of imprisonment, and its imprisonment binge has been accompanied by a halt to the post-war growth of crime. Whether increased punitiveness in the US was what caused the growth of crime to end is a central question, and perhaps *the* central question, for criminologists today. Crime also ceased to rise in Scotland a few years later than in the US, whereas it continued to rise in England and Wales and in many other European countries. Yet the end of the growth of crime in Scotland, unlike the US, was accompanied by no increase in the number of offenders punished, nor in the use of imprisonment. Instead, it was preceded, and accompanied, by a growing use of alternatives to prosecution, in part as a consequence of policies such as the establishment of the Children's Hearing System, the extension of fixed penalties, the introduction of fiscal fines, and the official encouragement of the use of discretion not to prosecute. On the face of the evidence, the Scottish example suggests that a policy of diverting many offenders from prosecution does not prevent rising crime from levelling off (to put it no higher) and that it is not necessary to increase the likelihood that offenders will be punished in order to stem the rise in crime. Further research is needed to show whether the detailed evidence supports this interpretation. Present evidence is enough to place firmly on the agenda the question whether diversion from prosecution in Scotland has been a successful method of stemming the post-war rise in crime.

Figure 2.1   Recorded crimes: Scotland, 1995

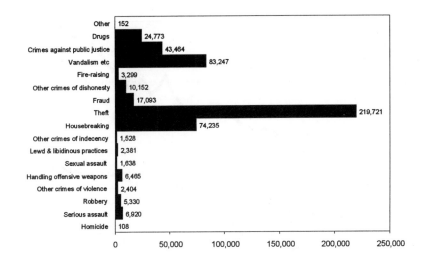

Figure 2.2   Recorded offences: Scotland, 1995

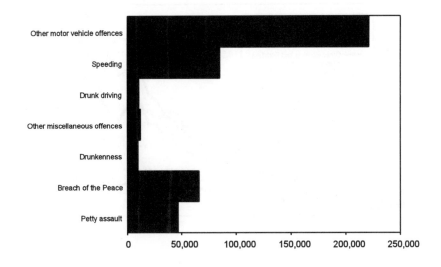

Figure 2.3   Recorded offences: Scotland, 1950-95

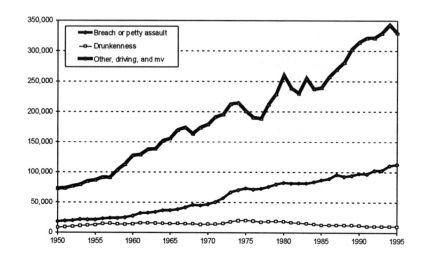

Figure 2.4   Recorded violent crimes and sexual assault: Scotland, 1950-95

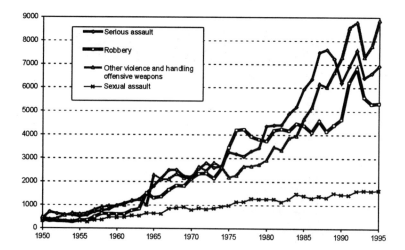

Figure 2.5   Recorded housebreaking and theft: Scotland, 1950-95

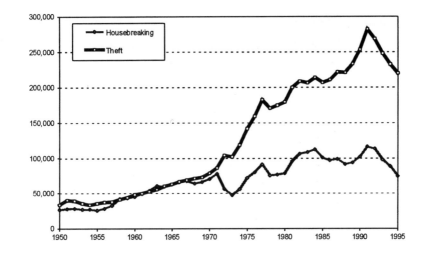

Figure 2.6   Recorded fraud and damage: Scotland, 1950-95

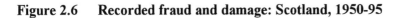

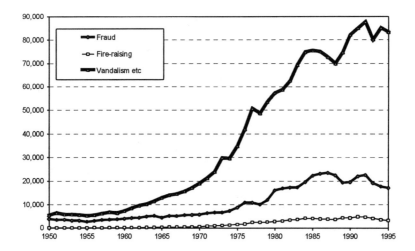

Figure 2.7   Increase in selected crimes: Scotland, 1950-71 & 1972-95

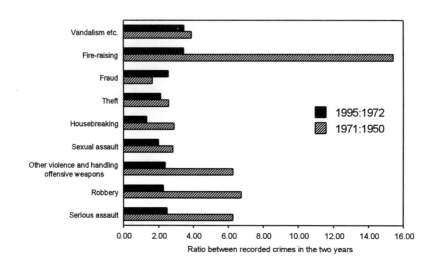

Figure 2.8   Indexed trends in crime: Scotland, 1981-95 (crime survey and recorded crime, 1981=100)

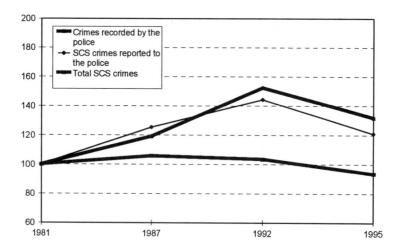

Figure 2.9   **Trends in survey and police-recorded crime: Scotland compared with England and Wales, 1981-95 (indexed, 1981=100)**

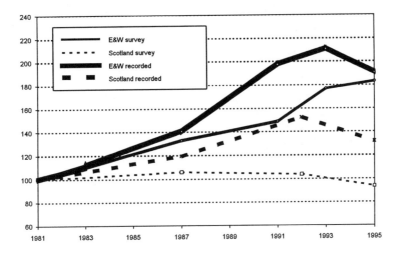

Figure 2.10   **Trends in acquisitive crime: Scotland compared with England and Wales, 1981-95 (indexed, 1981=100)**

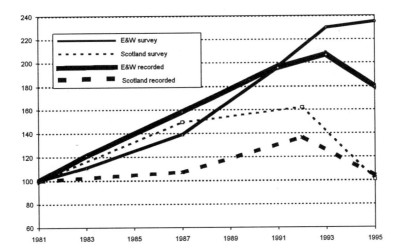

Figure 2.11   **Trends in vandalism: Scotland compared with England and Wales, 1981-95 (indexed, 1981=100)**

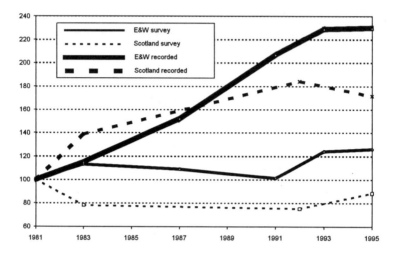

Figure 2.12   **Trends in violent crime: Scotland compared with England and Wales, 1981-95 (indexed, 1981=100)**

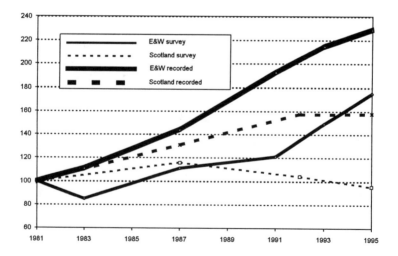

Figure 2.13   Survey victimisation rates: Scotland compared with England and Wales, 1995

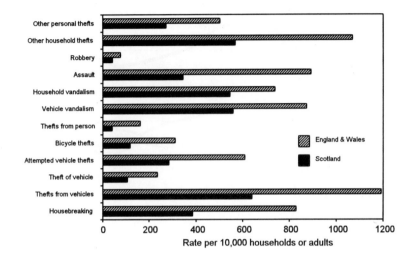

Figure 2.14   Average daily prison population: Scotland, 1950-94

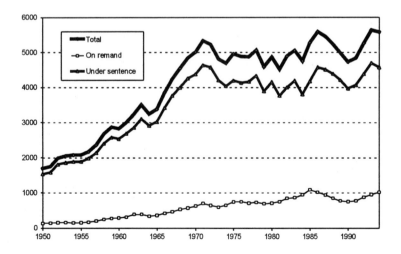

Figure 2.15 Receptions to prison: Scotland, 1980-94

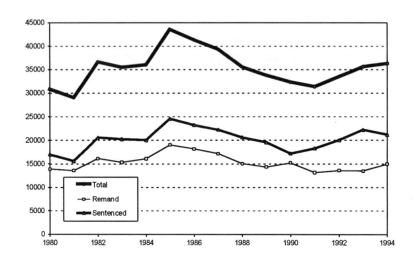

Notes

1. Other things being equal, crimes can be expected to rise or fall in line with changes in the population, so it is appropriate to express recorded crimes per head (or per 10,000) of the population. However, it happens that in Scotland there was virtually no change in the total population between 1950 and 1995 (over this period the population rose from an estimated 5.102 million to 5.137 million). Because expressing the counts per head of population makes no appreciable difference, we have preferred to show the actual counts of recorded crime.

2. Miscellaneous other offences are also included in this category. They were not shown separately from driving and parking offences until 1972, when they accounted for 16 per cent of 'other, driving, and motor vehicle' offences; by 1995, they accounted for only four per cent. Hence the rise is in driving and parking offences, not in miscellaneous other offences.

3. Breach of the peace and petty assault are lumped together in the statistics until 1972.

4. The official statistics group crimes into larger categories ('non-sexual crimes of violence', 'crimes of indecency', 'damage', 'other crimes') but we have preferred to base this analysis on smaller, less heterogeneous categories. Some crimes have been left out to simplify the presentation, and in two cases (crimes against public justice, and drugs) because they were not separately

identified at the beginning of the period. However, some statistics for recorded drugs offences from 1983 onwards will be quoted below.

5. The series for all notifiable offences in England and Wales has been constructed by Home Office statisticians, and is shown in *Criminal Statistics England and Wales 1993* (Home Office, 1994). The series for robbery in England and Wales was compiled without adjustment from the statistics published annually in *Criminal Statistics England and Wales*. For a presentation of these statistics, see Smith, D. (1996).

6. In fact, the change was in 1978, but the statistics for 1972-77 have been re-worked to fit the new definitions.

7. Including both murder and common law culpable homicide, but excluding causing death by dangerous or reckless driving.

8. Note however that these comparisons, which are based on World Health Organization statistics, refer to intentional homicide, whereas the statistics quoted elsewhere in this chapter also include manslaughter and infanticide (in England) and common law culpable homicide (in Scotland).

9. Some detailed inconsistencies between the methods used in the two surveys have been ironed out in the latest results (MVA Consultancy, 1997). For example, the recall period used to calculate the percentage of incidents reported to the police has now been standardised.

3 Crime Statistics and the 'Problem of Crime' in Scotland

SIMON ANDERSON

> Like all knowledge, official statistics must be analysed as a product. They are never mere givens to be taken as they are or else dismissed as inadequate. Like all products, they must be examined in terms of the conditions and instruments of their production.
> (Hindess, 1973, p.4).

Introduction

We spend both too much and too little time talking about crime statistics: too much, in the sense that they continue to be drawn on in popular, political and even academic debate as relatively straightforward reflections of 'crime reality'; too little, in that there is scant understanding of the important conceptual and technical issues which lie behind them.

The aim of this chapter is to encourage and facilitate a critical engagement with the main quantitative indicators of crime in Scotland. More specifically, I aim to do three things: first, to look at what it is that crime statistics actually represent and at why it is important that we understand the ways in which they are constructed and used; second, to provide an overview of the main indicators of crime in Scotland - the statistics of crimes recorded by the police and the national crime surveys carried out periodically by the Scottish Office since the early 1980s; and, finally, to highlight some of the questions that might be asked of these and other quantitative indicators of crime.

What I do not intend to do, for reasons which will become obvious, is provide a neat summary of the 'facts and figures' of crime in Scotland. I do not believe that such summaries are either valid or helpful - except as a means of prompting debate about their silences and limitations. It should also be emphasised that the chapter concentrates on incidents of crime or victimisation as recorded by the police or surveys, rather than on other sources of quantitative data relating to the criminal justice process, such as the statistics of persons proceeded against in court or held in Scottish prisons. These latter sources play a less significant role in debates about crime and are essentially less contestable, since they do not claim to be any more than indices of institutional activity.

Crime Statistics and the 'Problem of Crime'

In this part of the chapter, I want to look at what crime statistics actually are and at why they matter. The answers to these questions are, I think, less obvious than they first appear. I want to argue against an uncomplicated 'realist' view which treats crime statistics as measurements - albeit imperfect ones - of an objective 'crime reality'. But I also hope to rescue them from the 'institutionalist' critique which, in its most extreme form, sees them as little more than indices of the activities of the organisations which produce them.

Crime statistics matter for two main reasons: first, because they do tell us something real about the 'problem of crime', though we may need to rethink our understanding of that term; and second, because in seeking to describe that problem, they help to constitute it in the first place. I return to these themes below. First, however, I want to consider briefly how quantitative indicators of crime have traditionally been viewed.

'Consider Crimes as Things': Realism and the Dark Figure of Crime

In recent decades, the two main sources of quantitative information about crime in Scotland, as elsewhere, have been the statistics of crimes recorded by the police and the data offered by local and national crime surveys. These are generally seen as being in opposition to each other - understandably, since crime surveys developed largely in response to the perceived inadequacies of police-recorded crime statistics. There is, however, a greater degree of continuity between them than is usually supposed - what links them is an implicit realist perspective. I use the term here not in relation to left realism (a theoretical perspective strongly associated with the use of crime surveys at a local level) but in the sense in which it is employed by Biderman and Reiss (1967). A realist perspective, they suggest, emphasises the 'virtues of completeness with which data represents the "real crime which takes place"' (p.2).

This is, of course, an essentially positivist perspective - one which conceives of crimes as 'things' that can be objectively identified, labelled and tallied. It has two main consequences. First, it pushes us towards what has been termed an 'events-orientation' (Skogan, 1986) which focuses our understanding of crime on discrete 'acts' and 'incidents', abstracted from the context in which they occur.[1] Second, it defines the problem of the quantification of crime in essentially technical terms and establishes the so-called 'dark figure' - that sum of incidents 'missing' from the main quantitative sources - as the central problem of criminological enquiry.

Writing in the late 1960s, Biderman and Reiss noted a growing preoccupation with the pursuit of this figure; some 30 years on, in the words of two recent commentators, the discipline remains 'haunted' by it (Coleman and Moynihan, 1996). As a result, most discussion about quantitative sources of information about crime has remained technical in character. For the crime survey methodologist, the key problem is that of how to unearth the 'reality' of an incident in question. This point is well illustrated by Skogan (1986, p.80, emphasis added), who writes:

> Because the survey gathers data on events *external to the individual* and those events presumably have a reality apart from their description to an interviewer, the standard of accuracy in victimisation research is the match between *the reality of an incident* and its description.

While, in some ways, crime surveys have been used to challenge the 'official' picture of crime presented by the police statistics, in other ways they have served to reinforce the categories and definitions of formal criminal justice. This has been especially true of the national crime surveys (the British and Scottish Crime Surveys), which - in their pursuit of the dark figure - have attempted to classify incidents in exactly the same way that the police would have done. In fact, this is an impossible task, since the classification decisions made by the police reflect not only a set of formal decision rules, but also the social and institutional context in which those decisions are made. The very notion of the dark figure, however, pushes the crime survey in this direction. If we want to show how many crimes are 'missing' from the police statistics, we have to accept the boundaries and definitions employed in those statistics.

Some crime surveys - especially those carried out at a local level by researchers associated with Left Realism - have placed less emphasis on the need for an exact tie-up with the categories of formal criminal justice. They have disputed not just total numbers of incidents, but also the type of incidents that are recorded in the first place - including questions, for example, about sexual or racial harassment. What they have failed to escape, however, is the events-orientation referred to above. Ultimately, they, too, are trapped by their methods, which implicitly focus attention on the technical obstacles to an 'accurate' crime count and distract attention from serious conceptual debate about the construction of quantitative indicators of crime. While the more sophisticated proponents of the crime survey may not actually believe that it is possible to arrive at the 'true' level of crime, as Phipps (1988) notes, 'they seem to *proceed* as though this goal *were* attainable'.

The Institutionalist and Radical Critiques

The realist position has been - and continues to be - the perspective which dominates public and academic interpretations of crime statistics, but there have been some important critical voices. Perhaps the most influential of these has been the 'institutionalist' perspective, associated - initially at least - with the micro-sociological theories of Kitsuse, Cicourel and others. This sees crime statistics not as relatively straightforward measures of 'crime reality' upon which to base policy or causal explanation, but as products of social and institutional processes. As Kitsuse and Cicourel (1963, p.135) state:

> We suggest that the question of the theoretical significance of the official statistics can be re-phrased by shifting the focus of investigation from the processes by which *certain forms of behaviour* are socially and culturally generated to the processes by which *rates of deviant behaviour* are produced ... Rates can be viewed as indices of organisational processes rather than as indices of the incidence of certain forms of behaviour.

Kitsuse and Cicourel argue that attention should be directed, through qualitative and observational methods, to detailed study of the policies and processes through which crime statistics are produced. They place a particular emphasis on seeking to understand the background 'expectancies' and intellectual frameworks of individual actors within the 'rate producing process'. While the value and possibility of this latter approach was decisively criticised by Hindess (1973), the general argument - that crime statistics should be viewed not simply in terms of actions (i.e. criminal incidents) but in terms of individual and collective *re*actions - was very influential during the 1970s. Indeed, it was taken in a more radical direction by a number of critical criminologists who began to focus attention on the fact that crime statistics were the product not just of social processes but of *political* ones and who sought to highlight the way that class interests were represented in the criminalisation of certain acts and not others. The theoretical groundwork for such a reading of crime statistics was laid by Taylor, Walton and Young (1973) in *The New Criminology*, which sought to bring together elements of interactionist and Marxist theory. There were also empirical attempts to apply such a framework to particular types of crime, such as 'crimes of the powerful' (Pearce, 1976) and 'mugging' (Hall *et al.*, 1978).

Rethinking the 'Problem of Crime'

Where does this leave us, in terms of our attempt to understand what it is that crime statistics actually represent? The realist position, in its pure form, is clearly untenable. There is no 'true' level of crime, to which we can get ever closer through methodological innovation. The notion of the dark figure is, in itself, misleading, since it suggests a pre-existing pool of incidents, waiting patiently to be uncovered and assigned to their 'correct' categories. In fact, what different types of crime statistics offer us is not an ever more complete count of crime, but competing definitions of what we should count *as* crime in the first place.

So, if crime statistics are not a straightforward reflection of real events, is it more helpful to draw on the institutionalist or radical perspectives, which highlight the social and political processes through which 'crime rates' are constructed? The problem with this approach is that, ultimately, it obscures the fact that 'real things' do happen to 'real people'. It is doubtful whether even the most committed institutionalist could sustain a view of crime as a purely social construct in the face of a violent assault or having had their home broken into. Victimisation has a 'stubbornly concrete' quality. We cannot avoid the conclusion that, regardless of the filtering and definitional processes involved, however distant or distorted, the primary material from which crime statistics are hewn remains 'real life'.

If crime statistics are neither straightforward reflections of 'crime reality' nor wholly social or political constructs, how are we to understand them? I want to suggest that their significance lies in the concept of the 'problem of crime', though not perhaps in the conventional understanding of that term.

When we talk about crime statistics, we tend to invoke the concept of the 'problem of crime', though the precise meaning of that term is rarely articulated. It is assumed to be self-evident: crime is a problem, first, because it exists and, second, because we find it difficult to know what to do about it. The extent or seriousness of the problem is generally conceived in quantitative terms - the more crime, the bigger the problem. Crime statistics are, therefore, given a key role both as indicators of the problem itself and of the success or failure of our efforts to address it.

I want to suggest that we need to move towards a more complex understanding of the 'problem of crime' that does not equate its seriousness simply with quantity. This is not simply a call for academic criminologists to adopt a more theoretical and less 'administrative' approach, as such a move would have practical significance for crime prevention and policing too. As Muncie and Fitzgerald (1996, p.2) have pointed out, the 'problem of crime' is dual-edged. Crime is problematic in the obvious sense - that criminal acts create real difficulties for both individuals and communities - and in the less obvious sense, in that it is an essentially contested concept. In treating the problem of crime as a self-evident, easily quantifiable concept, we fail to do justice to people's actual experiences and risk creating policy outcomes which are inflexible or misguided.

We have seen that the 'realist' perspective conceives of an objective crime reality - a universe of 'things that happen' - while from the 'institutionalist' point of view, crime is largely the product of institutional activity and definition. I want to suggest, uncontroversially, that the 'problem of crime' involves elements of both - that real things do happen to real people, but that our understanding of those things is shaped and defined by institutional responses. But I also want to introduce a third element - one that is largely missing from the perspectives outlined so far - namely, the significance of the subjective response of members of the public. The missing element in the everyday construction of the problem of crime is a sense of the 'victim sensibilities' of the public - in other words, the capacity of individuals to *feel* victimised or to feel the threat of victimisation. In this sense, the problem of crime can intensify without any underlying change in the number of 'things that happen'. There is little evidence, for example, of a significant increase in the rate of crime in rural areas in recent years. Nevertheless, the capacity of rural communities to absorb or respond to those things which do happen has been reduced through changes in the nature of those communities themselves (Anderson, 1997). In that sense, the problem of crime has worsened, even if its actual prevalence has remained unchanged.

The problem of crime as a social phenomenon is, therefore, constructed in the space between 'things that happen' and the way that, collectively and *as individuals*, we respond to those things. Crime statistics matter because they are an imprint or expression of that construction, a relationship summarised in Figure 2.1.

Figure 2.1   The problem of crime

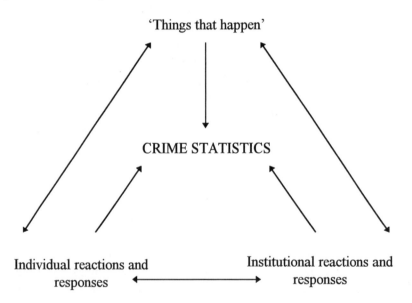

'Things that happen'

CRIME STATISTICS

Individual reactions and responses   Institutional reactions and responses

But crime statistics are important not only because they provide an indicator of the problem of crime; they matter because they help to constitute it in the first place. Despite the scientific veneer - and the image of an objective 'social barometer' - crime statistics (of whatever kind) are not separate from the world they seek to describe. Through their very existence, in fact, they help to shape it. When statistics are used to describe crime spiralling upwards, they contribute to a discourse of lawlessness and social mistrust. While such a discourse may not be inappropriate, in itself, it may make it more likely that crime actually does occur (for example, by reducing the number of people using the streets at night) or intensify the problem of crime by heightening public concern. Similarly, when the Chief Constable of Strathclyde announces that 'crime is down by six per cent', he is not only telling us something about the extent of the problem of crime, he is consciously attempting to shape it.[2]

Crime statistics not only shape our understanding of how crime is changing, they give us a particular image of what it consists of in the first place - one, as we have seen, that is based on incidents not processes, objective acts not subjective experience, and closely defined legal categories. Both police-recorded crime statistics and crime survey data emphasise certain types of crime and not others. For example, we hear much about street violence, but little about domestic violence, racial harassment or elder abuse; we hear about housebreaking, but not about tax evasion, wildlife crime or crimes against the environment. While crime statistics are generally honest about their limitations, this does not stop them from reinforcing a particular understanding of crime. This may be unavoidable, but we should at least be conscious that it is happening.

In reading crime statistics, of whatever kind, we should ask ourselves how the various elements identified above may be interacting to produce a particular picture. While there will be no definitive answers, the attempt in itself may be valuable, since it forces us to confront the way that the 'problem of crime' is constructed and the role that crime statistics play in that process. This is not an approach that denies the 'reality' of victimisation or its effects. It is one, however, which emphasises that the problem of crime is to be found not just in what happens, but in how, as individuals and collectively, we react and respond to those events. As a consequence, it suggests that sometimes the 'answers' to the problem of crime may be found in the base of the triangle (shown in Figure 2.1), rather than in its apex.

In the final section of this chapter, I return to this theme by showing some of the questions that a critical reading of crime data might involve. First, however, I want to offer an overview of the main sources of quantitative information about crime in Scotland: the police-recorded criminal statistics and the national crime surveys carried out by the Scottish Office.

Recorded Crime Statistics in Scotland

The first regular statistics relating to crime in Scotland were published in 1833 and consisted of annual court returns showing the numbers of people committed to prison, the nature of their crimes and the results of proceedings. Figures of crimes made known to the police - our concern in this section - were first published in 1868 and, following a review in 1895, remained broadly unchanged until 1978 when the current format was established.

The principal source of these statistics is the bulletin, *Recorded Crime in Scotland*, published annually by the Civil and Criminal Justice Statistics Unit of the Scottish Office.[3] This presents information on crimes and offences[4] 'made known' to the police under seven main headings:

(i) Non-sexual crimes of violence;
(ii) crimes of indecency;
(iii) crimes of dishonesty;
(iv) fire-raising, vandalism, etc.;
(v) other crimes;
(vi) miscellaneous offences; and
(vii) motor vehicle offences.

In total, there are some 320 individual crime and offence codes. Although these are usually presented in the form of the seven summary headings shown, there is also a more disaggregate classification containing 30 headings and statistics can be produced for any single code. The crime and offence figures included in the bulletin take two forms: 'counts' and 'rates'. Counts are straightforward tallies of the raw numbers of crimes and offences recorded by the police; rates express those totals in terms of numbers of crimes or offences per head of population (or, more specifically, per 10,000 people). This information is presented at three levels: for Scotland as a whole, by police force area and by local authority district. Information is also presented about trends in these figures over time.

The recorded crime statistics in Scotland (unlike in England and Wales) are technically offence rather than incident based. This means that when several crimes or offences occur in the course of a single incident (e.g. when the occupants of a house are assaulted in the course of a housebreaking), these are counted separately.

The other significant statistic contained in this bulletin is the proportion of offences 'cleared-up' by the police. Until 1996, a crime or offence was regarded as having been cleared up if one or more offenders had been apprehended, cited, warned or traced for it. Because of concern that this gave the police scope to record an incident as cleared up simply on the basis of suspicion, a revised definition was introduced which defines a crime or offence as having been cleared up 'where there exists a sufficiency of evidence under Scots law to justify consideration of criminal proceedings', even if a report is not actually submitted to the procurator fiscal.

The statistics are based on regular returns made by each of Scotland's police forces to the Scottish Office. Until 1994, these returns were made on a monthly basis. Forces now submit such figures on a quarterly basis, with the national bulletin generally being published in April following the end of the calendar year to which the statistics refer. The aggregate level information (relating to Scotland as a whole) is, however, sometimes published via a news release in advance of the main bulletin (especially, it seems, when the figures seem to contain 'good news'!).

Although *Recorded Crime in Scotland* presents most of the information in summary form, data at a more disaggregate level are available from the Civil and Criminal Justice Statistics Unit, who can supply figures for all 30 crime categories for each of the 32 local authorities. Such data are generally provided free of charge to universities and other non-profit organisations. A charge may be made to supply data for commercial use.

While the police recorded crime statistics are compiled centrally, it is important to trace their production backwards through the eight Scottish forces to their origins in every day police work. The point to note here is that there is a distinction between incidents 'logged' by the police and those recorded as crimes. A crime report is only raised if there is considered to be sufficient evidence that a crime has actually occurred. An incident can subsequently be 'no crimed' if - following further investigation - it becomes evident that no crime has actually taken place, although there are relatively strict checks on the level of 'no criming' within each force. The task of assigning incidents to a specific crime category belongs increasingly to centralised divisions within each force, though in some police force areas an initial classification is still undertaken by officers themselves.

National Crime Surveys in Scotland

Large-scale surveys of victimisation were pioneered in the United States, initially as part of President Johnson's National Commission on Crime, and in 1972 were institutionalised in the form of a National Crime Survey. During the 1970s, many other countries followed suit, including Canada, Israel, Australia and the Netherlands. In Britain, however, despite one or two small-scale projects, the government resisted calls for a national survey. They did so largely on grounds of cost, but also, it would seem, out of fear that the discovery of a vast well of undisclosed crime would cause undue political embarrassment.

The eventual launch of the British Crime Survey (BCS) in the early 1980s was the result of a number of factors: a build-up of pressure from the academic community; the feeling that Britain was lagging behind other countries; the influence of so-called 'administrative criminology', focused on questions of crime prevention and efficient resource allocation, within the Home Office Research and Planning Unit; and the prevailing climate of 'law and order' politics, heightened by the riots in many English inner cities in 1981. The first sweep of the BCS took place in 1982 and had separate samples of 10,000 in England and Wales and 5,000 in Scotland.[5]

In the period since, the BCS in England and Wales has been repeated on five occasions and has come to occupy a central position in both policy-based and academic debates about crime.[6] In Scotland, however, national crime surveys have had a far more patchy history. The Scottish Office chose not to participate in the second sweep of the BCS in 1984 - primarily on grounds of cost, though also, apparently, because it was felt to follow too soon after the initial survey. Although the Scottish Office did take part in the 1988 survey, the experience was an unhappy one - there were significant problems with completion of the fieldwork for the survey and long wrangles with the survey company over the calculation of victimisation rates. As a consequence, the results from the study were not published until 1992 (Payne, 1992; Kinsey and Anderson, 1992).

The experience of the 1988 BCS persuaded the Scottish Office that there would be considerable merit in running its own national survey, over which it would be possible to exert a greater degree of control. As a result, Scotland again sat out the next sweep of the BCS in 1992 and, the following year, launched its own survey, the Scottish Crime Survey (SCS). This exercise was repeated in 1996 and it is anticipated that there will be a third sweep in the year 2000.[7]

Although the decision to run a separate Scottish survey seemed to reduce the problems with the overall management of the project, it failed to address one of the underlying weaknesses of the survey - the relative lack of resources for analysis. For both sweeps of the SCS, publication of the main results has taken significantly longer than in England and Wales (where the Home Office has a larger team of researchers available to work on the study) and almost no use has been made of the datasets for secondary analysis.

The national surveys in Scotland have all taken the same broad form, consisting of a nationally-representative sample of *circa* 5,000 adults (aged 16 and over) resident in private households. Although the surveys cover a range of issues, including attitudes towards the police and anxiety about crime, their core function is that of crime counting.[8] The surveys provide estimates of the prevalence and incidence of two types of victimisation - that involving households (e.g. housebreaking, car crime) and that involving individuals (e.g. theft from the person, assault). They do not, of course, provide estimates of crimes in which there is no clearly identifiable individual victim (e.g. vandalism of public or business property), nor 'victimless' crimes such as prostitution, traffic offences or drug misuse.

Near the beginning of the interview, survey respondents are asked a series of 'screening' questions aimed at eliciting experience of different types of crime during the previous year (e.g. 'Since the first of January last year, has anyone entered or tried to enter your home and stolen or damaged anything that belonged to you?'). For each incident or series of connected incidents reported at a screening question, an additional set of questions (known as a victim form) is asked in order to establish further details about what happened. A complex set of decision rules is subsequently applied to this information in order to assign the 'correct' legal classification to the incident.

The results from the survey cover some 13 crime or offence types, five of which are 'directly comparable' with the statistics of crimes recorded by the police. This subset of the survey data is used in two main ways - as the source of the estimate of the size of the dark figure (equal to the crime survey estimate minus the police estimate) and to compare rates of change. Two points should be made about these comparisons. First, they are based on a very limited (and somewhat curious) set of offences - namely, housebreaking, theft of a motor vehicle, theft of a bicycle, vandalism and assault. Second, even for these offence categories, the comparison is somewhat arbitrary, since the police figures must be 'adjusted' to exclude all incidents without an individual victim or in which the victim was aged under 16.

The 'crime count' information from the surveys is presented in two main forms - as *incidence* rates and *prevalence* rates. Incidence rates are an expression of the number of incidents occurring per head of population (typically, per 10,000 households or 10,000 individuals) and form the basis of comparisons with police statistics. Prevalence rates are an expression of the proportion of the population (either households or individuals) that has been victimised. These have no equivalent in the police statistics and are usually expressed as a percentage. An incidence rate will generally appear higher than a prevalence rate because some members of the population will have been victimised more than once. Thus, the 1993 SCS suggested an incidence rate for housebreaking of 667 per 10,000 households and a prevalence rate of 4.9 per cent (or 490 victims per 10,000 households).

Towards a Critical Reading of Crime Statistics

By this stage it should be clear that crime statistics, of whatever kind, should always be subjected to critical scrutiny. This is not because they are potentially 'faulty' indicators whose 'biases' must be identified and taken into account in our pursuit of the 'real' level of crime in Scotland. Rather, as I suggested earlier, the reason for looking at broader explanations of change in such indicators is that it may tell us something valuable about the construction of the 'problem of crime' itself.

In this concluding section, I want to highlight the kinds of questions that we should be asking of police-recorded crime statistics and crime survey data in Scotland. In many ways, despite their obvious differences, these two types of data bear similar scrutiny, since, as we have seen, they also share a number of underlying assumptions about the nature and characteristics of crime. Several sets of questions suggest themselves.

First, there are those which relate to the subjective experience of victimisation by individuals. As Christie (1986, p.18) points out:

> Being a victim is not a thing, an objective phenomenon. It will not be the same to all people in situations externally described as being the 'same'. *It has to do with the participants' definitions of the situation.*

We need, then, to remain alert to the possibility that some sections of the population are more likely to see themselves as victims than are others or are more likely to appeal to formal criminal justice to address their victimisation. For example, it is possible that at least some of the gap between the level of police-recorded crime in urban and rural parts of Scotland can be accounted for by lower rates of reporting to the police in rural areas (see Anderson, 1997). Differences in 'victim sensibilities' may also show up in crime surveys: it is well known, for example, that there is often a so-called 'education effect' in relation to measures of violent victimisation, with the likelihood of reported victimisation rising with levels of educational attainment (see Sparks *et al.*, 1977). Thus, for any specific set of crime figures, questions should be asked about the consistency of individual response across different sections of the population.

Even more importantly, the same questions may be asked about changes in crime rates over time. Could it be that the dramatic growth in recorded crime in Scotland (as in most Western societies) since the Second World War can be partly explained by the growing willingness of individuals in a 'risk society' to see themselves as victims and by an increasingly 'police-centred' view of how we should respond to problematic behaviour? The results of the national crime surveys carried out in Scotland certainly suggest an increase in rates of reporting between 1981 and 1992 (from 38 per cent of all survey incidents to 52 per cent) - though, interestingly, the most recent survey, relating to 1995, suggests a slight decrease, which may help to explain why police-recorded crime statistics have themselves been falling in recent years.

A second set of questions relate to the capacity and willingness of the data collecting agencies to record incidents. It may seem facetious to point out that if there were no police officers there would be no crime, but this does illustrate an important point. The ability of the police to detect and record criminal incidents is highly dependent on their overall level of resourcing and on their use of those resources. In general, most crimes recorded by the police are brought to their attention via a member of the public. However, certain categories of crime are much more dependent on the actions of the police themselves. The main examples of these are so-called 'victimless' crimes, such as drug misuse and prostitution, and crimes which have no clearly identifiable individual victim, such as tax evasion or environmental degradation. Thus it is always important to ask the question: to what extent do police-recorded crime statistics reflect a concentration of police resources on particular issues? An increase in the rate of drug offences or public order offences, such as drunkenness, is very often simply a reflection of a police initiative aimed at tackling these issues. The opposite is also true. The relative invisibility in the police-recorded crime statistics of 'white collar' crimes, such as fraud or tax evasion, is a reflection of the fact that this is not an issue on which police resources are focused.

As noted above, members of the public bring most crimes to the attention of the police, but the simple act of reporting an incident is not sufficient to guarantee it a place in the criminal statistics. For a variety of reasons, the police may choose not to record an incident as a crime, or take the decision to record it under a different heading from that which might appear likely. For example, an attempted housebreaking may appear in the statistics as vandalism. It is important to take account of the various institutional factors which may shape the police's response to the recording of individual incidents. The need to maintain a healthy 'clear up' rate, for example, may exert a pressure to 'cuff' (i.e. not formally record) more trivial incidents for which it is unlikely that an offender will be identified.

Another issue to take into account here is the relationship between crime rates and police funding. Throughout the 1980s, a cynic might argue, the police in Scotland - as elsewhere in the UK - had a vested interest in seeing the crime rate increase, since the Conservative government of the time was willing to expand the funding available to the police, subject to evidence that the extent of the crime problem was continuing to grow. In recent years, however, there has been much less money available to the police and there has been a greater emphasis on value for money in public expenditure. The onus has, therefore, been on the police to show that they are providing an efficient and effective service. How better to show that than by delivering year-on-year decreases in the crime rate?

A third and final set of questions relate to the consistency with which data is collected and defined. In relation to both police statistics and crime survey data, methods of data collection change, definitions are altered and the confidence with which one can really claim to be comparing like with like diminishes over time. In 1990, for example, the police definition of serious assault was revised, meaning that figures for previous years had to be 'adjusted' to allow continued time-series analysis. At the same time, the gradual introduction of computer-based incident logging and crime reporting has had its own impact - not least in encouraging the inclusion of more minor offences and in enforcing greater consistency across the different Forces.

There are also important questions to be asked of apparent changes in crime survey victimisation rates over time. All other things being equal, such changes between surveys will still be subject to sampling error - and, in the case of less common types of crime, such errors may be sizeable. These errors are, however, at least known. The real problem is that all other things are generally not equal across different surveys carried out with several years between them. Some of the methodological changes worth considering are the following. First, there may have been a change in the sampling frame used - for example, the 1982 BCS used the electoral register, while subsequent surveys used either a hybrid between the electoral register and the Postcode Address File (PAF) or PAF on its own. Second, there may have been important variations in the wording or order of questions, which can have substantial effects on response. Third, since the four national crime surveys in Scotland have been carried out by three different fieldwork organisations, there may be significant so-called 'company effects', resulting from different standards or practices among the interviewers. Finally, it should be borne in mind that the process of incident classification is by no means straightforward - as with the police statistics, slight differences in decision rules over time may result in apparently considerable increases or decreases in victimisation rates for specific offence types.

While some of the above issues are undeniably technical in nature, they are also of conceptual significance, in that both the police-recorded crime statistics and the crime survey help to create a particular image of crime. To understand (or challenge) that image, we need to be clear about how it is constructed - hence the focus on its technical aspects. But, at the same time, we also need to remember that crime is not a given empirical category. The more we treat its quantification *solely* as a technical exercise, the less, ultimately, we will understand about it.

Further information about the police-recorded crime statistics can be obtained from the Civil and Criminal Justice Statistics Unit Branch 2, The Scottish Office Home Department, W1 (C) Spur, Broomhouse Drive, Edinburgh, EH11 3XD. Telephone: 0131 244 2225.

Further information about the Scottish Crime Survey can be obtained from the Criminological Research Branch, The Scottish Office Home Department, Broomhouse Drive, Edinburgh, EH11 3XD. Telephone: 0131 244 2114.

The data from the British and Scottish Crime Surveys are also available via the ESRC Data Archive (telephone: 01206 872001; e-mail: archive@essex.ac.uk).

Notes

1.   As Genn (1988, p.91) argues, in her study of victimisation on a North London housing estate, 'it is clear that violent victimisation may often be better conceptualised as a *process* rather than as a series of discrete events'. Because crime surveys tend to conceptualise continuing states as individual events, they cannot possibly reflect people's actual conditions of life or experience of victimisation.

2.   In a recent press release (Strathclyde Police, 1998), Chief Constable John Orr was quoted as saying, 'the fact remains that crime has not been lower in a generation and the people in Strathclyde are far less at risk of becoming victims of crime than they think. The Force will continue to do all it can to reduce needless over-anxiety among the citizens of the area because such fear limits their quality of life'. Interestingly, the police have started to use crime survey data on *perceptions* of crime to illustrate their success in this respect. The same press release contained survey results purportedly showing a reduction in fear of crime. For another example of the way that crime statistics can start to shape the social world they purport to describe, see the press reaction to the publication of the 1996 Scottish Crime Survey - in particular, 'Nine in ten Scots live in fear' (Daily Record, 1998); 'Scotland turns into a crime-fearing nation' (The Herald, 1998); 'Scared off the streets' (The Daily Mail, 1998).

3.   Two other bulletins are also published by the Scottish Office which relate to statistics of police-recorded events, rather than criminal justice processes. The first of these relates to incidents of homicide in Scotland and is published on a biennial basis. These figures are slightly unusual insofar as incidents initially included as homicide may subsequently be 'corrected back' on the basis of judicial findings (e.g. a 'not guilty' verdict) and excluded from subsequent counts. Thus, the homicide figures represent a unique combination of incidents classified by the police and the findings of the courts. The second additional bulletin published by the Scottish Office relates to incidents of crimes involving firearms.

4.   The distinction between 'crimes' and 'offences' for statistical purposes has little significance - in general, however, the term 'crime' is used for more serious criminal acts and the term 'offence' for less serious acts. The terms are used interchangeably in this section.

5.   For the results of the survey in England and Wales, see Hough and Mayhew (1983); for Scotland, see Chambers and Tombs (1984).

6.   This is reflected in the fact that citation analyses regularly place Pat Mayhew, the principal author of most of the reports from the BCS, near the top of the criminological citation 'league'. See, for example, Cohn and Farrington (1998).

7.   As well as the national crime surveys, there has been an irregular series of local crime surveys in Scotland. Local crime surveys have the advantage of being able to look in detail at the experience of particular communities, rather than at *types* of community constructed artificially from a sample stretched across the whole country. Typically, however, local surveys are less well funded - which means that the questionnaire tends to be shorter and the sample smaller - and ill co-ordinated, making it very difficult to make meaningful comparisons across different studies. Most of the local surveys carried out in Scotland have been associated with the Safer Cities Programme, funded by the Scottish Office (see chapter 5). They were intended to provide information to inform the development of community safety initiatives and a benchmark to allow the evaluation of those initiatives. Some of these studies have been published (see, for example, Anderson *et al.*, 1990; Jones *et al.*, 1994) or have been drawn on in evaluations of the Safer Cities Projects (e.g. Carnie, 1996) though the datasets have generally not been made available for secondary analysis.

8.   There is another, and equally important, discussion to be had about the interpretation and uses of other types of information from the survey - especially that relating to public perceptions of crime, which has played a central role in the construction of 'fear of crime' as a separate policy concern.

4 Classifying Scottish Criminal Procedure

CHRISTOPHER GANE

Introduction

There are many ways of classifying systems of criminal procedure. One of the most enduring is by reference to the distinction between 'inquisitorial' and 'adversarial' systems.[1] This is a distinction which has increasingly come under critical scrutiny in recent years (Di Marino, 1997), not least because of the modification in practice of procedural systems on both sides of the inquisitorial-adversarial divide (Coughlan, 1994; Fassler, 1990; Zappala, 1997). But provided it is recognised that no contemporary system (whether inquisitorial or adversarial) adheres fully to the ideal-type these terms remain useful analytical tools, not least because they retain a sound empirical foundation. It is important also to recognise the insights which are to be drawn from alternative typologies, in particular, the distinction drawn by Damaška (1975; 1986) between 'hierarchical' and 'co-ordinate' models of criminal procedure.

This chapter analyses the Scottish system of criminal procedure with reference to the typologies mentioned above. Its general conclusion is that while historically Scottish criminal procedure may have displayed some features which were of an 'inquisitorial' nature, in most important respects modern Scottish procedure is 'adversarial' in nature. Similarly, although some features of Scottish procedure display characteristics typical of Damaška's 'hierarchical' model of criminal procedure, for the most part the Scottish system conforms to Damaška's 'co-ordinate' model. The combination of these factors serves to place Scottish criminal procedure in the same 'family' as Anglo-American criminal procedure systems.

'Inquisitorial' and 'Adversarial' Models of Procedure

In addressing the distinction between inquisitorial and adversarial systems of criminal procedure, it is necessary to ask three related questions: What goal does the criminal process seek to achieve, who determines the scope of the inquiry in a criminal process and who determines the manner in which the conflict between the prosecutor and the accused is to be resolved?

The Inquisitorial Model

In inquisitorial systems, the fundamental purpose of the process of investigation and trial is the discovery of the 'objective truth' in relation to an alleged crime.[2] This is an inquiry which must be conducted on behalf of the state by an appropriate official, and, at least in the case of serious offences, there is a clear separation between accusation (which is the function of the prosecutor), and investigation (which is the function of an examining judge). The purpose of this separation is to ensure that weak cases are not presented to the trial court, and to ensure that the latter is fully appraised of matters which relate not only to guilt but also to exculpation.

This investigation into the truth takes place initially during a pre-trial phase, in which the investigator will examine all aspects of the case and all witnesses, including the accused. The accused's participation in the process of investigation is regarded as being in his interests, providing an early opportunity for the suspect to be heard in relation to the case being developed against him. While at one time the accused could be compelled to testify, under threat of prosecution, in general he will enjoy the right to remain silent (although he need not be informed of this fact).[3] The product of this investigation is a 'dossier', built up by the investigating judge, which, when complete, is transmitted to the trial court.

The trial takes the form of an examination of the accused and any witnesses by the court, based on the information contained in the dossier. It follows from the fundamental objective of the criminal process - the discovery of the truth - that the trial court is not bound by artificial limitations on the mode of proof, such as a requirement of corroboration, the exclusion of hearsay evidence, or the incompetence of certain categories of witness. Rather, the process is governed by the principle of the 'free evaluation of the evidence', according to which the trier of fact may have regard to any aspect of the evidence presented to the trial court giving such weight to the evidence as appears proper in the circumstances.[4] Indeed, the court has a duty to examine all available evidence, whether or not the accused or the prosecutor has asked the court to do so. The principle of the free evaluation of the evidence cannot, however, be invoked to permit reliance upon evidence which has been unlawfully obtained (Van den Wyngaert *et al.*, 1993; Vogler, 1996; Hüber, 1996).

Inquisitorial systems, being committed to a search for the material truth, and placing control of the case in the hands of an impartial third party - the judge - do not accord to the accused and the prosecutor any significant measure of control over how the case will be resolved (see, for example, Hüber, 1996, p.110). In particular, inquisitorial systems generally do not recognise the guilty plea, in the sense of a plea which relieves the prosecutor of the burden of proving the guilt of the accused. Without such a plea, inquisitorial systems find it difficult to accommodate consensual settlement of criminal cases by plea negotiation, and even where such settlement is achieved, it is generally regarded as anomalous and, indeed, a challenge to fundamental principles of legality (Hüber, 1996, pp. 159-161).[5]

The Adversarial Model

The adversarial system of criminal procedure differs from the above in virtually all respects. The purpose of the exercise is less of a search for the 'material truth', than an efficient settlement of a conflict between the prosecutor and the accused. The analogy with a 'game' or 'contest' is sometimes applied.[6] The search for the truth and the principle of the 'free evaluation of the evidence' give way to a complex of rules which restrict what evidence may be considered or otherwise regulate the weight to be given to evidence which is admitted. The roles of accuser and investigator are generally combined (in the office of the public prosecutor) and there is no concept of the impartial, judicial investigation of the case at the pre-trial stage. Responsibility for the investigation of the case lies with the 'parties': the case for the prosecution is developed by the prosecutor, while the case for the defence is prepared by the accused and his advisors. In the trial phase the evidence is presented by the parties and the court has only a limited capacity to pursue lines of evidence and should not explore issues not previously opened up by the parties in the course of the examination and cross-examination of the witnesses.

In contrast to inquisitorial systems, accused and prosecutor are accorded a significant measure of control over how to resolve the dispute between them. In reality, adversarial systems are not adversarial in the sense of both sides being committed to a contest the outcome of which will determine the disposal of the case. Rather, adversarial systems are highly dependent upon, and give formal recognition to, settlement of the case by agreement between the parties. Such settlement is dependent upon the possibility of the accused relieving the state of the burden of proving guilt by tendering a plea of guilty. In exchange for this plea, the prosecutor may agree to drop certain of the charges brought against the accused, or otherwise reduce the gravity of the case which he or she faces. Negotiated settlement has become so central to adversarial systems that it might fairly be described as the distinguishing characteristic of such systems in the inquisitorial-adversarial dichotomy.

Hierarchical and Co-Ordinate Models of Criminal Procedure

As indicated above, the dichotomy between inquisitorial and adversarial systems of procedure is not an entirely satisfactory one. Not only is it difficult to find in practice any system which conforms to these models, but they do not address certain other important features of the systems of procedure typical of either group. In particular, certain important structural features of the system are ignored, including the manner in which important elements of the criminal procedure system - such as the judiciary and the prosecutor - are ordered. The inquisitorial-adversarial dichotomy also focuses predominantly upon the trial as the normal outcome of the criminal process, whereas in practice a formal resolution by criminal trial may by no means be the normal outcome in either model.[7] In the light of such criticisms, Damaška has proposed a further, alternative, classification - that of 'hierarchical' and 'co-ordinate' models of criminal procedure.

The hierarchical model is typical of continental European procedural systems, and is characterised by 'the high premium placed on certainty of decision making' (Damaška, 1975, p.483). This certainty, in turn, requires the development of uniform policies, which in turn leads to a centralisation of authority (Damaška, 1975, p.484). This centralisation of authority is reflected in the structure and organisation not only of police forces and prosecution agencies but also in the judicial structures which, through easily accessible avenues of appeal, seek to ensure uniformity in the application of the law. Furthermore, judicial authority is placed within a defined legislative structure in which 'inherent powers' play no part.

In the hierarchical model there is a preference for 'determinative rules' (Damaška, 1975, p.502) as opposed to a system based on extensive discretion so that, for example, in many continental systems public prosecutors are bound by the 'principle of legality',[8] according to which they are required, where evidence of a crime is available, to prosecute.

The premium placed on certainty in decision-making also leads to another important feature of the 'hierarchical' model, and that is the limited opportunities for lay participation in the criminal justice process (Damaška, 1975, p.491):

> A pure hierarchical model regards with great misgivings any participation of lay people in the administration of justice. The reasons for this attitude are not difficult to see: Laymen are usually unable and often unwilling to look at criminal cases through the prism of general rules. To laymen each case is a crisis, a unique human drama, rather than a representative of a general class. Thus, no matter what form it takes, lay participation always injects an element of unpredictability into the criminal justice system.

In systems which conform to the 'co-ordinate' model the guiding aim is to reach the decision most appropriate to the circumstances of each case (Damaška, 1975, p.509). While certainty is an important value, it is less significant than in the hierarchical model. This is reflected in a much less centralised ordering of the police and other criminal law agencies.[9] Similarly, although courts at the higher level may be centrally-organised, the bulk of criminal business is in fact conducted in lower courts which, typically, do not form part of such a central hierarchy. Since certainty in decision-making carries less of a premium, there is a greater willingness to embrace lay participation, as exemplified by the jury, and reliance on lay justices, and there is generally a much greater degree of discretion and flexibility in the system, for police, prosecutors and judges.

Finally, it is worth observing that negotiated settlement of the criminal process, almost by its nature, is dependent upon the prosecutor enjoying a large degree of discretion. As one would expect, then, negotiated settlement

- plea bargaining - is typically found in systems arranged along co-ordinate rather than hierarchical lines.

Criminal Procedure in Scotland

Inquisitorial or Adversarial?

Inquisitorial forms: judicial examination in Scottish procedure Although Scottish criminal procedure is essentially adversarial in nature, it contains certain procedural forms which suggest a more inquisitorial process. The best example of this is pre-trial judicial examination in solemn procedure.

Before the development of efficient police services, and the emergence of the modern office of procurator fiscal, the investigation of crimes in Scotland was a judicial function, and that function extended to investigating all aspects of the case - both inculpatory and exculpatory. Judicial examination of all witnesses, including the accused, was a central feature of solemn proceedings until the latter part of the nineteenth century (Hume, 1844, i, pp.75-83; Alison, 1833, ii, pp.116-151).[10] The purpose of the examination was explained by Alison (1833, p.131) in terms which would be recognisable even today by anyone trained in the inquisitorial tradition:

> The Scotch law, differing in this particular from the English, allows and enjoins a declaration to be taken from a prisoner as soon as he is brought before the magistrate; and that for the double purpose of giving him an opportunity of clearing himself in so far as he can by his own allegations, and explaining any circumstances which may appear suspicious in his conduct, and of affording evidence on which the magistrate can with safety proceed in making up his mind whether or not to commit for trial. And experience has abundantly proved the wisdom of this assistance to an innocent man in clearing him from an unjust imputation, as it is a disadvantage to a guilty one in endeavouring to screen himself from punishment.

Judicial examination was intimately connected to the rights of the accused in the criminal process. Since, prior to 1898, the accused was not a competent witness at his own trial, judicial examination provided the sole opportunity for the accused directly to offer his version of events and to comment upon the evidence offered against him. When, following the

Criminal Evidence Act 1898, the accused became a competent witness at the trial, the *raison d'être* of judicial examination was effectively removed. Even before this date, however, the utility of judicial examination as a method of investigation had been substantially undermined. In *HMA v Brims*[11] the High Court held that an accused could lawfully decline to answer questions put to him at judicial examination, and thereafter those able to afford legal advice generally took advantage of this privilege. In 1887 the accused was given a statutory right to consult a solicitor before examination and to the presence of the solicitor during examination. The combination of these factors had, by the end of the nineteenth century, reduced judicial examination to 'a formality' (Gordon, 1978a, p.320) at which, typically, no plea or declaration was made by the accused, and the latter was either bailed, or committed into custody pending further investigation of the case. Judicial examination was in practice made obsolete by section 77(1) of the Summary Jurisdiction (Scotland) Act 1908 which, recognising the developments which had taken place in relation to judicial examination, provided that where the accused was brought before the sheriff and intimated that he did not wish to make a declaration, it was not necessary for the sheriff to take such a declaration.

Judicial examination was re-introduced into Scottish criminal procedure by the Criminal Justice (Scotland) Act 1980.[12] Although to some extent the purpose of judicial examination shares something in common with the former procedure - in the sense that it provides an accused person the opportunity to comment upon and explain certain aspects of the evidence against him - modern judicial examination differs significantly from judicial examination as it formerly functioned. In modern procedure, responsibility for the investigation of crime is no longer a judicial function, but rests rather with the police, under the control and guidance of the public prosecutor. This is reflected in modern judicial examination. The examination is today conducted *before* the sheriff, by the prosecutor, rather than by the sheriff. It is a process which follows upon, and, indeed, may be premised upon, the accused having been questioned by the police,[13] rather than being the suspect's first opportunity to give an account of himself. As was the case at common law, the accused may decline to answer questions put to him, but in modern practice this may, in certain circumstances, be made the subject of comment by the prosecutor, the judge or a co-accused at the trial.[14]

Does truth matter? If inquisitorial systems, in their search for the material truth, eschew what Damaška (1971) calls 'evidentiary barriers to conviction', Scots law has traditionally embraced these wholeheartedly. The best known example of this is adherence to the general rule requiring corroboration: evidence from a single source, no matter how credible, persuasive or reliable, must be disregarded if it is not corroborated by evidence from another, independent, source.[15] In similar fashion Scots law contains a number of exclusionary rules by virtue of which evidence such as hearsay may be excluded from criminal trials.

And yet, contemporary Scottish practice appears to be less committed than formerly to an adversarial game theory of criminal procedure. There are, for example, virtually no *mandatory* exclusionary rules of evidence, so that even evidence which has been unlawfully obtained may at the court's discretion be admitted.[16] Inroads have also been made into the rule requiring the exclusion of hearsay evidence. Subject to certain conditions, it is now possible for the court to admit hearsay evidence of statements by a person who cannot give evidence, where it is not reasonably practicable to secure his or her attendance as a witness, where the witness cannot be found, where he or she is entitled to refuse to give evidence on the ground that such evidence might be incriminating, or where the witness refuses to testify.[17]

Even the corroboration requirements have been substantially diluted in recent years by diminishing the rigour with which the requirement of 'independent' corroboration is applied. Thus the courts have increasingly been willing to accept the notion of a 'self-corroborating' confession, according to which theory, evidence which is made known to the investigating authorities through the alleged confession of a suspect may be regarded as corroborating that confession.[18] The courts have also developed the doctrine that the evidence of the distress of an alleged victim may be held to corroborate the elements of certain offences. Where, for example, the victim alleges that she has been raped, or been the victim of an assault, distress may corroborate the allegation that what took place happened without the victim's consent.[19] The so-called 'Moorov doctrine' which allows mutual corroboration of separate incidents to which only one witness testifies is also applied with increasing flexibility with regard to the requirement that the incidents be closely linked in terms of time, character and circumstances.[20]

These changes in the rules of evidence in criminal proceedings suggest that both the courts and Parliament are less willing than formerly to accept the contest theory of adversarial proceedings, and that they are more inclined to dispense with, or at least dilute the effect of, exclusionary rules or rules which would lead to evidence which is otherwise competent and reliable being discounted by the courts.

Who determines the limits of the inquiry? In this respect, Scottish procedure conforms to the adversarial model, prior to the trial and at the trial itself. The responsibility for developing the case lies with the parties, who decide which evidence they will present and which witnesses they will call. Although the court may be called upon to lend assistance to the parties in obtaining certain forms of evidence - such as statements from witnesses[21] - generally the parties are left to their own devices in the gathering of evidence.

At the trial, evidence is presented to the court through the examination and cross-examination of the witnesses led by the parties. The extent to which the trial judge may question a witness is circumscribed by the need for the judge to avoid the appearance of partiality, and the court should avoid assuming the role of examiner or cross-examiner.[22] The court has no power to call witnesses who are not listed by the Crown or by the accused, and may not even order the appointment of an expert witness.

Consensual settlement Consensual resolution of criminal cases is a normal feature of Scottish criminal procedure.[23] Recent legislative developments have tended to emphasise this. The most significant of these are the procedures introduced by the Criminal Justice (Scotland) Act 1995, relating to the obligations of the parties prior in the pre-trial stage. Section 257 of the Criminal Procedure (Scotland) Act 1995 provides that the prosecutor and the accused are obliged to identify facts, oral evidence of which can be dispensed with at the trial, and to secure the agreement of all parties to the case to those facts. The duty to seek agreement of evidence is reinforced by the introduction of pre-trial hearings,[24] the purpose of which is to ascertain, so far as practicable, whether the case is likely to proceed to trial on the date assigned for trial, and in particular, the state of preparation of the prosecutor and of the accused with respect to their cases, whether the accused intends to adhere to a plea of not guilty, and the extent to which the prosecutor and the accused have complied with the obligation to seek agreement of evidence.

At these hearings the parties are required to account to the court what steps they have taken to comply with this obligation.

These pre-trial hearings introduce into contemporary procedure a significant measure of judicial management of the pre-trial phase. They do not, however, represent a serious challenge to the extent to which the parties determine the scope of the inquiry. There is nothing in the judicial management of the pre-trial stage which changes this. Indeed, it is significant that the procedures relating to the pre-trial hearings specifically refer to 'the state of preparation of the prosecutor and of the accused with respect to *their* cases' (emphasis added), thus emphasising that, fundamentally, responsibility for determining the limits of the inquiry lies with the parties.[25]

Hierarchical or Co-ordinate?

In virtually all respects, Scottish criminal procedure displays the attributes of a system arranged according to the co-ordinate model. This is true particularly in relation to: (a) the absence of a centralised and hierarchical structure to important elements of the criminal justice system; (b) lay participation in the criminal process; and (c) the very considerable degree of discretion which operates throughout the system.

Centralisation and hierarchy With the exception of the public prosecutor's office, the main elements of the criminal justice system are not organised systematically in a hierarchy, although some elements of centralisation can be identified.

The absence of a centralised system is particularly marked in relation to the police. There is not a single national police force in Scotland but eight police forces, organised on a geographical basis which reflects in part the former boundaries of local government areas in Scotland (see chapter 6).[26] In so far as operational matters are concerned, the Chief Constable exercises considerable autonomy with regard to the deployment of personnel and other resources, and the Chief Constable is not subject to central direction (for example by the Secretary of State) in relation to such matters.

There is some measure of centralised control over the reporting of offences with a view to prosecution, the Chief Constable being under a statutory duty to comply with instructions from the public prosecutor in this respect.[27] But in general, police forces are free to act with a considerable degree of autonomy.

So far as concerns the criminal court, while the higher courts are centralised (in the sense that there is only one High Court of Justiciary having jurisdiction throughout Scotland), the lower courts - the sheriff and district courts - are dispersed widely throughout Scotland and organised on a local basis. Although the lower courts are subordinate to the High Court in terms of appellate and review jurisdiction, there is no other hierarchical link between the local and central courts. Thus, although there is no formal obstacle to advancement from the sheriff court bench to the High Court, with the exception of the occasional appointment of a sheriff as a temporary judge in the High Court, in practice sheriffs are not 'promoted' in this way. District Court justices, being lay persons[28] are as such not qualified to sit in the sheriff court or High Court.

The position with regard to the system of public prosecution is rather different. The public prosecution system, although decentralised at local level, is subject to strong central control by the Crown Office in Edinburgh, directed towards promoting uniformity of practice in relation to matters of prosecution policy. Although the office of the public prosecutor is decentralised, it is internally organised along hierarchical lines, each sheriff court district being presided over by a regional procurator fiscal, assisted by deputy procurators, procurators and procurators depute. In terms of structure, therefore, the public prosecution system is probably the only feature of the Scottish criminal justice system which displays the organisational characteristics typical of Damaška's hierarchical model.

Lay participation Although lay participation is less of a feature of Scottish criminal justice than it is of English law, its presence nevertheless serves to place Scottish criminal procedure amongst those systems which Damaška would describe as following a co-ordinate model of criminal justice. As in England and Wales, lay participation takes two forms: lay judges in the lowest tier of criminal courts, and the jury in more serious cases.

Lay justices are only found in the district court, and while the range of offences which may be tried in that court is quite broad,[29] an equally significant list of offences is excluded from the jurisdiction of the court,[30] and the powers of the court are limited,[31] the maximum punishment which may be imposed by the district court in general being 60 days' imprisonment.[32] The role of the district court justice in the Scottish criminal justice system is, therefore, much less significant than that played by the lay magistrate in England and Wales. Not only is the jurisdiction of the district court more limited, but the number of cases dealt with in the district court as a percentage of all summary criminal cases is significantly less than the figure disposed of by the Magistrates court.

So far as concerns the Scottish jury, only a small part of all criminal cases are heard by juries, and in this sense the jury's importance in the system as a whole may be more symbolic than real. Nevertheless, the jury is a distinguishing feature of the system which serves to place Scottish procedure amongst those systems which follow a co-ordinate model of criminal justice.

Although the Scottish jury performs the same role as its counterpart in England and other common law jurisdictions, there are certain features which distinguish it (see chapter 9). Thus the Scottish jury has fifteen members, making it rather larger than most other trial juries. It is entitled to reach a verdict by a simple majority of 8 votes to 7, although this is somewhat complicated by the presence of three verdicts - guilty, not guilty and not proven. A vote for 'not proven' is, in modern practice, a vote for acquittal, and for a verdict of guilty to be returned there must be at least eight votes in favour of that outcome. Probably the feature of jury trial which most serves to distinguish the Scottish conception of this institution from other jurisdictions influenced by the common law is that in Scotland the accused has no right to demand trial by jury (as opposed to trial by a judge or justice)[33] and it is only in respect of a limited number of crimes that trial by jury is required by law.[34]

Discretion It is in the place of discretion, as opposed to 'determinative rules', that the Scottish system of criminal procedure is most clearly allocated to the 'co-ordinate' model of criminal procedure. This can be seen most strikingly in relation to the powers of the public prosecutor, and in reliance upon certain 'inherent powers' by the criminal courts.

The Scottish public prosecutor certainly enjoys greater discretionary powers than are enjoyed by his counterparts in any system in continental Europe, and probably more than those enjoyed by public prosecutors in other systems based on the 'co-ordinate' model (see chapter 7).[35]

In deciding whether or not to initiate criminal proceedings the public prosecutor is subject to virtually no controls other than the internal policies of the prosecution service, although in certain cases the court may intervene to prevent a prosecution proceeding where it believes that the prosecutor is acting oppressively.[36] Equally, a decision not to prosecute is subject to virtually no external control. The High Court may grant authority to the victim of an offence to bring a private prosecution where the public prosecutor has taken a decision not to proceed, but as a measure of control over prosecutorial discretion this is available only in the most exceptional circumstances.[37]

In general, Scottish criminal procedure does not have a strict classification of offences according to which the mode of trial of an offence is determined. In general, therefore, it is the public prosecutor who determines the mode of trial. As was noted above, the accused has no say in determining this matter. So, for example, in a case of theft, it is for the public prosecutor to determine whether or not the offence will be prosecuted, and if so, whether it will be prosecuted summarily or on indictment. And in the latter case, it is for the public prosecutor to determine whether the prosecution will be brought in the sheriff court, or before the High Court. It follows from this that the public prosecutor has a substantial degree of indirect control over the sentence which may be imposed on conviction. By determining the form of procedure, and the court, the prosecutor is, for the ordinary run of cases, determining the sentencing parameters of the case. A case of theft tried under summary procedure in the sheriff court, for example, cannot attract a custodial sentence of more than three months' imprisonment, at least for a first offence.[38] A case of theft tried under solemn procedure in the same court is, at least in theory, punishable by up to three years' imprisonment.[39]

The extent to which Scottish criminal procedure permits the parties to enter into agreed settlement of a criminal prosecution has already been noted. The guilty plea is, of course, central to any consensual settlement of a prosecution, and in this respect Scottish criminal procedure is similar to other common law systems. What distinguishes Scottish criminal procedure in this respect is the complete absence of control over the public prosecutor's discretion in accepting or rejecting pleas of guilty. In other common law systems the acceptance of a guilty plea may be subject to a measure of judicial control, and, in exceptional cases, the court may refuse to accept a plea of guilty. That is not the case in Scottish procedure. The court has no control over what pleas the Crown is prepared to accept or reject.

Inherent powers of the criminal courts   The most striking example of reliance upon 'inherent powers' by any contemporary criminal court is the power of the High Court of Justiciary to create new crimes, by reliance upon the so-called 'declaratory power'.[40]   This power, strictly speaking, relates more to the substantive law than to procedural law, but provides an insight into a system in which reliance upon unwritten, discretionary powers, can be taken to extremes.   An almost equally striking example of the system's tolerance of discretionary procedures as opposed to 'determinative rules' is to be found in the *nobile officium* of the High Court.[41]   This is an equitable jurisdiction exercised by the High Court in criminal cases.   The *nobile officium* of the High Court may be invoked for the purpose of preventing injustice or oppression where the law does not otherwise provide for a method of appeal or review of a decision by a lower court, or even the High Court sitting as a court of criminal appeal.[42]   This power extends, for example, to making good a *casus improvisus* in a statute,[43] and generally to dealing with extraordinary and unforeseen circumstances in criminal proceedings.   It provides, in short, a method of addressing circumstances in which there are no 'determinative rules'.

Conclusion

The Scottish legal system is frequently thought of as a 'mixed' system, displaying characteristics of the two major legal 'families' - the common law and the civil law traditions.   Whatever may be the case in relation to the divisions and classification of private law, there is little to suggest that the criminal procedure law of Scotland is 'mixed'.   In terms of both the 'inquisitorial - adversarial' and the 'hierarchical - co-ordinate' dichotomies, contemporary Scottish criminal procedure has a great deal in common with systems of procedure which are 'adversarial' or which display 'co-ordinate' structures.   These are systems which are typically found in the common law world, and in terms of its criminal procedure Scotland must be regarded as forming part of the common law tradition.

Notes

1. The literature on this topic is extensive.   For useful introductions and overviews, see: Damaška (1971); Goldstein and Marcus (1977-78); Langbein and Weinreb (1977-78); Frase (1990); Osner *et al.* (1993); Van den Wyngaert *et al.* (1993); Hatchard *et al.* (1996).
2. *Cf* Huber (1996, p.89).   Article 81 of the French *Code de Procédure Pénale* provides that the purpose of the pre-trial *instruction* (judicial investigation) is the '*manifestation de la vérité*' - bringing out the truth.   According to Van den Wyngaert *et al.* (1993, p.18), 'the purpose of criminal proceedings is to find the material truth.   Everything is geared towards this end.   All participants in the proceedings, whether it be during the pre-trial stage of during the trial, must contribute to this purpose'.
3. *Cf* Vogler (1996, p.31).
4. See Van den Wyngaert *et al.* (1993) at pp. 21-22 (Belgium), 155 (Germany), 174 (Greece), 238 (Italy), 330-331 (Portugal), 390 (Spain); Vogler (1996, para. 3.11 at pp. 29-30); Hüber (1996, para. 3.7 at p.111).
5. See also Jung (1997).   Jung begins his discussion in the following terms: 'Criminal procedures seem to have been afflicted by a lingering disease; the US infection of plea bargaining'.
6. In Thomson v Glasgow Corporation 1961 S.L.T. 237 at 246, the Lord Justice-Clerk (Thomson) described the nature of a civil process in the following terms: 'A litigation is in essence a trial of skill between opposing parties conducted under recognised rules, and the prize is the judge's decision.   We have rejected inquisitorial methods and prefer to regard our judges as entirely independent.   Like referees at boxing contests they see that the rules are kept and count the points'.   With only a few adjustments to the language this *dictum* could be applied to the criminal process.
7. Vogler (1996, p.24) points out that in France 'it has been estimated that the decision not to prosecute is taken in at least 50 per cent of all possible cases'.
8. The so-called '*Legalitätsprinzip*' or *principe de legalité*.   The antithesis of this is the principle of opportunity or expediency (*Opportunitätsprinzip*; *principe de l'opportunité des poursuites*).
9. Thus, prior to the creation of the Crown Prosecution Service in 1979 there was no general public prosecution service in England and Wales, and there is still no national police force in the United Kingdom.
10. Hume and Alison describe in some detail the procedures to be followed upon the arrest of a suspect, and make clear that the first responsibility of the person making the arrest was to bring the suspect before a magistrate,

typically a sheriff, and that the first responsibility of the magistrate to whom the suspect was presented was to take from the latter a 'declaration'.

11.   (1887) 1 White 462.

12.   The procedure at judicial examination is now set out in sections 35-39 of the Criminal Procedure (Scotland) Act 1995.

13.   Criminal Procedure (Scotland) Act 1995, s.36(1) and (3).

14.   Criminal Procedure (Scotland) Act 1995, s.36(8).

15.   ·Hume (1844, i, p.383) states: '[N]o one shall in any case be convicted on the testimony of a single witness. No matter how trivial the offence, and how high soever the credit and character of the witness, still our law is averse to rely on his single word, in any inquiry which may affect the person, liberty or fame of his neighbour; and rather than run the risk of such an error, a risk which does not hold when there is a concurrence of testimonies, it is willing that the guilty should escape.' *Cf.* Alison (1833, ii, p.551).

16.   Lawrie v Muir 1950 J.C. 19; HMA v McGuigan 1936 J.C. 16; Bell v Hogg 1967 J.C. 4; MacNeil and Others v HMA 1986 S.C.C.R. 288.

17.   Criminal Procedure (Scotland) Act 1995, ss. 259-262. These provisions do not apply to statements made by the accused, except where a co-accused proposes to lead such evidence against another co-accused: Criminal Procedure (Scotland) Act 1995, s.261.

18.   Alison (1933, ii, p.580); Manuel v HMA 1958 J.C. 41; Gilmour v HMA 1982 S.C.C.R. 590; Wilson v McCaughey 1982 S.C.C.R. 398; Wilson v HMA 1987 S.C.C.R. 217; Sinclair v Tudhope 1989 S.C.C.R. 690; Woodland v Hamilton 1990 S.L.T. 565; McVeigh v Normand 1992 S.C.C.R. 272; Smith v Lees 1997 S.C.C.R. 139; Beattie v HMA 1995 S.C.C.R. 275.

19.   Smith v Lees 1997 S.C.C.R. 139; Cannon v HMA 1992 S.L.T. 709; Gedes v HMA 1996 S.C.C.R. 687; Stephen v HMA 1987 S.C.C.R. 570; Gracey v HMA 1987 S.L.T. 749; Moore v HMA 1990 S.C.C.R. 586; Gibson v Heywood 1997 S.L.T. 101.

20.   Moorov v HMA 1930 J.C. 68. See also, Ogg v HMA 1938 J.C. 152; Burgh v HMA 1944 J.C. 77; Tudhope v Hazelton 1984 S.C.C.R. 455; Hay v Wither 1988 S.C.C.R. 334; Russell v HMA 1990 S.L.T. 753; Pettigrew v Lees 1991 S.C.C.R. 304; Coffey v Houston 1992 S.C.C.R. 265; O'Neil v HMA 1995 S.C.C.R. 816. Although the modern doctrine is said to date from the case of *Moorov*, the possibility of cumulative corroboration was recognised much earlier: Mackenzie (1678, xxvi, section iv); Hume (1844, ii, p.385), Alison (1833, ii, p.551). Hagart v Hog and Souter, Hume, ii, 385 (1738).

21.   At common law the Crown could apply to the sheriff to have a witness examined on oath. Section 291 of the Criminal Procedure (Scotland) Act 1995 provides for a similar application by an accused person.

22. Livingstone v HMA (1974) S.C.C.R. (Supp) 68; Tallis v HMA 1982 S.C.C.R. 91; Nisbet v HMA 1979 S.L.T. (Notes) 5.
23. In 1983 the then Lord Advocate issued a statement concerning the practice of plea negotiation which began with the words 'Plea negotiation is encouraged by the Lord Advocate with a view to avoiding inconvenience to witnesses and waste of resources'. It concluded with the following words: '[The Lord Advocate] hopes that the arrangements which have been made for pre-trial consultation between prosecutor and defence will be fully used ... Any plea that is at all realistic will be seriously considered by the prosecutor'. The full text of this statement can be found at 1983 S.L.T. (News) 47.
24. These are mandatory in summary proceedings and in solemn proceedings in the Sheriff court. They are optional in High Court proceedings. In summary proceedings they are known as 'intermediate diets', in solemn proceedings in the sheriff court they are known as 'first diets' and in the High Court as 'preliminary diets': Criminal Procedure (Scotland) Act 1995, ss. 71, 72 and 148.
25. The extent to which the parties may determine the scope of the inquiry is further reflected in the terms of section 256 of the Criminal Procedure (Scotland) Act 1995 which provides for the agreement of evidence between the parties. Where evidence on which the parties is agreed is recorded in accordance with section 256 'any facts and documents admitted or agreed thereby shall be deemed to have been duly proved'. A less obvious, but potentially significant, legislative development is to be found in section 196 of the Criminal Procedure (Scotland) Act 1995 which provides that in determining sentence where the accused had pled guilty, the court may take into account the stage in the proceedings at which the offender indicated his intention to plead guilty and the circumstances in which that indication was given. This provision is a novelty in Scottish procedure, which in general has rejected overt sentence-discounts (in contrast to the practice in England and Wales): Strawhorn v Mcleod 1987 S.C.C.R. 413. *Cf* Young v HMA 1995 S.C.C.R. 418. See also R v Williams [1983] Crim L.R. 693.
26. The police forces in Scotland are Central, Dumfries and Galloway, Fife, Grampian, Lothian and Borders, Northern, Strathclyde and Tayside.
27. Criminal Procedure (Scotland) Act 1995, s.12.
28. With the exception of the District Court in Glasgow where a small number of professionally qualified stipendiary justices sit.
29. Criminal Procedure (Scotland) Act 1995, ss. 7(3) and 7(4).
30. Criminal Procedure (Scotland) Act 1995, s.7(8).
31. Criminal Procedure (Scotland) Act 1995, s.7(6).

32. When constituted by a stipendiary magistrate, the district court has the same summary jurisdiction and powers as a sheriff: Criminal Procedure (Scotland) Act 1995, s.7(5).
33. Dunbar v Johnston (1904) 4 Adam 505.
34. Whether a case is tried by a judge or by a jury is determined by the public prosecutor. Jury trial is required in any case over which the High Court has exclusive jurisdiction (in modern practice, murder, rape, deforcement of court officers and offences which by statute are reserved to the High Court). The explanation for this is that the High Court sits only as a court of solemn jurisdiction.
35. These powers were summarised by Lord Cameron in the case of Boyle v HMA 1976 J.C. 32, at p. 37: 'In Scotland the master of the instance in all prosecutions for the public interest is the Lord Advocate. It is for him to decide when and against whom to launch prosecution and upon what charges. It is for him to decide in which court they shall be prosecuted. It is for him to decide what pleas of guilt he will accept and it is for him to decide when to withdraw or abandon proceedings. No only so, even when a verdict of guilt has been returned and recorded it still lies with the Lord Advocate whether to move the court to pronounce sentence and without that motion no sentence can be pronounced or imposed'.
36. Renton and Brown (1996, paragraphs 9-21 and 29-38). See also Mowbray v Crowe 1993 S.C.C.R. 730 at 735; Hamilton v Byrne 1997 S.C.C.R. 547; Latto v Vannet 1997 S.C.C.R. 721.
37. J & P Coats Ltd v Brown 1909 S.C.(J) 29; McBain v Crichton 1961 J.C. 26; Trapp v M, Trapp v Y, 1971 S.L.T. (Notes) 30; Meehan v Inglis and Others 1974 S.L.T. (Notes) 61; H v Sweeney and Others 1983 S.L.T. 48; McDonald v Lord Advocate and Another 1988 S.C.C.R. 239. *Cf* C v Forsyth 1995 S.C.C.R. 553.
38. Criminal Procedure (Scotland) Act 1995, s.5.
39. Criminal Procedure (Scotland) Act 1995, s.3(3).
40. Hume, i, 12; Bernard Greenhuff (1838) 2 Swin. 236; Grant v Allan 1987 S.C.C.R. 402.
41. Renton and Brown (1996, chapter 34) and the authorities there cited.
42. McLellan, Petr. Dec. 4, 1990.
43. Lloyds and Scottish Finance v HMA 1974 J.C. 24.

5   The Politics of Crime Prevention: The Safer Cities Experiment in Scotland

JAMES CARNIE

Introduction

In a recent article, David Garland reflects that high crime rates have become a 'normal social fact' and that the 'threat of crime has become a routine part of modern consciousness' (Garland, 1996). He argues that over the last few decades successive governments have taken a dualistic, ambivalent and often contradictory approach to crime control. On the one hand an authoritarian punitiveness has come to characterise certain aspects of government rhetoric, policy and action (for example, in terms of sentencing), but on the other the state's claims in respect of crime control have become more modest, with 'a more limited sense of the state's powers to regulate conduct and prohibit deviance'. The limits of criminal justice based on a traditional penal-welfare strategy have thus become increasingly apparent, prompting a belief that government agencies by themselves cannot succeed in controlling crime.

The problem for governments today, asserts Garland, is the need to 'withdraw or at least qualify their claim to be the primary and effective provider of security and crime control', while at the same time minimising the political costs of such action. This new mode of governing crime is characterised as a *responsibility strategy* which 'involves the central government seeking to act upon crime not in a direct fashion through state agencies (police, courts, prisons, social work, etc.) but instead by acting indirectly, seeking to activate action on the part of non-state agencies and organisations'. Garland argues (at p.451) that this shift can be explained by the *new criminologies of everyday life* which begin from the premise that crime is a normal, commonplace aspect of modern society:

> The new criminologies of everyday life have been taken up by policy makers to reorient government action and to create new techniques for acting upon

the problem of crime. In particular, it is significant that many of the programmes of practical action which flow from these theories are addressed not to state agencies such as the police, the courts and the prisons, but beyond the *state* apparatus, to the organisations, institutions and individuals of civil society ... The new programmes of action are directed not towards individual offenders, but towards the conduct of potential victims, to vulnerable situations, and to those routines of everyday life which create criminal opportunities as an unintended by-product ... This is, in effect, 'supply side criminology'.

Consequently, over the last 20 years or more, there has been a marked growth in crime prevention initiatives. These initiatives have encompassed a wide range of activities. High profile media campaigns, for example, against car crime, drug misuse and domestic violence have flourished and have sought to command public attention often through the use of dramatic and striking imagery. Closed circuit television cameras (Honess and Charman, 1992) are now commonplace in both private and public sites; Neighbourhood Watch Schemes (Brown, 1992) operate in numerous communities; and experiments like the Safer Cities Programme, the subject of this chapter, have been promoted. The recurring message embedded in these activities, reflects Garland, is that 'the state alone is not, and cannot effectively be, responsible for preventing and controlling crime'. How effectively agencies, businesses, community organisations and citizens themselves have responded to this challenge will be considered in the following case study.

The Safer Cities Programme

A Safer Cities Programme in England was announced in March 1988 as part of Action for Cities. Over the next three years, 20 Safer Cities Projects were established by the Home Office in areas which had been identified as suffering from high levels of deprivation. Projects were set up across the country in locations such as Birmingham, Salford, Bristol, Hull and Islington. In Scotland, the Scottish Office announced its own Safer Cities Programme in 1989 and after a phased introduction four projects were established in Central Edinburgh, Castlemilk, Greater Easterhouse and Dundee (North East). The projects were originally scheduled to run for three years, but with additional funding from The Scottish Office they were extended to five years. A fifth project was introduced in Aberdeen in 1992.

Common objectives were set: to reduce crime; to lessen the fear of crime; and to create safer cities in which economic enterprise and community life could flourish. Nonetheless, differences did exist between projects in terms of operational style. Further, the Glasgow projects - Safe Castlemilk and Safe Greater Easterhouse - negotiated with The Scottish Office a wider 'community safety' remit in line with Strathclyde Region's 'Safe Strathclyde' initiative.

Local 'Politics'

The Scottish Office announcement that Safer Cities Projects were planned for Central Edinburgh, Castlemilk, Greater Easterhouse and Dundee (North East) was met with some suspicion in each of the localities. There were concerns by some local politicians and activists that the Scottish Office planned in the longer term to off-load crime prevention responsibilities to local authorities without providing the commensurate level of resources. Further, in some of the proposed Project Areas, fears were expressed by some local activists that the Project was no more than a thinly disguised exercise in police control.

Each of the Projects was distinct. The Safer Edinburgh Project was distinct demographically in that it was situated, not in a large peripheral housing development like the other Projects, but in the bustling centre of Scotland's capital city with its historic sites, prime residential properties, social amenities and thriving commercial outlets. Castlemilk, too, was distinct in that it already had a well developed network of community organisations which were committed to halting a spiral of decline through the redevelopment and regeneration of the area. The Castlemilk Partnership, one of the Scottish Office's urban renewal initiatives, was at the forefront of this regeneration.

Greater Easterhouse also had its unique characteristics in that it comprised a collection of 15 neighbourhoods, each with its own traditions and sense of identity. While there was no longer the major gang warfare which had in the past contributed to Glasgow's 'violent city' image, flashpoints still occurred between local youths. Further, there was some resentment by local activists that, yet again, Greater Easterhouse was being stigmatised as 'unsafe' and was to be the subject of another central government 'experiment' in social policy. Of all the Projects, Dundee (North East) was, perhaps, the most receptive to the Safer Cities idea, but this area also lacked a clear sense of identity. Made up initially of four large housing estates, Mid Craigie, Linlathen, Fintry and Whitfield, with Douglas and Mill o' Mains being added mid-way through the Project, local residents did not immediately relate to the Dundee (North East) tag.

That initial reservations and suspicions were overcome in all the Project Areas was due in no small measure to the work of the respective Co-ordinators and their Management Committees who quickly established Project credibility, instilling a sense of purpose into the Projects' work on crime prevention and community safety. Of course, that is not to say that everyone was in accord with the direction taken by individual Projects, but when it became apparent that the Safer Cities Projects would have significant budgets to spend directly in and on their respective communities, lingering reticence about motives gradually gave way to warm enthusiasm for funding local initiatives.

Project Strategies

Each Project developed a strategy aimed at serving the needs of the community in which it was set. Based on research and consultation exercises, Projects outlined action plans through which community problems were to be addressed. While a number of similar themes prevailed, important differences also existed. The balance which was struck in each of the Projects between pursuing crime prevention and community safety was influenced by four main factors: the socio-economic and demographic characteristics of the Project Area; the findings of research and consultation exercises; the input of community activists on Management Committees; and the personal interests and 'agenda' of each Project Co-ordinator.

Safe Castlemilk was quick to develop its agenda because it already had a strategy in place before Safer Cities status was conferred upon it. An inter-agency group operating under the auspices of the Castlemilk Area Liaison Committee had developed a mission statement and a ten point strategy in which crime prevention was to be addressed within a broader community safety agenda. Key areas identified for action were: Safe at Play; Safe on the Roads; Safe at Home; Safe from Fire; Safe beside Water; Safe at Work; and Safe to Complain. Underpinning the strategy was the belief that crime prevention could not be viewed in isolation, being inextricably linked to wider welfare and socio-economic concerns of local people (Graham and Fehilly, 1990-95). Also there was a concern that a project dedicated only to crime prevention might not have commanded respect within the community where suspicions about the role and influence of the police were apparent. However, criticisms were voiced by some professionals on the Management Committee that the approach had been too diffuse and insufficiently focused. Tensions developed, then, between those favouring a 'holistic' approach covering a broad range of community safety issues and those favouring a more focused approach covering fewer topics in greater depth and giving greater prominence to crime and its prevention.

In Edinburgh, a narrower remit was adopted based on information obtained from the Household Crime Survey (Anderson *et al.*, 1990) and the local Crime Profiles (McGowan and Slater, 1988-94a; 1988-94b). These showed an above average incidence of violent crime taking place in the city centre after dark and high levels of public concern about disorderly conduct, drunkenness and vandalism. Women in particular expressed considerable anxieties in relation to 'fear of crime' in the central area. Responsive to these research findings, the Safer Edinburgh project developed an 'Action Plan' which focused on three main themes: late night alcohol related violence and disorder; 'fear of crime' and women's safety; and young people and crime. Safer Edinburgh, therefore, adhered largely to a crime prevention agenda, although community safety issues were not entirely ignored. Considerable effort was expended by Project staff to assimilate the views of local people into the planning process through Community Forums. Although response rates were often poor, credence was given to the concerns expressed and wherever possible the Project did attempt to prompt appropriate agencies to take action.

The Dundee (North East) Safer Cities Project also adhered closely to a crime prevention agenda. On the basis of local knowledge available to it (Thomson *et al.*, 1989-94), together with research data (Jones *et al.*, 1991), the Project outlined a four point strategy on which to base its activities: physical crime prevention; social crime prevention; fear of crime; and community safety. Given the high levels of housebreaking prevalent in the area it was not surprising that 'target hardening' should form the basis of the Project's approach to crime prevention. High priority was given to making people feel more secure in their own homes with solid core doors, door chains, spy holes and window locks being fitted by the Project in collaboration with Dundee Housing Department, Scottish Homes and the Whitfield Partnership. Additionally, it was recognised that since young people were responsible for a great deal of local crime, especially vandalism, 'social crime prevention' measures were also required. To this end the

Project was committed to working with youth clubs and schools to promote various initiatives to encourage local children to participate in positive activities which would divert them away from potentially mischievous or delinquent behaviour.

In Greater Easterhouse a balance was struck between pursuing crime prevention initiatives and pursuing community safety matters, although both Project staff and Management Committees were acutely aware that since funding emanated from The Scottish Office Crime Prevention Unit, the emphasis needed to be placed on the former. An action plan was implemented (Daly, 1991-95a) which combined physical crime prevention measures, including a comprehensive home security programme and an innovative business security scheme, with social crime prevention measures such as engaging people in sports and leisure activities. Additionally, since local residents themselves had raised specific concerns about fire safety and road safety within the Greater Easterhouse area (Daly, 1990-95b), Project staff and Committee felt obliged to address the problems identified.

Physical Crime Prevention Initiatives

Home security (Bannister, 1991) was a significant part of the strategy in three out of the four Projects, that is, Greater Easterhouse, Castlemilk and Dundee. Undoubtedly, it was a major 'coup' on the part of Safe Greater Easterhouse to secure £680,000 over three years from the Urban Programme to fund an initiative which offered home security equipment free of charge to all 16,000 households in the area. The Project surpassed the crime reduction targets set for this initiative - the number of recorded incidents of domestic housebreaking in the area fell from 1,235 in 1991 to 635 in 1994 (Daly, 1990-94b), which represented a 49 per cent decrease in housebreakings to domestic dwellings over the period.

In Castlemilk and Dundee (North East), where home security programmes were also undertaken, a decline in the number of housebreakings was also recorded. From 1989 to 1994, housebreaking in the Castlemilk area (Ditton, 1990; 1994) declined by 56 per cent and in Dundee (North East) recorded housebreaking decreased by 17 per cent (Jones *et al.*, 1991; 1994) in the same period. Of course, all these figures need to be put into some perspective. First, although figures for housebreaking at National and at Regional levels (Strathclyde and Tayside respectively) showed an upward trend until 1991, thereafter the number of recorded incidents fell. Second, even although the decreases recorded in Greater Easterhouse, Castlemilk and Dundee (North East) were greater than that prevailing at Scottish, Strathclyde or Tayside levels, such decreases might not be solely attributable to the home security programmes as other factors might also have impinged, such as the impact of demographic shifts and changes to housing stock. Nevertheless, it does not seem unreasonable to suggest that various home security programmes, through their 'target hardening' measures contributed in part to the improving trend.

Similarly, the business security programmes run in Greater Easterhouse and Dundee (North East) were also effective in improving the security arrangements of local businesses participating in the scheme. Within specified limits, applicants to the respective schemes could receive a grant of 50 per cent towards the cost of approved security equipment. Non-domestic break-ins in the Greater Easterhouse area decreased by over 40 per cent between 1991 and 1994 (Ditton *et al.*, 1991; 1994) and while disaggregated figures were not available for Dundee (North East), verbal feedback from the recipients of scheme grants indicated that shops were now more secure against break-ins, although still liable to high levels of vandalism to the external fabric of the properties. While of course caveats apply to the 'success' of these physical crime prevention measures, the business security schemes do seem to have played a part in helping specific traders to continue operating in their respective areas (Burrows, 1988; 1992). Moreover, the scheme was a good example of the 'cross-fertilisation' of ideas between Co-ordinators involved in different Projects. Safer Greater Easterhouse initially developed the scheme, with Dundee (North East) later adapting the initiative to meet the needs of its own locality.

Social Crime Prevention Initiatives

All of the Projects invested time and resources in youth work, placing particular importance on occupying young people in positive pursuits as one method of diverting them from potentially mischievous or delinquent behaviour. Children were thought to be at their most 'restless' during school holidays, particularly the long summer break, when, generally speaking, their daily activities were both unstructured and unsupervised. It was recognised that inactivity amongst the young could lead to boredom and frustration which resulted in many instances in anti-social behaviour and minor crime. To combat the problem each of the Projects devised its own summer activities scheme to occupy local youngsters - in Dundee it was known as 'Passport to Sport'; in Castlemilk, 'Pass to Safe Play'; in Greater Easterhouse, 'Safe Sports'; and in Edinburgh, 'Leith Youth Links'.

Although no specific targets were set, it was hoped that each of the initiatives would help to reduce vandalism and malicious mischief. To attract youngsters, local sports and leisure facilities were made available at reduced costs to those who held the appropriate credentials in the form of a 'Pass' or 'Passport' issued by the Projects, usually via local schools. These initiatives were well supported in each of the Project Areas with high take-up rates being recorded each year. Some initial teething difficulties were experienced by the schemes, however, in targeting specific age groups and in timetabling events. Transport problems also arose and there were difficulties in Greater Easterhouse and Dundee (North East) where the Project Areas encompassed a number of separate neighbourhoods. Children frequently showed themselves unwilling to cross territorial 'boundaries' for fear of being bullied or attacked while in another part of the estate. Yet, any such disadvantages were far outweighed by the advantages which the initiatives bestowed, with the vast majority of local children participating in activities with great enthusiasm.

Projects attempted as best they could to monitor and assess the effect of these diversion initiatives. It is, of course, difficult to make any direct correlation between any downturn in local crime and the introduction of such schemes. However, from the evidence that is available, especially from Dundee (North East) and Castlemilk, such initiatives can certainly help to minimise errant behaviour by providing the opportunity for children and young people to become engaged in positive recreational activities. In Dundee (North East), total reported crime in the Project Area fell by 25 per cent when the summer holiday period of 1994 (when 'Passport to Sport' was run) was compared to the equivalent weeks in 1993. The reduction in the remainder of Dundee was a more modest one per cent. Vandalism was also down in the Project Area (by 18 per cent) during this 1994 summer period, and the number of complaints about youths made to and recorded by the police decreased, lending support to the view that the area was 'quieter' than normal. It needs to be noted, however, that when the initiative was repeated in the 1994 October school holidays, results were not so dramatic. Nonetheless, experiences in Castlemilk also suggest that initiatives of this type can be an effective method of social crime prevention.

Projects also attempted to meet the needs of local children and young people in a variety of other ways. Safer Edinburgh, for instance, devoted a significant part of its budget to the building of all weather kick-pitches at a cost of £25,000 each (McGowan and Slater, 1988-94). Each pitch was located in an area where residents had identified a particular need for youth facilities. These pitches represented tangible evidence of the Project's activities and were designed to give local youngsters better opportunities for sport, diverting them away from potential mischief. Although crime statistics for the relevant Police Beats taken before and after the building of the kick-pitches were inconclusive in respect of the impact of the new facilities upon crime, other indicators, such as feedback from community organisations directly involved in their management, suggested the pitches were providing a valuable social amenity and were making a contribution to occupying children and young people in positive pursuits.

Safe Castlemilk, on the other hand, eschewed large capital projects of this kind, preferring instead to devote resources to numerous community safety initiatives and campaigns aimed at young people (Graham and Fehilly 1990-95). The video package 'Jamie and the Buzz' was one example of the Project's work in this respect. It highlighted the many dangers and temptations facing youngsters in the modern world and sought to focus young people on taking responsibility for their actions by making appropriate choices, emphasising the need to turn away from anti-social activity, dangerous behaviour and crime. Safety education packs for younger children such as STARS (Stop, Think and Remember Safety) and CATS (Choose, Act, Think Safety) were also developed and distributed by the Project. Feedback from teachers involved in promoting these campaigns in local schools was very positive, indicating that the children had benefited from the experience through gaining real insights into the choices that needed to be made. A growth in the children's self esteem and increased confidence in their own decision-making was reported. Yet, there was an understanding that although awareness had been raised and practical situations experienced, it was impossible to predict what the long term impact of such campaigns on pupils' behaviour would be.

Unsuccessful Initiatives

Of course, not every initiative promoted by the Projects was an unqualified success. Some were disappointingly ineffective in achieving any impact. Although not so much an initiative in its own right, but more a mechanism through which it was hoped to engender grassroots support and interest, the

Community Forums promulgated by the Safer Edinburgh Project failed to live up to expectations. A considerable amount of staff time was invested in developing Safer Community Forums as a vehicle for embracing local views. However, low levels of community interest were displayed and the prevailing view within the Project Steering Committee was that the 'return on investment' was disappointingly poor.

Other projects also had their share of ineffectual initiatives. Both Safe Castlemilk and Safe Greater Easterhouse established in conjunction with the local police a Drugs Line facility. Neither line proved to be as successful as had been hoped for and quickly became known among locals as 'grassing lines'. Dundee (North East) also had limited success with its women's self defence courses in the Whitfield area and its car security promotion saw a disappointing return on the effort expended.

Fear of Crime

All of the Projects identified reducing fear of crime as an important strategic objective (Anderson *et al.*, 1990; Bennett, 1991; Williams and Dickson, 1993). It was well understood that people's quality of life may be seriously affected if they are fearful of crime. Residents can be reluctant to leave their homes and their movements may be restricted to avoid areas or situations which they see as unsafe. Anxieties may occur about being home alone, especially at night. While a certain level of fear may be a sensible safeguard which encourages people to be more careful and to engage in protective behaviour, fear of crime can become a problem when the anxiety which people experience is out of all proportion to the actual risk of being a crime victim.

Fear of crime can also have wider costs to the community. Public facilities such as car parks and public transport may not be fully utilised and excessive money can be spent on security devices for the home and person. Where fear of crime is widespread within a community it can lead to isolation, especially amongst groups which perceive themselves to be particularly vulnerable such as women and the elderly.

Fear of crime can be influenced by a number of factors such as gender; age; level of home security; the local physical environment ('signs' of disorder including derelict property, graffiti, rubbish in the streets); direct or indirect experience of victimisation (as a victim, witness or acquaintance of a victim); and media treatment of crime issues. These factors can combine to create a climate of alarm about crime in which 'irrational' fears are often held. In such a climate it can be difficult to convey accurate and realistic information about the appropriate use of law enforcement resources and about crime and its prevention. While well designed and targeted policing strategies can help reduce public anxiety about crime, it is unrealistic to expect the police by themselves to have a major impact on levels of fear in the community. In this respect, Projects recognised the need to co-opt local authority departments, other service providers and community organisations to combat the problem on a wider front.

Fear of crime in the city centre was a particular problem for Safer Edinburgh. The Edinburgh Crime Survey revealed high levels of anxiety; fear of sexual assault and sexual harassment were found to be key concerns. Media attention on sexual crimes could influence perceptions of the problem, as could direct experience of victimisation or of witnessing a crime. Moreover, fear could be instilled through experience of, or knowledge of, general incivilities in the community such as drunkenness, rowdiness and harassment.

The Safer Edinburgh Project attempted to tackle the problem on a number of fronts. It argued for 'high visibility' police patrolling at appropriate times and locations, and in an effort to curb late night disorder which was contributing to high levels of fear, it lobbied and exerted pressure (successfully) on the Edinburgh District Licensing Board to adopt a policy of Zone Closing (The Portman Group, 1993) of public houses in the central area (that is, all pubs within a given vicinity were required to close at a designated time). Additionally, the Project worked collaboratively with both local statutory services and voluntary agencies to develop practical initiatives to address the problem. Priority themes were identified concerning environmental factors such as street lighting and transport provision; publicity material; and direct work with local women. Emphasis was placed on a pragmatic approach with concentration on small scale initiatives.

It was not possible, however, to assess precisely the impact of Safer Edinburgh's initiatives in reducing women's fear of crime. Certainly, the Second Household Crime Survey (Kinsey, 1994) revealed that fewer women in 1994 (37 per cent) worried about sexual assault than in 1989 (45 per cent). However, slightly more women were worried about sexual harassment (44 per cent in 1994; 40 per cent in 1989). The influence of Safer Edinburgh's work is not easily separated out from other high profile initiatives such as the District Council's 'Zero Tolerance' Campaign.

Moreover, in such a sensitive area as fear of crime, attempts to raise public awareness on the issue, even in a measured way, may also concomitantly serve to heighten latent anxieties.

Other Projects also attempted to deal with fear of crime, especially in relation to women and their safety. Safe Greater Easterhouse ran a self defence and assertiveness programme for women together with workshops on domestic violence. In addition to educational programmes and campaigns, Safe Greater Easterhouse offered a practical response to victims of domestic violence by supplying and fitting home security items and by providing personal attack alarms to women in need. Personal alarms were also provided by the Dundee (North East) Project, where over 2,000 alarms were distributed to vulnerable groups in the community. In Castlemilk, the Project produced and distributed leaflets and help cards explaining women's rights in situations of domestic violence and listing the names, addresses and telephone numbers of key services which could offer immediate help and support.

Again, it is difficult to judge what effect these and other initiatives had in tackling fear of crime in Project Areas. The Second Household Surveys (Ditton, 1994; Ditton *et al.*, 1994; Jones *et al.*, 1994) in each of these localities showed, in general terms, mixed responses. In Greater Easterhouse slightly fewer respondents in 1994 appeared to worry about being harassed or assaulted by a stranger. Similarly, in Castlemilk fewer citizens in 1994 worried about becoming a victim of street assault or robbery. Of course, as noted, a wide range of social and environmental factors can impinge upon people's perceptions of crime and their resultant anxiety levels. The extent, therefore, to which any single Project initiative can impact meaningfully on 'fear of crime' is perhaps open to question. Yet, the Projects, in working collaboratively with a range of service-providers and with local community organisations themselves, nonetheless, made a serious attempt to instil in local citizens a more realistic appreciation of prevailing crime trends which might enable people to make more rational decisions concerning the conduct of their daily lives.

Projects as Honest Brokers

One of the main functions expected of Projects was to act as a 'broker' or 'catalyst' to bring together local service providers and community organisations to work collaboratively (Berry and Carter, 1992; Tilley, 1992; 1993). Each of the Projects recorded both success and failure in this regard.

Whether projects were successful or unsuccessful in their attempt to 'broker' collaborative responses to crime prevention and community safety depended to a great extent on local conditions and the nature of relationships between key players in the area. Some common factors may be distilled. Conditions which seemed to contribute towards effective partnership were: where objectives were commonly held and priorities agreed beforehand; where initiatives were orientated to fulfilling a special task; where initiatives were service driven with community backing; where there was a general empathy with the aims of Safer Cities; where a spirit of compromise prevailed when problems arose; and where tangible benefits were perceived to accrue from co-operation.

On the other hand, failure to promote co-operation arose: where different perspectives on a 'perceived' problem were held; where intransigence was deeply entrenched; where co-operation on an initiative was seen as duplication of effort; where the work of Projects suggested criticism of indigenous service providers; where agencies were concerned about having to commit resources; where the contribution of existing well established community organisations was overlooked; and where attempts were made to generate interest at grassroots level in matters which were not specifically issued based or of local relevance.

Each of the Project Management/Steering Committees attempted to strike a balance between the need for professional Project staff to manage and direct affairs while at the same time acknowledging the wishes and aspirations of the community as voiced through its representatives. Sometimes this could create tensions as the expectations of the community were tempered by what professionals believed to be achievable. Nonetheless, each Management Steering Committee was reasonably effective in reaching the necessary compromise, although each adopted its own individual style for conducting business and resolving disputes.

Theoretically there can be different levels of involvement by the community in Projects of this kind. At the very lowest level 'information sharing' ensures that people living in the area are kept informed about what is happening. 'Consultation' allows local people to say what they think about proposals, plans or initiatives being put forward by the Project with public meetings convened specifically to discuss matters providing forums for community debate. 'Participation' offers community representatives the opportunity to take part in discussions about Project activities at regular meetings. 'Decision making' empowers community representatives not only to take part in discussions leading up to decisions but to vote to influence outcomes and the use of resources. 'Power sharing' involves those representing the community in having an equal say with agency personnel regarding proposals for the implementation of a strategy. 'Community control' gives local representatives an active role in the design and implementation of strategic goals and control over funding and the allocation of resources.

Community input varied between Projects. Even within Projects there was far from uniform agreement about the contribution made by local representatives. The Committee of the Safer Edinburgh Project was arguably the most 'senior' in composition. The Chief Constable of Lothian and Borders Police chose personally to sit on the Steering Committee with the Regional and District Councils and other agencies also sending along top officials. This undoubtedly gave the Committee an 'authority' which helped to expedite action after decisions had been reached. However, it also laid the Steering Committee open to the criticism of being 'elitist'. Nonetheless, in Edinburgh, community input can be said to have hovered around the 'decision making' level.

Greater community input was exerted in Castlemilk where the constitution of Safe Castlemilk permitted only community representatives to vote and excluded professional service-providers (Blake-Stevenson Consultants, 1993). Also, given that Safe Castlemilk had already established itself and its community safety agenda through a process of local consultation prior to the Safer Cities Project being 'absorbed' into the area, it is tempting to argue that Castlemilk was the Project which most closely approximated a model in which 'community control' was exerted by local representatives over the design and implementation of strategy and in the allocation of resources.

In Greater Easterhouse the situation was close to local people 'sharing power' with professionals. Constitutionally, all members of the Management Group were eligible to vote although it seems that few decisions proceeded to formal divisions. In Dundee (North East) there also appeared to be little in the way of contentious debate between community representative and agency personnel. For the first three years of the Project a formal constitutional mechanism for resolving disputes was deemed unnecessary. Local representatives themselves were content that they had a fair share of influence over decisions affecting initiatives and the allocation of funding so in this respect community input in Dundee (North East) was pitched at the 'decision-making' level.

In all of the Projects, the Management/Steering Committee attempted, wherever possible, to liaise with existing community organisations to advance common objectives. Certainly, the experience of the Edinburgh Project suggested it was more productive and effective to collaborate with *existing* groups to develop initiatives than to try to create *new* amalgamations of residents based around 'Community Forums'. Yet care had to be taken that Projects were not seen to be duplicating or usurping the endeavours of already well established organisations. For instance, in Castlemilk, some local groups saw the involvement of the project as an implied criticism that their own efforts were somehow falling short of the mark. Umbrage could also be taken when a Project sought to take undue credit for initiatives to which others had made a significant contribution.

Notwithstanding some of these difficulties, the 'community' would certainly appear to have had the opportunity to participate in the Projects and where appropriate influence matters. Whether or not they chose to participate was their decision. The Projects were never likely to generate mass interest, so the fact that the community was 'represented' in many instances by core activists should not come as a surprise.

While Projects needed to acknowledge community wishes as expressed through local organisations, it was nevertheless incumbent upon the professional staff employed by Safer Cities - the Co-ordinator and Assistant Co-ordinator - to give a direction and lead on crime prevention and community safety and to manage Project affairs. There was little evidence of any real tensions or rivalries between professionals sitting on Management/Steering Committees since most were open-minded and flexible in their approach to issues. Although they had departmental or agency interests to safeguard this did not preclude a commitment to the wider objectives of the Project, with most professionals being accommodating by providing funding or assistance in kind from their own agency's resources.

Differences of opinion did arise, but perhaps not as many as might have been expected in Projects with a five year lifespan. Occasionally, divisions of opinion arose between service-providers and community representatives over the appropriate course of action to take to resolve perceived problems. Frustrations were evident when community protests about a 'problem' site did not match the definitional criteria used by professional analysts. In this way community 'expectations' were sometimes at odds with professional 'expertise'. Holding such different perspectives, positions could become entrenched and confrontational, stifling any collaborative response to address the situation.

'Conditions for Success'

It is difficult to say precisely what impact the Projects had on crime prevention and community safety since it is impossible to know what would have occurred had the Safer Cities Projects not existed. However, notwithstanding this obvious caveat, Projects undoubtedly helped to stimulate and co-ordinate inter-agency activity and were instrumental in propelling forward key initiatives to tackle community problems (Berry and Carter, 1992). It is also difficult to generalise why some schemes were effective and others less so, but some common factors can be distilled.

Home security programmes were effective, insofar as Crime Profiles and Household Surveys reveal, in the 'peripheral' housing estates of Castlemilk, Greater Easterhouse and Dundee (North East). This is perhaps an unsurprising finding given the condition of some of the housing stock and the socio-economic profiles of these areas. People have a basic right to feel secure within their own homes; if they do not feel so then it is unlikely they will feel secure or confident in other contexts within the community (McAllister *et al.*, 1993). The anxieties of many local residents appear to have been assuaged through the fitting of comparatively simple security devices. Not only did such measures make people feel safer at home, it also reassured them that service providers took their concerns seriously and were at least attempting to remedy them.

Business security schemes were also effective in those localities where they were implemented, that is, Greater Easterhouse and Dundee (North East). Local traders and shopkeepers were able to benefit from funding to improve the security of their premises. It is arguable that small local businesses should have been entirely responsible for financing their own security arrangements, but given limited profit margins this was perhaps not a realistic proposition. While there is little evidence to suggest that the availability of such funding has attracted businesses into the respective areas, the security schemes do appear to have helped a number of local enterprises to remain open and to continue trading.

Youth work was undertaken by all of the Projects and the vast majority of such initiatives proved successful because they were able to 'engage' children and young people in positive pursuits. Especially effective were the school holiday diversion schemes which gave pupils opportunities to pursue their favourite sports and leisure activities. A key to the success of these schemes was that activities were either free or affordable to the children through the subsidies provided by the Projects. Instead of idleness and boredom during the holiday periods, which could lead to mischief and delinquency, young people were presented with attractive choices which they were able to opt into. Collaborative work between the Projects, other service providers and commercial concerns was instrumental to the success of such initiatives.

The provision of physical amenities was also an effective mechanism for engaging young people. The building of new all weather kick-pitch facilities and the refurbishment of boys clubs provided communities with valuable assets. Again, it is arguable that local authority departments should have been responsible for the provision of such amenities. However, competing demands on Parks and Recreation Departments' budgets precluded this option and without Safer Cities' funding the amenities would never have materialised. Such facilities provided a focal point through which local youngsters could channel their sporting energies.

Projects achieved varying degrees of success in publicising their activities in the communities in which they were set. Quite marked differences existed between each of the Project Areas. In Castlemilk, for example, 64 per cent of respondents to the Second Household Crime and Safety Survey indicated that they had heard of Safe Castlemilk, whereas in Central Edinburgh only 15 per cent of residents interviewed had heard of the Safer Edinburgh Project. In Greater Easterhouse, 38 per cent of residents indicated awareness of Safe Greater Easterhouse and in Dundee (North East) 32 per cent of people knew of the Safer Cities Project's existence.

Safer Edinburgh's limited success in promoting the public profile of the Project and its activities may be attributable to its location in the city centre of Scotland's capital. The Project undoubtedly faced difficulties in attempting to make a public impact in the context of Edinburgh city centre where there was already in existence a profusion of publicity material promoting domestic and international events of every conceivable type. Conversely in an area like Castlemilk, where there was a greater sense of identity, a plethora of issue-based local organisations and a history of community activism, people may have been more receptive to the various high profile promotional activities of Safe Castlemilk.

Greater Easterhouse and Dundee (North East) faced similar problems in publicising their activities since both were large 'composite' areas comprising a number of different local neighbourhoods. Both Projects, initially at least, had difficulties in convincing residents, who identified principally with their immediate neighbourhood, that Safer Cities had a relevance to their daily lives. Public awareness of the Projects in these areas tended to result from specific high profile initiatives which reached a large number of people.

There is, of course, a need to differentiate between the Projects' profiles and credibility with the general public, and with active community groups and local statutory agencies. Notwithstanding some of the difficulties the Projects experienced in trying to reach a mass audience, they were all successful in promoting a credible image with the community activists and professional service-providers with whom they collaborated. Occasionally, petty rivalries could emerge, but, by and large, local representatives and professional personnel viewed the Projects positively and were enthusiastic in their support.

'Lessons Learned'

In each of the Projects there were undoubtedly some things that might have been done better. A number of important lessons have been learned.

The Projects' own attempts at monitoring and evaluating their performances were at best ad hoc and uneven (Youell, 1991). Some initiatives were evaluated quite fully while others received scant attention. Admittedly some, like home security programmes, were easier to evaluate because 'before' and 'after' small area crime statistics were available through which an informed conclusion might be drawn. Others, especially in the field of social crime prevention with young people, were more difficult to measure, since it was not always clear what criteria could be used to evaluate outcomes. Certainly, initiatives involving larger amounts of expenditure tended to be more closely monitored than those involving lesser sums. But overall, Projects did not routinely or systematically subject themselves to evaluating performance. While there was an expectation that Projects should monitor their activities no official guidance on how to do so was issued by the Scottish Office. This may be seen as an oversight since the Home Office had chosen to circulate very specific guidance on monitoring and evaluation to Safer Cities Projects south of the border.

Clearer 'central' direction from the Scottish Office might also have helped Projects to 'balance' their activities between crime prevention and community safety. Projects were funded from the Crime Prevention Unit's budget. It was therefore implicit that crime prevention was a priority. Yet from the outset, Safe Castlemilk 'negotiated' a wider community safety remit while other Projects also broadened their agendas to include at least some aspects of safety. There is evidence to suggest that Scottish Office officials were concerned that the drift towards community safety became too pronounced. Some unease existed about crime prevention money being spent on things such as fire safety and road safety. Greater intervention on the part of the Scottish Office may have left it open to criticism for being overly directive, but clearer guidance on the balance to be struck between crime prevention and community safety might have been helpful.

The importance of harnessing both the goodwill and experience of established community groups cannot be emphasised enough. The community, through its representatives and organisations, needs to feel it has a proper voice in decision-making over events which will impact on residents' lives. It needs to have a sense of ownership of the initiatives which are being implemented on its behalf. A delicate balance has to be struck between the 'top down' managerial role of Project Co-ordinators and the 'bottom up' representations of community activists. To assist this process it is beneficial for a Project to create a distinctive 'image' and role for itself within the community so that local people can clearly identify with its aims and objectives. Some Projects managed to achieve this more easily than others with the effectiveness of Project publicity depending to a great extent on the nature of the community in which it was set.

Lines of communication between professional service providers and community representatives need to be clear so that tensions do not arise over the quality or effectiveness of service delivery. When professional 'expertise' is clearly at odds with community 'expectations', some degree of compromise is necessary on both sides. Professional reasons for proceeding or not proceeding with a particular course of action need to be explained fully, wherever possible with supporting data, to the community affected. Similarly, local representatives need to appreciate more readily some of the constraints under which service providers must operate and be more accommodating of advice based on wider professional knowledge and experience.

While the Safer Cities experiment in Scotland has now come to an end, there is evidence to suggest that many of the new local authorities have assimilated the ethos of Safer Cities by establishing Community Safety Units. Further, there is a growing consensus amongst academics, politicians, service-providers and others that the 'problem of crime' and the 'fear of crime' need to be tackled at the 'front end', in the community through a partnership approach of local agencies and citizens. Safer Cities provided the catalyst for crime prevention and community safety activities tailored to the needs (assessed through consultation and research) of the communities in which they were set. The challenge facing central and local government, statutory and voluntary agencies and communities themselves, is to develop inter-agency structures which provide the necessary platform to promote collaborative, focused and appropriately directed crime prevention efforts.

6   Situating Scottish Policing

NEIL WALKER

Introduction

The policing of Scotland, like the policing of any territory with its own
political and cultural identity, consists of a distinctive but broadly familiar
set of social practices informed by a distinctive but broadly familiar pattern
of historical development. As Marenin (1996a, p.309) has argued:

> Policing is a field of contest among the state, private interest groups... and
> communities over the division of authority and responsibilities for
> constructing and protecting secure routines of daily life.

This suggests general and particular reasons for the distinctiveness of
policing. In any socio-political order, the state, private elites and wider civil
society each have their own culturally specific characteristics, and the
overall balance of power and influence between them is struck in a manner
which has implications for the organisation of the public sphere and for
public policy generally. As for the particular focus of policing - the
protection of the secure routines of daily life - since this task concerns the
micro-dynamics of social reproduction, its refinement and pursuit is likely to
be closely informed by local circumstances (demographic patterns, economic
opportunities, housing conditions, balance between public and private space,
and so on) and coloured by local cultural preferences and sensibilities
(traditions of self-policing, tolerance of rule infraction, deference to public
authority, and so on).

The differences between policing systems should not, however, be
exaggerated, and again Marenin is helpful in demonstrating this. He claims
that the police typically perform a dual function, protecting both the
'specific order' and the 'general order' within a defined territory, with the
first referring to the particular interests of dominant political and economic
groups and the second referring to the interest of *all* social constituencies in
living in conditions of public tranquillity and personal security (Marenin,
1982, p.258). On this view, provided the policing system associated with a
particular socio-political order has developed to the point where it is more

than simply a tool of a ruling faction,[1] then it tends to harbour the same broad aspirations (crime prevention, crime detection, protection of life and property, and so on), exhibit the same internal tensions[2] and face the same basic dilemmas and trade-offs in its pursuit of general order as does any similar system.[3] Local social conditions and attitudes may add their own particular gloss to the policing mandate and to the choice of policing methods, while the configuration of authority and the balance of special interests within the political system may significantly influence the institutional arrangements through which policing is regulated, but the underlying security problematic remains the same.

Another homogenising factor is more closely tied to the circumstances of 'high modernity' (Giddens, 1991, p.4). In the contemporary world, every agency - including the state - operates in an intensely reflexive manner. The growth of transnational markets and capital movements, the development of mass communications and other 'globalizing' trends, such as the emergence of international and supranational normative orders, reflect the gradual 'disembedding' of social and political relations from immediate contexts of interaction. Government techniques and 'rationalities' (Foucault, 1991) are now informed by international example and global trends, and are less likely to remain tied to the self-corroborating imperatives of direct experience and local tradition. From this perspective, policing, like every other area of criminal justice policy, becomes more susceptible to critique and revision in accordance with transnational norms and practices.[4]

Furthermore, the susceptibility of Scotland to non-local policy influences is greatly accentuated by its constitutional position as part of the larger British state. Many commentators (see, for example, Kellas, 1989; Paterson, 1994) have sought to emphasise the continuation of a separate Scottish social and political system after the Union with England in 1707, focusing upon the preservation of indigenous Scottish traditions in key areas such as law, religion and education and the development of a substantial framework of devolved administrative authority in the 19th and 20th centuries. Yet while it is important to distinguish Britain as a 'union state' from 'unitary states' with 'one unambiguous political centre' (Rokkan and Urwin, 1982, p.11), it is just as important that the consequences of vesting ultimate legal and political sovereignty in Westminster and Whitehall over almost three centuries are recognised (Midwinter *et al.*, 1991; Nairn, 1997). As we shall see, the status of Britain as a single constitutional state pre-dates the origins of the 'new police' both in Scotland and in England and Wales by around a century, thereby restricting the scope for separate policy development from the outset. Moreover, continuing constitutional unity entails that the first point of comparative reference within the reflexive politics of high modernity is likely to be the alternative, and dominant tradition within the same state.

In what follows, the question of distinctiveness versus homogeneity is addressed by situating Scottish policing within a historical, cultural and institutional context. It is argued that Scotland, like many modern democratic countries, has 'reached a watershed in the evolution of [its] systems of crime control and law enforcement' (Bayley and Shearing, 1996, p.585). However, although the diagnosis of the condition of Scottish policing may have much in common with that of the policing system of many liberal democracies, England in particular, the prognosis need not be the same. There is no historical law of inevitable convergence. Indeed, the present conjuncture may offer an opportunity for Scottish policing to forge a *more* distinctive identity in adapting the old security imperatives to the demands of a new age.

Historical Context

Origins of the New Police

In view of the 'remarkably early growth' (Carson, 1984, p. 207) of Scottish policing, it is especially to be regretted that its history is under-researched in comparison to the policing of the rest of the British Isles (Emsley, 1996, p.25).[5] The establishment in the towns of 'new police' forces of professional officers with a clear public mandate took place through a series of private Acts of Parliament at the turn of the 19th century. Aberdeen led the way in 1795, followed by Glasgow in 1800, Edinburgh in 1805, and, in rapid progression, a cluster of smaller urban centres, until in 1833 the first public Act enabling the establishment of police forces in all royal burghs or burghs of baronny was passed. Equally, in rural Scotland, as many as a dozen counties had, through their Commissioners of Supply, established police forces prior to the enactment of general enabling legislation in 1839. While organised police forces had been established earlier in France, Russia, Germany and Austria, the Scottish initiative was, with the exception of abortive experiments in Ireland in the last years of the 18th century, the first in the British Isles, in its embryonic stage significantly predating a much more familiar historical landmark - the establishment of the Metropolitan Police in London in 1829.

The poverty of serious historical investigation and analysis hinders attempts to account for this early development, but, drawing upon Carson's work (1984; 1985), at least two partial explanations may be offered. First, the relevant legislation could be enacted so early because it continued to chime quite closely with the old police idea. In particular, the police provided for under the early urban statutes were not merely specialists in the maintenance of order and the prevention of crime, but continued to provide a broader measure of public welfare in matter such as road maintenance, lighting and public health. This does not imply, as some have suggested (see, for example, Hart, 1981, pp.158-69), that the early Scottish forces may be dismissed as an inconsequential legacy of the old police; in particular, their full-time, professional status sets them apart from their predecessors. It does, however, demonstrate the lack of any clear historical rupture between old and new in the development of Scottish policing,[6] and explains how a broader conception of the police task - one which has remained under serious contemplation in the modern age - retained a toehold in Scottish policing discourse and practice well into the 19th century.

In as much as the early Acts were genuine harbingers of the new police, a second strand of explanation has to do with the peculiar pattern of economic growth in Scotland. As Carson notes (1984, p.218), there appears to be broad consensus that the major agricultural and industrial developments which ushered in the age of capitalism took place rather later in Scotland than in England, but accelerated more rapidly. In consequence, the effects of economic transformations, in terms of social dislocation and altered routines of daily life, and in terms of new insecurities attendant upon these changes, 'were experienced much more acutely north of the border' (*ibid.*). Rural depopulation in the Lowlands and, later, in the Highlands was precipitated by the actions of Scottish landlords, unhampered (unlike their English counterparts) by the need to proceed through costly and difficult acts of enclosure, in developing large-scale commercialised agriculture and thereby dispossessing large numbers of small tenants. The absence under the Scottish poor laws of a compulsory safety-net for the able-bodied pauper together with the thickening flow of immigration from Ireland in the first half of the 19th century dovetailed with these changes in the rural economy to provide mid-century Scotland with a large migrant population. In turn, this created a sizeable pool of cheap labour to service the textile, chemical and iron industries of the rapidly expanding lowland towns.

Reiner (1992, p.40) has argued that policing in its new mode was required 'to deal with conflicts, disorders and problems of co-ordination which are necessarily generated by any complex and materially advanced social order'. Scotland of the early-to-mid 19th century certainly fitted this description. The migrant population produced high levels of vagrancy in the countryside and new towns, precipitating a competitive struggle amongst urban mad rural authorities over the management and exclusion of the travelling population. An organised police presence was also required to maintain order in the new and densely populated urban communities, and to provide an alternative to the crude and increasingly unacceptable imposition of military force to quell unrest associated with the discipline of the industrial workplace and with the traumas of rural dispossession. Moreover, and further reinforcing their support for the new capitalist order, the police were actively employed in the suppression of activities such as begging, hawking, poaching and grazing of cattle on public land which were subjected to increasingly draconian regulation as the 19th century progressed, and which had traditionally provided alternative forms of subsistence to wage labour (Carson, 1985, pp.3-12).

The development of nineteenth century policing also reflects the struggle between different groups over control of the state. The new police clearly served the 'specific order' requirements of both the traditional landed classes and the new industrial *bourgeoisie*, but the institutional politics of the new police nevertheless reflected the shifting balance of political power between these groups. For much of the nineteenth century, despite the democratic reforms of 1832, the landed interest continued to dominate the national level of politics, and so bourgeois strategies for gaining political influence tended to be locally concentrated. Even here, though, it proved difficult to remove the traditional unelected power base of the landowners in the magistracy or the town councils, or in the counties as Commissioners of Supply. The institution of local police forces - particularly through private legislation in the towns - promised an alternative source of municipal power for the new bourgeois and professional interests who sought to control such forces, and provided a particular incentive to define the new police mandate as widely as possible. After 1833 when generic local government began to develop its own limited democratic franchise on the basis of property ownership, the *bourgeoisie* began to strengthen its grip on local political power, and this encouraged the gradual integration of policing into the general system of local administration (Carson, 1984, pp. 220-222).

A Century of Consolidation

In the century from 1850 until the post-war years, we can trace two significant graphs in the development of the Scottish police - one cultural and the other structural. Culturally, it is often assumed that the relatively benign image of the British police during this period reflects the underlying cohesiveness of our social order. However, as Reiner (1992, p.61) argues, the negotiation of policing by consent was no mirror of basically harmonious social relations; rather it was a studied and strategically adept response to the depth of class divisions. The growing acquiescence and support of the working class was based upon its maturing perception, influenced by the policing authorities' careful cultivation of a non-partisan image, that the police were no mere instrument of the gentry and manufacturing classes, but could be useful to all classes in the suppression of crime and the maintenance of general order.

For example, during the Highland Land War of the 1880s, while the central authorities were aware of the danger of resorting to the brute force of the military, they were equally ambivalent about heavy-handed policing in the suppression of protesting crofters, recognising the strong legacy of suspicion that the police were tools of the landed classes (Carson, 1985, pp.5-8). If this exercise in the legitimation of policing was not an unqualified success, other efforts to fashion the police as custodians of impersonal authority were more measured and more effective. There are numerous reported examples in the latter half of the 19th century of the police distancing themselves from the narrow interests of landowners in deterring poachers and of factory owners in suppressing organised labour. There is also clear evidence of a project, involving both the central Inspectorate of Constabulary and local police authorities, to mark out a distinct organisational and cultural space for policing. Gradually, the police became a body apart; well-trained, subject to quasi-military discipline, reasonably well-paid and housed separately from the population policed. These various trends dovetailed with a wider process of incorporation of the working class into the political and economic institutions of Scottish society and a broader 'pacification of relations between social classes to enhance the legitimacy of the police as the increasingly professionally autonomous arm of an increasingly legitimate state' (Carson, 1985, pp.12-15).

Alongside these cultural changes, complementary institutional changes took place in the form of 'a number of interlocking processes such as consolidation, administrative rationalisation, more centralised control and clarification of function' (Carson, 1984, p.214). Following the general enabling legislation in the towns in 1833 and the counties in 1839, the facility to establish a police force was extended to smaller conurbations in 1847 and 1850, while in the counties comprehensive policing coverage was obtained after 1857 when the maintenance of a force became compulsory. That same year saw the establishment of the office of Inspector of Constabulary (HMIC), whose power to withhold government grant for reasons of inefficiency and whose influential role in the framing of detailed regulations on conditions of service, allowed the embryo of a centrally authorised model of good police administration to develop. Rationalisation continued with the repeal of the few remaining local police Acts in 1892 and a more general streamlining of local administration from which gradually emerged the shape of the modern tripartite relationship of control over policing, day-to-day operational control resting with the chief constable, material support and advice emanating from the police committees of the town or county councils, and general policy guidance and administrative direction coming from central government.

A final important thrust in the drive towards a uniform model of policing was the gradual consolidation of forces into larger and larger units. The pressure to amalgamate began as early as 1857, and from over 90 forces in mid-century, the Scottish police organisation was reduced through progressive rationalisations to 64 forces in 1900 (Murdoch, 1995), 49 at the end of the Second World War, 22 in 1968, and, finally, to the present figure of eight following the introduction of regional government in 1975. This trend, like the other institutional shifts towards increased uniformity, helped to foster and reinforce the image and practice of detached professionalism and cultural autonomy described in the previous section.

The Contemporary Watershed

The cultural and institutional developments set out above describe a familiar story in the development of policing systems within liberal democracies. In particular, the degree of convergence with English policing arrangements over the century of consolidation of new policing is marked. Although contemporary cultural and institutional developments also follow a recognisable pattern, there are some interesting variations in the Scottish experience.

Beyond the Golden Age

It has been persuasively argued that in the last 30 years the British police have passed the peak of their social legitimacy (Reiner, 1992; 1995; 1997). It is said that they no longer occupy the 'sacred' (Reiner, 1995) position as part of the awe-inspiring centre of society which they did in the early post-war years when they were seen as disciplined bureaucratic professionals, faithful to the rule of law and operationally impartial, committed to preventive policing and the minimal application of force, wedded to a service ethos, properly accountable, and - perhaps most significantly of all - effective in preventing and clearing up crime. Revisionist historians have remained sceptical about this account (see, for example, Roberts, 1973; Storch, 1975; Brogden, 1982; 1991), but even if it overstates the depth and breadth of the legitimacy of the police, and even if such approbation as did exist owed as much to dramaturgical devices - to astute self-presentation and skilful image management - as to concrete practice, there can be little argument that the middle years of this century were the closest approximation to a golden age of policing that Britain and other liberal democracies have known.

It is equally undeniable, however, that the golden age has passed, its demise most fully documented in the context of England and Wales. Corruption scandals have tarnished the image of professional integrity and shown the limits, and in some cases the pathologies, of bureaucratic discipline. Examples of serious rule infraction and a more aggressive approach towards the extension of police powers have revealed a strategic attitude towards law as a resource rather than a reverence for the rule of law. Serious public disorder in the 1980s, both in an industrial context and in the context of the policing of the inner-cities, has sullied the police reputation for minimal force, the development of new quasi-military forms of clothing and accoutrements appearing to provide sartorial confirmation of this. The increasingly explicit involvement of the police in the politics of law and order, particularly in the supportive environment provided by the early years of the Thatcher government, has compromised their position of political neutrality, aided and abetted by a series of running disagreements with local police authorities in urban centres such as Manchester and Liverpool. The movement from the 1960s onwards away from localised foot patrol as the fulcrum of deterrence, response, reassurance and information-gathering and towards car-based 'fire-brigade' response and the formation of new specialisms in proactive criminal intelligence and community relations, has led to more distant and fragmented police-public relations and a declining emphasis upon a broad service role and a preventive philosophy. Finally, the deterioration in the ability of the police to prevent and to detect crime, marked by the accelerating rise in serious crime and fall in the clear-up rate since the 1950s - and itself a function of deepening social divisions and new forms of political and economic marginalization which have exacerbated public disorder and strained police commitment to the rule of law - has demystified the police's key claim to form the vanguard in a successful war against crime by the state (Reiner, 1992, ch.2). This, then, is the 'watershed' alluded to by Bayley and Shearing, a mutually reinforcing combination of public alienation from, and dwindling support for, a more distant and more authoritarian police system, and a declining capacity on the part of that system to fulfil its core, crime-fighting mandate.

There is compelling evidence to suggest that the Scottish police have been affected by this general decline in police legitimacy. Many of the specific causes are clearly present in the Scottish context. Scotland, too, has been affected by the more explicit politicisation of the debate over police powers, most notably in the vigorous campaign to introduce a legal status of pre-arrest detention under the Criminal Justice (Scotland) Act 1980 (Baldwin and Kinsey, 1982, ch.6). The major industrial dispute of the last 20 years, the miners strike of 1984-85, included the Scottish coalfields and involved the police in a number of public order flashpoints. The decline of local beat policing and the marginalisation of the broader service role has been just as pronounced in Scotland as elsewhere (Baldwin and Kinsey, 1982, ch.2). So, too, until the mid 1980s, was the increase in crime levels and the decrease in clear-up rates (Chambers and Tombs, 1984); and as Fyfe and Bannister have fully documented in their contribution to this volume (see chapter 19), this decline, together with the imposition of new financial disciplines on the public sector generally, has led, as in England and Wales, to a rationalisation and reduction of the public police role in crime-fighting and increasing scope for private or collaborative initiatives - developments which further deflate the myth of the police as the central agency in a project of 'sovereign crime control' (Garland, 1996).

Furthermore, evidence from crime surveys seems to bear out a general reduction in support for policing and significant levels of dissatisfaction with police presence in the neighbourhood, with the outcome of police-public encounters, and with the propensity of the police to disobey rules (Allen and Payne, 1991, chapters 2-3). These figures and trends are broadly comparable with similar data for England and Wales, as is the concentration of greatest dissatisfaction and of abrasive police contacts amongst the young (Anderson *et al.*, 1994; Loader, 1996) and socially and economically vulnerable groups (Kinsey, 1992).

On the other hand, some of the available evidence implies that the decline in the legitimacy of Scottish policing may be less pronounced, more nuanced, and more amenable to stabilisation or even reversal than is the case for England and Wales. To begin with, many of the specific causes of decline are less emphatic in the Scottish setting. The major corruption scandals of the past 30 years have been concentrated south of the border, and in the Metropolitan Police in particular. Similarly, the main incidents of police subversion of the rule of law in pursuit of convictions in Irish terrorist cases and other major crimes have occurred in England. Equally, the periodic urban disorders since the summer of 1981, while not excluding Scotland, have mainly focused upon English cities and towns, and have often been sparked by confrontation between the police and young Afro-Caribbean or Asian populations. It is also the case that the politicisation of policing has generally been less explicit in Scotland. After the miners' strike, for example, a number of Scottish chief constables spoke openly of the need to restore good relations with the mining communities and to reaffirm their reputation for impartiality, and there have been no disputes between forces and local police authorities over police accountability of the intensity experienced in England. If these examples tend to concentrate on the ideological superstructure of police-public relations - on the vivid dramas of consent and confrontation - they are no less significant for that. The centrality of policing to basic questions of social order and state security, and, consequentially, the intensity of public preoccupation with policing institutions and the importance of mediated as well as direct experiences[7] of these institutions, is such that the symbolism associated with policing is highly significant in the process of its legitimation (Manning, 1977; Walker, 1996; Loader, 1997a). In addition, ideological forms tend to reflect and reinforce underlying practices and relations. In this context, it is at least arguable that the absence of intense local political conflict and of recurrent urban disorder is in some part attributable to the lesser salience in Scotland of a new urban underclass marginalized from mainstream political and economic institutions and practices, the growth of which in the English cities in the 1980s was linked to the demographic concentration of second generation ethnic minorities (Lea and Young, 1982; Kinsey *et al.*, 1986, ch.2; Brogden *et al.*, 1988, pp.124-142; Keith, 1993; Holdaway, 1996).

Less speculatively, and consistently with the above hypotheses, we may note that recent crime surveys in Scotland do suggest a significant divergence from England and Wales as regards levels of victimization and the reporting of crime. Whereas in 1981, levels of personal and household victimisation were broadly comparable, from the mid-1980s there has been an increasingly marked divergence, with Scottish levels now considerably lower (Anderson and Leitch, 1994, p.5; MVA Consultancy, 1997, pp. 4-5). Recent surveys also reveal the maintenance of markedly higher levels of reporting crime to the police in Scotland (Anderson and Leitch, 1994, p.3; MVA Consultancy, 1997, p.6). Taken together, these findings imply that Scotland differs subtly from England on both sides of the police legitimacy equation. The underlying crime rate is lower, suggesting that a higher level of credibility continues to attach to the police claim to pre-eminence and reasonable effectiveness in crime control. By the same token, reporting levels are healthier, which implies both a better informed police - and so better able to respond to crime - and a police which continues to inspire sufficient confidence amongst most sections of the population to provide the natural repository of crime complaints.

Institutional Flux

If the matrix of police legitimacy has altered significantly in recent years, so too have the structures through which policing is provided and regulated. In this respect, the differences between Scottish and English policing are, if anything, more marked than in the cultural domain. Taking as our point of departure the modern refinement of the tripartite relationship under the 1962 Royal Commission on Policing, we can identify three related patterns of institutional development which lend a distinctiveness to the contemporary structure of Scottish policing. First, there is a general mismatch between institutional capacity and formal powers within the tripartite relationship, leading to an incoherent division of labour and an uncertain co-ordination of responsibilities. Second, there is the increasing subordination of concerns about 'good governance' of the policing to concerns about its 'good management' in the identification of the optimal size of organisational units (Mair and Wilkie, 1997). Thirdly, and at the macro-structural level, there is the position of the Scottish constabulary within an emerging multi-tier framework of policing.

The tripartite framework under stress   Under the Royal Commission settlement of 1962 (Royal Commission on the Police, 1962), which continued the trend of increased uniformity between Scotland and England and was given statutory form in Scotland by the Police (Scotland) Act 1967, the power of the chief constable to direct the force was confirmed, with the local police authority largely confined to operational support functions. These included partial funding of the force, the settlement of its established strength and rank structure, the appointment and discipline of senior officers, the provision and maintenance of buildings and equipment, and the supply of civilian back-up personnel. The local police authority was also entitled to be kept informed of the manner in which the force was being run. As the third point of the triangle, the Secretary of State for Scotland not only made regulations for the government and administration, and, through his appointee, the Chief Inspector of Constabulary, ensured the overall efficiency of the police force and its buildings and equipment at pain of withdrawal of central police grant, but also provided an ever-increasing level of central services in matters such as training, technical back-up and specialist operations.

As the label implies, this 'explanatory and co-operative' (Marshall, 1978) model of police accountability presupposed a basically harmonious framework of relations within the tripartite system. The legal regime was facilitative and open-textured rather than prescriptive and precise. Further, the Royal Commission settlement arguably failed to match institution appropriately to function (Walker, 1995). The discretion it conferred on chief constables appeared to extend beyond particular operational decisions to embrace policy matters such as geographical deployment, crime-fighting priorities, and general policing style (for example, the balance between reactive and proactive modes), while the powers of the police authority were generally concerned with the nuts and bolts of operational capability. In legal terms, each party seemed to have what the other wanted, the chief constable as operational expert denied the means to support and maintain his force, and the police authority and - to a lesser extent - the Secretary of State, as the legitimate political voices denied the scope to make the hard value judgements in the domain of policy.

In an inhospitable climate such as developed in many metropolitan areas in England and Wales, this combination of legal permissiveness and functional mismatch could and did generate mutual frustration and led to the adversarial deployment of the law by the various parties to the tripartite system (Oliver, 1987, pp. 208-236). The broad groundswell of criticism eventually provoked the Conservative government into producing a new White Paper on reform of the tripartite system (Home Office, 1993), and this, together with the recommendations of the Sheehy Report (1993), which sought to overhaul the traditional bureaucratic structure of police organisation in accordance with a quasi-market philosophy, provided the ingredients for a revised constitutional settlement in the Police and Magistrates' Courts Act 1994.

There is no scope in the present context to examine the 'calculative and contractual' (Reiner, 1993, p.19) model adopted in this Act in any detail. Very briefly, however, we may note that as it applies to England and Wales, it rests upon the application to a streamlined organisation (reduced from nine to seven ranks) of clear and measurable standards in terms of which the quality of policing can be judged, and upon the use of contractual mechanisms (short-term contracts for senior officers and dismissal on grounds of incompetence for other ranks to replace the previously high level of security of tenure for all ranks) to control and sanction individual behaviour. The model combines market economics with the politics of centralisation, central government acquiring the power to establish national policing objectives and targets, to impose cash limits on force spending, and, through the HMIC, to give specific directions to police authorities to remedy inefficiencies. If this provides a more explicit policy-making role for the central democratic body, the local democratic body is also allocated a policy brief, albeit at a subordinate level, through its new power to devise local policing objectives and to issue local policing plans. To complete the re-allocation of responsibilities, the chief constable is now given control over the necessary resources for operations, including the provision of buildings and equipment, the specification of the size and rank profile of the force, and the direction of civilian support staff.

While considerable reservations may be expressed at the centralising trend of the new provisions (Morgan and Newburn, 1997, p.147; Oliver, 1997, p.184), they do at least address the complaint of functional mismatch levelled at the Royal Commission settlement. Operational support functions are transferred to the chief constable, while the police authority assumes a modest policy role. In Scotland, by comparison, the incoherent entanglement of functions remains, and the centralising drift is arguably just as pronounced and less democratically defensible.

The quasi-market initiatives of Sheehy in streamlining the bureaucracy and linking job security to performance have been applied in Scotland, but they do not interlock with a coherent model of political accountability. The chief constable is granted operational support powers over manpower, but not resources. Conversely, the police authority is denied most of its operational support powers, but, despite remaining partial paymaster, is still denied an explicit role in policy formation. Only central government has a role which clearly suits its institutional capabilities, with most of the powers available in England and Wales extended to Scotland. Yet even here, unlike the Home Secretary in England, the Secretary of State for Scotland lacks explicit responsibility to formulate policing objectives. This absence raises concern about the transparency of the Secretary of State's own accountability for his role in police governance, and also sits uneasily with the rational managerialist assumptions underlying the Sheehy reforms.

What explains the apparently ramshackle nature of the Scottish reforms? In part, it may be the product of complacency. Absent the institutionalised conflict which characterised relations between police authorities and central government in some parts of England, the tripartite system might have been viewed as being in less urgent need of repair north of the border, although the same in-principle objections applied. This is borne out by the fact that the 1993 White Paper on reform of the tripartite system was explicitly confined to England and Wales.

The other, more significant, explanation has to do with the peripheral nature of the Scottish political system. As is well-known, the marginal status of the Scottish Office within the British executive and the absence of an independent law-making process for Scotland means that Scottish legislation has to fight an unequal battle for its place within the government's legislative programme (Finnie, 1991). As a result Scottish legislation is often delayed, or is included within a wider statute which is primarily concerned with England and Wales and which often fails to acknowledge fully the peculiarities of the Scottish position. This structural deficiency blighted the passage of the 1994 Act. Sheehy, as an expression of the free market orthodoxies of the Conservative Government, was always intended to apply North and South of the border. The White Paper, as already noted, was not, but after its publication the Scottish Secretary of State briefly announced that some of the White Paper measures would be so applied. There had been no prior consultation, and, with the normal priority given to the English provisions in Parliament, there was subsequently only limited scope for debate and amendment of the Scottish provisions, despite the hostile reaction of both police and local authorities. The net result of this undesigned and hastily compromised package was a drift towards 'a kind of constitutional no man's land' (Walker, 1995, p.204) - a destination which none of the parties to the tripartite relationship in Scotland found particularly satisfactory.[8]

Management versus governance   Statutory developments in recent years have exacerbated another trend which began with the Royal Commission settlement, namely the delocalization of policing at the expense of accountability concerns.   As we have seen, the delocalization of policing started at least a century before the Royal Commission, but it was only with the application of the Report's conclusion that the optimum size of a police force was 'probably 500 or upwards' (Royal Commission on the Police, 1962, p.85), that managerial imperatives seriously began to interfere with the capacity of local communities to hold their police to account.   The introduction of regional government in 1975 and the matching, with two exceptions, of police forces to regional boundaries, underlined the decoupling of accountability and managerial concerns, particularly in the case of Strathclyde force and region which services 2.3 million people - almost half the population of Scotland.   The reintroduction of unitary authorities in 1995 prompted a further attenuation of the link between force and community.   The regions were abandoned but the eight regional forces were maintained; in consequence, the preservation of democratic accountability to the 32 new unitary authorities required the creation of joint boards for all but two of the forces.   Evidence from other jurisdictions, most pertinently England (Loveday, 1991), suggests that joint boards are more fragmentary and less vigilant supervisors of policing than unitary authorities - a consideration which particularly affects the Strathclyde force, now extending over twelve separate local authority areas.

A number of by now familiar factors explain this transformation.   A growing concern with mangerialist conceptions of efficiency is one.   Larger forces certainly attract economies of scale in terms of administration and technology and allow for greater pooling of knowledge and expertise.   Yet this cannot be the whole story, as force size is by no means uniform, ranging from under 400 officers in Dumfries and Galloway to over 7000 in Strathclyde today.   The local government re-organisations of the 1970s and 1990s which have produced this state of affairs have not simply, or even primarily, been concerned with the disinterested application of management science to local administration.   Just like the early new policing initiatives, they have also reflected a continuing struggle between powerful political interests over control of the local state and the balance of power between centre and locality (Paddison, 1997).

Further, the themes of complacency and an underdeveloped Scottish political system explored in the previous subsection are again pertinent. In England, too, there has been a progressive delocalization of the police and, earlier than in Scotland, a loss of direct accountability through the introduction of joint boards. In 1984, however, in the wake of serious inner-city disorders, some effort was made to refill the local accountability gap through the introduction of a statutory requirement for local consultative committees to complement the work of the police authorities. Despite representations from many interest groups, particularly ethnic minority groups,[9] the Scottish Office decided that the state of police/public relations did not demand a similar response in Scotland, a decision which is echoed in the repeated refusal of the Scottish Office to follow the English lead in introducing an independent element of accountability within the police complaints system (Uildriks and Mastrigt, 1991, pp. 40-42). Finally, the absence of a more fully developed political system is significant to the extent that there is scant evidence of the processes of police reform and local accountability reform being mutually informed and co-ordinated. This was particularly evident in 1994, when the Bills restructuring the tripartite system and introducing unitary authorities passed their legislative stages in close proximity to one another. There is little indication from the parliamentary debates or elsewhere that the ramifications of their interaction had been taken into account, and in particular, that their combined effect was significantly to undermine the position of police authorities (Walker, 1995, p.203).

Multi-tier policing The delocalization of the basic organisational unit of policing is one feature of a deeper structural trend towards the organisation of policing at different planning scales and for different functional tasks. A number of writers have linked this new institutional diversification to the conditions of high modernity (or postmodernity) (Reiner, 1995; Bayley and Shearing, 1996; Walker, 1996; O'Malley and Palmer, 1996; Loader 1997a; 1997b). In a more fragmented, pluralistic and internationalist culture, the idea of a unitary police with an 'omnibus mandate' (Reiner, 1997, p.1039) becomes symbolically redundant and instrumentally inadequate; symbolically redundant because the notion of a single body guaranteeing harmony and security becomes implausible with the fading of the project of sovereign crime control (Garland, 1996; Walker, 1996; Loader, 1997a; 1997b); instrumentally inadequate because the increasingly insistent demand for measurable effectiveness and efficiency prompts a range of initiatives which are not co-terminous with traditional territorial and task boundaries, such as neighbourhood policing and extended jurisdictions to deal with the problems of international and organised crime.

In Scotland, this process is gradually producing a system of multi-tier policing. At the local level, many forces have introduced devolved structures and moved to a local command unit style of operation (HMIC, 1996). Together with devolved budgeting, this allows local commanders to develop modes of policing which are sensitive to community needs and which can seek to restore security at a local level. At the supra-force level, there are a number of sites of development. The Scottish level continues to gain in significance, covering expanding training and technological facilities, the growing supervisory authority of government and inspectorate, and the investigation of drugs crimes and other serious crime by the Scottish Crime Squad - an agency whose profile was heightened by the decision under the recent Police Act 1997 not to include it along with the other regional crime squads within England and Wales in the new National Crime Squad (Uglow and Telford, 1997). Yet in other respects the British level thrives. An earlier decision in favour of Scottish participation in the UK-wide National Criminal Intelligence Service was endorsed under the 1997 Act, while recent legislative and administrative changes have expanded the policing capability against drugs and organised crime of two British agencies traditionally at the shadowy edges of security policy, namely the security service and HM Customs and Excise (Walker, 1993; Lustgarten and Leigh, 1994). Finally at the European and international levels, there are further developments. For example, Europol, an EU wide policing information exchange and intelligence support function presently operating in the transitional form of the Europol Drugs Unit, was allocated significant new operational powers in the 1997 Treaty of Amsterdam which will allow it to take the initiative in the preparation of transnational investigations (Walker, 1998a).

The emergence of these new institutional tiers compounds the problems of transparency, co-ordination and accountability associated with complex modern policing systems. If anything, the intricacy of Scotland's multi-tier arrangements outdoes that of other multi-layered territories, because the sub-state national level - the Scottish level itself - becomes a key site of authority alongside the supranational, state and local levels. Again, however, the absence of a mature Scottish policy framework obstructs efforts to establish a coherent link between the structure of Scottish policing and policing pitched at higher levels. For example, the decision to locate the UK-based Scottish NCIS and Customs and Excise alongside the Scottish-based Scottish Crime Squad in the same purpose-built accommodation near Glasgow (HMIC, 1996) raises questions about their interrelationship, and the adequacy of the accountability mechanisms for tracing this. Equally, the relationship between the fast-expanding European dimension and the state and sub-state level remains largely uncoordinated and unmonitored (Anderson *et al.*, 1995).

Future Tense

In both its cultural and institutional dimensions, Scottish policing has, since its emergence in the early 19th century, displayed and retained certain distinguishing characteristics. Even at this contemporary watershed, when policing world-wide is being transformed by powerful international forces, the distinctiveness of Scottish policing from policing South of the border remains, and in some respects may be more pronounced. However, two ironies attend this observation. In the first place, what remains most immediately distinctive about Scottish policing in cultural terms, namely its marginally better standing than its English neighbour in terms of effectiveness and social legitimacy, is so *in spite of* what distinguishes Scottish policing in institutional terms, namely an incoherence of approach and a weakening of local accountability. In the second place, its contemporary institutional distinctiveness is in a large part a function of its secondary status and marginal treatment within the British political system; it is, in short, a distinctiveness born of dependence and neglect rather than independence and close attention.

Yet the same deep forces which have questioned the legitimacy and efficacy of policing within the sovereign crime control model and which have encouraged the de-centring of the tripartite system may also provide the opportunity to address these ironies and the tensions which they contain. 1997 has witnessed an important British landmark in the long critique of the centralised sovereign statehood (Himsworth, 1996) with the election of New Labour and a commitment to the dispersal of constitutional authority, including a devolved Parliament for Scotland (Scottish Office, 1997g;

Walker, 1998b). Unlike its abortive predecessor scheme of 1979, where, revealingly, responsibility for law enforcement would have been retained by Westminster on the basis that 'key law and order functions are basic to sovereignty'[10] - an explicit endorsement of the sovereign crime control model (Jones, 1997) - the 1997 scheme, which has been emphatically endorsed by referendum, transfers all policing functions except those associated with national security and border controls to the new Edinburgh Parliament. As the anticipatory move of the Scottish Office in 1998 to establish a systematic review of the organisation of Scottish policing indicates,[11] this surely will provide an opportunity to address the drift in institutional arrangements away from a coherent model of local accountability, to discover an appropriate balance between democratic and managerial imperatives, and to harness and direct the development of multi-tier policing. In turn, this may help to safeguard or re-inforce police legitimacy, since publicly acceptable arrangements for providing and accounting for policing services can trigger a 'virtuous circle' (McLaughlin, 1996, p.62) of increased confidence in policing, greater appreciation of its potential and limits, and more effective public support in crime control and detection.

It would be naive to assume that the redesign of the procedures and institutions for holding Scottish policing to account can overcome all the problems posed by profound international changes in the ways in which we understand and are capable of pursuing security as a public good. On the other hand, it would be fatalistic to conclude that the availability of an indigenous deliberative and legislative forum is incapable of making a positive difference in managing the local solution to a global predicament.

Notes

1. Comparative studies of policing remind us that liberal democratic regimes with policing systems more committed to the service of general order than to the defence of specific interests remain the exception rather than the rule. See, for example, Bayley (1985); Mawby (1991); Marenin (1996b).
2. In particular, there is a voluminous literature which seeks to explain the differences and tensions between the 'cop culture' of the lower ranks of the police and the 'management culture' of more senior officers. Basically, these tensions reflect the fact that each internal sector sets different priorities in addressing the complex problem of securing the optimal degree of special order and general order. The lower ranks tend to emphasise the importance

of basic prevention and detection in the day-to-day reactive routines of policing, whereas their more senior colleagues are more concerned with managing external relations and achieving a broad consensus in a context where various constituencies are vying for a greater allocation of scarce policing resources and some constituencies are critical of the tendency of operational practices associated with prevention and detection to interfere with individual and community rights and freedoms. Unsurprisingly, as these structural problems are generic, the attendant organisation and cultural tensions within any particular jurisdiction tend to be very similar. For an overview, see Reiner (1997); for analysis of cultural tensions within Scottish police forces, see Baldwin and Kinsey (1992); Walker (1994); Loader (1996).

3. For a discussion of the perennial and pervasive difficulties of reconciling or balancing the various sub-goals within the general police mandate, see Bradley *et al.* (1986) ch.3.

4. Bayley's (1994) study is highly revealing in this regard, providing both a sophisticated example of internationally-informed reflexivity, and supplying considerable evidence of the extent to which policing methods and practices such as community policing, neighbourhood watch schemes and problem-solving community are already cross-fertilised throughout the international policing community. A recent Scottish example of cross-fertilisation is the adoption by Strathclyde Police in 1996 of a 'zero tolerance' strategy, adapted from the practice of a number of American forces including the New York Police Department, which involves rigorously enforcing the law within a particular area as a means of breaking a self-reinforcing cycle of community acquiescence in neighbourhood crime and vandalism and diminishing informal social controls. The academic source of this approach is Wilson and Kelling (1982).

5. Apart from Carson's work, there are very few historical analyses. Brief overviews are provided by Gordon (1980) and Murdoch (1995), while Smout (1970) is valuable for its contextualization of policing within a broader social history.

6. Although recent histories of the English police have also questioned the received wisdom of a sharp break between old and new systems. See, for example, Emsley (1983; 1991).

7. For example, the 1988 British Crime Survey in Scotland revealed that far more people gained their knowledge of policing from the media in general or from talking to other people than from personal experience (Allen and Payne, 1988, p.5).

8. Arguably, this continuing tension and confusion of functions contributed to the controversy surrounding the resignation of Ian Oliver, chief constable of Grampian Police, in April 1998. The police authority and the Secretary of State for Scotland appeared dissatisfied, *inter alia,* with the force's

efficiency in responding to the murder of a child in the Summer of 1997, and with the chief constable's continuing insistence that his conduct and the conduct of his force during and after the investigation of the murder had been professionally adequate. In turn, the chief constable was critical of the police authority and the Scottish Office ministers on account of their public denunciation of his conduct and that of his force, and on account of their aggressive, and, in his view, incorrect exploitation of the procedures under the 1967 Act concerning the resignation or dismissal of the chief constable (see White, 1998). On the one hand, one might sympathise with the frustrations of the police authority and the Scottish Office in the face of the absence of a clear legal mandate to influence the review of policy within a local force. On the other hand, one might sympathise with the chief constable that these frustrations were vented through a personal attack on his position.

9. The author was given access to the responses to the consultation procedure initiated by the Scottish Office in 1983 when deliberating whether to introduce statutory consultative committees on the English model.

10. 59 H.C. Debs. vol. 903, col. 737, January 15, 1976, *per* Ronald King Murray (then Lord Advocate).

11. Speech by Donald Dewar, Secretary of State for Scotland, to the Scottish Police Federation (*The Scotsman* 23rd April 1998). The announcement, which came the day before the resignation of Ian Oliver (see note 8 above), makes clear that the review was being established with a view to the new Scottish Parliament ultimately legislating for structural reform.

7 The Prosecution Service: Independence and Accountability

PETER DUFF

Introduction

Lord Stott, in his reminiscences, recalls 'a most interesting murder case' which arose while he was Lord Advocate. It involved the demise of a 'cantankerous old man', with nowhere to go, who had been 'dumped' in the household of his son, a teacher. Initially, the old man's death had been certified as due to natural causes but further investigation revealed that this source of 'endless trouble' must have been injected with a fatal dose of insulin by his diabetic daughter-in-law. Lord Stott (1995, pp. 42-43) explains:

> It seemed obvious that the young woman had acted only when driven to distraction by the old man's tantrums; and I soon made up my mind to mark the papers 'No Pro' - after which (the Crown Agent) and I set about finding sufficiently good reasons in law for this decision, which we had little difficulty in doing.

Apparently, therefore, it is possible to 'get away with murder' in Scotland, as long as the Lord Advocate sympathises with your motives!

The significance of this anecdote is that it reveals the extent of the discretion possessed by the Scottish prosecutor. As in most jurisdictions, decisions made by Scottish prosecutors are relatively unstructured and are of low visibility, compared with those made by the legislature or judiciary. Yet prosecutors' decisions may have similar effects. For instance, prior to the reduction in the age of consent to homosexual activity from 21 to 18 (under the Criminal Justice and Public Order Act 1991), it was revealed in *Scotland on Sunday* (14th April 1991) that the Lord Advocate was about to issue guidelines to procurators fiscal which rendered it unlikely that those aged between 16 and 21 would be prosecuted for consensual homosexual activity, except where advantage had been taken of a relationship of trust or there was some other aggravating feature. In effect, the Lord Advocate appeared to be decriminalising such conduct, theoretically a function reserved for the legislature.[1] Similarly, as we shall see below, Scottish prosecutors are increasingly involved in determining the appropriate sentence, traditionally the province of the judiciary.

Until recently, very little was known about the way in which prosecutors exercised their discretion. In Scotland, the first and only major investigation of this topic was carried out by Moody and Tombs (1982) towards the end of the 1970s, although some subsequent research has focused upon particular aspects of the use of prosecutorial discretion. More recently, Fionda's (1995) comparative study of prosecutorial involvement in sentencing contains a lengthy chapter on the Scottish prosecution system. It is the purpose of this chapter to describe the role of the prosecution service in the Scottish criminal justice system and, in particular, to summarise what is known about its exercise of discretion.

Most accounts of prosecutors begin by contrasting the principles of 'legality' and 'expediency'. Under the former, the prosecutor must prosecute in every case where there is sufficient evidence of criminal conduct. This absence of discretion is thought to prevent the possibility of arbitrary, politically motivated or biased decision-making and to ensure that the prosecutor does not usurp the legislative or judicial functions. In contrast, the principle of expediency allows the prosecutor a broad discretion to waive prosecution where this is considered to be in the public interest. Such circumstances might arise where the offence is so trivial that it would be a waste of public funds to proceed in court, or the offender is mentally disturbed and prosecution would serve no useful purpose, or the matter would be resolved better in a civil action brought by the victim.

In practice, the distinction between these two principles is purely academic because no modern criminal justice system has the resources to prosecute every possible act of criminal behaviour (even if this were desirable). (Consequently, it has been observed that the *de facto* prosecutorial discretion which operates under the principle of legality is more difficult to monitor and control because, in theory, its existence cannot be admitted and, in practice, its use has to be disguised, often under the heading of 'insufficient evidence'.) Rather, the real clash of principles which emerges from an examination of the prosecution process is the extent to which prosecutorial decision-making can be rendered independent from political and other extraneous pressures and, yet, can be held accountable to the body politic in order to ensure that prosecutorial discretion is exercised in a just manner (Di Federico, 1998). While the primary purpose of this chapter is to describe the Scottish prosecution system, I shall also touch upon the difficulty of reconciling the independence of the prosecutor with an adequate measure of accountability, although reasons of space preclude development of this topic.

Public Prosecution in Scotland

In Scotland, virtually all criminal prosecutions have long been conducted by a public prosecution service to whom the police report possible cases of criminal conduct (Moody and Tombs, 1982; Sheehan, 1990; Renton and Brown, 1996). Such services are common in the rest of Europe but, in England and Wales, until the recent establishment of the Crown Prosecution Service, it was the police, or solicitors instructed on their behalf, who conducted most prosecutions. In Scotland, a few statutory offences may be prosecuted by a public body - for instance, Customs and Excise or an education authority - but, in practice, such proceedings are normally undertaken by the public prosecutor, who also receives occasional reports from other agencies such as the Television Licence Records Office and Health and Safety at Work Inspectorate. Private prosecutions of one individual by another are extremely rare. The right of private prosecution was recently abolished in summary cases (Criminal Justice (Scotland) Act 1995, s.63) and in solemn cases such proceedings require the concurrence of the Lord Advocate or High Court. There have only been two instances this century where the necessary permission has been granted, the most recent being the infamous 'Glasgow Rape Case' in 1983.[2] In this instance, the Lord Advocate had decided not to prosecute the three accused because the victim's mental state cast severe doubt upon her ability to give evidence. Subsequently, he gave her permission to bring a private prosecution and her assailants were duly convicted and ultimately sentenced to long terms of imprisonment.

The Scottish prosecution service is headed by the Lord Advocate, a government minister, and his deputy, the Solicitor General, also a government appointee. At least one is always a member of one of the Houses of Parliament. The Lord Advocate appoints several members of the Scottish Bar to act as Advocates Depute, these senior law officers being known collectively as Crown Counsel. Their task is both to prosecute in the

High Court, where the most serious cases are heard, and to provide advice to local prosecutors about various other categories of case. Most prosecutions take place in the Sheriff Court or District Court, and, in these instances, the Lord Advocate acts through local prosecutors, known as procurators fiscal. There are 49 procurators fiscal spread across urban and rural Scotland. Their offices have case-loads of very different complexions and sizes: several of the smallest receive under 1,000 crime reports a year while the largest office receives around 80,000. In some of the smaller offices, the procurator fiscal is the only legally qualified member of staff whereas in the largest office there are around 60 other legally qualified prosecutors - known as assistant fiscals and depute fiscals - and nearly 400 administrative staff. In administrative and financial terms, the prosecution service is run by Crown Office in Edinburgh and headed by the Crown Agent, who is accountable to the Lord Advocate.

The most significant aspect of the Scottish system of public prosecution is its complete independence, a status which has long been established and frequently emphasised. The service operates under the principle of expediency - that is, the decision whether to prosecute is discretionary - and prosecutors act in what they consider to be the 'public interest', in practice, a broad, catch-all notion which allows them considerable freedom of action. The prosecution service does not have to account for its actions to the police, the courts or the individuals concerned, nor does it have to provide reasons for its decisions. It is accountable solely to Parliament through the Lord Advocate. Consequently, the Scottish prosecutor, as 'master of the instance', alone determines how to 'mark' a case: that is, whether to prosecute; what charges will be brought (unlike in England where the police are still responsible for charging the accused); and in what forum. The prosecutor possesses a similarly wide discretion in deciding whether to modify or drop some charges in return for a guilty plea (a 'plea-bargain'). In most cases, the local fiscal will act alone but, in the most serious of cases, the advice of Crown Counsel will be sought. Finally, the prosecution service may issue instructions to the police both about the general approach to be taken to particular types of crime and ask for particular steps to be taken in individual cases - for example, further investigations may be requested. In England and Wales, in contrast, it is not clear whether the Crown Prosecution Service is empowered to instruct the police in this way.

In theory, therefore, decisions made by prosecutors are entirely independent but, in practice, they usually rely solely on the information conveyed to them by the police. In a recent study of the prosecution process south of the border, McConville *et al.* (1991) argue that every criminal case - embodied in a file - is 'constructed', in the sense that the information presented to the prosecutor is controlled and shaped by the police. In other words, the report received by the prosecutor does not necessarily represent the objective reality of the incident with which it is concerned; instead it may well be geared to producing the outcome the police wish to secure. While the prosecution service in England is very much the 'junior partner' of the police and this is not so in Scotland, the research carried out by Moody and Tombs (1982) does confirm that the role of the police is crucial in the supply of information to fiscals. Other Scottish research indicates that when selecting alleged offenders for diversion from prosecution for social work intervention or psychiatric treatment, fiscals are heavily influenced by the information contained in the police report (Stedward and Millar, 1989; Cooke, 1990; Duff and Burman, 1994; Duff, 1997). In essence, therefore, the police, as the main source of information for the prosecution service, do exercise a considerable measure of control over the progress of criminal cases.

The Alternatives to Prosecution

As a result of the wide discretion traditionally possessed by fiscals, it has always been regarded as permissible for them to adopt some alternative to prosecution. As little as 15 years ago however, Moody and Tombs (1982, p. 79) commented: 'Scottish prosecutors seemed to regard the option not to prosecute ... as a marginal issue with little relevance to the processing of most criminal matters'. At that time, the 'prosecution rate' was over 90 per cent but in the early 1990s this dropped to around 50 per cent. As Tombs and Moody (1993) argued, this meant that prosecutors had in effect redefined their notion of the 'public interest' so that it no longer required almost automatic prosecution. The prosecution rate has subsequently increased to around 75 per cent, as a result of the massive delegation to the police of the power to offer fixed penalties for road traffic offences (see below). This recent increase in the prosecution rate does not mean that fiscals are prosecuting more cases; it is simply that the number of cases that they are not prosecuting has decreased because many such cases are filtered out of the system by the police issuing fixed penalties rather than passing the cases to fiscals to do likewise, thus causing an apparent rise in the prosecution rate.

This dramatic shift in policy was encouraged by the recommendations of the Stewart Committee (1980; 1983), set up by the government in 1977 to study alternatives to the prosecution of 'minor offences' in an effort to ease the pressure of work upon both the criminal courts and the prosecution service. It published two reports, the first of which recommended extending the use of fixed penalties for road traffic offences and the second of which suggested various methods by which prosecutors could divert a much wider range of offences. As a result, much of the sentencing function formerly exercised by the lower courts has in effect been devolved to the prosecution service. This trend, which is common throughout Europe, owes much to the desire to process cases through the criminal justice system in a cheaper and more efficient manner, although humanitarian considerations have also had some influence. Fionda, in her recent study of prosecution systems, characterises Scottish fiscals as 'reluctant sentencers' (1995, p.65) but, in my view, this is something of an overstatement. While some fiscals are reluctant to trespass into what they regard as judicial territory, the majority are enthusiastic about the recent changes (Duff *et al.*, 1996, pp. 21-22). The startling drop in the proportion of cases prosecuted bears testimony to this. What then are the alternatives to prosecution?

'No Pro'

Historically, around 10 per cent of cases reported to the procurator fiscal have always been marked 'no pro' (no proceedings), often as a result of there being insufficient evidence to proceed. This proportion began to rise at the beginning of the 1980s, primarily as a result of the increasing volume of petty crime and the inability of the system to deal with the increased workload. The no pro rate hit a peak of almost 20 per cent in 1986 but has since declined steadily to around 12-13 per cent (Crown Office and Procurator Fiscal Service, 1995; Duff, 1993).[3] The recent decrease has come about for two interlinked reasons: first, there was considerable political pressure to reduce the no pro rate, as a result of public concern that too many criminals were 'getting away with it' owing to resource constraints; and, second, the increasing availability of other alternatives to prosecution flowing from the Stewart Committee's (1980; 1983) deliberations. As a result of criticism of wide variations in no pro rates returned by different offices, Crown Office now requires fiscals to record their reasons for not proceeding. In 1993/4, the two principal reasons were: 'triviality' - 29 per cent; and 'insufficient admissible evidence' - 23 per cent (Crown Office and Procurator Fiscal Service, 1994, p.9).

Warning Letter

If the procurator fiscal feels that something more than a no pro is required, he may choose to issue a warning to the accused. Around five per cent of cases reported to the fiscal are now dealt with in this manner and this proportion rose dramatically after the use of warning letters was encouraged by the Stewart Committee (1983). In the vast bulk of cases, the warning is issued simply through the dispatch of a standard letter but it is open to the procurator fiscal to call the accused to his office and issue the warning personally. Whatever method is used, the recipient is told that his conduct was unacceptable and any repetition will result in prosecution. While a warning should not be issued if there is insufficient evidence to prosecute, it is not necessary that the accused has admitted his guilt. For this reason, a procurator fiscal warning does not count as a criminal conviction - obviously, the accused has not had the opportunity to deny the conduct alleged. Consequently, the issue of a warning is not revealed to third parties, including the victim. It is, however, recorded by the procurator fiscal for future reference.

Diversion

The fiscal may also offer the accused 'diversion' from prosecution to receive social work help, psychiatric attention or to participate in a mediation/reparation scheme. This occurs in only a tiny proportion of cases. In 1994/95, 971 cases were diverted, less than 0.5 per cent of the total reported to the prosecution service. Until recently, many fiscals would have diverted the occasional case on an informal *ad hoc* basis (and hence recorded it as a 'no pro' or warning letter). However, since the Stewart Committee (1983) recommended that such practices should be encouraged and formalised, the majority of the 49 procurator fiscal offices have instituted formal social work diversion schemes with the co-operation of their local social work departments, three have set up formal psychiatric diversion schemes with the co-operation of local psychiatric services, and three have formed links with mediation/reparation schemes, set up in conjunction with local authorities and the voluntary sector.

The Fixed Penalty

The 'fixed penalty' system for minor road traffic offences enables fiscals to offer alleged offenders the opportunity to pay a fine - of £24 or £48 - without the necessity for a prosecution or court hearing. As with other alternatives to prosecution, use of the fixed penalty increased considerably following the Stewart Committee's recommendations. In 1992/93, 101,633 fixed penalties were issued, representing over one-quarter of cases dealt with by fiscals during that year. (It should be noted that these cases do not include illegal parking and the like which were dealt with under a separate scheme operated by the police and traffic wardens). Since then, the number of fixed penalties issued by fiscals has declined drastically as a result of the delegation to the police of the power to issue fixed penalties for a wider range of traffic offences. In 1994/95, only 8,966 fixed penalties were issued by fiscals, representing just three per cent of cases reported to them. Unlike other diversionary mechanisms, a fixed penalty does count as a criminal conviction.

The Fiscal Fine

The fiscal fine, or prosecutor fine as it is called upon the continent (Duff, 1994), works in a similar way to the fixed penalty. It applies to minor non-traffic offences - for example, breach of the peace, shop-lifting, urinating in a public place - but it does not count as a criminal conviction. This measure was introduced to Scotland, on the recommendation of the Stewart Committee (1983), at the beginning of 1988. Originally, the fiscal fine was restricted to a fixed sum of £25 and could only be used for offences triable in the District Court. This excluded various minor statutory offences, most notably possession of a small amounts of cannabis. Since 1st April 1996, however, the Criminal Procedure (Scotland) Act 1995 has empowered fiscals to operate a scale of penalties - £25, £50, £75, £100 - and has allowed all statutory offences to be dealt with by the District Court, thus rendering the fiscal fine an option in a much wider range of cases (Duff,

1996a). Preceding this expansion of the system, fiscal fines were being used in around five per cent to six per cent of cases and it is obvious that there will now be an increase in that number. Clearly, as with the fixed penalty, the measure represents something of a 'half-way house' between the no pro or warning letter and prosecution. It is seen by fiscals as allowing them to mark society's disapproval of the accused's actions without taking the ultimate - and occasionally damaging - step of mounting a full-scale prosecution, with its attendant resource implications.

Prosecution

Where prosecution is the chosen option, the prosecutor as 'master of the instance' determines the charges and the court. A few offences, principally murder and rape, must be heard before the High Court but generally the prosecutor will select the venue thought appropriate for the gravity of the offence, paying particular attention to the sentencing powers of the various courts. Thus, unlike in many other jurisdictions, the accused has no say in the matter and may not, for example, demand that his case be heard before a jury.

The importance of the prosecutor's right to choose the venue is well illustrated by the recent debate over the 'two strikes' policy contained in the Crime and Punishment (Scotland) Act 1997. This provision - which is in abeyance following the election - required the High Court to impose a life sentence on those convicted of certain serious offences if they had a previous High Court conviction for a similar offence. Essentially, this meant that if an accused was being prosecuted for a second offence, the prosecution could determine whether he faced an automatic life sentence, by prosecuting in the High Court, or a maximum of five years, by prosecuting in the Sheriff Court.[4] There was concern that this would give considerable power to the prosecution to influence the sentencing process, albeit indirectly, through the exercise of discretion, while curtailing dramatically the discretion of High Court judges to determine for themselves the appropriate sentence (McCluskey, 1997). In this context, it is worth noting that mandatory sentencing guidelines in the United States have tended simply to replace judicial discretion with prosecutorial discretion rather than securing their intended purpose of removing such choices from those who operate the criminal justice system (Remington, 1993).

Once a prosecution has been launched, the most significant aspect of prosecutorial discretion relates to the negotiation of guilty pleas or, as it is commonly known, 'plea-bargaining'. Contrary to the popular stereotype of the criminal justice process, the vast majority of prosecutions are concluded by a guilty plea rather than a trial and many such pleas result from some kind of agreement between the defence and the prosecution. As Moody and Tombs (1982; 1983) demonstrate, plea-bargaining in Scotland manifests itself in charge-bargaining. For instance, in return for a guilty plea, the prosecutor may, for instance: reduce a charge of assault to the danger of life to one of assault to severe injury; or amend a charge of 'repeatedly kicking and punching' to one of 'kicking and punching'; or drop either of the charges of assault and breach of the peace stemming from the same incident (Moody and Tombs, 1982, pp.106-8). While this type of bargaining is perfectly legitimate in Scotland, it is extremely informal and entirely at the discretion of the prosecutor. Frequently, negotiations will be conducted at court, often by a junior fiscal with no opportunity to take advice or clear the matter with a superior, and frequently at the last moment before the trial begins. As Moody and Tombs (1982, p.105) comment:

> The negotiation of pleas is essentially an informal, private matter so that there is little case law on the subject or public awareness of the prevalence of such arrangements (and) no published figures.

Another type of plea-bargaining, more influential in other jurisdictions than in Scotland, is sentence-bargaining, whereby the prosecutor promises a particular (and reduced) sentence in exchange for a guilty plea. This is facilitated in those jurisdictions which explicitly practice 'sentence discounting', whereby the sentence is reduced if the offender pleads guilty. In England and Wales, for instance, the discount for a guilty plea is between one-quarter and one-third of the sentence. In Scotland, however, there is no formal system of sentence-discounting, although it was recently recognised that, in practice, Scottish judges do sometimes impose lesser sentences on those who have demonstrated remorse by pleading guilty (Scottish Office, 1994f, paras. 4.10-4.14). Further, section 33 of the Criminal Justice (Scotland) Act 1995 now makes it clear that the court in determining sentence may take account of the 'stage' and 'circumstances' in which a guilty plea is given. The effect, if any, of this legislation has not yet been examined. In some jurisdictions, particularly in the United States, sentence bargaining is further encouraged because the trial judge may be involved in the negotiations and will indicate the likely sentence if a plea is forthcoming. In Scotland, this practice has not found favour with the judiciary and this attitude is unlikely to change.

Why does charge-bargaining take place in this country? The principal advantage for the prosecution is that it eases the pressure of work; the system simply could not cope if everyone who initially pled guilty went to trial. It is a device for coping with otherwise unmanageable caseloads. Negotiating a plea also circumvents the uncertainty attendant upon the trial process, ensuring that there is at least a conviction and, particularly in certain types of case - for example, sexual assaults - it saves the victim from the ordeal of giving evidence. It is true to say, however, that fiscals feel constrained by the need to ensure that the nature of the adjusted charges will still result in what they see as a just sentence. From the accused's perspective, the main advantage is that less serious or fewer charges will produce a less serious sentence and that some credit may be given by the judge for a guilty plea. More cynically, it also allows the defence solicitor or advocate to persuade a recalcitrant offender that 'a good deal' has been secured and that the best option is now to plead guilty. Obviously, the defence lawyers may also benefit from the reduction in work-load (McConville *et al.*, 1994, p.186).

Plea bargaining raises various concerns which have been extensively discussed in the literature (Remington, 1993; Ashworth, 1994, chap.9; Sanders and Young, 1994, pp. 269-281, 303). For instance, it allows the experienced criminal (or defence solicitor) to 'play the system' by pleading not guilty until the last minute in the hope that excessive case-loads will force the prosecution to accept a plea to a charge which does not really reflect the gravity of the crime. This does not serve the interests of justice and may well upset the victim who feels that his suffering is insufficiently recognised by the amended charges and resulting sentence. On the other hand, it may lead to the prosecutor proceeding with a weak case in the hope of 'bluffing' the accused into a guilty plea or 'over-charging' in order to create some leverage to extract a guilty plea to the appropriate, and less serious, charge. In particular, the 'two strikes' rule would have enabled the prosecution in relevant cases to threaten the accused with a High Court prosecution in the hope of extracting a guilty plea which, it might be indicated, could be dealt with by the Sheriff Court. Further, the nature of the working relationship between prosecutors and defence solicitors, may lead the latter sometimes to pressurise an accused to plead guilty, when there is actually a strong defence. At worst, plea bargaining may lead to the innocent pleading guilty in order to 'cut their losses'.

Controlling the Prosecutor's Discretion

Broadly speaking, the very nature of a discretionary power renders it difficult to monitor and control (Galligan, 1987). In this instance, as we have seen, many discretionary decisions are made by the prosecution service every day, usually on an informal and private basis, and frequently at a relatively low level. In theory, the Lord Advocate is accountable to Parliament for all such decisions but, in practice, unless there is some really startling abuse or high-profile case, such matters are extremely unlikely to be raised in Parliament. As we have seen, the importance placed on the independence of the prosecution service dictates that there is no accountability to any other external body and I shall shortly discuss whether there are any remedies available to individuals dissatisfied with prosecutors' decisions. First, however, it is useful to examine the way in which Crown Office (formally, the Lord Advocate) is increasingly attempting to render fiscals internally accountable for the exercise of their discretion. Essentially, two methods are used: first, the frequent issue to fiscals of instructions or guidelines on policy matters and the handling of cases; and, second, the requirement that fiscals' offices submit detailed monthly statistics on the disposal of cases to Crown Office.

Internal Controls

First, the constant flow of circulars which emit from Crown Office have 'become embodied in . . . *the fiscal's bible*, the Book of Regulations' which will be regularly consulted by most prosecutors (Moody and Tombs, 1982, p.20). This remains confidential and it is normally impossible for anyone outwith the service to discover the precise policy on any particular topic. Occasionally, the contents of a Crown Office circular are made public: for instance, after a number of high-profile and controversial cases, the Lord Advocate recently issued guidelines on the action to be taken as regards violence on the sporting field.[5] Further, the recently instituted Annual Report of the Crown Office and Procurator Fiscal Service sometimes provides more general indications of current policies: for instance, the

1992/3 Report listed the most common criteria used by fiscals in deciding whether to prosecute, although these are couched in very general terms. Nevertheless, these instances of the disclosure of the way in which prosecutorial discretion is exercised are very much the exception to the rule. The comparative secrecy of the guidelines, however, does serve to emphasise the independence of the prosecution service, in that Crown Office does not think it necessary to reveal or explain its policy to any external body, but this reticence also reduces accountability, in that it is obviously difficult for anyone outwith the service to comment upon unknown guidelines or determine whether they are actually being followed.[6]

Second, Crown Office also monitors various statistics which fiscals' offices are required to return. These enable the comparison, for instance, of 'no pro' rates or usage of the fiscal fine across the 49 separate fiscals offices and allow investigation of any apparent divergences in approach. This process of monitoring fiscals' activity was increased following an investigation of the service by the National Audit Office (1989) which revealed, *inter alia,* that the 'no pro' rate varied widely between offices, ranging from 2.5 per cent in Forfar to 25.5 per cent in Edinburgh in 1987. At that time, Crown Office could provide no explanation for such variations and, hence, fiscals are now required to record their reasons for marking a case 'no pro'. The collection and collation of such statistics undoubtedly helps Crown Office monitor and influence fiscals' use of their discretion. Unfortunately, however, these detailed statistics are not released into the public domain. While the service's annual reports do contain some figures, these are invariably aggregated into national and regional totals, preventing identification of differences in approach by different offices and, almost certainly, 'smoothing out' any such discrepancies.

External Controls

Thus, there are some internal controls on prosecutors' use of discretion but what of the individual who is dissatisfied with the decision whether to prosecute? The accused who has been informed by the prosecutor that there will be no proceedings against him has a valid defence to any subsequent prosecution,[7] but otherwise the dissatisfied individual has few options. The victim of an assault, for instance, might be dissatisfied with the decision not to prosecute his assailant, or an accused might be aggrieved by the decision to prosecute him rather than adopt some alternative approach, like a fiscal fine.   In some jurisdictions, those dissatisfied with such decisions are explicitly entitled to go to court to challenge them but, in Scotland, there are no such rights.   Normally, all the dissatisfied individual can do is to ask for the procurator fiscal or Crown Office to reconsider the decision, in which case it will usually be reviewed by the decision-maker's superior. Ultimately, however, the position is that the prosecution service is simply not accountable to individuals and, normally, no explanation will be given for a particular decision.   Various justifications are used for this policy: the reason for the particular decision might prove embarrassing to those involved; witnesses' trust might be betrayed; to state that there is insufficient supporting evidence might amount to condemning the accused without trial; casting doubts upon the victim's account might prove damaging to the victim (Crown Office and Procurator Fiscal Service, 1993, p.15).

Nevertheless, there are other avenues through which prosecutorial accountability may be pursued.   As regards the dissatisfied victim, there is the vestigial right of private prosecution in solemn cases.   On closer inspection, this route would usually be blocked by the need to obtain the consent of the Lord Advocate or the High Court which would be unlikely to be forthcoming where the prosecution service had already decided not to prosecute.   Admittedly, this did happen in the exceptional circumstances of the Glasgow rape case (see above) but such consent has been refused in a number of subsequent cases.   As regards the aggrieved accused, it could be argued in court that the Crown decision to prosecute was 'oppressive' but the circumstances would have to be extreme in order for this plea to have any chance of success (McCluskey, 1992, p.182).

There is also the possibility that the aggrieved party - whether victim or accused - might seek judicial review of the prosecutorial decision.   There are no Scottish precedents, and the conventional view is that such a remedy is not available.   On the other hand, the courts might be influenced by recent developments in England, where several recent cases have established that the courts will review decisions by the prosecution at the behest of both victims and the accused.   At one stage it appeared that Duncan Ferguson, the footballer, was going to seek judicial review of the fiscal's decision to prosecute him for violence upon the playing field but the challenge never materialised.   Under the rules of administrative law, a prosecutorial decision may be quashed by the reviewing court only if it can be demonstrated that it was wholly unreasonable, procedurally improper or illegal (for instance, if irrelevant factors were taken into account).   An English commentator has observed that this barrier renders any such application very unlikely to succeed (Hilson, 1993) but decisions not to prosecute were recently quashed in two English cases because the prosecutor had not followed the Code for Crown Prosecutors.[8] In Scotland, the difficulties would be exacerbated by the lack of published prosecutorial guidelines because it is obviously much easier to demonstrate that a decision is unreasonable if it appears to conflict with demonstrable criteria.

Finally, the victim who is unhappy with the prosecutor's decision to accept a plea bargain has no possible remedy. In some jurisdictions, the prosecutor has a duty to consult the victim before accepting such a bargain but that is not the case in Scotland and many other places. In this context, it is interesting that in *HMA v McKenzie*,[9] the Court of Appeal made it very clear that it was wholly against the victim having any kind of say in the sentencing process. The main problem in this area is that victims' inclinations may conflict with offenders' rights and they are not necessarily coterminous with the public interest (see Maguire, 1991; Zedner, 1994; Moody, 1997; chapter 18).

Thus, given the absence of effective external control over the use by prosecutors of their very wide discretionary powers, considerable confidence must be placed in the competence, professionalism and incorruptibility of the prosecution service. It is fair to say that, at present, the Scottish public prosecutor is generally held in sufficiently high esteem, by both the general public and other participants in the criminal justice process, for the necessary trust to be granted.

Notes

1. The accuracy of the newspaper's account of the guidelines was disputed by Crown Office some six years later in McDonald v HMA 1997 S.L.T. 1237 but another example of prosecutorial guidelines being made public is cited in the case. In any event, the essential point is that through the issue of such guidelines, the Lord Advocate can in effect change the criminal law.
2. HMA v Sweeney and Others 1983 S.L.T. 48.
3. Exact comparisons are difficult because the effect of the delegation to the police of the power to deal with certain fixed penalty traffic offences 'artificially' inflates the 'no pro' rate. For example, the 'no pro' rate was 14 per cent in 1994/95 but, once the above is taken into consideration, it comes down to the equivalent of twelve per cent.
4. Section 13 of the Act increased the Sheriff's sentencing powers to five years. This provision has also not yet been implemented and the maximum

sentence the Sheriff may impose under solemn procedure remains at three years.

5.   1996 S.L.T. (News) 228. Another example of such guidelines being made public is provided by the Crown Office Circular on Warning Letters (reproduced in Gane and Stoddart, 1994, pp.44-45). See also MacDonald v HMA 1997 S.L.T. 1237 which is discussed in note 1 above.

6.   A useful discussion of the very real disadvantages of publishing prosecutorial guidelines can be found in Pizzi, 1993, p.1363ff. It is interesting to note that in England, the CPS is legally obliged to publish its *Code for Crown Prosecutors* and this is really quite detailed (Ashworth and Fionda, 1994; Crown Prosecution Service, 1994).

7.   Thom v HMA 1976 J.C. 48; McDonald v HMA 1997 S.L.T. 1237.

8.   R v DPP *ex parte* Chaudhary 1995 Current Law 26, 28 and R v DPP *ex parte* Treadaway Times 1st August 1997.

9.   HMA v McKenzie 1990 S.L.T. 28.

8 Criminal Justice Responses to Bail Abuse

FIONA PATERSON

Introduction

When police, prosecutors and courts make decisions about how to respond to people accused of crime but not yet convicted or sentenced, they must strike a delicate balance between fairness to the accused, whose cases are still being considered within the due process of law, and their duty to act in the public interest by not placing the public at undue risk from criminal activity. Bail is a feature of the criminal justice process which allows for the conditional release of untried and unsentenced prisoners, allowing them to remain in the community rather than to be remanded in custody.

Particular decisions to release or detain accused not only have an immediate effect on the accused, they also impact on the later action of other criminal justice agencies in relation to that accused. Thus police decisions to detain or release accused are signals to the prosecutor. The prosecutor may not agree with that signal (for example that someone need not be in custody), but the prosecutor's action will need to relate to the initial police decision (for example by issuing a warrant for the arrest of the released person). Similarly, when the court makes a custody or release decision about someone prior to conviction, then it must take into account the prosecutor's attitude to release. A court decision to attach an order, such as a bail order, to an accused's release, signals to that person that their release is conditional and, as will be illustrated later, it also signals a particular course of action to police and prosecutors if the accused has further criminal justice contact. In particular, it may lead to 'net-widening' (Cohen, 1985) or 'up-tariffing', whereby, for instance, an accused already on bail may find himself remanded in custody for a subsequent minor offence simply because he was already on bail rather than because the subsequent offence in itself merits that course of action. Decisions about the use of bail also provide an example of how different criminal justice agencies interact through their work in individual cases. They illustrate the way in which decisions in one part of the criminal justice system help to shape the responses of others.

While the use of bail or remand in individual cases reflects criminal justice responses to the circumstances of the alleged offence and of the accused, the level of use nationally reflects wider social and political responses to crime. Prior to the 1990s there were concerns about Scotland's high use of custodial remand (Wozniak *et al.*, 1988) but during the 1990s the level of offending on bail became a focus of attention. Crimes of offending while on bail (an offence in itself), as recorded by the police, rose steadily throughout this period from 2,765 in 1983 to 27,105 in 1995 (Scottish Office, 1997k). At the same time information about the use of bail was very limited. There were no statistics available about the number of bail orders issued by Scottish courts and this meant that it was not known whether courts' use of bail had changed. It was therefore difficult to interpret the recorded figures for bail abuse.

In order to develop a clearer understanding of the use of bail, in the early 1990s the Scottish Office commissioned a study of the bail decision making process (Paterson and Whittaker, 1994). In this chapter, results from the research are used to consider recorded offending while on bail. Following a description of how bail is operated in Scotland, there is an examination of the level of bail abuse identified in the study and its significance in relation to criminal justice decision making in the study areas. Finally there is a brief discussion of the implications of legislative changes since the completion of the study.

The study was carried out between 1991 and 1993. It focused on sheriff court cases and its purpose was to develop both a description and an explanation of bail practice. As part of the study, police and prosecutors (procurators fiscal) were asked about their Bail Act decisions over a twelve week period in each of three areas (Doon, Tweed and Braid). Court practices in these areas were observed and interviews were carried out with sheriffs. To compensate for the absence of reliable official statistics about bail in Scotland, during the period of the research, information about the use of bail was collected from police detention sheets and from a census of bail decisions which was carried out in the sheriff courts. This provided a broad picture of decision making and made it possible to identify the population of decisions from which the sample for detailed study was drawn.

Bail in Scotland

Although in Scotland only a court can grant bail, decisions ultimately affecting bail are made daily by police and prosecutors. For example, the police may release an accused unconditionally and report the incident to the procurator fiscal (who may have the accused summonsed to court); they may release the accused on undertaking to appear at court on a specified date (which must be within one week of arrest); or they may detain the accused in custody to appear at court on the next lawful day, in which case alone bail becomes an issue. Prosecutors may reverse police decisions by releasing people whom the police have kept in custody or by issuing a warrant for the arrest of someone whom the police have released. If a case goes to court, which is at the discretion of prosecutors, the latter have a key role prior to conviction since they can decide to oppose the release of anyone who pleads not guilty, or, if they are agreeing to release an accused, they may ask for this to be subject to bail conditions.

The court has a number of options, including the use of bail, if at its first calling the case does not reach final disposal. It can ordain an accused to appear at court on a certain day - if they subsequently fail to appear they may be charged with contempt of court, but there are no other restrictions on the accused. Alternatively the accused may be granted bail with standard conditions, which are: to appear at court on a certain day; not to commit an offence while on bail; not to interfere with witnesses or otherwise obstruct the course of justice; to be available for enquiries for a report to be prepared to assist the court in dealing with the offence.[1] The court can attach any other, special, condition(s) to the bail order in order to secure the protection of the public and the administration of justice. The final option is to remand the accused in custody. The accused must apply to the court if they are seeking bail and case law has established that if an accused enters a plea of not guilty the sheriff can only refuse bail if the prosecutor opposes bail in court. If the accused enters a guilty plea the remand decision is totally at the discretion of the sheriff.

The framework within which bail decisions are made in Scotland is set out by both statute and case law[2] and police and prosecutors have their own regulations for interpreting the legislation. At the time of the research, there was a presumption in favour of bail, except in cases of murder or treason. The main grounds for not releasing an accused on bail were: the identity of an accused was in doubt; the continued presence of the accused was necessary for further enquiry; the accused's liberation might have impeded continuing enquiries; the accused had no fixed abode; the police had reason to believe that the accused might interfere with witnesses, commit another offence, or abscond and not turn up for trial; and the accused appeared to be unable to understand the terms of a bail undertaking which might be required to be given.

Bail Offences

Bail abuse refers to the breach of any condition of a bail order. The 1980 Bail etc. (Scotland) Act created a new offence whereby anyone failing to comply with a bail order or undertaking was considered to have committed a further offence. In Scotland during the 1980s and most of the 1990s breaches of bail conditions could involve: failing to appear at court at an appointed date and time; committing an offence while on bail; interfering with witnesses or evidence; or failing to adhere to a special condition imposed by the court. The most commonly recorded of these breaches was committing an offence while on bail.[3] This is the breach which is often referred to in discussions of bail abuse and on which this chapter will focus.

Initially, when the Bail Act had come into force, there was some uncertainty about the propriety of libelling both the substantive charge and a charge of offending while on bail when someone was accused of having committed an offence while on bail. Procurators fiscal had to choose which offence they would libel.[4] The belief at this time was that libelling both charges would constitute double jeopardy. However, after a High Court ruling[5] it was decided that it was competent to libel both the substantive and the breach of bail charges.[6] The explanation was that if someone had committed an offence while on bail then they had breached the trust of the court and a sentence for this type of offence was a sentence for the breach of trust rather than an additional sentence for a substantive offence. Separate recording of offending on bail started in 1983 but variation in recording practices contributed to making the figures unreliable and this remained the case into the 1990s when recording of this offence ceased. The most accurate measure of the extent to which the court's trust is being breached would be provided by looking at the proportion of those granted bail who were subsequently found to have offended while on bail. However, these figures have not been collected.

Patterns of Bail Decisions and Criminal Justice Cultures

The formal position for police, prosecutors and courts, in all areas at the time of the research was that custody should be the exception to the normal rule of accused being released.[7]   Breach of bail was not, of itself, automatically a reason for detaining someone in custody.   If someone arrested was found to be on bail then police force standing orders generally indicated that they should be detained in custody only where the offence for which they had been arrested *in itself* justified custody, or where the bail order related to a serious crime or offence and the nature of the breach of conditions necessitated detention, such as when the breach involved a similar offence.   However, the formal regulations recognised the importance of discretion in individual decisions and in each area this was used differently.

Police Decisions

The police are the first point of criminal justice contact for accused and, as such, police decisions help to define the input to the rest of the criminal justice system.   During the three month study period around 500 people were arrested at Doon, 900 at Tweed and around 1200 at Braid. In Doon 36 per cent of those arrested were detained in custody compared with 28 per cent in Tweed and 18 per cent in Braid.   Data recorded on police detention sheets showed that 12 per cent of accused at Doon compared with 3 per cent at Tweed and 8 per cent at Braid[8] were identified as being on bail at arrest. Figure 8.1 compares police action for those with and those without bail orders.

In all areas those accused already subject to bail orders when arrested were more likely to be detained in custody than accused without bail orders. However the existence of a bail order had varying significance for police in each area.   In Braid the bail order had a lesser influence on decision outcomes and over half of those with bail orders were reported for summons.

Figure 8.1   All arrested by police during the twelve study weeks (police action on cases with and without bail orders)*

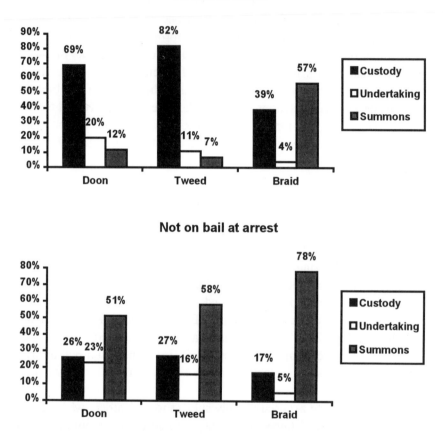

On bail at arrest

Not on bail at arrest

* Doon excludes 70 cases where it was not stated whether the accused was on bail. On Bail Doon n=61; Tweed n=28; Braid n=91; Not on Bail Doon n=380; Tweed n=872; Braid n=1102.

In interviews there, the police said that the existence of a bail order did not affect their decision to detain or release accused and observation confirmed this. This is in marked contrast to Tweed and Doon where most accused on bail were detained in custody.[9] In these areas police said they detained in custody anyone found to be on bail when arrested.

To understand the significance of these differences we need to consider the types of cases being dealt with in the study areas as well as the approaches which criminal justice practitioners took to dealing with them. The study examined in detail the circumstances of cases and the custody/release decisions made about those accused whom police detained for custody court during this period. This resulted in a sample of 139 custodies at Doon, 203 in Tweed and 157 in Braid.

Characteristics of Sample Accused

Table 8.1 shows key features of the criminal histories of the sample.

Table 8.1   Percentage of sample with particular characteristics

	Doon (%)	Tweed (%)	Braid (%)
Convictions in last 3 years	82	70	78
% with convictions who have served custodial sentence	31	41	49
Analogous pending case	46	38	42
Non-analogous pending case	16	11	17
Subject to current court order (not bail)	27	32	27
Currently on bail	33	28	18
Alleged to breach study bail order[10]	43	29	35

Consistent with the information collected from police, the sample over-represented accused with outstanding bail orders. Though most in the sample had convictions within the previous three years and most had a pending case, fewer than half had served a custodial sentence or were subject of a current court order. The criminal record profile of the sample at Doon and Braid was similar, though those in Braid were more likely to have served a custodial sentence. Importantly, while accused at Doon and Braid were just as likely to have cases pending against them, accused at Doon were much more likely to be on bail in connection with these.

Table 8.2   Features of criminal justice cultures*

Culture type	Police	Prosecution	Court
Bail (Doon)	Policy and practice of detaining those on bail; high use of custody.	Presumption of bail for police custodies; bail history interpreted relative to other elements of record.	Most cases to court in 24 hours. High use of bail (66%); low use of remand (12%) and ordain (22%); low use of custodial sentences.
Liberation (Tweed)	Practice of detaining those on bail; medium use of custody.	Presumption of ordain unless police custody; bail history interpreted relative to other elements of record.	High use of ordain (37%); medium use of bail (47%); low use of remand (16%); low use of custodial sentences.
Remand (Braid)	Bail irrelevant to custody decision; low use of custody; high use of release for summons.	Regular opposition to bail for cases released by police; any bail history likely to lead to opposition.	High use of remand (34%); medium use of bail (47%); low use of ordain (20%); high use of custodial sentences.

* The percentages in Table 8.1 for accused dealt with at court derive from the bail census. It is important to note that the bail census identified that a high proportion of accused appearing personally at Doon (nearly a quarter, compared with twelve per cent in Tweed and ten per cent in Braid) were ultimately found not guilty. This suggests that in Doon the statistics for offences committed on bail which were recorded prior to court outcome would significantly overstate the level of bail offending.

Information was also collected about the incidents which had resulted in the arrests[11] and overall it was found that seriousness of record or of incident was not sufficient to account for the pattern of police restriction of liberty which was identified in each area. We therefore examined criminal justice decision making more closely and also found variations in approach to custody and release amongst prosecutors and the courts. Each area was characterised by a distinctive criminal justice culture and Table 8.2 summarises their key features.

The distinctive features of the criminal justice cultures operating in the individual study areas had consequences for the level of bail abuse identified in the study sample.

Offending on Bail

In order to identify (alleged) further offences, the police checked accused's records with the Scottish Criminal Records Office in order to identify charges libelled between the date of liberation by the court on the initial offence and the date of its final disposal.[12] For all accused in the sample who were released during the process of their case, information was collected on the number of charges[13] libelled as having occurred during their release.

Most accused were not alleged to have abused their release. Few of those who were ordained to appear or who were remanded and later released on bail had further offences libelled. However, around 40 per cent of those initially released on bail at Doon and Braid, and 30 per cent of those given bail at Tweed, had subsequent charges. Most of those with further charges had one or two new charges, however a few in each area had a larger number of offences subsequently alleged.

Further charges were alleged for 42 accused on bail at Doon, 25 at Tweed and 23 at Braid. In all areas most of those with further charges were alleged to have offended within eight weeks of their release on bail. Just over half of those with further charges at Doon, where the use of bail was highest, were alleged to have offended within four weeks, and a further quarter within eight weeks, of their release on bail. This compares with around a third of this group at Tweed and Braid alleged to have offended within four weeks. A further fifth at Tweed and a further third at Braid were alleged to have offended within eight weeks.

There was a significant relationship between the age of accused and whether they had further offences libelled or whether they had cases pending at the time of being charged. In each area around half of accused aged under 21 had allegedly committed further offences. This is similar to findings of previous research that young offenders are more likely to be involved in allegations of offending on bail.

Doon had a particularly high proportion allegedly re-offending within the first four weeks and many of these were within two weeks of release by the court. In Tweed and Braid few accused aged 16-20 appeared in the sample more than once but, in Doon, three accused appeared twice, three appeared three times, one four times and another five times, during the twelve week period.

This does not necessarily mean to say that there was a greater incidence of re-offending in Doon. It must be remembered that there was little difference between areas in the likelihood of people in the sample having cases pending (Table 8.1) and that in general police at Doon detained people in custody at twice the rate of police at Braid. The release of more accused at Braid for summons (77 per cent compared with 43 per cent at Doon) meant that accused who were likely to be dealt with as custodies or undertakings in Doon may have been released by the police at Braid. At the time of the research, police in Braid stated that it was taking about five weeks for them to send a report to the procurator fiscal on summons cases in that area. This meant that, unlike their counterparts in Doon who were in court within 24 hours of arrest, many accused at Braid who may have been involved in further incidents at that stage would not yet have been to court in connection with the initial incident and could not therefore have been subject to bail orders at the time. As a result, they would not be identified in the official statistics in a way which would indicate that they had recently had contact with the criminal justice system. This suggests that the higher level of recorded offending on bail at Doon may in part have been a result of police practices of detention, fiscal practices in seeking bail for police custodies and the greater court use of bail. This meant that the behaviour of those initially detained in that locality was monitored in a way which did not happen in localities with different criminal justice practices which released more people for summons to court and which made less use of release on bail.

Protection of the Public: Likelihood of Custodial Sentence

In view of the concerns about the risk posed to the public by those released on bail, it is important to look at whether this group of people were considered, at the end of their initial case, to be people from whom the public needed to be protected by the court passing a custodial sentence. In interview both prosecutors and sheriffs said that the likelihood of a custodial sentence was a factor taken into account at the time of considering whether bail should be granted for an accused. If a custodial sentence is unlikely, then the only alternative justification for remanding someone is to enable the case to be properly processed (that is, to prevent interference with witnesses or evidence, to enable further enquiries to be made, or to ensure appearance at court).

The outcome of the initial case[14] was that, of those facing further charges, most (around 70 per cent) in Braid and around half in Tweed ultimately received either a custodial sentence or a community service order (which is considered to be an alternative to custody). (As a result of the small numbers involved, only in Braid was the figure statistically significant.) This contrasts with outcomes from these courts for those in the sample with no further charges - around 20 per cent of these offenders received either a custodial sentence or a community service order. There was little difference in the outcomes at Doon for those who were alleged to have committed further offences and those who were not - around ten per cent of each group ultimately received either custody or community service. Whatever kinds of problems may have been posed by the pre-trial or pre-sentence release of those who received a non-custodial disposal, a remand to protect the public would not have been consistent with the final outcome of their case.

Protection of the Public: Repeat Offending

Anxieties about bail abuse are anxieties about repeat offending. The official police category of '*re-offending while on bail*' presupposed that people were guilty of both the initial offence for which bail was granted and the subsequent offence on the basis of which it was alleged that bail had been breached. But a high proportion of accused in the sample at Doon (38 per cent, compared with eight per cent at Tweed and 13 per cent at Braid) were either not guilty or their case was not proceeded. Even if they had been guilty of the subsequent charges, although they would have committed an offence while on bail, they could not accurately be described as having *re-offended*.

Proportions of alleged *further* offences were calculated by removing those accused found not guilty or whose case was ultimately not proceeded with. Tweed and Braid were found to have a similar percentage of alleged further offending (respectively, 30 per cent and 29 per cent) and Doon had a lower rate (24 per cent). This implies that the higher use of remand at Braid was not necessarily providing greater protection for the public from repeat offending there, and neither was there evidence that the higher use of bail at Doon and Tweed was placing the public at greater risk of a high volume of crime.

Bail Abuse: Types of Offences

It is important, nevertheless, to look beyond the volume of offences and to consider in more detail the types of offences both for the original charges and for the subsequent charges, in order to assess further the risk at which the public was being placed.[15]   Previous research has found that those charged with crimes of dishonesty were more likely to breach their bail (Morgan, 1992). With the exception of the small number of accused at Tweed and Braid whose alleged offences were classed as 'other', the findings of this study confirm this for Doon and Tweed, though for Braid those charged with breach of the peace were more likely to have further offences alleged. In all areas crimes of dishonesty were the most frequently libelled for people at liberty. In addition, those with further offences alleged and who were originally charged with dishonesty were the most likely to have offences alleged which were analogous to the original offence (58 per cent of such accused in Doon, 83 per cent in Tweed and in Braid 90 per cent).

Recording Bail Abuse

Following the 1980 Bail etc. (Scotland) Act, for just over 15 years Scotland had a specific offence of breaching bail by committing an offence while on bail. Prior to this statute there was no information collected about the extent of offending on bail. Such information was not in fact gathered nationally until the High Court had clearly signalled that an offence under this section of the Act indicated a breach of the court's trust and could not therefore constitute double jeopardy. Once in use, this offence allowed the criminal justice system to make recidivism of bailees statistically visible in a way which had not previously been possible. Thus, an unintended consequence of the provision which created a specific offence of breaching bail by committing an offence while on bail, was to contribute to public alarm about crime and the criminal justice system's response to crime.

During the 1990s levels of recorded offending on bail were often discussed as if they signified the level of repeat offending. The rising figures for offending on bail fuelled anxiety about risk to the public by those who repeatedly offend. However these statistics recorded alleged breaches of the court's trust; they were not a reliable indicator of recidivism. Most important, the results of the research discussed here show that in areas with a culture of bail there was likely to be increased awareness of offending while on bail. Further, the offending while on bail statistics were recorded by the police at the point of arrest and at that stage no account could be taken of whether accused would ultimately be convicted. They assumed that the accused would be convicted of the original offence and, in addition, took no account of those who were not convicted of the further offence. The research found that guilt was not established for around ten per cent of those in the sample at Tweed and Braid and in Doon, where more people were on bail, this figure rose to 30 per cent.

The provisions of the 1995 Criminal Justice (Scotland) Act have removed the difficulty associated with having a specific offence of committing an offence while on bail. Under the new provisions which came into force in April 1996, if someone commits an offence while on bail then the court must take this into account when sentencing for the new offence. This means that the court may impose a more severe sentence than it would otherwise have done for the conviction. The new arrangements therefore have removed the problems associated with the separate recording of offending while on bail, while enabling criminal justice practitioners to continue to respond to the problem posed by those who commit crime while released on the trust of the court.

Notes

The study was funded by the Scottish Office Home Department and was conducted with the research assistance of Claire Whittaker. I would like to acknowledge the help of police, prosecutors and court staff in the study areas.

1.   Now set out in s.24(5) of the Criminal Procedure (Scotland) Act 1995.
2.   At the time of the research the most notable were the Criminal Procedure (Scotland) Act 1975, as modified by the Bail etc. (Scotland) Act 1980, and Smith v McCallum 1982 S.C.C.R. 115 (sometimes known as the Wheatley guidelines). Since the study, the 1980 Act has been modified by the Criminal Justice (Scotland) Act 1995 and previous legislation has been consolidated in Part 3 of the Criminal Procedure (Scotland) Act 1995.
3.   This latter type of breach ceased to be a separate offence when the Criminal Justice (Scotland) Act 1995 was implemented (becoming an aggravating factor as regards the subsequent offence) and thus these figures are no longer recorded.
4.   Amendment to Crown Office Circular No. 1671 in May 1980.
5.   Aitchison v Tudhope 1981 S.L.T. 231.
6.   Amendment to Crown Office Circular No. 1671 in May 1982.
7.   The Criminal Justice (Scotland) Act 1995 s.3 has now removed the presumption of bail for people accused of attempted murder, culpable homicide, rape or attempted rape, where they have a previous conviction for any of these in the case of culpable homicide involving a custodial sentence, or murder or manslaughter or treason.
8.   However, these figures need to be treated with caution since the 'not known' figure for Doon is high (21 per cent of cases) and the low figure for Tweed (three per cent) may be a result of recording practice because the fact that the accused was on bail was not routinely recorded on the police detention sheet in that area.
9.   In areas where the police keep more people with outstanding bail orders for custody court, the sample can be expected to contain more people with outstanding bail orders than will the sample drawn from elsewhere.
10.   As the study has not measured the extent to which those in the sample were found guilty of these subsequent offences, these percentages are likely to overstate the level of bail abuse in the sample. Figures may also be affected if the police record was not correct, for example, if pending charges had not been recorded on the computer at the date of checking.
11.   Chapter 3 of Paterson and Whittaker (1994) provides more detail about differences in cases between areas.

12. The discussion of bail abuse here focuses on accused involved in summary cases. This is because in the Braid sample, no solemn cases where the accused had been at liberty reached their final disposal within the time-frame of the research. There was a shorter period of time than there was for the other areas, between the end of fieldwork and the end of the study.

13. Because of the level of concern about offending on bail at the time of the study we tried to consider the most serious picture of this problem which could be generated by our sample. It should be emphasised that we recorded *charges* rather than *cases*. That is a case often consists of more than one charge. This inflates the levels of bail abuse in the discussion.

14. For more detailed figures, see Paterson and Whittaker (1994, p.107).

15. The following figures have not excluded those found not guilty or whose cases were not proceeded. Arguably these accused ought to be removed from this section, however, since responses to the generalised 'problem of bail abuse' are based on statistics which assume guilt and neither take into account guilt and innocence nor whether the offences are indeed *further* offences, the statistics here have not been adjusted and will therefore over-state levels of bail abuse.

9 Courts

CLARE CONNELLY

Introduction

Focusing on the rules of criminal procedure to gain an insight into court processes may give the impression of an ordered system, with rules which govern time limits, procedures, evidence, and so on. Supplementing this with the view of court processes presented in television and film productions, one would expect to find that all accused stand trial with a judge and jury.[1] The defence solicitor or advocate and prosecutor, aided by a whole team of researchers, would be working on only one case. In most cases, the accused would be acquitted as a result of a clever piece of evidence discovered near the end of the trial, expert cross-examination of witnesses or the summing up by the defence. This fictional world does not involve long delays, courts and lawyers overburdened by case loads and discretionary decision making. This chapter will examine the courts: the processes and personnel involved; how accused plead and the factors affecting pleading; lay input in the court process in the form of justices and juries; and the appeal process.

Court Processes

The court process is concerned with establishing the guilt or innocence of an accused, in respect of the charges brought by the procurator fiscal, and consequently punishing or releasing the accused. This process is based on an adversarial system, which involves two representations of reality being presented to the court and the judge or jury choosing between them. (In practice, of course, the vast majority of accused plead guilty, as will be seen below, so sentencing becomes the main issue.) The court is dominated by criminal justice professionals with lay input restricted to the role of accused, victim, witness, juror and justice. The physical lay-out of all courts is structured so that the criminal justice professionals are contained within one area with the justices, sheriff or judge, on a platform above the others. The accused will also be within this area of the court as will the jury, if present. Witnesses only enter this area of the court while giving their evidence, thereafter, they are permitted to join the general public and the press in the public area towards the rear of the court.

The procurator fiscal decides which court the accused appears in (that is, the sheriff, district or high court) at the stage of 'marking'. The question of whether the case will be tried summarily or by jury[2] is also decided at this stage. The distribution of business amongst the various courts is shown in table 9.1. The majority of business is conducted in the Sheriff Court which deals with both solemn and summary cases, by far the greater number being summary (see below). The smallest number of cases are heard by the High Court, reflecting the fact that only the most serious offences are heard in this court.

Table 9.1   Distribution of business amongst the various courts

	All court types	High court*	Sheriff court	District court	Stipendiary magistrate court	Unknown
1985	210,067	1,186	111,892	78,681	18,308	-
1986	204,321	1,183	108,434	77,728	16,976	-
1987	199,334	1,252	104,060	78,591	15,431	-
1988	197,805	1,062	103,866	81,063	11,785	29
1989	193,162	1,056	103,150	80,153	8,745	58
1990	199,722	1,099	101,678	83,591	11,300	54
1991	199,866	1,220	100,121	86,973	11,497	55
1992	198,038	1,419	100,109	84,704	11,732	74
1993	183,038	1,601	96,391	74,920	10,472	290
1994	178,067	1,228	97,579	68,183	10,893	184
1995	176,420	1,390	98,304	66,036	10,649	41

* High Court figures include cases remitted to the High Court from the Sheriff Court.

Source: Figures published by the Scottish Office in *Statistical Bulletin, Criminal Justice Series,* HMSO, March 1997.

Legal Representation

To date no research has been carried out in Scotland which provides a comprehensive overview of the extent of legal representation in the criminal courts. Table 9.2 shows the total number of Legal Aid applications granted for summary cases in the period 1991-1997.

Table 9.2   Total number of Legal Aid applications granted for summary cases in the period 1991-1997*

	District court	Sheriff court summary
1991/92	18,612	39,716
1992/93	20,212	43,646
1993/94	18,772	42,542
1994/95	21,555	45,465
1995/96	20,779	46,603
1996/97	17,622	44,214

* These figures do not include Legal Aid awarded by the courts in solemn and summary proceedings under the Legal Aid (Scotland) Act 1986 s.23(1)(b).

Source: Figures published by the Scottish Legal Aid Board in Annual Reports 1992/93 to 1996/97.

These figures provide information in respect of those accused who were represented by a solicitor as a result of full Legal Aid being awarded. A recent Scottish Office paper suggest that around 30 per cent of those prosecuted under summary procedure are granted Legal Aid (Scottish Office, 1993f). Despite the majority of accused charged with summary offences falling outwith the Legal Aid scheme, very few accused in summary proceedings are unrepresented if they go to trial. This may be explained by many accused changing their initial plea to guilty, and they then qualify for Advice By Way Of Representation (ABWOR).[3] Further, anecdotal evidence suggests that some solicitors will, without payment, represent existing clients or those who are deemed to be good future clients, who have been refused Legal Aid. Such clients would normally fulfil the financial requirements of the Legal Aid Board, but have had their application refused on the basis that it is not in the 'interests of justice'. As the majority of accused charged summarily plead guilty, this 'free' legal representation merely involves the defence agent presenting a plea in mitigation on behalf of their client. Paterson and Bates (1993, p.99) suggest that most of those who stand trial under solemn procedure are legally aided, and consequently are represented in court.

The Role of the Accused

The court process is an alien environment to most accused. The trial is constructed around the legal rules of evidence and procedure, which tend to only be known by legally qualified personnel, and this formal set of rules is supplemented by wide ranging discretion. The case presented by the prosecution and the defence is constructed in accordance with these rules of procedure and evidence. If the accused does not have legal representation, he will participate in the adversarial system against a professional prosecutor, even though the accused will rarely have any substantial knowledge of legal procedure or the rules of evidence. Within this process, the accused, if legally represented, plays a very minor role. The whole trial may take place without the accused speaking or participating in any way. Indeed, if legally represented, the only participation the accused will have in this process, is if he elects to give evidence as part of his own defence.

Guilty and Not Guilty Pleas

A critical part of the court process which fundamentally effects the format of the proceedings is the pleading diet. If an accused pleads guilty to the charges contained in the complaint or the indictment, this is followed by the court disposing of the case. If the accused pleads not guilty, however, the court will arrange to have an intermediate diet, where, amongst other things, evidence may be agreed and a trial diet fixed. A non-guilty plea tendered at the pleading diet, can be changed later to one of guilty.

The factors which affect the way accused plead are difficult to ascertain as little research has been carried out in this area, either in Scotland or elsewhere. Much of the discussions which take place around pleading will be low visibility, that is, they do not take place in the public forum and are not governed by the formal rules of criminal procedure or evidence. These would include those taking place between police and a suspect or accused person, discussions between an accused person and their solicitor and discussions between a solicitor or defence advocate and procurator fiscal.

Guilty Plea

The reasons why an accused person may plead guilty are numerous. The most obvious reason is that the accused is prepared to admit liability for the charges brought against them. It might be assumed that this is the only reason an accused would plead guilty but there are other possibilities. A study of prisoners in Holloway (Dell, 1971) who had pleaded guilty, despite maintaining their innocence after disposal, found that inconsistent pleading was most commonly found with first offenders rather than recidivist offenders. The majority of these prisoners gave police advice or pressure as their reason for pleading guilty. Research carried out in England by Bottoms and McClean (1976), Cain (1973) and Laurie (1970), all found evidence of the police, at times, negotiating a guilty plea or confession on the basis of the persuasiveness of evidence they had, or on the basis of a concession which they were offering, such as a reduced charge or release on bail. The role of the police in Scotland in securing such confessions and admissions of guilt is not clear. The Scottish police are less centrally involved in the prosecution process than England and in the context of a trial, their role is that of a witness. In addition, the Scottish rules of corroboration would prevent conviction on the basis of an uncorroborated confession and consequently, there may be less incentive to obtain one.

Other possible explanations for an accused offering a guilty plea include the wish to have the matter dealt with as soon as possible and avoid any adverse publicity, which may arise from a trial. The accused may be advised by their solicitor to plead guilty, for example because the defence case is weak or on the basis that some discretion will be applied in sentencing an accused who admits guilt and avoids the time and public expense of a trial and possible trauma to witnesses (Moody and Tombs, 1982, pp.124-7). Particularly in the lower courts, lack of Legal Aid which enables legal representation, may be an factor influencing guilty pleas.[4]

Plea bargaining   Another significant explanation for guilty pleas, particularly those which occur later in the court proceedings and involve a change from an initial plea of not guilty to guilty is plea bargaining (see also chapter 7). Plea bargaining is not governed by the formal rules of criminal procedure, but relies upon the discretion of the prosecutor and negotiation between the prosecutor and defence agent. As a result of the informal nature of these negotiations very little is known about them and no official statistics on the extent of plea bargaining are recorded. Moody and Tombs examined the process and extent of plea bargaining in Scotland and suggest, on the basis of routinely collected Crown Office statistics, that 'in about a third of all solemn cases and a tenth of all summary cases the accused changes his plea from one of not guilty at first appearance to a guilty plea at a later stage' (1982, p.105). Not all of these changes of pleas will be due to bargaining[5] although it is assumed that most will be. Bargaining may also take place earlier in the process, between the complaint or indictment being served and the accused appearing in court to plead to the charge.

Plea bargaining involves the adjustment of charges, which is accepted by the fiscal in exchange for a guilty plea by the accused. It can take the form of adjustment of charges resulting in trial avoidance; the deletion of certain charges from the complaint or the indictment; altering the wording of charges to make them less serious, (e.g. amending a charge of 'attempted murder' to 'assault to severe injury') and the agreement that certain information is either included or excluded from the presentations by the defence and prosecution[6] to the court. As noted above, there are no formal rules governing plea bargaining. It does not take place in the open court or any other public place but rather, may take place during a telephone conversation between the defence and prosecution or an informal meeting of these two people in the court just before the case calls or in the fiscal's office.

A significant difference between plea bargaining in Scotland and England is the absence of sentencing bargaining. The latter exists in England but has never formed part of the bargaining process in Scotland. In the recent Scottish Office (1993g) *Review of Criminal Evidence and Criminal Procedure*, the possible introduction of sentence bargaining was raised with the question of whether late cancellation of trials could be avoided by introducing sentence discounting. This proposal did not receive support from the Scottish Law Commission (1993) in their response to this document and did not form part of the subsequent criminal justice legislation. The Scottish Law Commission suggests that unless the right to innocence until proven guilty and the right to a free trial are removed, there would be no justification for punishing a person who is found guilty after trial more severely than a person who pleads guilty at an earlier stage in the court process. The remit of plea negotiation consequently remains unchanged in Scotland.

The foregoing paragraphs may suggest an ordered, homogenous system of plea bargaining. The reality however, is that rather than a consistent set of negotiating criteria being applied by fiscals throughout Scotland, the process of plea bargaining is instead haphazard and strongly influenced by the workloads of defence agents and fiscals amongst other factors (Moody and Tombs, 1982).

A dichotomy exists in the central role that plea negotiation has come to play in a criminal justice system which is adversarial in nature. Yet to run efficiently, this system relies on these negotiated agreements and their central role is founded upon an acceptance and utilisation of plea bargaining by both the prosecution and defence. Moody and Tombs (1982) found that prosecutors gave caseload pressures as their primary reason for plea bargaining together with the unpredictability of trial verdicts and the difficulties both of witnesses attending to give evidence and the quality of that evidence. It was also recognised, however, that the fiscal had a responsibility to pursue a charge and sentence appropriate to the person's culpability and not to automatically mitigate this by plea bargaining. Some cases were identified as unsuitable for negotiation.

Defence agents recognised plea bargaining as an integral part of their job. This would be used where a plea of guilty appeared as appropriate and the solicitor would advise or possibly attempt to persuade their client to plead guilty. Plea bargaining was viewed as beneficial as it may reduce the overall number of convictions recorded against the accused or the nature of those offences recorded. It was also felt that a negotiated plea resulted in only the abbreviated facts of the case being presented to the judge prior to sentencing and avoided evidence detrimental to the interests of the accused, being heard by the judge. The ultimate motivation for the defence agent in plea bargaining is to reduce their client's sentence. As noted above, sentence reduction is not formally part of plea negotiation in Scotland. However, if the severity of the charges are reduced, the sentence would be appropriate to the lesser charge. Defence agents also expressed the view that sentencers looked favourably on those who admitted liability.

From the accused's point of view, Moody and Tombs (1982) suggest that the individual's lack of legal knowledge results in the accused relying upon the advice of their defence agent in relation to plea bargaining. Quotes from defence agents suggest that this advice is not always given primarily in the accused's interest. It is suggested that in some instances pressure of work may motivate a defence agent to persuade a client to plead guilty to an amended charge. This may take the form of persuading the client that the deletion of minor charges may result in a more favourable disposal even although both the defence and prosecution agents know that this will not be the result.

The discretionary nature of this plea negotiation has attracted criticism. As noted above, the process is not controlled by rules of procedure. However, the Crown Office have issued several circulars to fiscals which recommend consulting with a senior fiscal and/or the marking depute before plea bargaining. There has also been a call to encourage defence agents to negotiate pleas at an early stage. Many plea bargains take place on the date of the trial, resulting in witnesses attending court for a trial which does not proceed. Consequently, the expenses of witness and, potentially, jurors may have to be met and one of the benefits of plea bargaining, economic efficiency, is lost. As noted above, the suggestion contained within the Scottish Office (1993g) *Review of Criminal Evidence And Procedure* to resolve that problem by introducing sentence discounting for guilty pleas, has not been incorporated in the latest criminal procedure legislation.

Not Guilty Plea

The extent of not guilty pleas is unclear in Scotland. Scottish Office statistical services do not collect current figures on pleading diets. However, information collected prior to 1988 indicates that pleas of not guilty are more common in serious offences, such as homicide (Scottish Office, 1987c, p.7). One explanation for this may be that in solemn matters where there is a possibility the accused may receive a custodial sentence, Legal Aid will not be refused on the basis that it is not in the interests of justice. Legal representation may encourage an accused to go to trial and as this situation would apply to more serious offences, an accused may wish to stand trial in the hope of an acquittal rather than pleading guilty and receiving an onerous punishment.

Lay Input - Justices and Jurors

Lay people become involved in the court process in the role of the accused, witnesses, jurors and, if they have been appointed, Justices of the Peace. In particular, lay justices and jurors have some power within the court process to determine the guilt or innocence of an accused. Lay justices also have the power to punish the accused in the District Court. Both of these bodies clearly have a considerable amount of power and the fact that they are not legally or otherwise 'professionally' qualified makes them unique actors within the court process.

Justices of the Peace

Justices of the Peace or, alternatively, a Stipendiary Magistrate perform the judicial role in the District Courts. As Stipendiary Magistrates[7] are legally qualified they will not be examined here, as this section will focus on lay input in the court process. Justices of the Peace are appointed by the Secretary of State on the recommendation of the Justice of the Peace Advisory Committee (JPAC). Lay justices have a role equivalent to a sheriff in the Sheriff summary court, namely the arbiter of both fact and law and are responsible for the disposal of the case. A clerk of court, appointed by the local authority assists the lay justice(s). The clerk must be an advocate or a solicitor and has the role of legal assessor[8] as well as having the administrative role of a clerk. The role of the clerk is strictly limited to matters of law but research (see, for example, Moody and Toombs, 1982, ch.5; Bankowski *et al.*, 1987, ch.2) has shown that in practice, some clerks become involved in determining issues of fact and advising on an appropriate disposal.

The jurisdiction of the District Court is restricted to offences which are generally deemed to be the least serious of those committed. As stated above, the fiscal decides which court will hear the case at the stage of marking. The common law crimes which cannot be heard in the District Court are described in section 7(8) of the Criminal Procedure (Scotland) Act 1995. This list includes murder, culpable homicide, rape and theft by housebreaking. All statutory offences which can be tried summarily may be tried in the District Court unless the statute indicates to the contrary.

A court may consist of one or more justices. Justices hearing a case alone are found to be more common in the city courts whereas up to three justices sitting together are more likely to be found in the county courts (Jones and Adler, 1990, p.39). Justices' powers of punishment in relation to common law offences are restricted in respect of financial penalties of up to level four on the standard scale and up to 60 days of custodial sentence. The justice can also ordain the accused to find caution of an amount not exceeding level four on the standard scale for his good behaviour for a period not exceeding six months and can also impose a sentence of imprisonment in the event of the accused failing to pay a fine or find caution.[9]

The recruitment and training of justices has in recent years come under review. One of the principles behind having lay justices is that the accused appears in court before someone from the same community and that the justices are from a range of social backgrounds. Research by Bankowski *et al.* (1987) revealed that the average age of justices was 65 years, there were more justices in rural than urban areas,[10] and less than 15.5 per cent of the total population of justices in Scotland were female. Those people recommended as suitable justices to the JPAC during the period 1976-1981 had an average age of 48.7, only 14 per cent were women and, although those recommended came from a broad range of occupations, they were concentrated in the middle ranges of occupations and professions. The 'Perth Experiment' in 1985 involved replacing the traditional method of recommendation of new justices by drawing on a wider group of locally important individuals and organisations. Jones and Adler (1990, p.51) suggested that 'even when the net of recruitment is widened, if the *method* of recruitment remains the same, the composition of JPs will remain fairly static'.[11] The extent to which the lay justices have a practical everyday knowledge of the way of life and social conditions in the local community to which those who appear before them belong remains questionable as long as the current methods of recruitment and training are employed. In addition, as justices are appointed for life it may take not only a change of policy but also the passing of a substantial period of time before the body of justices changes shape.

The response to the use of lay people as judges in the District Courts has been mixed. The legal profession has generally held the view that this role is inappropriate for lay personnel. This was apparent when the role of lay justices was considered when District Courts were introduced in 1975.[12] Subsequent research has shown that the legal profession is still critical of, if not opposed to, the idea of lay justices. Lack of legal knowledge and an absence of professional approach together with a view that lay justices are lenient sentencers are some of the criticisms which have been made by fiscals. Some defence agents suggested that they required less preparation for a District Court case, they needed to explain matters more clearly to a lay justice than a sheriff and they felt that their client was more likely to be acquitted in the District than the Sheriff Court (Bankowski *et al.*, 1987, pp.157-9). Most defence agents expressed that 'they felt more comfortable with a sheriff' (*ibid.*, p.158).

The source of this dissatisfaction amongst legal personnel appears to be based upon the lack of legal knowledge and qualification of the justices and also the fact that District Courts tend to deal with less serious matters which are often viewed as trivial. Bankowski *et al.* (1987, p.181) note that the role of justices is often viewed as analogous to the jury but this is not wholly accurate, as the jury are confined to assessing only the facts while the justice is the arbiter of both fact and law and also sentences the accused. The similarity, however, is that both are 'supposed to provide a common sense lay element into the system'. The operation of any lay input is always within the confines of the legal definitions of crime and the rules of evidence and procedure and consequently, the District Court and the lay justices are not a form of community justice divorced from the wider legal system. The role of the assessor advising the lay justice underlines the legal confines within which lay justices are expected and permitted to operate. The fear that non legally qualified participants in the court process will or have subverted the law arises in relation to both lay justice and jury decision making. In respect of lay justices the conclusion reached by Bankowski *et al.* (1987, p.183) is

> The rule of law is not subverted by this injection of the lay element. On the contrary, this lay element is necessary for its full and proper working. This is not something sinister but rather the only morally acceptable way a society based upon the rule of law can be organised.

Juries

For many, the jury symbolises justice and safeguards in the court process. This lay input is deemed to protect the rights of the accused in a criminal trial. Indeed, for the public it has been suggested, by Findlay and Duff (1988), that the jury helps to legitimate the criminal justice system overall. The symbolic role of the jury is consequently very important even though its actual role is very small in the overall court process. The limits of the jury's role can be attributed to at least two factors. Firstly, in Scotland, unlike England, an accused has no right to jury trial. The decision whether an accused will be tried by solemn procedure, thus involving a jury, is made by the procurator fiscal at the stage of 'marking'. Juries are only employed in a minority of cases, as most criminal cases are tried summarily. In 1980, 4,097 cases were tried under solemn procedure compared with 257,265 under summary procedure and in 1990, 4,280 were tried under solemn procedure compared with 185,288 under summary procedure (Paterson and Bates, 1993, p.87).

Despite this numerical insignificance, the existence and role of the jury has been far from uncontroversial. The attention given to the jury is perhaps reflective of its symbolic rather than actual role. The controversy has focused on the selection of jurors, the qualification of jurors to participate in the court process, their role and the verdicts returned.

Selection of jurors Juries in Scotland have 15 members, selected at random from the list of eligible jurors who are cited for possible service. The list of eligible jurors is drawn from the voters' roll in the jurisdiction of the court where the accused is to be tried. The prosecution and defence are provided with only the names and addresses of jurors. Prior to the 1995 Criminal Procedure (Scotland) Act, the occupations of jurors were revealed on this list and each party in a jury trial had a right of peremptory challenge. This right allowed both the prosecution and defence to object to three jurors each, without stating any reason for doing so. Jurors can now only be excluded if good cause is shown or, alternatively, if all parties agree to the unsuitability of one person.[13] This removal of the peremptory challenge within the limits outlined, is believed by Ferguson (1997) to remove one of the means by which the randomness of the jury may be interfered with. Methods of jury selection other than random selection are possible. It has been suggested that juries of peers would be more appropriate, for example, for all female juries in trials involving women who have killed their violent partner. Views on the appropriate form of jury selection are based on views of community and representation. The randomly chosen jury, according to Bankowski (1988), implies the existence of a community which is diverse, and supports the scientific impartiality of random polling.

Legal qualification and the role of the jury The suitability of a non legally qualified jury has been subject of debate. A conflict exists between those who view juries as symbolic of freedom and justice, and those who believe that these non legally qualified amateurs are incapable of the role of arbiter. Lack of legal knowledge is deemed to result in wrong verdicts being returned. This conflict highlights two areas for investigation. Firstly, what is the role and responsibilities of the jury and, secondly, what is the effect of the dynamics of the court process on jury decision making? The jury in the trial process is viewed as the arbiter of fact whereas the judge is the arbiter of law. If this distinction of duties is accepted, then the lack of legal qualification of the jury becomes unproblematic. The extent to which this is an accurate description of the role of the jury is less straightforward.

The role of the jury is to consider the evidence heard in court and thereafter return a verdict in respect of the accused's liability for the crime. The jury may be requested to return either a special or general verdict. The special verdict demands adjudication on a specific question of fact (e.g. 'did the accused on the date and time libelled enter the bar and punch Mr Brown?') and is very rare. The general verdict, however, asks the more complex question (e.g. 'is the accused guilty of the murder of the deceased?'). The special verdict relies wholly on fact, whereas the general verdict involves the consideration of facts and whether these satisfy the legal definition of the crime charged. The modern court process normally demands a general verdict from a jury, and this is where the lack of legal knowledge may be seen to be problematic. This is only problematic, however, if the jury are seen as central in the decision making process of the court. The most powerful of the legal personnel in the court, the judge, has the role of legal interpreter and advisor to the jury. The jury rely on the judge to translate the alien environment of the court, constructed as it is around knowledge of legal rules and procedures (Mungham and Bankowski, 1976). This is not to suggest that all juries accept the advice and direction of the judge. Jurors do not arrive at court as blank sheets. As citizens, they will come to serve as jurors with existing ideas on the legitimacy of law and the criminal justice process. In particular, they may have specific ideas regarding the legitimacy of the law they are considering and return a verdict which is reflective of the validity of that law rather than the accused's legal liability for the crime committed.[14] This type of action by the jury, for some, threatens both the order of the court and the rule of law. For others it is reflective of the jury operating appropriately, as such action 'can help lead to the cultivation of alternative realities in the courtroom' (Mungham and Bankowski, 1976, p.222).

Verdicts Due to the historical development of the role of the jury and the verdicts available, the modern court process offers three verdicts to the jury: guilty, not guilty and not proven.[15] A majority verdict is accepted in Scotland[16] and the foreman of the jury will indicate, in court, whether the verdict is by majority or unanimous. No oral or written explanation is provided, in respect of the verdict, by the jury. The question the jury address is whether or not the prosecution have proved their case beyond reasonable doubt. Consequently, if the jury opinion is split into seven supporting a verdict of guilty, five a verdict of not guilty and three a verdict of not proven, the correct verdict would be not guilty. Maher (1988) suggests that any possible confusion which may arise from this system is diverted by the terms of the standard charge made by the judge to the jury, namely, that an accused should not be convicted unless eight find him guilty. The majority verdict has been criticised because any lack of unanimity demonstrates evidence of a reasonable doubt existing amongst some of the jurors. This challenges the principle that an accused must be found guilty beyond reasonable doubt.[17] Maher (1988) suggests that the additional safeguards built into the system namely, the requirement of corroboration of evidence and also the third verdict of not proven, protect and uphold the principle of 'proof beyond reasonable doubt'. He rejects that lack of jury unanimity is inconsistent with this principle.

In recent years the media debate on juries in Scotland has not been on majority verdicts but, rather, the not proven verdict. High profile murder cases in the early 1990s launched, once again, a 'moral panic' around the third verdict.[18] Media coverage included the campaigning by families of the murder victims to have the third verdict abolished and programmes, for example BBC Scotland's *Focal Point*, exposed the level of ignorance amongst members of the general public as to the effect of such a verdict.[19] Once again in 1997, a similar media response followed the verdict of not proven in the case against James Dunn and John Ferrier who were accused of murder.[20]

The not proven verdict results in the acquittal of the accused and the principle of *res judicata* means that the accused can not be retried for the offence. In terms of the outcome of the trial the effect of a not proven and not guilty verdict are identical. There is suggestion that a verdict of not guilty is representative of the fact that the judge or jury think that the accused definitely did not commit the offence. The not proven verdict is viewed as a poor alternative, as it is deemed to represent some doubt as to the accused's guilt rather than being confirmation of his innocence (Duff, 1996b). This 'panic' around the third verdict and the fact that the accused cannot be tried again for the same offence, omits to address the essential nature of the criminal trial. The criminal trial is not to determine whether the accused is innocent or guilty, but rather to assess whether the prosecution have proved beyond reasonable doubt that the accused committed the offence charged. If the prosecution fail to convince the jury of the accused's liability, then acquittal should follow. Willock (1993) suggests that the logical way forward is to dispose of the not guilty verdict and return to the historical verdicts of proven and not proven. This would remove the dilemma where the jury are asked to consider if the prosecution have discharged the burden of proof which is upon them or, if they believe the case is not proven, if the accused is not guilty. Willock is of the view that the question of the accused's innocence is not one which should be considered or commented upon by the jury.

Further illustration of the media lead 'moral panic' around the third verdict is demonstrated by the fact that this verdict is most commonly returned by judges sitting summarily and the lack of attention paid to this.[21] This lack of media attention may be due to the fact that there is a presumption that the judge has returned the correct verdict, that cases being decided under summary procedure are less serious, or alternatively, that there is less mileage in suggesting a judge, rather than a jury, has got it wrong. The third verdict fuels the notion that the jury can make a mistake. This verdict was considered during government consultation (Scottish Office, 1994g) prior to the recent reform of the criminal justice system. Responses to the government consultation were in favour of the retention of the third verdict.

Appeals

The right of appeal of the accused against sentence, conviction or both is upheld within the court process in Scotland. Such a right of appeal is recognised as central to any system of justice (Scottish Office, 1994f), but the right of appeal against sentence under summary proceedings was only introduced in 1980 by the Criminal Justice (Scotland) Act. This legislation also removed the requirement in solemn cases to seek leave to appeal from the High Court. This extension of the right of appeal was followed by an increase in the total number of appeals. Appeals against sentence under summary procedure between 1981 and 1992, rose by approximately 300 per cent, with 3,510 appeals being lodged in 1992 (Scottish Office, 1994c, p.26). The prosecutor has identical rights of appeal as an accused except that an acquittal by a jury cannot be appealed against. The prosecutor, however, does not need to obtain leave to appeal.

Little empirical research has been carried out into the appeal process in Scotland,[22] but the information which is available reveals that appeals against conviction are rare. Millar (1993) calculated that such appeals occurred in 1.8 per cent of cases in 1991, a higher figure than in previous years. This accounts for approximately 12 per cent of all appeals. Since 1985, approximately 70 per cent of all appeals have been against sentence and 10-15 per cent against sentence and conviction. The percentage of appeals emanating from all cases tried under solemn procedure in 1991, was higher (20 per cent) than for summary procedure (one per cent). The higher percentage of appeals in solemn cases may be explained by the greater seriousness of the offences committed which will attract more onerous sentences. Numerically, however, most appeals come from summary cases, reflective of the fact that most cases proceed under summary procedure. In 1991, 2,313 summary cases were the subject of appeal compared with only 695 solemn cases.

The rate of success varied between appeals against sentence and those against conviction. Appeals against sentence were successful in 20 per cent of cases in 1991 and most of these successful appeals came from summary procedure and related to a non-custodial sentence (Millar, 1993, pp.21-2). In these cases the sentence was either quashed or a lesser sentence substituted. The Court of Appeal is empowered, in the case of an unsuccessful appeal, to increase the original sentence but this power is rarely exercised.[23] Duff and McCallum (1996) found the overall success rate of appeals against conviction to be around ten per cent. If abandoned appeals are discounted, the Court of Appeal allowed 30 per cent of the appeals which actually came before it. The two most popular grounds of appeal, in the sample examined, were 'insufficient evidence' and 'refusal of no case to answer submission'. This level of success may appear to be very low but it may be due to a number of reasons. The appeal process may be inadequate in addressing wrong decisions on conviction and sentence made by the court of first instance or most appeals may be weak in that there may be no legitimate grounds of appeal because the court of first instance has correctly decided the case. The most significant reason for the low rate of successful appeals is the level of cases abandoned either before or during the appeal hearing.

Around two thirds of all appeals studied by Duff and McCallum (1996) were classified as abandoned. This figure included those cases abandoned using the set procedure but also those where the appellant failed to turn up or abandoned the appeal at the outset of the hearing. The latter two would officially be classed as dismissed appeals. Millar (1993) found the level of abandonment for 1986-1991 to be approximately 40 per cent. This figure was based on those cases that would procedurally be termed as abandoned. The reasons for abandonment were identified as: the accused accepting or being persuaded that the initial impulse to appeal was misconceived; counsel's opinion being unfavourable in respect of the appeal; Legal Aid being refused; the stated case or judge's charge to the jury being unhelpful to the appeal; the accused being denied interim liberation pending appeal; and the grounds of appeal being weak (Duff and McCallum, 1996).

The increased number of appeals was recognised as a burden on the Appeal Court in the Government consultation paper, *Sentencing and Appeals* (Scottish Office, 1994h) and the response to the consultation paper, *Firm and Fair* (Scottish Office, 1994f). Consequently, the government introduced the requirement to obtain leave to appeal in the 1995 Criminal Procedure (Scotland) Act (ss.107, 180, 187). The application for leave to appeal applies to appeals arising from both solemn and summary appeals and is considered by a single judge, whose decision can be challenged. The motivation behind this change was to reduce the workload of the Appeal Court. Stewart (1997) suggests that the burden has merely shifted to those judges who consider applications for leave to appeal.[24] This procedure highlights a tension in the court process which is becoming more common, namely, the tension between achieving efficiency and economy and maintaining the rights of the accused. The removal of the automatic right of appeal may make the process more efficient and reduce the number of poorly prepared or 'weak' appeals being lodged by the defence and subsequently abandoned. The question begs, however, whether it is in the interests of justice to have a 'gatekeeper' system of appeals rather than one which is automatically available and supported by Legal Aid?

Conclusion

This chapter has provided an overview of the court process and examined some of the aspects of this process. The court process itself is socially constructed around the rules of evidence and procedure and is dominated by legal expertise. Supplementing this legal dominance is the use of discretion, for example plea bargaining and lay input in the form of justices and juries. Lay input has aroused suspicion that the rule of law is being subverted and concern that criminal justice disputes are being decided by amateurs. Despite these criticisms, lay input continues and is viewed by some as symbolic of a democratic legal system.

The criminal justice system and the court process (e.g. the appeal process) have been the subject of much government review and change in recent years. Other changes which were considered, such as sentence reduction in relation to plea bargaining and the removal of the not proven verdict, have not been implemented. The result of the pilot scheme, involving public defenders being used for the first time, may also produce dramatic changes in both the funding and form of defence agents. Despite these and possible future changes, the court process will continue to be constructed within rules of evidence of procedure, albeit that these may be altered over time. The tension between economy and the rights of the accused will remain.

Notes

1. Jury trial will always be the form of trial used in the High Court. The figures shown in Table 9.1 indicate that it is only the minority of trials which take place in this court. Some of the trials which take place in the Sheriff Court will take the form of jury trial.
2. This differs from the procedure employed in the English courts where the accused can elect to be tried summarily or by a jury.
3. Advice by way of representation, (ABWOR), may be available to an accused who initially pleads not guilty. An accused may plead not guilty and apply unsuccessfully for Legal Aid. He may not be granted Legal Aid on the basis, for example, that it is not in the interests of justice. The interest of justice criteria is laid down in s.24(3) of the Legal Aid (Scotland) Act 1986. If the accused changes his plea, to guilty, within 14 days and meets the financial criteria, ABWOR will be granted.

4. Approximately 20 per cent of those who stand trial under summary procedure are legally aided. A significant majority of accused charged with summary offences plead guilty. ABWOR may be available to an accused who pleads guilty within the criteria outlined at note 3, above.

5. As suggested above, in summary cases, the lack of availability of legal aid may influence a change of plea.

6. Following a plea of guilty the prosecution will present an outline of the offence to the court. Negotiation may take place regarding the information which is included in this presentation normally with a view to mitigating the accused's liability. This will be followed by a plea in mitigation, presented by the defence agent, on behalf of the accused. The purpose of this plea in mitigation is to seek leniency in sentencing.

7. Stipendiary magistrates are only found in Glasgow District Court although other courts are empowered to appoint them.

8. The role of Legal Assessor involves advising the Justice of the Peace on matters of law.

9. Criminal Procedure (Scotland) Act 1995, s.7(6)(a)-(d). Powers of punishment for statutory offences are detailed in each particular statute.

10. This may explain why it is more common for three justices to hear a case in rural areas whereas a single justice is more common in urban or city areas.

11. More information on the 'Perth Experiment' can be found in McManus and Greenhalgh (1988).

12. The District Courts (Scotland) Act 1975 replaced the previous lay courts of the burghs and counties with the district courts. During both the passage of the legislation and also after the provisions were introduced it became apparent that while local authorities supported the continuation of lay justice involvement, the legal profession was opposed to any such continuation.

13. Criminal Procedure (Scotland) Act 1995, s.86

14. See, for example, HMA v Greig 1979, unreported (Gane and Stoddart, 1991, pp. 526-527). June Greig killed her violent husband after years of abuse. No violence occurred at the time of the killing which would have been necessary to satisfy the legal requirements of the defence of provocation. The judge, Lord Dunpark, directed the jury that if they could find some evidence that the requirements of the provocation defence had been established that they were entitled to return a verdict of culpable homicide. He also stated that he did not accept that the grounds had been established. The jury returned a verdict of culpable homicide, ignoring the Judge's direction.

15. See Willock (1966) for an outline of the historical development of juries and verdicts.

16. In England ten of the twelve jurors must agree on the verdict whether it be guilty or not guilty. If a minimum of ten jurors cannot agree on a verdict the accused will be retried.

17. See Maher, (1988, pp. 45-49), for an outline of the discussion on majority verdicts and the principle of proof beyond reasonable doubt.

18. The response to these cases by both the media and the legal profession are discussed at length in Duff (1996).

19. Duff (1996, p.9). The BBC commissioned a poll which revealed that 48 per cent of those questioned believed that following a not proven verdict the accused could be retried on the same charges if new evidence emerged.

20. This verdict was widely reported in Scottish newspapers on October 23 1997.

21. Figures collected between 1988 and 1992 by the Criminal Justice Statistics Unit of the Scottish Office Home and Health Department, revealed that between four per cent and five per cent of those prosecuted are acquitted after trial. A not proven verdict has been returned in 21 per cent of these acquittals. Juries make proportionally more use of the verdict returning it in 42 per cent of High Court cases and 33 per cent of Sheriff Court cases. Sheriffs and justices who hear cases summarily only used the verdict in 21 per cent of cases, however, as more cases are tried summarily than by solemn procedure, 88 per cent of all not proven verdicts are returned by justices or sheriffs sitting alone (Scottish Office, 1994c, p.27).

22. Millar's (1993) study examined the nature and scale of appeals in the period 1981-1991 and conducted a more in-depth study on appeals lodged in 1985. Duff and McCallum (1996) sought to provide a 'comparison of successful and unsuccessful grounds of appeal against conviction or conviction and sentence'.

23. Millar (1993, p.23) found that over the eleven year period of her study that an increase in sentence occurred in 0.5 per cent of unsuccessful appeals.

24. As noted above, the requirement to obtain leave to appeal does not apply to the prosecution.

10 Sentencing in Scotland

NEIL HUTTON

Introduction: Sentencing in Context

Sentencing is the allocation of an appropriate penalty to a convicted offender. It is thus a crucial decision which has a major impact on the overall pattern of punishment in Scotland. This chapter will show that sentencers in Scotland exercise considerable discretion and are not required to implement any government 'sentencing policy'. If there is such a thing as a 'sentencing policy' then it is made by the judiciary. I argue in this chapter that sentencing has avoided the modern rationalising reforms which have affected most other areas of criminal justice in Scotland. On a more descriptive level, the chapter provides a very brief account of the law governing sentencing, the penalties available to sentencers and the recent trends in their use, as well as reviewing the limited research into sentencing in Scotland and describing some recent movements in the direction of reform. The chapter begins looking at sentencing in Scotland in the context of some important themes from the sentencing literature.

Philosophical Justifications

Sentencers in Scotland are held to be guided by the same philosophical principles of punishment as those of other western common law jurisdictions which are discussed in the standard penology texts (Ashworth, 1997, p.1096). Offenders are punished: because they have broken the law and deserve it (desert or retribution); because society requires protection from their offending (incapacitation); because it is hoped that crime can be reduced by transforming offenders into non-offenders (rehabilitation); because society needs to deter others from offending (deterrence); or because society hopes to repair some of the damage done to the victim (reparation or restorative justice). As we shall see, however, these philosophical principles do not help us to explain how sentencers choose an appropriate sentence in a particular case. Sentencers in Scotland are not obliged to provide a written justification of the sentence unless the case goes to appeal. In these written

166

judgements, as in the judgements of the Court of Appeal itself, these philosophical principles are rarely mentioned. It is not clear to what extent these principles, either alone or in combination, inform the decision-making of sentencers in Scotland.

In addition, Hart (1968) has argued that the general justifying aim of punishment is to control crime. There is probably a widespread belief in the community that punishment should 'do something' about crime. In practice, only around four per cent of all crimes and offences reported by the public to the police, and two per cent reported to the British Crime Survey (see chapter 2), result in convictions or court sentences (Ashworth, 1997, p.1103). This suggests that sentencing may have much less impact on the level of crime than has traditionally been assumed. It also places the onus on proponents of the various theories described above to provide evidence that sentencing does in fact achieve the various utilitarian aims that they attribute to it. For example, we should not simply assume that sentences are effective deterrents, or that incapacitative punishments make a significant impact on the overall level of crime.

However even if the crime control function of punishment is commonly exaggerated and the philosophical justifications of punishment are more usually the subject of academic debates than matters of routine concern for sentencers, sentencing is still a very important decision in the criminal justice process for a number of reasons.

Sentencing as Communication

Sentencers' choice of punishment in a particular case is an expression of the nature and extent of the disapproval of the community towards an offender. In using a particular sanction for a particular case a sentencer 'knowingly deploys a conventional device for the expression of meaning, and engages in a symbolic communication of greater or lesser significance.' (Garland, 1990, p.257). The meaning of the sentence depends on the context. For example, a fine may be described as an opportunity for a first-time offender to learn from his mistake, may be treated almost as an administrative fee for a minor road traffic offence, or intended to be a painful deterrent in the case of a heavy fine. Although the significance is variable and indeed this flexibility can be seen as one of the strengths of sentencing, the communicative aspect of sentencing should not be underestimated (for a thorough elaboration of this idea, see Duff, 1995).

Justice in Punishment

Sentencers are responsible for delivering justice in punishment. There is no space here to discuss the considerable theoretical literature on the difficulties of producing justice in punishment (see Duff and Garland, 1994; Hudson, 1996). However, from the sentencers' point of view, the pursuit of justice in sentencing may be characterised as a tension between the claims of 'tariff sentencing' which tries to ensure that similar cases are dealt with in a similar fashion and 'individualised' sentencing which requires each case to be dealt with on the basis of its distinctive facts and circumstances. Sentencers try to produce just sentences by balancing these competing principles (Hutton, 1995, p.557). Some jurisdictions have introduced sentencing guidelines which have placed strict limits on the extent to which sentencers can exercise their discretion to individualise sentences in this balancing act (Clarkson and Morgan, 1995). However, as we shall see, in Scotland, there has been no significant reform of sentencing and sentencers retain very wide discretion.

Prison Population

The decisions of sentencers play an important part in determining the size and composition of the prison population. This is of particular importance in those 'marginal cases' which lie on the border between a custodial sentence and a community sentence. A recent study has shown differences between sheriff courts in Scotland in the use of custodial sentences in such marginal cases (Creamer *et al.*, 1992a). In these cases, and also in cases where an offender is being sent to prison for the first time, the decision making of sentencers has a major impact on the prison population. Scotland's prison population has been rising steadily in recent years, as have prison populations all over the western world (see chapter 13). One of the recurrent aims of penal reformers has been to reduce prison populations. Clearly, if any reduction of the prison population is to take place, the role of sentencers is vitally important.

Sentencing as a Social Practice

Sentencing is normally a solitary business. Most sentencers make these decisions without consultation;[1] however, they do not make these decisions in a vacuum. They hear cases which have already been interpreted and processed by police officers, prosecutors and sometimes social workers. They work routinely with other professionals in a local criminal justice culture and they may informally discuss their work with their judicial colleagues in their chambers or at judicial seminars and conferences. Sentencing is a social practice like any other decision in the criminal justice process.

There is no sentencing policy in Scotland, in the sense of a systematic and coherent approach to the allocation of punishment to achieve particular penal purposes, set out by Parliament and implemented by the judiciary. Like prosecutors (see chapter 7), sentencers exercise wide discretion and have not been subjected to the managerialist reforms experienced by other criminal justice agencies in Scotland such as the police (see chapters 6 and 19), social work (see chapter 12) or the Scottish Prison Service (see chapter 13). Sentencers do not operate to a mission statement nor is their work measured by performance indicators. However, the practices of sentencers exercising their discretion unfettered by many legislative restraints, might be said to constitute a sort of 'de facto' sentencing policy.

Although the social practice of sentencing is very important, there has been relatively little research conducted on sentencing in Scotland. We know remarkably little about the ways in which sentencers go about making their decisions by comparison with what we know about other decision makers such as police officers, fiscals and social workers (see, respectively, chapters 6, 7 and 12). This is a part of the criminal justice process which is likely to come under increasing scrutiny from a variety of sources. The greater demand for value for money in the expenditure of public funds may put pressure on the government to justify expenditure on the courts and thus focus attention on sentencing outcomes. The media and the public may also want to know more about alleged disparities arising from judicial discretion in sentencing. For a long time sentencing has been an under-researched area of the criminal justice process in Scotland, however there have been some recent developments, described below, which suggest that the area is beginning to open up.

Sentencing in Scotland

The following sections provide a brief description of the sentencing powers of the courts in Scotland, a review of the types of sentence available, their relative use and a brief consideration of recent sentencing trends.[2] The chapter concludes with a review of the research on sentencing and an account of some recent research and policy developments.

Sentencing Powers

Although there are maximum penalties laid down for certain statutory offences, most of the criminal offences in Scotland are common law offences rather than statutory offences. In any case, since sentencers very rarely use the maximum penalty, these cannot be considered to do more than set a penalty ceiling and do not give sentencers any guidance as to the appropriate penalty in a given case.

The jurisdiction of the court does place some restrictions on the sentencing powers of judges. In the District Court, judges are lay persons[3] appointed by the Secretary of State for Scotland or the local authority and known as justices of the peace. They are the Scottish equivalent of magistrates in the English Magistrates Courts. The District Court operates only under summary jurisdiction, that is without a jury, and sentencing powers are restricted to a maximum fine of £2,500 and to a maximum prison sentence of 60 days. The Sheriff Court sits under summary and solemn jurisdiction. Sheriffs sitting under summary jurisdiction may pass a maximum period of imprisonment of three months unless the offender has been convicted for a second or subsequent offence of either dishonesty or personal violence, where the judge can pass a sentence of six months. The maximum level of fine for common law offences in the sheriff summary jurisdiction is £5,000.

In the Sheriff Court, under solemn jurisdiction, that is with a jury of fifteen members, the maximum period of imprisonment which can be imposed is three years[4] and there is no limit to the amount of fine for common law offences. If the sheriff considers his powers of sentence to be inadequate he may remit the case to the High Court for sentencing. The High Court may impose a custodial sentence of any determinate length. The only indeterminate sentence available is the life sentence which is mandatory for a person over 21 convicted of murder.[5]

There are a variety of other pieces of legislation which place some limits on the use of custodial sentences but these are piecemeal and give no general guidance to sentencers as to when a sentence of imprisonment is appropriate (see chapter 13).

Sentences Available to the Court

Absolute discharge The accused is not convicted but discharged from the court with no offence recorded against him or her. This disposal was used in less than one per cent of all cases in 1995.

Admonition The accused is convicted but dismissed with an admonition which may include a verbal warning. An admonition is recorded as a conviction. It was used in around ten per cent of all cases in 1995. This proportion has remained fairly steady over the last ten years although there has been a small decline in the use of admonition since 1991.

Fine In 1995 the fine was used for 70 per cent of persons against whom a charge was proved in Scottish courts (Scottish Office, 1997c). This continues a downward trend in the use of the fine which is partly caused by an increase in the use of other sanctions and partly due to the introduction of fiscal fines[6] and fixed penalty notices which apply to cases which are diverted from the court process (Nicholson, 1994). Nevertheless the fine remains by far the most commonly used disposal in Scotland as it has been for most of this century (Young, 1989; chapter 11). The fine is the routine punishment for most of the cases under summary jurisdiction.

Although there is a statutory maximum fine under summary jurisdiction, the maximum penalty is very rarely used and sentencers have considerable discretion in deciding the level of fine. Section 395(1) of the Criminal Procedure (Scotland) Act 1975 requires the sentencer to 'take into consideration amongst other things, the means of the offender so far as known to the court'. The offender may be allowed time to pay, or to pay by instalments; in either case the offender must be allowed at least seven days before the first payment. At a later date the court may allow further time to pay or change the instalment plan.

The sanction for non-payment of fine is normally a period of imprisonment related to the size of the fine outstanding[7] but the court may not impose a custodial sentence for fine default without holding a Means Inquiry Court into the financial circumstances of the offender. Section 35 of the Criminal Justice (Scotland) Act 1995 allows supervised attendance orders to replace imprisonment as a means of dealing with those in default of fine (see chapter 12). These orders can also be used as a sentence in their own right, replacing a fine for 16 and 17 year old offenders who would not have the means to pay a fine.

The imprisonment of fine defaulters appears to be a particularly serious problem in Scotland. Around six per cent of all those who are fined receive a custodial sentence for fine default. Around 42 per cent of receptions into penal establishments in Scotland in a year are fine defaulters (the comparable figure for England and Wales is 26 per cent) and around six or seven per cent of the average daily population are in prison in default of payment of fines or compensation orders (see chapter 13). Nicholson suggests that this may be explained by greater levels of poverty in Scotland and the existence of a more punitive attitude amongst sentencers as evidenced by the highest rate of imprisonment per head of population in Europe (Nicholson, 1994, p.60)[8].

Compensation order   This sanction was introduced in part IV of the Criminal Justice (Scotland) Act 1980. It requires convicted offenders to pay compensation for any personal injury, loss or damage caused by the offending acts. The money is payable to the victim through the clerk of court. Compensation orders were used as the main penalty for one per cent of persons against whom charges were proved in 1995. This proportion has been fairly steady for the last eight years. However compensation is more commonly imposed along with another sentence, typically a fine. Taking both primary and secondary figures together, compensation orders were used in 4.7 per cent of cases in 1995. They are most commonly used for offences of vandalism, less frequently for offences of dishonesty and very infrequently for offences of violence against the person (Hamilton and Wisniewski, 1996).

Community service orders and probation orders   Probation is an order of the court requiring the offender to be under supervision for a specified period of not more than three years and not less than six months. It may contain special requirements and may have a community service order or a compensation order built in. Community Service can be imposed on a person over the age of 16 for offences punishable by imprisonment. It is essentially an order to perform unpaid work. The minimum period is 80 hours, and the maximum periods are 240 hours under summary jurisdiction and 300 hours under solemn jurisdiction.

Taken together these constitute the community based sanctions available to sentencers in the Scottish courts. In 1995 Community Service Orders comprised three per cent of all court disposals and Probation Orders comprised four per cent. The use of these community sentences appears to be growing slowly but steadily (see chapter 13).

Custodial sentences Only adults over the age of 21 may be sentenced to imprisonment. Offenders between 16 and 20 may be sentenced to detention in a Young Offenders Institution. A sentence of detention may not be imposed on a young offender, nor may any offender be imprisoned for the first time, unless the court is satisfied that no other method of dealing with the offender is appropriate. The court may be assisted in making this judgement by the provision of a social enquiry report.

There has been a steady increase in the proportionate use of custodial sentences in Scotland since 1990. The latest available figures for 1995 show that 16,221 offenders, (11,571 adult offenders and 4,650 young offenders) received a custodial sentence. This is around ten per cent of all those convicted of crimes and offences. Custody is the most common sentence for those convicted of offences of violence, although almost half of all those given custodial sentences were convicted of crimes of dishonesty.

Sentencing Principles

Scottish sentencers enjoy a very wide discretion in their choice of sentence. The standard scholarly textbook on sentencing in Scotland, written by Sheriff Principal Gordon Nicholson (Nicholson, C.H.B., 1992, p.177) and now in its second edition, argues that the Scottish appeal court has:

> traditionally adopted an individualised approach to questions of sentence, and has always tended to decide cases on their own facts and circumstances rather than on the basis of any declared principles.

This could be held to apply more generally to all Scottish criminal courts where an individualised approach to sentencing prevails.

In England and Wales, Thomas (1979) has produced what amounts to a scholarly jurisprudence of sentencing based largely on the decisions of the English Court of Appeal. However there is no Scottish equivalent. The Court of Appeal in Scotland has not followed the practice of its English counterpart of issuing guideline judgements for particular classes of case.[9] As Nicholson, C.H.B. (1992, p.177) notes, judges in the Court of Appeal in Scotland generally restrict their remarks to that which is strictly necessary for the disposal of the case. As a result it is not possible to describe any systematic set of principles to which judges refer when selecting sentence. Nicholson C.H.B. (1992, pp. 177-178) and Kelly (1993) have carefully examined the decisions of the Court of Appeal in Scotland and reported the views of the court on sentencing, but neither of these books could be described as describing a systematic approach for sentencers in Scotland to follow.

There have been a number of pieces of research which have included, as part of their methodology, interviews with judges (usually sheriffs) about their approach to sentencing. The responses provide further support for the general proposition that sentencers in Scotland have very wide discretion and that there is no rational, systematic sentencing policy. The familiar aims of retribution, deterrence, incapacitation and rehabilitation are all referred to by sentencers as appropriate but the responses of judges indicate that these are applied on a case by case basis. Judges found it difficult to specify the general circumstances or conditions under which a particular penalty would be appropriate. For example, asked when the sentence of probation was appropriate, sheriffs talked in general terms about balancing the type of offence, the needs of the offender and the public interest (Ford *et al.*, 1992). However, sheriffs said that supervision should be geared to prevent further offending and, in addition, offer something positive tailored to the needs of the offender, which suggests that a supervisory disposal is more clearly intended to rehabilitate the offender. In other words judges may agree that the main aim of a sentence of supervision is rehabilitation, but they find it difficult to specify what sort of case is appropriate for a sentence of this kind.

Another study reported that sheriffs were unable to specify the sort of case in which deferment of sentence was appropriate. Their view was that it depended on the circumstances and background of the offender and the nature of the offence and they reported that the sentence could be used as a vehicle for retribution, rehabilitation, or reparation (Nicholson, L., 1992). This echoes findings of other research. Young (1989) notes that sheriffs regard the fine as a flexible sanction which is capable of serving any of the main justifications for punishment and similar views were expressed by district court judges in an earlier study (Bankowski *et al.*, 1987). Other studies which have dealt with sentencing as part of a larger project include work on community service orders (Carnie, 1990), probation (Creamer *et al.*, 1992a) and drug offenders (Haw, 1989).

There has been one recent Scottish study which focused on the issue of disparity in sentencing. A study of patterns of custodial sentencing in three sheriff courts found evidence of both consistency and disparity in sentencing (Hutton and Tata, 1995). The study examined the custodial sentencing of ten sheriffs and developed a means of controlling for seriousness so that the sentencing of different sheriffs for broadly similar cases could be compared. The average length of sentence passed by most judges was broadly consistent; there was one judge however whose sentences were consistently higher than those of his colleagues. The methodology of the research was not designed to explain how sheriffs produce a consistent pattern of sentencing given the absence of formal rules and the lack of useful information about sentencing available to them. It may be that information about sentencing practices circulates around sentencers but there has been no research into how this informal 'tariff' works. The divergence of one judge from most of his colleagues would seem to be clear evidence of the sort of disparity in sentencing which has led to reforms in other jurisdictions designed to reduce or eliminate judicial discretion from sentencing. The study by Creamer *et al.* (1992a) compared the sentencing practices of different courts using an index developed to predict risk of custody (DUNSCORE) as a means of controlling for seriousness. The study found that 'differences in custodial sentencing rates can be attributed largely to differential court responses to relatively similar circumstances' (Creamer *et al.*, 1992a, p.12).

Sentencing Reform

The principle of judicial independence has a long history in Scotland (Hume, 1955) and judges appear to retain a strong allegiance to this principle. Unlike most other common law Western jurisdictions, there has been no programme of sentencing reform in Scotland. Elsewhere in the world, from the beginning of the 1970s, discretion in sentencing was held to produce unacceptable levels of disparity and governments sought to develop methods of restricting judicial discretion. Since around 1975 many US state jurisdictions, and the federal jurisdiction, have introduced some form of sentencing guidelines (Frase, 1995). These are intended to reduce the extent of judicial discretion and thereby to improve consistency in sentencing. The reform movement has been based on the Just Deserts approach to punishment which proposes that sentences should be proportionate to the seriousness of the offence (Von Hirsch, 1976). This neo-classical approach rejects the offender-centred approach of rehabilitation and concentrates instead on the offence although, in practice, all systems of guidelines take account of the criminal history of the offender. The guidelines take the form of a grid which ranks offences in order of seriousness on the vertical axis and the criminal history score of the offender on the horizontal axis. Sentencers plot a point on the grid which corresponds to the seriousness of the offence and criminal history of an offender in a particular case and this gives a presumptive sentence from which a judge may only depart under specific circumstances. The range of discretion given to judges within the presumptive sentence varies across jurisdictions. Some guidelines are voluntary but most are presumptive.

There has been some research on the effectiveness of sentencing guidelines. Much of this claims to demonstrate that disparities have been reduced but as Doob (1995) has pointed out, this is hardly surprising given that before the guidelines existed there were no rules to provide consistency in sentencing. There is evidence from research on the US Federal guidelines that both prosecutors and judges have been able to find a way around the guidelines where they feel that the guideline penalty is substantively unjust (Nagel and Johnson, 1994). Indeed judges and legal academics have been very critical of numerical guidelines which is perhaps one reason why this approach to sentencing reform has not been used in jurisdictions outside the US.

Several other jurisdictions have used a narrative guidelines approach which tries to articulate a principled approach to sentencing which guides sentencers while leaving their discretion broadly intact. This type of approach has been successfully implemented in Sweden and Victoria in Australia, and somewhat less successfully in England and Wales in the controversial Criminal Justice Act 1991 (Thomas, 1995).

Sentencing Information Systems

The most recent style of sentencing reform has used computer technology to provide sentencers with information about the past sentencing practices of the court. The aim is to assist judges to pursue consistency in sentencing without any formal interference with their discretion. The idea of providing judges with information is not new (Morris, 1953), but it is only relatively recently that technological advance has made access to such information a practical possibility. Early versions of these systems were pioneered in Canada (Hogarth, 1988; Doob and Park, 1987; Doob, 1990) but for various reasons including a lack of consultation with judges who would be using the systems, excessive cost and the cumbersome early technology, none of these are still in use. A system was developed in New South Wales in the late 1980s. This system has been successfully used and expanded to form part of a wider Judicial Information Research System (Schmatt, 1996).

At the time of writing (December 1997) the High Court in Scotland has started to use a Sentencing Information System (SIS) which has been developed in collaboration with the University of Strathclyde. Until this system was developed, there was relatively little systematic information available to sentencers about sentencing practice. Indeed, outside the High Court, nothing has changed. Sentencers who seek information about sentencing are able to read the reported criminal cases in the *Scottish Criminal Case Reports* which report a selection of cases, predominantly from the Court of Appeal, although they also report some cases from the High Court sitting at first instance and occasionally cases from the Sheriff Court. There is also *Green's Weekly Digest* which publishes short reports of similar criminal cases. However, the vast majority of criminal cases are unreported.

Sheriff Courts are privately circulated with tables, produced by the Scottish Office and by some Regional Social Work Departments, which seek to describe sentencing in different courts. However, the data does not take any direct account of variations in the gravity of offences that come before different courts and so the information is of limited use to sentencers. For some years now the Sheriffs' Association has organised 'sentencing exercises' for sheriffs who attend the annual conference.[10] However these are a limited source of information covering only a small range of cases, dealing with hypothetical examples and available to a limited number of sheriffs.

In the first edition of his book (though this claim does not appear in the second edition), Nicholson argued that since Scotland is a small jurisdiction and has a relatively small legal community, sentencers are aware of each other's approaches to the problems of sentencing. He argues further that although courts would deny that a 'tariff' exists, 'all judges, and many criminals, have a fairly clear idea, based on experience and practice, of the range within which a custodial sentence for a particular crime will normally fall' (Nicholson, 1981, p.206). There is no indication whether this tariff varies from one court to another nor of the extent of any systematic variation from the tariff by individual sentencers.[11] In any case, even if an unofficial tariff exists, information about the sentencing practices of judges is, as yet, not available in any systematic manner. Thus sentencers have very limited opportunities to find out about the sentencing practices of their colleagues.

The Scottish High Court Sentencing Information System

The design of this system began in 1993 and the first stage of implementation has recently been completed. It now contains around 6,000 cases and is being used by half of the 26 High Court judges (Hutton *et al.*, 1996; Tata *et al.*, 1997). A final phase of the project due to start in 1998 will extend the system to all High Court judges. The aim of the system is to provide sentencers with information about the penalties passed by the court for 'similar' cases. A judge can enter information about a particular case into a personal laptop computer and the screen will display the range of penalties passed by the court for previous cases which share the same characteristics. This allows judges to continue to use their discretion to select an appropriate sentence but to do so against the background of accurate information about the previous sentencing practices of the court. This might also be described as providing support for judges as they seek to balance the demands of individualised sentencing with the importance of pursuing consistency.

The system was designed in close consultation with the judiciary. In particular, judges were very actively involved in the vital decisions about how to represent the 'similarity' of cases (Tata, 1997). This is perhaps one explanation for the continued success of the system. Another reason might be that the system is voluntary and descriptive and does not interfere with judicial discretion. Judges are not obliged to consult the system nor are they obliged to change their sentencing practices in response to the patterns they see on the screen. For this reason some would argue that the system should not really be described as a 'reform' of sentencing (Hutton *et al.*, 1995). It is certainly a very different approach from the sentencing guidelines used in the USA which are directly intended to place clear limits on judicial discretion and which inevitably transfer power over sentencing policy away from judges and into the hands of state and federal legislatures.

Conclusion

Although predictions are always dangerous, there seem to be reasonable grounds to suggest that the SIS will become established in the High Court. There are no indications that this kind of system will be extended to the lower courts where most of the sentencing goes on. There is much speculation about what the forthcoming Scottish Assembly will do but it seems unlikely that any 'guidelines' style of sentencing reform will occur.

On the assumption that the High Court SIS becomes established and Scotland therefore proceeds along the road of information provision as a means of addressing public concerns about justice in sentencing, there are a number of interesting potential implications. Now that Pandora's box has been opened, it seems unlikely that the existing absence of research and information and the secrecy and mystery which surround the sentencing decision making process will be able to continue. There is likely to be a demand for access to the SIS from other agencies and individuals; for example defence agents, the Crown Office, journalists and the general public may all have an interest in examining the system. It is arguable that the data in the system is a matter of public record and that there would therefore be no impediment in opening up access to the system. However, for the moment it remains accessible only to the judiciary. It may be that at some point in the future, the government may wish to consider how the system might be used pro-actively to provide information about High Court sentencing to the public.

With the possible exception of the development of the Sentencing Information System, sentencing in Scotland is one part of the criminal justice process which has avoided the modernising transformations which have taken place elsewhere. Managerialism has penetrated the provision of social work services for offenders, the police, the Scottish Prison Service and, to a lesser extent, the Procurator Fiscal Service, but it has had little impact on sentencing. The Just Deserts approach which has had a major impact on sentencing in the United States and some influence in England and Wales has made virtually no inroads to sentencing in Scotland. The legitimacy of sentencing in Scotland is still based on the traditional authority of the exercise of judicial discretion. It remains to be seen how long this local cultural difference can survive against the global trends described by Walker in chapter 6.

Notes

1. The exceptions are the Court of Appeal which sits as a bench normally of three High Court judges and some District Courts where justices of the peace also sit on benches of three.
2. For a thorough exposition of the law of sentencing in Scotland see Nicholson, C.H.B. (1992) and Renton and Brown (1996).
3. In Glasgow District Court there are three stipendiary magistrates who are qualified lawyers and have the same sentencing powers as a sheriff under summary jurisdiction.
4. Section 13 of the Crime and Punishment (Scotland) Act 1997 raises the limit for sheriffs under solemn jurisdiction to five years, and for sheriffs or stipendiary magistrates under summary jurisdiction to six months for a first conviction and twelve months for a second conviction for violence or dishonesty.
5. Sections 1 and 2 of the Crime and Punishment (Scotland) Act 1997 require a judge to impose a sentence of life imprisonment for a second or subsequent High Court conviction for a serious violent or sexual offence. This is the introduction of the 'three strikes' policy (in this case two strikes) to Scotland. However, subsection 1(3) allows a judge not to impose a life sentence where such a sentence would not be in the interests of justice. This substantially dilutes the mandatory nature of these provisions. No commencement orders have been passed by the new government for this Act at the time of writing.
6. Procurators Fiscal were given powers to deal with offenders without resorting to prosecution in section 56(1) of the Criminal Justice (Scotland) Act 1987 (see chapter 7).
7. Currently the guidelines are: up to £200 (seven days); between £200 up to £500 (14 days); over £500 (28 days).
8. In 1993 the figure was 115 per 100,000. Only Northern Ireland was higher. Home Office figures quoted in Cavadino and Dignan (1997, p.13).
9. There has been one exception to this practice: Nicholson v HMA 1991 S.C.C.R. 606 where the Appeal Court gave guidance at pp 609-610A as to the approach to sentencing in cases of child stealing. This indicates that the

High Court has always had the power to issue guideline sentences. Thus the provision in section 34 of the Criminal Justice (Scotland) Act 1995 to allow the High Court 'to pronounce an opinion on the sentence ... which is appropriate in any similar case' was arguably unnecessary. As yet the High Court has not issued any guideline judgements.

10. A Judicial Studies Committee for Scotland has recently been established. The intention is to develop a body similar to the existing Judicial Studies Boards in England and Wales and Northern Ireland. One of the main responsibilities of this committee is to develop judicial training in Scotland.

11. With the single exception of the local study of sheriff's custodial sentencing described above (Hutton and Tata, 1995).

11 The Fine as an Auto-Punishment: Power, Money and Discipline

PETER YOUNG

Introduction

In this chapter I want to discuss the question of how the fine fits into the contemporary penal system. I am aware, compared to some of the big questions asked in the literature on punishment - such as the causes and consequences of the rise in prison populations, whether prison works or the debate over the emergence (or not) of a new type of penality - that this one hardly seems pressing and that little, therefore, seems to hinge on the answer to it. I believe that the question is worth persevering with, however, for two different but related reasons. First, the fine, along with other monetary sanctions, is the most commonly used of all penal measures. This can be illustrated by a brief examination of the use made of penal measures in Scotland. Although it has unique features, the Scottish penal system is typical of penal systems in western Europe and this is particularly true of its sanctioning structure - the long-term patterns or shapes that can be observed in the use of penal sanctions. In 1994, 71 per cent of all disposals in Scotland were fines; the fine was used most in relation to offences, where it was used to deal with over 80 per cent of cases, but it was the most common sanction for crimes also, where 48 per cent of cases were dealt with this way (Scottish Office, 1995c). In contrast, the prison amounted to just seven per cent of all disposals, to which should be added the three per cent of disposals consisting of the detention of offenders in young offender institutions (admonition and caution, in fact, constituted ten per cent of all disposals in 1994 as well). Although these are the most up to date figures available for Scotland, they do not describe a recent phenomenon. In many respects, the shape of the sanctioning structure has not changed since comprehensive statistics were first compiled, in 1897; then, the fine was used as a disposal in 71 per cent of crimes and offences and detention in nine per cent and this seems to suggest that there has been no real change in the sanctioning structure at all (Young, 1987).

As was said, this sanctioning structure is not unique to Scotland but is, with minor variations, typical of many western societies. It follows, therefore, that, empirically speaking, the fine constitutes the hub of the modern penal system. Punishment, in modern society, in other words, typically consists of a monetary exchange; most of the harms dealt with by criminal courts involve a routine pricing of harm, settled by the payment of a sum of cash.

The second reason for persevering with my question concerns the theoretical implications of the above. While there is now an extensive and ever growing literature on punishment and penal systems, there are grounds, I think, for doubting its power to explain that much about the fine. These doubts revolve around the suitability of what David Matza (1964) once called the 'exemplar' case in constructing theories. Exemplars, according to Matza, play a key role in theory construction, indeed in the formation of whole traditions or programmes of research. Exemplars are like background images, or assumed focal meanings of the key social relationships and practices, that the job of a particular theory or wider tradition of research is to explain. Their importance is that they effectively come to govern what a community of researchers takes to be the explanatory agenda of a discipline or area. As Matza argued, the strength of exemplars is that they give direction and purpose; their danger is that, through a process of accretion - one research study in the tradition builds upon another - they come to be treated self referentially, as being beyond question or revision. How does this apply to the literature on punishment?

The exemplar case in the literature on punishment is undoubtedly the prison and the types of social relationships upon which it is based and to which it gives rise. There is now a large, empirical and theoretical knowledge about the prison and there have emerged a number of interlinked and very sophisticated vocabularies in which to talk about it, how it works, what its effects are and the role the prison plays in the penal system and in the wider society. Within the social sciences, the most prominent of these vocabularies is probably that which places the study of the prison in the wider context of a concern with power. At this time, the particular vocabulary that has animated and enlivened studies of the prison and punishment is that which derives from the work of Michel Foucault. Concepts such as power (as Foucault uses it), discipline, power-knowledge, disciplinary society, normalisation, the carceral archipelago and governmentality have become part of the working vocabulary; and, if these terms are not used directly, then they at least provide a central point of reference. While Foucault's vocabulary is distinctive and original, it is, I suggest, all too easy to overlook its similarity (at least family resemblance) to more traditional moral and political ways of talking about the prison and punishment. As Gresham Sykes (1958) argued, in one of the established classics of the field, the sociological, moral and political fascination of the prison is that it raises, perhaps more acutely than any other institution in civil society, the question of power - how power is constituted, its limits, its effects on individuals both in terms of their bodily and self integrity, and how power is resisted. The prison fascinates thus, because it is like reading about the nature of liberalism from the underside, its dark side - and here there is a clear convergence between Foucault's work and that which belongs to the mainstream.

It is not surprising, therefore, that the prison and the vocabularies in which we talk about it have become the exemplar case in the literature on punishment. They resonate with deep seated notions about the nature of modern liberal societies; the image of the prison serves simultaneously as a metaphor for power, as one of how cruel we can be to one another and also as one of how individual autonomy and selfhood can be stripped down sometimes beyond the bare essentials. The problem I have with this literature, with this way of looking at and talking about punishment, is not that it is wrong (although some of its claims are exaggerated) but that it is a partial and inappropriate way of thinking about other penal sanctions, how they work, how they fit into the penal system and their broader social functions. The prime reason that it is inappropriate can be simply stated. While all penal sanctions share at least one characteristic - they are enforced deprivations and thus involve an exercise of power - it does not follow that their nature and how they work can be explained just in these terms. Different sanctions deprive individuals of different things and it seems perfectly reasonable to suggest that an acceptance of this difference should be the starting point for understanding and explaining them. The prison deprives individuals of their liberty and all that we associate with this; the fine deprives individuals of a resource they may or may not have - money. Now, unless it is said that liberty and money are the same thing, or that one can be reduced to another, then it seems to follow that we need a different vocabulary for talking properly about and analysing each, including how they surface or figure in the institution of judicial punishment. My point is that this does not happen in the literature on punishment. Rather, explanations work as though a conceptual framework developed to describe and explain one, is appropriate to the description and explanation of the other. For example, one very common way of organising discussions of the penal system is to make a distinction between custodial (the prison) and non-custodial sanctions (the rest, including the fine). This is a very odd distinction. It defines non-custodial sanctions not by reference to what they are, but by reference to what they are not. The fine, for example, is characterised not by what is essential to it - that it is a deprivation of money - but in terms of something which is external to it - liberty.

This would not matter if it could be shown that deprivations of liberty and of money work the same way and have the same effects. But this is not so, either with regard to the individual punished or with regard to the penal system or the wider society. The differences between depriving individuals of their money on the one hand and their liberty on another can be shown by reflecting on a unique characteristic of the fine. The fine is the only penal sanction someone else can pay for you. It is quite common, for example, for courts to allow one person's fine to be paid by another - a parent or a friend. This is a fairly routine feature of how fines are administered and collected. By contrast, it is really not imaginable, in a modern penal system, for one individual to legitimately substitute their body and their liberty for another person's when a sentence of imprisonment is imposed. The difference between the two sanctions flows from the different relationship that the 'commodity' being removed has to the body and the person of the individual being punished. Money, as a resource, is easy to conceive of as being separate from the body and as not being tied in directly to an individual's sense of self or basic autonomy. Liberty, in contrast, is tied to the body of the person and to concepts of autonomy and self. Being able to control one's body is an essential component of what is it to be considered a free, autonomous person. This difference allows for the possibility that someone can walk away from a fine (although not without consequence) while they cannot avoid a sentence of imprisonment. Fines may thus be conceived of as 'resource based' punishments and imprisonment as a 'bodily punishment'. The appropriate vocabulary for the latter is one which rightly gives a central place to the concepts of power, liberty and body and the relationships between them. The appropriate vocabulary for the former, however, has yet to be fully developed but it should be relatively clear already that the triumvirate relationship of power-liberty-body will be configured quite differently.

Auto-Punishments: Punishment Effects and Penal Sanctions

The problem, of course, is what this vocabulary should look like and this is where my concept of auto-punishment comes in. It is an admittedly ambitious attempt to begin to develop a more sensitive, appropriate and better vocabulary for talking about the use of money as punishment and, therefore, about the penal system more generally. The notion of auto-punishments aims to pick up on what I see as the crucial aspects of the nature of the fine. As will be seen, the concept of auto-punishment was developed from an empirical study of how fines are imposed and enforced and the middle sections of the paper will report on this. First, however, it will be helpful if I provide an initial rather abstract outline of what I mean by the concept of auto-punishment.

The most convenient way of explaining what I mean by the term is to contrast the ways in which the fine and the prison achieve what I call their 'punishment effect'. While the defining feature of the punishment-effect of the prison - deprivation of liberty - works whether or not the offender resists or co-operates (although it is better if there is a degree of co-operation), this is not the case with the fine. In contrast, the punishment-effect of the fine, the deprivation of money, always depends on the co-operation of the person fined. As has been said, this aspect of the fine is made most clear when somebody pays another person's fine for them, but the element of co-operation is, in fact, a general feature. These days, when somebody is fined, the court is required to allow that person time to pay the fine and will normally also offer the possibility of payment by instalments. These are everyday, routine aspects of the fine and can be observed daily in most criminal courts. The everyday nature of these aspects of the fine should not lead to them being overlooked. Their importance is that they create a space within which the administration of the fine is effectively handed over, in large measure, to the person who is being punished. Individuals who are fined end up, in a real sense, with a choice of whether or not to pay. If they do not pay then they stand, particularly in Scotland, a high chance of being imprisoned - but what happens in these circumstances, as will be illustrated, is that the person effectively trades with the system. The exchange is one in which individuals balance a portion of their liberty against a sum of money and, in many cases, reach the decision that the exchange is worthwhile. The conditions surrounding this exchange, it is true, are not completely of the individual's choosing but, as will be shown, individuals do control these conditions more than is commonly realised. My point here is that, while this trading may be an unintended consequence, it is nevertheless only made possible by two things coming together. These are, first, the nature of the fine as a resource based punishment, coming together with, second, the way the fining process is administered and organised. The co-operation of the offender with his or her punishment in the case of the fine thus ought not to be seen as a by-product of the fining system but rather as a de facto presupposition. Without it, the present day fine could not work and alternative systems, such as the immediate coercive extraction of money in the court or the translation of the fine into a bodily punishment, would have to be invented. The costs of such alternatives would, however, likely prove to be unacceptably high and cancel out many of the well known advantages of the fine (for example, its relatively low costs of administration).

As was said, the idea of auto-punishments grew out of an empirical research project and I will now turn to a description of this project and in particular that part of it which examined fine default, the most clearly policy driven aspect of the research. This part of the research generated results which seemed to me to be anomalous and which thus worked as a spur to conceptual revision. Before doing this, a final word is necessary as to what I see to be at stake here theoretically. The most immediate issue is, of course, to do with the fine but beyond that there are broader questions. As was said in the introduction, the fine is the most common sanction in use in most western penal systems; the fine is the hub of modern penal practice. A good case can also be made out - although the details cannot be provided here - for the fine and other types of monetary settlement being the most common means of dealing with crime historically (see Young, 1987). Viewed in this light, the history of punishment, it follows, would be more accurately written and better conceived of as a type of cash nexus, in which money is brought into differing relationships with what have come to be conceived of as criminal harms rather than as a process in which the prison holds centre stage. Indeed, what I argue points in the direction of a history of punishment which explores how it developed along two vectors, one consisting of resource based punishments, of which the fine is the best example, and the other vector consisting of the bodily punishments, such as prison but also torture, branding and execution. This is a much broader theme but this paper can be seen as an attempt to develop a vocabulary to facilitate its exploration.

Fine Default in Scotland

As may be known, Scotland has a particularly deep seated and long standing problem with the imprisonment of fine defaulters (see chapter 13). A high proportion of the prison reception population is composed of them. In 1992 the figure was approximately 43 per cent of the reception population and, over the last four decades, with some ups and downs, has steadily grown (there was a recent fall it should be noted between 1992-1993 but this has been reversed). In comparative terms this is an unusually high figure. In England and Wales, the corresponding figure is about 26 per cent and in most continental countries it is significantly lower. The only jurisdictions with higher proportions are Northern Ireland with 55 per cent of prison receptions being composed of fine defaulters and Ontario, which for a short period in the 1950s, had a reception population that was composed 70 per cent of fine defaulters.

It appears that this is not a new problem but one that has bedevilled the system since at least the early 1900s. For example, in 1902, the commentator to the Criminal Statistics in Scotland (1904, p.11) argued:

> This point has been dwelt upon at some length, because the non-payment of fines is for some reason an outstanding feature of Scottish Criminal Statistics when compared with those of other countries, and it may not have received that amount of attention which it deserves.

Or again, in 1906 (Criminal Statistics in Scotland, 1907, p.10):

> It will be seen that those sentenced to imprisonment remain at the previous figure of nearly 11,000. It has often been pointed out that the sentences of simple imprisonment give no idea of the numbers received into prison, as they are increased five times their number by the addition of persons sentenced to pay a fine, but who fail to do so, and are on that account imprisoned in lieu.

This commentator went on to quote an 'American writer':

> There is something essentially unreasonable and absurd in the effort to collect a fine from men and women who have just spent their earnings in a drunken debauch. Such a demand on the morning after arrest is, in the case of many working people, a formal mockery; and the imprisonment which is yearly meted out to tens of thousands of often poor people for failure to make

such immediate payment is little less than imprisonment for debt under peculiarly exasperating circumstances.

This was the context in which I began to reflect on the problem of default. As can be seen, it showed fine-default to be an endemic feature of the modern Scottish system, as it is of all systems which rely on the fine, although to differing degrees in different systems. The questions now became why this should be so, what could be done about it and what general lessons about the nature of the fine could be gleaned. The research questions to which an answer seemed to be required I took to be these: why do some people pay their fines and others not pay them? and, why, is the use of imprisonment for fine-defaulters higher in Scotland than elsewhere? It was in seeking answers to these questions that anomalies became apparent.

One immediate issue that struck me was that the first question was strange. One of the general views of the nature of punishment that is deeply rooted in the literature is that punishments are not the sorts of thing about which there is supposed to be a choice, once they are imposed. There is a Kantian strain in the literature which says that individuals will their punishments by willing their crime, and this raises the interesting possibility that people do their punishments because they accept them. But the issue I was faced with seemed to be a different one, at least in some ways. The question seemed not to be one of accepting or not accepting punishment, although I do not want completely to lose sight of this. Rather, the question was that, with the fine, we seem immediately to accept that there is the possibility of paying or not paying. In other words, there is an acceptance, in the case of the fine, that the very form of the punishment and the way it is administered, cedes the possibility that it will not achieve its punishment effect.

So the first question seemed to point to there being something different about the fine and the way we talk of it. The sense of oddness and difference grew as the empirical work progressed. There were two bodies of empirical data that contributed to this stretching process. First, and probably most dramatically, there were the results of a series of interviews conducted with a group of fine-defaulters in Edinburgh prison. This was a small exercise involving just 21 prisoners. The interviews were free-form and for various reasons we were not allowed to tape record them. Nevertheless, even given their limitations, including the possibly unrepresentative nature of the 'sample', the interviews produced some very interesting and illustrative results. Secondly, data was collected about how the enforcement process worked, including the views of sheriffs on it. These two bodies of data proved to be mutually re-enforcing in important ways.

First, the interviews with prisoners. In demographic terms, the type of person most likely, in absolute numbers, to be imprisoned for fine default is a young male. For example, in 1992, 93 per cent of those imprisoned for fine default were male; 74 per cent of those received for fine default were under the age of 30, most (54 per cent) being between 21 and 30. The most common crimes originally committed will be theft of a motor vehicle and housebreaking. The group interviewed (in 1983) were very similar in profile to this; most were between 21-30, with a few young offenders and just two who were significantly older (one was in his 40s and the other was in his 50s). The average sum owed in fines at the point of imprisonment was £162, but it must be pointed out that this figure was greatly inflated by the unpaid fines of just two prisoners who owed well over £1000 each for various frauds and confidence tricks (1983 prices). Most were unemployed and on social security payments.

The most significant conclusions drawn from these interviews were that the men did not see themselves as being unable to meet their fines because they were poor in some absolute sense; the non-payment of fines was not the direct result of a simple lack of money. They did not see themselves as being unable to pay their fines only because they lacked funds. Rather, their reasons were altogether more complex. They did think that they lacked resources but this was very much a relative judgement. The crucial consideration for all of them was where the fine fitted into their budget and lifestyle; the issue was one of what priority they chose to give to the fine in the context of their other commitments as they saw them. There were certain material factors that affected their reasoning, such as how many fines they owed, how big they were, whether they could trade off fines they had recently incurred but had not yet been pursued for and whether or not they had a family of their own. The time of the year also influenced their decision in that, if they received a fine near Christmas or near what they described as their holidays, then it was a common practice to make a few payments but then to desist. The general view was that if there was only one fine of about £50 or if the accumulated total was below £50 (1983 prices), then it was worth trying to pay by instalments, but above that sum it was seen not to be worthwhile at all.

There were several interconnected things that I found interesting about what these men said. First, it appeared they treated the fine as simply another item on their budget, to be dealt with in the same way as others -

that is, you meet the debt only if the opportunity costs of doing so are acceptable. Paying the fine obviously meant that no advantage could be gained by using that sum of money for another purpose. If the other purpose was evaluated more highly, then the obligation to pay the fine fell down the list of priorities, sometimes to the point where the men entered what was a trade. The trade here was between control over their money and their liberty. Essentially, these men were trading with the criminal justice system and it was clear that, even though this was sometimes inarticulately expressed, they often saw themselves as being in control of the process - they saw themselves as calling the shots. These men, in other words, saw themselves as in a real sense choosing to go to prison rather than pay their fines; in a cost benefit way, this was, sometimes, both the least troublesome and the most profitable thing to do.

It would be wrong to overstate the sense of cold rationality with which these men made their decisions. Some of them, particularly the young, single ones and the eldest person interviewed, did not use economic terms like budget; indeed, their finances tended to be in a state of disorganisation and muddle and their sense of ordinary economics was topsy turvey. But, it was clear that they nevertheless did discriminate between their priorities in a balance sheet way. They certainly traded with the system in the controlled fashion described. For example, one young man, who was already a veteran of the system, said he tended to regard the many fines he got as what he called, 'a deferred prison sentence'. This was not meant at all to refer back to his lack of money; rather, he said he preferred to build up a healthy balance sheet of partially unpaid fines so that he could control when he traded them in with the local sheriff court. He said he felt he had reached an understanding with the local sheriff about timing (he came from the Borders) and that both were happy for him to pick up fines, most of which in his case were for breach of the peace (shorthand for drink related offences), as long as he did not get 'out of order', as he put it.

It should be evident from my description that these men were experienced and knowledgeable about how the criminal justice system worked. Many of their calculations depended upon quite detailed knowledge of how long the system took to do certain things; how long, for instance, it took for the local court to write to them reminding them that they had not met an instalment, how long they could afford to ignore this letter, when they were likely to be called to a means inquiry court or to be imprisoned for non-payment and so on. They sometimes got things wrong, and many of them related tales of this, but that they possessed knowledge and could use it to work the system to their advantage was clear.

Apart from the intrinsic interest of the interviews, they also gave rise to a number of more general questions. The interviews provided, perhaps on the basis of an unrepresentative population, an indirect but crucial insight into how the fine works as a sanction. They also provided direct evidence of how those who are fined view the punishment imposed on them. If these are put together, the picture that is painted is a rich and challenging one. It shows on the one hand, that the way the fine is administered provides room for those who are punished to exercise a surprising amount of control over the process. What I earlier called the punishment effect of the sanction seems very much to depend on choices the men made; if the men chose not to co-operate with the conditions attaching to the fine then it was not paid. In a real sense the men were controlling the enforcement process, particularly in its earlier stages - that is in meeting instalment payments and themselves effectively controlling the time to pay element - but also in the later stages of the process as well. In this sense, the men were self-administrating their own punishments. Furthermore, it ought to be apparent that this was not simply a result of them manipulating the system - although, of course, this is what they were doing - but a product of the very way the fine is organised which creates the space within which this could happen.

Auto-Punishments, the Fine, Money and Discipline

In this last section I return to the central question posed earlier - how does the fine fit into the modern penal system? - and begin, on the basis of the data described and the vocabulary developed, to begin putting together an answer. In doing this I want also to touch the broader theoretical questions about the role and applicability of exemplar cases in explanations. My consideration of both questions can, in fact, be advanced by examining the issue of whether the fine can be conceived of as disciplinary sanction in the Foucaultian sense. This is, I think, more than a semantic or purely liturgical debate in Foucaultiology. Discipline is a central concept in Foucault's own work, especially in *Discipline and Punish* (1979), and it has come to play an equally central role in a wide range of literature about punishment thereafter. Perhaps, most importantly, the concept of discipline has come, as exemplars do, to denote a certain way of approaching the study of punishment, almost without regard to the precise meaning that may reasonably be given to the term. In this tradition, the presumption seems to be that punishment is best theorised within a vocabulary organised around what I described, as the triumvirate of power-liberty-body. As was argued earlier, Foucault's concept of discipline is a contemporary exemplification of this tradition, so to test its applicability to the data described here clearly has wider implications as well as allowing me to advance my central aim of understanding better how the fine fits into the modern penal system.[1]

The core image, the exemplar case of discipline, in Foucault's work, is of a series of quite specific techniques of instruction which work through or on the body and which are aimed at producing particular effects or outcomes. While disciplines and outcomes may thus be quite specific in nature, there is nevertheless said to be a general aim - that of normalisation. In itself, normalisation works at the specific level, but all normalisations are related in that the purpose is to create conformity and obedience - to create what Foucault called 'docile bodies' and this is achieved through the training of the 'soul' (self). The wider context of disciplinary techniques is that they are an application of power and thus themselves a particular type of power; disciplines, at the most general of levels, are a way(s) of managing populations and individuals. While this seems to me to be the core of what Foucault means by discipline, there are a number of what I see as ancillary concepts which are sometimes brought into the picture but other times not. For example, it is quite possible to use the concept of discipline without requiring there to be an actual agent present who is actively engaged in surveillance - for Foucault, it is that individuals feel that they are under a 'gaze' or are trained in a regime that is important.

My contention is that it is not reasonable to interpret the data in such a way as to make it fit with this image of a discipline. The picture that is painted by the interviews shows clearly that fine defaulters were not acting as 'docile bodies'. The men's bodies were not being trained, they were not subject to a process of continuing surveillance (although this would not be a requirement) and their actions were not being normalised through a special technique or application of power. Their bodies were not directly captured by 'the carceral texture of society' or 'its perpetual observation' (Foucault, 1979, p.304). Rather, it makes more sense to describe what was happening as quite the reverse. The men were not captured by the system but rather used their bodies and their liberty to trade with it. They were not normalised, if by this is meant the inculcation of values and norms the purpose of which is to make them obedient or passive. Rather, they responded to the situation in a way which seems to assume an active subject

- that is, an individual who was able to exercise power and to make choices about courses of action on the basis of the relative costs of the various options available. In this sense, the men willed many of the outcomes in the process.

Moreover, it is difficult to interpret what was going on in the fine process, as it is portrayed in the interviews, as a search for the 'soul' of the subject. Indeed, the search for such 'deep' things in this mode of punishment - the most common in the penal system - appeared to be singularly absent; or, to put this more precisely, the fine as a penal sanction seems to be remarkably indifferent to the 'soul' or the subjectivity of the offender. Rather, the aim of the fine, even on these occasions where it had 'failed', was to extract a resource, money, hopefully with as little administrative effort as possible.

So there was no soul searching, no direct capture of the body of the offender unless this was the product of a trade-in, no specific technique of training and apparently no explicit normalisation. It follows, therefore, that there was no disciplining going on in the Foucaultian sense. This is not, of course, to say that there was no controlling of the men's behaviour evident. The men were being punished and, in this sense, they were responding to an exercise of power. By itself, however, this could hardly be taken as an sufficient ground upon which to define what was going on as 'discipline'.[2]

This is not, of course, the first time that an argument about the disciplinary nature of the fine has been debated. In a pioneering essay, Tony Bottoms also argued that the fine is not a disciplinary sanction on grounds very similar to those advanced here. He too noted, in the case of the fine, the absence of an agent directly surveying or observing the offender and more importantly, the absence of a regime of training. Bottoms rightly concluded that if these characteristics of discipline are not present, then the fine (along with some other sanctions, like community service orders) cannot be conceived of primarily as a disciplinary sanction. Rather, Bottoms claims it is more of a classical punishment (calculable, public, non-arbitrary) which, he argues further, can best be characterised, in Weberian terms, as a gelleschaft type penalty consistent with the rational bureaucracy as the predominant mode of organisation in modern society (Bottoms, 1983).

By itself I take Bottoms' argument as support for the case advanced here and this essay can be seen to build on his. I want, however, to push the case further than Bottoms in two respects. First, it should be noted that the object of Bottoms' attack turns out not so much to be Foucault's work as that of what thereafter came to be known as the 'dispersal of discipline' thesis advanced in particular by Cohen (1985). Secondly, and this follows, there remains a degree of ambiguity about how far Bottoms thinks that the notion of discipline can be taken as an account of modern penality. In an intriguing couple of pages (pp.194-196), Bottoms does say that he can see no reason why his Weberian derived account of the contemporary penal system is inconsistent with Foucault's thesis. This, however, is not really directly related to the debate about the disciplinary (or not) nature of the fine but more to a recognition that in Foucault's later work less attention is placed on discipline and more on the range of practices (risk management, insurance, and so on) now associated with the idea of governmentality. This is fair enough but it is also a bit of a fudge. Whether or not Foucault moved on (which, of course, must be recognised) does not alter the significance of the account of penality given by Foucault (especially given its influence on contemporary penology) which is, it seems to me, organised around the concept of discipline and which draws from the power vocabulary described above. It is as though Bottoms too accepts that the most persuasive account of penal practice is one which comes from this stable, so to speak. To put this slightly differently, the account of the non-disciplinary nature of the fine which comes out of Bottoms appears to be based on the idea that it is non-disciplinary because there is something like a short-fall or a lack of reach in power.

The problem I have with this, as ought to be evident, is that I see it to be a partial and in some senses wrong view of the nature of the fine and of the way power is enmeshed in the penal system. My contention is that the non-disciplinary nature of the fine is not a product of a short-fall in or lack of reach of power but is more related to its monetary nature. The fact that the fine is what I have called a resource based punishment alters very significantly how power and the body come in both empirically and at the level of explanation. The data described here show how the body is not the central object of the fine and it provides grounds also for arguing that power, understood as a force which captures bodies, is not central either.

The general implication of this is that a theory of the penal system which proceeded from the commodity which is primarily involved (i.e. money) would be different from one which proceeds from a vocabulary of power. Money works differently from power. As Simmel argues, the controlling aspect of money is that it requires us to enter into exchange relationships in which we are faced with a constant whirl of choice; money forces us continually to evaluate what we do against market mechanisms and against differing opportunity costs. It requires us continually to evaluate those other commodities and relationships with which it is proposed at this or that point to strike an equivalence. If we decide one way, we pay our money and we have to accept the loss of opportunity - but there is always the possibility of difference, of different outcomes (Simmel, 1978). This account of the nature of money works well, it should be noted, as a summary of the picture of the fine process which emerges from my interviews with fine defaulters.

In terms of the vocabulary that I have used here, a theory of the penal system which proceeded from its base in money would push the concepts of power and body out of the centre and more to the periphery of explanation. This does not mean, it must be stressed, that power and the body become thereby redundant. Punishment is an expression of power and, as has been made clear, resource based punishments can and are quite routinely transposed into bodily ones. The point is, rather, that in a money based account of the penal system, these key relationships are significantly altered with the effect that an account of the penal system which just gives centre place to the power-body relationship is shown to be radically incomplete.

So, what would a money based account of the contemporary penal system look like? This is where my concepts of resource based punishments and auto-punishments are relevant. I earlier defined an auto-punishment as one in which the person punished self administers the punishment; I argued also that auto-punishments are made possible where certain administrative aspects of the penal system come together with punishments based on the deprivation of resources. While the fine is the best example of an auto-punishment it is not the only one. Many of what are conventionally called 'non-custodial' sanctions also hand over the administration of the punishment to the offender or centrally presuppose his/her co-operation. There are in fact many examples of punishments which work this way. In Scotland, both community service orders and probation orders require the consent of the offender and thus have a family resemblance which allows one to conceive of them as auto-punishments (see chapter 12). Neither, of course, directly extract money but they do work with a money type analogy in that the labour/time of the offender is parcelled out as though it is a type of resource.

The account I have given here is obviously incomplete. It does, however, open up a different and, I would claim, more accurate way of thinking about the penal system. My account also has the virtue, I suggest, of being based in an empirical description of penal practice, rather than being written, as so many others are, from an essentially document/policy perspective. It is hoped that it works as a partial corrective to them.

Notes

1.   There is, however, a real problem with 'testing' the concept here. Foucault tended not to evolve concepts in a way which permits others to engage with them in a precise fashion, empirically or conceptually. Rather, the key concepts in his work tend to rely for their meaning on the way they fit into a broader conceptual scheme with the result that attempts to take one concept out, so to speak, to investigate it are made difficult. This difficulty is compounded by the looseness with which Foucault defines concepts. This was, as many commentators with varying degrees of sympathy have noted, all intended - it is part of the Foucault effect. This may be so, but it should not divert attention away from the fact that many of Foucault's key concepts are high in empirical content, in the sense that they state propositions about the social world, down even to the level of descriptions of how individuals behave. This seems especially true of the concept of discipline. While Foucault may have used the concept in slightly different ways at various points of *Discipline and Punish* and while, in his later work, he may even have somewhat distanced himself from the concept, it still nevertheless, I suggest, has a core meaning.

2.   It seems to me that unless Foucault's concept of discipline is given a more restrictive meaning than it being used as a synonym for control, it lacks real analytical bite. Unless the meaning of the term is made more definite, then, there is a danger, that 'discipline' will become the sort of mickey mouse concept that Stanley Cohen claims social control has already become (Cohen, 1985).

12 Community-based Disposals

GILL MCIVOR AND BRYAN WILLIAMS

Introduction

In Scotland, community based disposals are run by local authority social workers, who have been responsible for the provision of a range of statutory services to the criminal justice system since the absorption of the former probation service into the newly created generic social work departments in 1969. This remit includes the supervision of offenders subject to social work disposals imposed by the courts. Since 1991, however, the Social Work Services Group (SWSG) of the Scottish Office has re-imbursed to local authorities the full costs of providing these services: '100 per cent funding'. A significant practical consequence has been the creation in all but the smallest social work departments of specialist arrangements for the delivery, and in many cases management, of social work services to the criminal justice system.

The introduction of 100 per cent funding by central government formed one part of a broader strategy aimed at reducing the numbers of offenders who were imprisoned for short periods of time. In 1988 the then Scottish Secretary delivered the Kenneth Younger Memorial Lecture to the Howard League (Scotland) (Rifkind, 1989). In this address he outlined the government's commitment to reducing the use of custody at the remand stage, for fine default and at first sentence. The majority of those imprisoned serve relatively short sentences and it was those who were not considered to pose any undue risk to the public for whom the increased use of community-based social work disposals was considered appropriate. The Scottish Secretary rejected the possibility of increasing the range of alternatives to custody available to the courts. Instead he sought to strengthen existing measures - probation and community service - by providing full central funding and requiring that they operate within a nationally agreed framework of objectives and standards. In this chapter we consider the philosophy and operation of both of these measures and of a relatively recent addition to the armoury of community-based disposals available to the courts: the supervised attendance order.

Probation Orders

A Brief History

Initially, probation was an informal procedure whereby a court would allow an individual (usually a young offender) a specified period in which to prove that they could act in a law-abiding manner if given the guidance of a responsible person. Successful completion of this 'proving' period would result in no further action by the court. In the early years, probation (which is thought to have originated in the mid-nineteenth century in England and the USA independently) was confined to first offenders, and supervisors were volunteers appointed by religious bodies such as the Church of England Temperance Society (King, 1958). Pressure from organisations like the Howard Association to formalise the use of probation resulted in the passing of the Probation of Offenders Act 1907 (Bochel, 1976). Thus probation became a statutory function and the first probation officers were appointed and paid from public funds.

In following years, the organisation, training and deployment of probation officers were gradually standardised and the Criminal Justice Act of 1925 laid down an organisational framework for the probation service in England and Wales. The same was achieved in Scotland six years later by the passage of the Probation of Offenders (Scotland) Act 1931 (Bochel, 1976). Full-time probation officers were appointed in Glasgow to take over work originally begun by police officers (Murphy, 1992). Further expansion of probation in Scotland was brought about by subsequent legislation relating to children and young persons (notably the Scottish Act of 1937) and by the early 1960s, there was a heavy emphasis on work with young offenders (*ibid.*).

Enactment of the Social Work (Scotland) Act 1968 brought about disbandment of the Scottish Probation Service in 1969. This had been resisted unsuccessfully by many probation officers and judges during the deliberations of the Kilbrandon Committee and subsequent legislative process (Murphy, 1992). It may have been this experience which led to consideration of probation functions being specifically excluded from the terms of reference of the later Seebohm Committee in England and Wales. In the years following, there was much debate within Scotland about the allegedly deleterious effect of this organisational change on the nature of community-based services like probation. Attention focused on whether the new Social Work Departments, with their characteristic social welfare orientation, placed enough importance on criminal justice functions; had staff with sufficient experience of dealing with adult offenders; and who were sufficiently in tune with the principles and values underpinning criminal justice (Marsland, 1977; Nelson, 1977).

Developments in probation (such as groupwork projects, hostels and day-centres) were widely thought to have been inhibited by the absence of a specialist probation service and sentencers' confidence in these measures was said to have been undermined (see Howard League, 1976; Moore, 1978). Despite such negative views (e.g. Moore, 1980), Curran and Chambers (1981) found that sheriffs were generally satisfied with the standards of the court reports prepared by non-specialist social workers. More recently, Ford *et al.* (1992) also reported largely positive shrieval attitudes towards probation supervision.

Introduction of 100 per cent funding arrangements and National Objectives and Standards (Social Work Services Group, 1991; 1996a) have brought about increasing specialisation in criminal justice within Social Work Departments, which has largely silenced criticisms concerning the location of probation supervision within mainstream social work services. At the time of writing, however, plans for radical changes in the training of probation officers and the organisation of criminal justice services in England and Wales, together with the prospect of devolved government in Scotland, have re-focused attention on the question of whether a separate criminal justice agency would add greater credibility to the supervision of offenders within the community.

The Nature and Purposes of Probation

The definitive Morison Committee (Report of the Departmental Committee on the Probation Service, 1963) defined probation as

> The submission of an offender whilst at liberty to a specified period of supervision by a social caseworker who is an officer of the court; during this period the offender remains liable if not of good conduct to be dealt with by the court.

Given that the courts have been giving offenders this type of 'second chance' since the turn of the century, it is perhaps rather surprising that, despite many changes in political and penological thinking, the duties of both probation supervisors and probationers have remained relatively unaltered.[1] Similarly, the pre-requirement of consent by the offender to being put on probation and the power of the supervisor to return him to court for punishment for his original offence in the event of him breaching the requirements of the probation order, or committing a further offence, remain key features of contemporary probation legislation and practice.

It can be argued that these somewhat imprecise requirements have endured because they allow the maximum possible scope to probation supervisors and thereby continue to permit probation orders to be made in a wide range of circumstances (Ditton and Ford, 1994). The supervision relationship established between probation officer and probationer remains the mainstay of probation practice (Hill, 1991; McIvor and Barry, 1996), although modern conceptualisations tend to de-emphasise the treatment-oriented and rehabilitative connotations of this notion, originally rooted in psycho-analytic theory. Similarly, despite the introduction of programmes of groupwork, most of the work carried out with probationers in Scotland remains in the context of face-to-face supervision sessions, normally on a one-to-one basis (Williams *et al.*, 1988; McIvor and Barry, 1996).

A probation order can be made in any case for which the penalty is not fixed in law (for example, murder and certain Road Traffic Act offences). The court must view this action as 'expedient ... having regard to the nature of the offence and the character of the offender'.[2] In order to investigate these matters a Social Enquiry Report must be obtained and considered. The order itself can be for any specified period between six months and three years.

To address special circumstances in a case, additional requirements may be inserted into probation orders. The most common are those requiring: residence in a specified place (such as a hostel); medical or psychological treatment for a condition considered to be related to offending (such as drug or alcohol misuse); attendance on a programme designed to address aspects of behaviour (such as anger management, illegal driving, victim awareness); the undertaking of unpaid work; and the payment of compensation or other restitutory measure. To safeguard the probationer's interests certain restrictions exist as to when such conditions may be added and what they may require of him/her. Probation orders may be discharged early for good progress and may be transferred to a new local authority (or across the Border to England or Wales) should the probationer move his/her place of residence.

The Use of Probation

General considerations and trends The Morison Committee (Report of the Departmental Committee on the Probation Service, 1963) concluded that probation should be considered when the following conditions are met:

(i) That the circumstances of offence and offender should not be so serious as to warrant a more severe penalty;

(ii) that the risk to society of releasing the offender should be outweighed by the moral, social and economic arguments for not depriving him of his liberty; and

(iii) that the offender is in need of continuing attention; and that he is capable of responding to such attention.

Nicholson (1981) in his authoritative book on sentencing in Scotland and Moore and Wood (1981) in their influential practice manual on social work within the Scottish criminal justice system do not depart significantly from this view, which suggests that probation is suitable in a very wide range of cases.

The number of probation orders made in Britain rose steadily for several decades, reaching a peak in the early 1970s, following which its use suffered a noticeable decline.[3] The decline in England and Wales was attributed to the development of other non-custodial measures such as community service and suspended sentence supervision orders. In Scotland it was widely attributed to the alleged loss of confidence following the disbandment of the Scottish Probation Service discussed earlier. Since the trend was UK wide, however, this suggests that more than these 'local' factors were involved. One explanation relates it to growing disenchantment at that time with rehabilitative models (Bottoms and McWilliams, 1978; Hudson, 1987). The decline in probation usage may also have been related to social workers' practice in not recommending this disposal (Williams *et al.*, 1991; Ditton and Ford, 1994).

More recently, there has been an increase once again in the use of probation orders. 6,071 probation orders were made by Scottish courts in 1995 (over twice the number recorded in 1986), representing 3.9 per cent of all disposals (compared with 1.6 per cent in 1985) (Scottish Office, 1997c). This increase appears to be associated with greater shrieval confidence in probation as a disposal, its more frequent use in more serious cases (e.g. in so-called 'intensive' probation projects) often in combination with a requirement for unpaid work and better targeting of probation resources. Even at this level, probation and community service combined represent only 7.4 per cent of disposals, compared with custody at 10.4 per cent, admonition and caution at 10.3 per cent and financial penalties at 70.4 per cent (*ibid.*). Increases in probation and community service since 1985 are paralleled by an increase in the use of custody of 2.2 per cent. Thus, despite some success in using probation as a direct alternative to imprisonment (Williams and Creamer, 1997), its increased use appears to reflect a decrease in the use of financial penalties. This may be a sign of courts' reluctance to fine those already in reduced financial circumstances, as recommended in several reports (see, for example, Association of Directors of Social Work, 1987).

In the most recent Scottish study, 85 per cent of probation orders were made by sheriffs in summary proceedings and 69 per cent of these were for one year or less (McIvor and Barry, 1996). Just over half of the orders contained one or more additional requirements as compared with only one in six reported in an earlier study (Williams *et al.*, 1988). This increase seems likely to be related to the introduction into Scotland, during the last ten years, of various 'intensive' or 'enhanced' probation projects, for which additional requirements are normally added to probation orders.

Within these overall figures, there appear to be significant variations in the patterns of probation usage by different Scottish courts, even at the same level, both in terms of the type of case considered appropriate and in the use of 'higher tariff' probation as an alternative to custodial sentences (Creamer *et al.*, 1992a). These differences reflect not only local historical sentencing patterns and priorities, but also differences in the pattern of social workers' recommendations for probation within court reports (Williams *et al.*, 1988; Williams and Creamer, 1989).

Tariff considerations With a growth of interest in the use of probation as an alternative to custody, the notion of 'tariff' (the seriousness of a case in respect of likely sentencing outcomes) has become important. Employing a validated risk-of-custody scale (Creamer *et al.*, 1994; Creamer and Williams, 1996), cases in a study (based on a sample of social enquiry reports) focusing specifically on this issue were split into higher and lower tariff categories. Table 12.1 shows the distribution of probation and other cases in the research sample.

Table 12.1 Higher and lower tariff cases

	Probation orders	Other disposals	Totals
Higher	32 (39%)	51 (61%)	83 (100%)
Lower	41 (48%)	45 (52%)	86 (100%)

n=169

As can be seen, the cases fell evenly between the higher and lower tariff categories. Despite a tendency for more probation disposals to be within the lower tariff group, orders were made in nearly two out of five higher tariff cases. Nearly one third of the probation orders were made in cases where the accused was facing three or more charges and the median number of charges was two for both probation and non-probation disposals. There were also no obvious major differences between probation and non-probation disposals in respect of the number of libelled previous convictions and it was striking that one sixth of the probation orders were made on individuals with ten or more previous convictions. It was concluded that courts at that time were certainly not confining probation to the less serious cases (Williams *et al.*, 1988).

More recently, McIvor and Barry (1996) found that the probationers in their sample had an *average* of eight previous convictions (half had six or more) and had served an *average* of nearly four previous custodial sentences. One third had previously been sentenced to community service and a similar proportion had previously been placed on probation. These findings reinforce the picture of probation often being used in higher tariff cases (a product of *both* the offending history of the probationer and the seriousness of the probation-generating offence).

Official figures show that probation is used widely for crimes of dishonesty, such as burglary (16 per cent) and theft and fraud (28 per cent); breaches of public order (23 per cent); non-sexual crimes of violence (seven per cent); and road traffic offences (six per cent) (Scottish Office, 1997c).

Gender and age   Since men represent some 85 per cent of all those appearing before the Scottish courts (Scottish Office, 1997c), it is not surprising that men constitute the vast majority of those given probation - 85 per cent in the Scottish Office study (*op. cit.*) and 82 per cent in McIvor and Barry's (1996) study. Considered overall, men are as likely as women to be given probation (approximately four per cent of the whole group in each case). It would appear, however, that women appearing before *some* courts may be given probation more frequently than men in similar circumstances (Williams *et al.*, 1988). In a similar vein, McIvor and Barry report that the proportion of women probationers in their study varied between 31 per cent and 14 per cent, which suggested differential practice across the four courts studied (McIvor and Barry, *op. cit.*). Without matching for factors such as case seriousness, it is not possible to be entirely clear as to why this is so. Women probationers demonstrate different characteristics from men, for example they are more likely to be older, married or cohabiting; to have dependent children; and to have fewer previous convictions (especially to be first offenders). The implicit and explicit reasons given in court reports as to why probation should be considered a suitable disposal, tend to differ from those cited in the cases of men (McIvor, 1997). Finally, the probation orders of women are more likely to be discharged earlier than those of men, whereas men are more likely to be breached for non-compliance (McIvor and Barry, *op. cit.*). Taken together, these findings suggest bigger gender differences than the overall statistics indicate and it seems clear that more detailed investigation is needed.

A not dissimilar pattern also exists in respect of age in relation to probation. The overall sentencing statistics for 1995 suggest that, proportionately, younger men and women (i.e. those aged 20 and under) are more likely to be placed on probation - eight per cent, compared with two to three per cent for those aged 30 plus (Scottish Office, 1997c). By contrast,

Williams *et al.* (1988) found a statistically significant trend towards probation for those in the older age groups (over 30, but most noticeably 40 plus) and against probation for those aged under 21, for both males and females. McIvor and Barry (1996) reported that less than half (48 per cent) of their probation sample were aged under 21 (52 per cent male, 32 per cent female) and that the average age for probationers was significantly over 21 (27 for females, 23 for males). Furthermore, age-offence patterns for probationers seem to be important in both cited studies. In view of these apparently discrepant findings, it may be that the aggregated figures tend to mask important local variations in sentencing practice.

The Realities of Probation Supervision

Theoretical background The 'traditional' probation literature tends to stress supervisors' role authority as 'officers of the court' (Monger, 1964; Foren and Bailey, 1968) and to dwell on the relationship between 'care' and 'control' in supervision (Haxby, 1978; Harris, 1980; Coker, 1982). The original duties of probationer supervisors, as defined in the Probation of Offenders Act 1907 (to 'advise, assist and befriend'), have been reappraised and re-worked many times to fit within changing political and penological climates of opinion (Senior, 1984).

Much of this debate (as with the parallel debate concerning 'welfare' and 'justice' within juvenile justice), was conducted at rather an abstract level. Empirical studies have tended to show that in practice these allegedly dichotomous concepts are frequently conflated or coexistent (Hardiker, 1977; Day, 1981; Fielding, 1984). Raynor (1985) argued that much of the traditional debate has been misplaced because of the failure sufficiently to keep the criminal justice context firmly in mind. His views on this matter are worth quoting (Raynor, 1985, p.105):

> Although there may well have been plenty of examples of inappropriate coerciveness by probation officers, the view that this is somehow inherent in the role depends on a misreading of the probation relationship as a transaction between only two parties in which one makes demands and the other complies or rebels. In fact both officer and client are part of a far wider pattern of transactions and contracts ... The role of the probation

officer ... can be more fruitfully understood as that of negotiator or mediator in the decision-making process rather than as decision-maker or source of coercive authority in his own right.

Using this conceptualisation, he makes a link between the earlier 'officer of the court' literature and the 'non-treatment' literature of the 1980s (Bottoms and McWilliams, 1978). The combination gives rise to a broader view of probation objectives, encompassing both individual (micro) and societal (macro) elements (Harris, 1992; Williams and Creamer 1997).

What happens in practice? Whatever the theoretical analysis, the practical realities are likely to determine the nature of probation supervision and to set limits as to what is achievable within this type of community sanction. Despite diversification in probation practice, the vast bulk of supervision in Scotland is still carried out by means of face-to-face meetings between supervisor and probationer. The following account of the practical realities of supervision is based on the two empirical studies which have contributed most to our detailed factual knowledge of Scottish probation practice (Williams, Creamer and Hartley, 1988 (WCH); McIvor and Barry, 1996 (MB)).

Who, when and where? WCH found that in three out of five of the cases the author of the court report was also, subsequently, the probation supervisor and this appeared to make a difference to the approach taken towards supervision. MB reported that 90 per cent of supervision sessions involved only the offender, WCH's comparable figure being 71 per cent. In both studies, where a third party was present, it was generally a member of the probationer's immediate family or a relative. Relatively little use was found to be made of other agencies, although where this was the case (most often in dealing with employment, alcohol, drugs and health issues), these agencies tended to become sole service providers (MB).

National Standards require initial contact within a week and a further eight contacts within three months (weekly for one month and fortnightly thereafter). Following this initial period, contact between supervisor and probationer is expected to take place at not less than monthly intervals

(Social Work Services Group, 1991, para.62.1). The most recent study (MB) reported that two thirds of new probationers were first seen within one week and the initial three-months targets were largely met, although there were variations between areas. Over the whole duration of probation orders, the average period between contacts was reported as slightly less than a month. The average contact reported in the earlier (pre-National Standards) study (WCH) was fortnightly (frequency ranged from one week to twelve weeks), with contact generally decreasing as the probation order progressed. There was no clear evidence to suggest that the seriousness of the case significantly affected the frequency of contact between supervisors and probationers.

The majority of supervision interviews in the earlier study (WCH) took place in the supervisor's office, with less than half of the probationers receiving a home visit during the three-month research period. In general terms, this pattern appears not to have changed significantly: the later study (MB) reports an overall ratio of two office interviews to one home visit, although the variation between different areas was striking. National Standards require two home visits within the initial three months - a ratio of three office interviews to one home visit. Interestingly, the main criticisms made by probationers of the probation supervision experience in the latter study related principally to the fixed pattern of interviews (location, frequency, structure). One in eight standard probation interviews were reported as lasting more than 50 minutes and the most common duration of interview was found to be between 20 and 35 minutes (WCH). The time accorded to interviews varied not so much between probationers as it did for each probationer.

Focus of supervision sessions   MB reported that the main priorities identified in probation action plans were offending behaviour (73 per cent); relationships (50 per cent); practical problems, such as employment (36 per cent), accommodation (23 per cent) and finances (26 per cent); and drug or alcohol problems (29 per cent and 26 per cent respectively). During supervision, practical problems were found to be the most likely additional issues to emerge. They also noted that 83 per cent of their sample were unemployed at the point of sentence. The most commonly reported explanations for offending concerned links with alcohol and drug abuse (34 per cent and 21 per cent respectively); impulsiveness or lack of control (21 per cent); financial gain (19 per cent); and peer group pressure (17 per cent). Finally, the main reasons given in court reports for recommending probation as the preferred option were: to address/monitor offending behaviour itself (62 per cent); to address factors associated with offending, such as drug/alcohol abuse or lack of impulse controls (70 per cent); to provide practical help, such as with employment, accommodation or finances (54 per cent); and to provide general help or support (73 per cent). All of these factors varied significantly with the type of offence and the age and sex of the offender.

WCH found that the most commonly reported main focus of supervision interviews was on family relationships. Offending behaviour also featured relatively frequently, although for over two thirds of the cases studied, this matter was not given priority. Practical and material problems received considerable attention; employment, accommodation and financial difficulties comprised the main focus in two fifths of interviews. Probation supervisors did not appear to focus on one area of difficulty, but rather to deal with a variety of problems in turn. The vast majority of the areas of difficulty which social workers had reported the probationer to be experiencing were actually addressed within the interviews studied. There were, however, an appreciable number of interviews in which the matters addressed did not coincide with these, suggesting that the interviews themselves were surfacing new issues. Although there appeared to be considerable agreement between supervisors and probationers as to the most significant difficulties, the rate of disagreement was such as to suggest at least a measure of conflict regarding the direction and focus of supervision.

Those made subject to probation orders with specific conditions, requiring time-limited participation in intensive probation projects, are likely to have experienced an added focus on issues such as their offending behaviour, drugs/alcohol misuse, use of leisure time, impulse control/problem solving strategies and victim awareness (MB; Wilson, 1997).

The Effectiveness of Probation

There is a growing literature concerning the evaluation of court disposals such as probation and the criteria on which measurement of effectiveness should most appropriately be based (Raynor, 1996; Mair, 1997b). Given the wide range of legitimate probation objectives referred to earlier, attention needs to be paid to such matters as: rates of successful completion (*levels of compliance and enforcement*); individual and aggregated reconviction rates, including changes in offending frequency and patterns (*containment and reformatory effects*); amelioration of social and emotional problems associated with offending (*rehabilitatory effect*); changes in offender attitudes and behaviour (*reformatory effects, risk reduction*); and overall impact on sentencing patterns, especially the use of custody (*diversionary effects*).

Compliance and completion rates McIvor and Barry (1996) reported that nearly one half of probationers in their sample received at least one formal warning and full breach proceedings were taken in one third of cases. Just under one half of the latter resulted from the commission of further offences, a further third for non-compliance with basic requirements (e.g. keeping in contact with the supervisor) and the remainder for breaches of additional requirements. Of those cases breached, the vast majority (83 per cent) resulted in revocation of the probation order and sentence for the original offence. In total, two thirds of the orders were successfully completed, with 16 per cent being discharged early on the basis of good progress.

Reconviction rates Despite important reservations about using reconviction rates as a measure of probation effectiveness (Mair *et al.*, 1997), there is little doubt that, as with all court disposals, recidivism cannot be ignored as a crude indicator of relative success or failure, if only because of media presentation and its impact on public opinion. Two methodological problems, however, frequently intervene to complicate the issue. Firstly, it is not always practical to track offenders for long enough after the end of their probation orders to gain a sufficiently long-term view of their offending. Secondly, to produce reliable figures, probation samples have to be matched not only for case variables such as seriousness, but allowance has to be made for the 'incapacitation effect' of sentences such as imprisonment. In the absence of such controls, interpretation of reconviction figures remains fraught with problems. Furthermore, as Walker (1983) and others have suggested, aggregated reconviction figures may mask important differences in effectiveness with different types and ages of offenders at different points in their offending histories.

Table 12.2 1996 study of reconviction rates

Disposal	Reconviction rate (%)
Standard probation	47
Probation with groupwork requirement	41
Probation with day-centre requirement	63
Imprisonment	63

Source: Kent Probation Service 1996

Table 12.3 1995 study of reconviction rates

Disposal	Reconviction rate (%)
Probation (all types)	41
Community service	37
Imprisonment	64

Source: Cleveland Probation Service 1995

Having made these caveats, it would seem that there is something of a consensus of evidence suggesting that reconviction rates following probation are generally better than those following imprisonment. Tables 12.2 and 12.3 show the results of two recent studies, based respectively on five-year and two-year follow up periods.

There is also evidence that, even in the case of serious offenders sentenced to intensive probation, that the longer term effects are at least as good as those associated with imprisonment, although short-term 'incapacitation effects' are not as readily evidenced (Brownlee, 1995). If relative costs are considered, the argument in favour of community disposals is considerably strengthened. Recent official figures show that current average costs (per month) are: £2,190 (prison), £105 (probation) and £100 (community service) (Home Office, 1995). There is no compelling reason to consider the case to be significantly different in Scotland.

Problems solved or ameliorated In one Scottish study (Williams *et al.*, 1988), one in seven probationers were reported as having had a specific problem resolved and 70 per cent were judged to have shown some improvement in at least one problem area by the end of the three month research period. In contrast, one in six probationers was considered to have shown deterioration in at least one aspect without improvement being apparent in any other. The most common focus in supervision (family relationships) was observed to demonstrate the lowest rate of improvement, whilst the areas which received least attention (such as social isolation) showed the highest improvement rates. This pattern was so ubiquitous that it was concluded that supervisors typically directed their efforts towards amelioration of those problems they had assessed as being the most difficult to resolve.

McIvor and Barry (1996) reported a reduction, over the period of supervision, in unemployment (nine per cent) and a decrease in the number with housing problems (for example, the proportion in independent accommodation increased by 15 per cent). Overall, they recorded a relatively high success rate in the achievement of objectives specified by supervisors in relation to specific probation orders (an average success rate of 62 per cent, ranging from 80 per cent success for provision of practical support, change in attitudes towards offending and promotion of personal development to 38 per cent for accommodation problems and 33 per cent for employment difficulties). Offending objectives were considered to have been achieved in 56 per cent of probation cases studied. Not surprisingly, perhaps, success of this kind was found to be more frequent for early offenders than for persistent offenders. As with most other in-depth studies of this kind, however, the small numbers in each category in both cited studies suggest the need for caution in drawing firm conclusions.

Changes in offenders' attitudes and behaviour The vast majority of probationers in the earlier study (WCH) were reported by their supervisors as having positive attitudes towards the matters addressed in supervision. In all, some 70 per cent of the interviews studied were shown to have been conducted in a positive climate, suggesting that probationers are not on the whole a reluctant group. Supervisors in a fifth of the cases considered that the probationer was at considerable risk of re-offending during the probation period but no clear relationship was found to exist between the perceived level of risk and the stage the probation order had reached. This risk was adjudged to be contained or reduced over the supervision period in all but one of the 36 cases studied.

Supervisors in the later study (MB) generally rated probationers as motivated to address both offending behaviour and other problems. Only a minority were not considered to be thus motivated (one in seven in respect of offending; one in five in respect of other problems). Perceived motivation/positive attitude were found to be closely correlated with positive outcome (successful completion and early discharge), although the nature of this connection was not explored. Women were generally considered to have responded better to probation and younger males less so. Factors most commonly associated with poor response were considered to be continued substance abuse, lack of interest, personal or practical problems and immaturity/lack of self-esteem, rather than active opposition. In addition to a good level of motivation, a fear of/desire to avoid negative consequences (breach proceedings, custodial sentence) was considered to be the main factor associated with a positive outcome.

Asked to assess the risk of further offending, probation supervisors considered 42 per cent unlikely to re-offend and 17 per cent very likely to do so. Young offenders were generally considered to be at higher risk, whereas the converse was the case for women probationers. Nearly three quarters of probationers were considered by their supervisors to be less likely to reoffend at the end of their order than at the start. Motivational and circumstantial factors, both actual and envisaged, appear to have been drawn on by supervisors in making these assessments. It would seem, therefore, that probation supervisors hold positive views concerning the capacity of supervision to modify the attitudes and behaviour of most probationers, provided that they have been correctly identified on the basis of their motivation to tackle their problems.

Impact on sentencing   As noted earlier, the existence (and modest expansion) of community measures such as probation does not itself impact significantly upon the use by courts of these disposals. This may be because sentencers have in mind an informal 'profile' of those most suitable for probation which is relatively independent of the probation policies pursued by social work agencies (Poole, 1991; Ditton and Ford, 1994). Creamer *et al.* (1992a), however, in an evaluation of four early Scottish intensive probation schemes, reported that the introduction of these initiatives was accompanied by a fall in the proportion of cases resulting in a custodial disposal in each of the study areas. The relationship, however, was found not to be straightforward or linear and the authors attributed the effects to both direct and indirect factors, including the creation of what they termed 'an alternative to custody ethos' (Creamer *et al.*, 1992b; Williams and Creamer, 1997).

Developments in Probation Practice in Scotland

The introduction of thematic inspections by the Social Work Services Inspectorate to underpin the 100 per cent funding arrangements, together with ongoing revision of National Objectives and Standards, have focused attention on the importance of *consistency* in probation practice. In time, this process may help to eliminate what, in the past, have been found to be significant variations in the use of probation and the standards of probation supervision (Williams *et al.*, 1988; Ditton and Ford, 1994). Sentencing practice, however, is unlikely to be influenced directly by these processes and so local variations in the use of probation by the courts can be expected to continue. It is, nonetheless, true that sentencers and probation supervisors and the latter's managers have been brought into more constructive dialogue as a result of these developments.

The growing call for probation to be used for higher risk cases has further called into question the *credibility* of this disposal with the courts and the public. In order to overcome the all-too-prevalent view of probation as being 'let off', and the consequent inhibition in its use in more serious cases, both enforcement (i.e. supervision and breach practices) and the nature of the demands made on offenders have been brought into sharper focus. Whilst the 'punishment in the community' debate has not been pursued in quite the same manner in Scotland as south of the border, the greater use of additional probation requirements (especially those involving unpaid work in the community and compensation to victims and those directly restricting the freedom of the probationer) may be seen as indications of this process at work. Although not yet reached, it seems likely that there are natural limits to the use, in this way, of probation as punishment, given its historical development and the social welfare principles underpinning most supervision practice.

Increased interest in the 'What Works?' debate (McGuire, 1995) has led progressively to policy and practice in probation designed to *target* supervision at those considered most likely to be affected positively by the experience and where damaging custodial sentencing can be avoided. Part of the consideration here has been to avoid so-called 'tariff escalation' or 'net-widening' (i.e. inappropriately serious consequences on breach, resulting from use of probation too early in an individual's career, brought about by a predominance of 'welfare' ideology). Accompanying this development has been a growing interest in service-level *monitoring*, designed to provide a readily-available basis for judging whether objectives are actually being met in practice. To generate consistent baselines for comparison, measures of case seriousness such as the DUNSCORE have become widely employed (Creamer *et al.*, 1994).

Finally, there has been an increase in the number of shorter, more focused probation orders, with an emphasis on directly addressing offending behaviour and modifying offender attitudes (for example, towards their victims). This has found expression in the growth of *intensive and enhanced* probation projects, based on group activity rather than individual one-to-one supervision. Indications are that these are proving generally successful (Mair, 1996) but inevitably more resource intensive. Hill (1991) suggests that intensive probation is five times more expensive than standard probation and this alone is likely to impose upper limits on the expansion of schemes of this kind. Another important issue relates to whether sufficient links for the offender exist between the intensive activity and support available whilst on an intensive probation programme and the more infrequent contact with supervisor, characteristic of subsequent probation supervision.

Community Service by Offenders

Nature and Historical Development

Local authority social work departments in Scotland are also responsible for the administration and operation of community service orders, although in practice and in philosophy community service differs significantly from probation. Community service orders require offenders to perform a specified number of hours of unpaid work of benefit to the community. Although the origins of community service can be traced to the USA (see McDonald, 1986), it was first introduced in England and Wales in 1973 on the recommendation of the Advisory Council on the Penal System chaired by Baroness Wootton. Responsibility for the administration of schemes and the supervision of offenders fell to the probation service. Against a background of growing disenchantment with the rehabilitative efficacy of imprisonment, increasing recognition of the detrimental effects of imprisonment upon prisoners and their families, high levels of overcrowding in penal establishments and concern about the increasing costs of incarcerating offenders, the Wootton Committee was set the task of devising alternatives to custodial sentences and expanding the range of non-custodial disposals for offenders who would not, in any case, attract a sentence of imprisonment.

Community service was described by Baroness Wootton as the 'most imaginative and hopeful' of the Committee's recommendations (Advisory Council on the Penal System, 1970, p.v) but it was characterised from the outset by a confusion of purpose (Pease *et al.*, 1975) which could be traced to the Wootton Committee's proposal that the community service order could appeal to different varieties of penal philosophy and could fulfil, though not necessarily simultaneously, a number of sentencing aims. Community service, it was suggested, could punish offenders by requiring that they sacrifice some of their leisure time; it could enable offenders to make amends to the community for their wrongdoing; and it might, in some instances, promote a changed outlook on the part of the offender. There was, in addition, ambiguity about whether community service should be regarded as a sentence in its own right or as a tariff measure intended for use only if a custodial sentence would otherwise be imposed, an ambiguity which was reflected in wide variations in practice (Pease *et al.*, 1975; Vass, 1984). Despite this, community service proved to be a popular new sentencing option in England and Wales and its availability was quickly extended beyond the initial experimental schemes. National standards were introduced in 1989, while the 1991 Criminal Justice Act re-defined community service as a community sentence which could be imposed in conjunction with other community sentences, including probation, with the latter arrangement being referred to as a 'combination order'.

Community service was initially introduced in Scotland in 1977 through the establishment of five pilot schemes and was subsequently extended throughout the country so that community service schemes are now available to all sheriff courts. The 1978 Community Service by Offenders (Scotland) Act enabled courts to order offenders aged 16 years and over who had been convicted of an offence punishable by imprisonment to perform between 40 and 240 hours of unpaid work, subject to the offender being considered suitable for such an order, a work placement being available and the offender consenting to a community service order being imposed. Once sentenced to community service an offender could be asked to perform unpaid work alongside other offenders in a supervised community service work team, in a voluntary or statutory agency setting where the work would be supervised by a member of agency staff or, less usually, in a community service workshop. Offenders who failed to comply with their orders (by, for example, not turning up for work as instructed or failing to inform the supervising social worker of a change of address) could be returned to court and, if the breach was found proven, be fined, have extra hours added or be re-sentenced for the original offence.

In the absence of specific enabling legislation, the first community service orders in Scotland were made as a requirement of probation but the 1978 Act enabled the courts to impose 'stand alone' community service orders, although the opportunity to combine community service with probation supervision - widely referred to as a Section 7 Order after the relevant section in the 1978 Act - was retained. Duguid (1982) identified the main features of community service as punishment, rehabilitation, reparation, community integration and, in comparison to prison sentences, cost effectiveness and concluded from his evaluation of the experimental schemes that this new sentencing option was operating broadly as planned. With partial funding provided by the Scottish Office the availability of community service was extended to other parts of the country and by 1986 community service was available in 50 sheriff court districts. However, despite the issuing of operational guidance by central government, wide variations in practice across, and indeed within, social work departments emerged with respect to issues such as enforcement and breach, placement availability and methods of assessing offenders for orders (McIvor, 1992). Moreover, the funding arrangements were recognised to be preventing the expansion of schemes to enable them better to meet the growing demand for community service orders by the courts.

On 1 April 1989, the Scottish Office assumed full responsibility for the funding of community service and introduced national objectives and standards for community service schemes (Social Work Services Group, 1989), the intention of the former being to increase the availability of community service places to the courts and latter being designed to ensure greater uniformity of practice (Scottish Office, 1987f). One of the main operational objectives of community service would be to ensure that orders were used as a means of diverting offenders from short sentences of imprisonment. Although the primary purpose of the community service order was defined as punishment, the punitive element of the order would lie in the deprivation of the offender's free time and, in accord with research (McIvor, 1992), the work itself would, for both the offender and the beneficiary, be meaningful, constructive and worthwhile.

Use of Community Service by the Courts

General considerations The use of community service by the courts increased steadily from its inception until the implementation of the new funding arrangements, largely as a consequence of the incremental introduction of new schemes. By 1987, the number of persons with a charge proved who receive community service exceeded the number who were given probation and by 1990 three per cent of persons with a charge proved received a community service order. Since 1989, the number of community service orders made annually has continued to increase, from 4,135 in that year to 5,506 in 1995, though the number of probation orders made since 1993 has exceeded the number of community service orders, no doubt as a consequence of the extension of 100 per cent funding and national objectives and standards to cover probation supervision and other statutory social work services to the criminal justice system (Scottish Office, 1997c).

The probation order, which had doubtless suffered through the creation of generic social work departments in 1969, was described by one sentencer as having become by the 1980s the 'sick man of the criminal justice system' (Lothian, 1991). By contrast, however, community service immediately proved to be a popular sentence with the courts (Carnie, 1990). Moreover a programme of research conducted shortly before and after the introduction of 100 per cent funding and national standards had demonstrated the benefits to the community of unpaid work by offenders and the cost effectiveness of this measure in comparison with imprisonment. Offenders were found, in the main, to value their experience of community service and, more crucially, although community service is not an explicitly rehabilitative disposal those who perceived their experience as more worthwhile - for instance, those who had contact with the beneficiaries of their work or acquired new skills - were reconvicted on fewer occasions and were less often reconvicted of offences involving dishonesty than those who found their experience less worthwhile (McIvor, 1992).

Community service has been least successful, it seems, in meeting its operational objective to serve as an alternative to imprisonment. By allowing the courts to impose community service orders upon offenders who had been convicted of offences that were punishable by imprisonment, the legislation lent itself to varied interpretation and use. This had been found to occur in the experimental schemes in England and Wales (Pease *et al.*, 1975) and was a feature of community service from its initial introduction in the Scottish context. Duguid (1982), for example, presented data which suggested that orders made in the second year of the experimental schemes had less often diverted offenders from custodial sentences than those made in the previous twelve months. McIvor (1992) estimated that by the mid-late 1980s only around two-fifths of community service orders in Scotland were direct alternatives to custody and Carnie's (1990) interviews with sheriffs confirmed that they differed according to whether they perceived community service as an alternative to custody or as a sentence in its own right which might usefully be applied across the sentencing tariff. Keen to justify the increased expenditure on community service on the grounds that it replaced the more costly option of imprisonment, and in line with the then Scottish Secretary's apparent commitment to reducing the use of short and unnecessary sentences of imprisonment by the courts, the government's response was to amend this unhelpfully ambiguous aspect of the legislation.

Section 61(3) of the Law Reform (Miscellaneous Provisions) (Scotland) Act 1990, which came into effect on 1 April 1991, sought to ensure that courts imposed community service orders only upon offenders who would otherwise have been dealt with by an immediate sentence of imprisonment. Subsequent research suggests that the diversionary impact of community service has been increased somewhat by the new legalisation, although as many as one- third to two-fifths of orders are still likely to have been made in lieu of other non-custodial penalties (McIvor and Tulle-Winton, 1993).

Age and gender considerations　A significant feature of community service is that it has been used by the courts predominantly as a 'young man's punishment' (Worrall, 1995).　In 1994, for instance, women accounted for 14 per cent of persons sentenced by the Scottish courts but only seven per cent of those given a community service order (Scottish Office, 1995c). A similar picture is found in England and Wales (Hine, 1993).　Gender differences in the relative use of community service are greatest among younger offenders. Thus, in 1993 males aged 16-17 years were more than three times as likely to receive community service in Scotland than were females of the same age (Scottish Office, 1995f).

Although there is some evidence that when age, current offence and criminal history are taken into account, women are as likely to receive community service as men (Mair and Brockington, 1988) and also that women who are referred for community service assessments are as likely to receive community service orders as men so referred (Scottish Office, 1995f), there are, nonetheless, clear differences in the characteristics of men and women referred for and sentenced to community service.　For example, in comparison with men, women referred for a community service assessment in three sheriff court areas in 1992 had fewer previous convictions, were more often first offenders, were facing sentence for less serious offences, had a lower average DUNSCORE rating[4] and were less often thought by the social worker preparing their social enquiry report to be at risk of receiving a custodial sentence (McIvor, forthcoming).　In support of their argument that women offenders in Scotland are being placed at risk of custody because community service does not accord with the conventional welfare model of female offending, Asquith and Samuel (1994) report that in 1988 16-17 year old females against whom a charge was proved were five times as likely to receive a custodial sentence than a community service order.　Males of the same age, on the other hand, were only twice as likely to be detained in custody than ordered to perform community service. More recent revisions of the National Standards for community service have sought partially to redress this imbalance by emphasising equality of access to community service by male and female offenders although it is unlikely that varied and flexible placement provision and the availability of child care facilities alone will tackle what appear to fundamental differences in the construction of male and female criminality.

Developments in Community Service Practice

Other recent developments in respect of community service - very much in accord with central government policy in the mid 1990s - have been characterised by increased emphases upon punitiveness and upon the assessment and management of risk. The Criminal Procedure (Scotland) Act 1995 vested power in the Secretary of State to amend, via statutory instrument, the minimum and maximum numbers of community service hours that could be ordered. As a consequence, the minimum number of hours has been increased to 80 and the maximum to 300, although orders in excess of 240 hours can only be imposed by the sheriff court under solemn procedure or by the high court. The latter adjustment was intended to increase the proportion of orders made as alternatives to custody by encouraging their greater use by the higher courts.[5]

Although the commission of offences against the beneficiaries of community service work is rare (McIvor, 1990b), serious incidents do occasionally occur. The 1995 Act introduced a provision aimed at addressing this issue. The commission of an offence against a recipient of community service, either while the order is being completed or within the subsequent three months, can now be considered by the court as an aggravating factor when passing sentence for the offence. The spirit of this provision, in attempting to provide greater protection for the beneficiaries of community service, is similarly reflected in the most recent version of the National Standard (Social Work Services Group, 1996a) which places an obligation upon local authorities to consider the risk posed by offenders when reaching decisions regarding placement allocation and when supervising offenders on community service orders.

Further changes to the operation of community service were introduced in Circular no. SWSG 12/96 to local authorities (Social Work Services

Group, 1996b). The circular encouraged a greater emphasis upon physically demanding work, with local authorities urged to pay particular attention to the development of environmental improvement projects. It also demanded formal involvement of Victim Support Scotland in the local authorities' strategic planning process to obtain comment on the range of community service placements to be made available. In this way, according to the recent White Paper, *Crime and Punishment* (Scottish Office, 1996f, para.9.7), 'the range of placements provided by local authorities will ... reflect the views of victims of crime and their perceptions of the kind of work which should be undertaken'.

The Social Work Services Group circular further encouraged local authorities to ensure that community service was visible and that projects carried out were known in the local community. To achieve this, social work departments were urged: to seek every opportunity to publicise the benefits produced by community service schemes in the local media; to identify projects, where appropriate, by signs indicating that the work is being or had been carried out by a community service scheme; to ensure that vehicles used by community service schemes are marked to indicate this; and, most controversially, to provide offenders with protective clothing which is clearly and visibly marked with the wording 'community service scheme'. This latter requirement for marking clothing and vehicles has now been revised.

These changes were, in the words of the circular, intended to ensure that community service is 'both visible and testing' and in this latter regard further changes aimed at tightening up the administrative arrangements for community service are likely to be introduced in the next revision of national standards following the Inspectorate report on discipline and enforcement of community service orders (Social Work Services Inspectorate, 1996).

The Supervised Attendance Order

Historical Context

As we noted earlier in this chapter, by the end of the 1980s the Scottish Office had articulated a clear commitment to reducing the use of short periods of imprisonment through encouraging the increased use of community-based alternatives. One issue which appeared to cause particular concern was the number of offenders received into custody as a consequence of fine default: although the percentage of defaulters was low, this group represented a high proportion of prison receptions - 62 per cent of all sentenced receptions in 1992 (Scottish Office, 1993d).

In 1987 a working party on fines and fine default commissioned by the Association of Directors of Social Work (1987) (ASDW) produced a number of recommendations aimed at reducing the unnecessary imprisonment of offenders for failure to pay their fines. Acknowledging that many people default on their fine repayments not because they are unwilling to pay, but because they have insufficient income to meet the instalments imposed, the ADSW working party encouraged further debate on the possible introduction of a unit fine system which would gear the level of monetary penalties more realistically to the offender's ability to pay. The Government agreed that a unit fine system 'might make it easier to mark the gravity of the offence without setting unrealistic fines for poorer offenders' and this, in turn might result in 'fewer defaults, less need for enforcement measures and a reduction in the prison population of fine defaulters' (Rifkind, 1989, p.86).

Other possibilities discussed by the ADSW working party were the introduction of an attendance centre order, or some similar measure, to expand the range of non-custodial options and reduce the courts' reliance upon financial penalties for offenders without the necessary means to pay and to provide the option for courts, in cases of default, to impose another non-custodial sanction such as community service or probation. The extension of community service to fine defaulters - an option which had also been debated in England and Wales (see, for example, West, 1978) - was rejected by the Scottish Office both on practical grounds and on the basis that the credibility of community service was an alternative to custody might be undermined if it were to be used in this way.

A framework for the introduction of unit fines in Scotland was included in the 1990 Law Reform (Miscellaneous Provisions) (Scotland) Bill but failed to gain legislative expression. The subsequent Act did, however, introduce a new option for use by the courts in dealing with fine defaulters. Initially conceived of as an extension to the existing range of non-custodial sanctions, both at first sentence and in cases of fine default, the supervised attendance order was considered appropriate for offenders for whom probation was not deemed necessary but who lacked financial resources to pay a monetary penalty commensurate with the gravity of the offence. The supervised attendance order was subsequently introduced solely as an option for fine defaulters who would otherwise be imprisoned.

Operational Features

The new legislation enabled the courts to order offenders who were in default of their fine repayments, and who faced imprisonment as a result, to undertake 10-60 hours of specified activity supervised by the local authority social work department. The aim of the new order, according to the Social Work Services Group of the Scottish Office (Social Work Services Group, 1991), was 'to provide constructive activity which is likely to include sessions on life skills as well as unpaid work, carried out wherever possible on a group basis'. The supervised attendance order would not be 'geared to tackling individual offending behaviour' but would, like community services, 'constitute a fine on the offender's free time' (para. 6.3). As with probation and community service, the offender's consent was required before a supervised attendance order could be made. Breach of an order was punishable by imprisonment, with the maximum custodial penalty available on breach being determined by the amount of fine outstanding when the supervised attendance order was imposed.

An evaluation of the three pilot schemes (Brown, 1994) suggested that the availability of the supervised attendance order could impact positively upon the numbers of offenders received into custody for fine default, though the study was unable to identify which model - one based upon social education and life skills or one more akin to community service - was more effective. Since then, supervised attendance order schemes have developed across the country - with 100 per cent central government funding - often in partnership with independent sector agencies such as APEX.

Several significant changes to the legislation were, however, contained in the Criminal Procedure (Scotland) Act 1995. These included the removal of the need for the offender's consent prior to the imposition of a supervised attendance order; an increase in the maximum number of hours that could be ordered to 100; and changes in the method of calculating the maximum penalties available on breach. Courts are now able to impose a prison term on breach up to the maximum custodial sentence available to that court. Other provisions contained in the 1995 Act include making the supervised attendance order available on first sentence for 16 and 17 year olds and as the sole penalty for fine default in respect of this age group and, for offenders over 17 years of age, the sole penalty available to the courts where the amount of fine outstanding is less than £500.

In 1995-6 1,400 supervised attendance orders were made in Scotland, with the expectation that this figure would rise to 3,000 in 1996-7 (Scottish Office, 1996f), and the expansion of this measure was identified as a service priority in the Social Work Services Group National Planning Statement for 1997-8. Certain provisions in the 1995 Act could have a significant impact on the number of prison receptions for fine default, which currently constitute around 40 per cent of all admissions under sentence to penal establishments in Scotland, but they have yet to be implemented and to do so would have enormous practical and resource implications for central and local government. Despite the inherent potential for the supervised attendance order to offer a more constructive response to fine default and to widen the repertoire of disposals available to the courts for young offenders who often have no income or other means of financial support (Kennedy and McIvor, 1992), the ability of this relatively new measure to impact significantly upon the prison population will be adversely influenced to an unknown extent by the new powers vested in the courts to impose custodial sentences on breach which are far in excess of those which would have followed from the earlier requirement to link the length of custodial penalty imposed to the amount of fine outstanding.

Community Disposals - Contemporary Issues

A number of recurrent themes can be discerned within contemporary criminal justice social work policy in Scotland. The first is a lessening preoccupation with the concept of risk of custody and an increased emphasis upon the assessment and management of risk of re-offending and risk to the public, highlighted in the 1997-8 National Planning Statement as a key priority for training on a national level.

The mixed economy is a second area which is likely to be accorded greater priority, with the independent sector becoming increasingly involved in what Christie (1993) has termed the 'crime control industry'. The introduction of 100 per cent funding and national standards served to formalise the role of the independent sector in the provision of services and development of new initiatives, though not to the extent that it has been formalised in England and Wales where probation services are now expected to devote five per cent of their budget to partnership projects. Local authorities continue to hold statutory responsibility for the supervision of offenders, but they are also encouraged to make the most effective use of voluntary organisations and to stimulate new initiatives from these organisations where this seems appropriate. Local government re-organisation has posed fresh challenges to local authorities to maintain and enhance the quality and range of services they provide to the criminal justice system. To do so will often require partnerships to be developed between the new authorities and independent sector service providers and between local authorities.

Increased accountability is a third theme which characterises community based social work disposals in Scotland. The introduction of associated National Objectives and Standards was, in essence, aimed at increasing the accountability of criminal justice social work services by ensuring that they were provided in accordance with certain nationally agreed criteria. To encourage compliance with the procedural aspects of national standards, monitoring arrangements were introduced at the local and national level and a system of inspections has been introduced.

Although it would appear that many of the developments which have taken place in recent years have had little empirical grounding, it is also the case that community based social work disposals currently operate within a context of both increased optimism regarding the ability of supervision to impact positively upon offenders' attitudes and behaviour and increased understanding of what the most effective elements of the supervisory relationship might be. The crucial test over coming years will be whether their effectiveness in reducing re-offending and protecting the public from harm can be demonstrated and whether the support and confidence of the public, the criminal justice system and policy makers consolidated and sustained.

Notes

The bulk of the work reported on by both authors in this chapter has been funded by awards made by the Home Department of The Scottish Office. Bryan Williams wishes to acknowledge the long-term assistance of Anne Creamer in collecting and analysing much of the data included in the chapter and that of Linda Hartley in contributing to the studies.

1. The current regime is set out in the Criminal Procedure (Scotland) Act 1995, ss. 228-234 and sch.6.
2. Criminal Procedure (Scotland) Act 1995, s.228(1).
3. Scottish Office statistics show the number of probation orders made by Scottish courts to be 3053 in 1971; 2364 in 1977; and 2757 in 1985.
4. A standardised method for assessing risk of custody based upon key sentencing variables. Developed by Creamer *et al.* (1993), a higher Dunscore value indicates a greater risk of attracting a custodial sentence.
5. A similar intent lay behind the withdrawal of community service as a sentencing option in the district courts.

13 Imprisonment and Other Custodial Sentences

JIM MCMANUS

Introduction

Imprisonment, for those over 21, and detention, for those under 21, is the ultimate sanction available to the Scottish criminal courts. Far from all persons in prison are serving sentences for crime however. Between 20 and 25 per cent of the average daily population in Scotland's prisons have been remanded to prison awaiting trial or after conviction pending sentence. A further six or seven per cent are in prison in default of payment of fines or compensation orders. Smaller numbers are detained under the Immigration Acts, pending the outcome of deportation proceedings, or for contempt of court, or because a sheriff has decreed that they are between the ages of 14 and 16 and 'unruly'. Custody is thus used for a variety of purposes and it should come as no surprise therefore that the only consistent principle which appears to underlie the use of imprisonment is a felt need to keep persons in secure conditions. The reasons for this need can be many and varied.

Determining the rationale for the use of imprisonment in particular types of case is only to a very limited extent facilitated by reference to the legislation enabling imprisonment and to the case law developed by our courts. Thus 'unruly' children can be sent to prison only when they are so unruly or depraved that they cannot be dealt with by a place of safety order (Criminal Procedure (Scotland) Act 1975, ss. 24, 297); persons awaiting trial or sentence can only be sent to prison when the Wheatley guidelines on bail are followed;[1] fine and compensation order defaulters benefit from a variety of protections before imprisonment can be imposed (Criminal Procedure (Scotland) Act 1975, ss. 396, 398, 400; Criminal Justice (Scotland) Act 1980, s.41); and civil imprisonment is available in only very restricted circumstances, imprisonment for debt alone in Scotland having been abolished in 1932. The law regulating the use of imprisonment for convicted offenders also reflects some confusion in thinking. Thus offenders under the age of 21 cannot be sentenced to detention unless the sentencing judge is of the opinion that no other sentence is appropriate and before reaching this conclusion the judge must consider the background of the offender (Criminal Procedure (Scotland) Act 1975, ss.207, 415). Persons over the age of 21 cannot be sentenced to imprisonment for the first time before the court has received a background report and the sentencing court in summary cases must certify the reason why it does not consider that a non-custodial disposal is appropriate (Criminal Justice (Scotland) Act 1980, s.41). The law does not, however, define 'appropriate'. The confusion and potential for circularity become evident when we note that a community service order can only be imposed as a direct alternative to custody (Community Service By Offenders Act 1978, as amended). Since a summary court cannot think of imprisonment if any other disposal is appropriate, community service orders can never, in strict legal logic, be used by other than the solemn courts. As to the length of custodial sentences, the law provides for a mandatory life sentence for those convicted of murder. Otherwise it confines itself to establishing maximum periods for statutory offences with no indication given of the factors to be used in decided the actual periods. Decisions of the courts, including the court of criminal appeal, do not fill this lacuna. The appeal court in particular has gone to some lengths to stress that it makes decisions in individual cases and has refused the invitation to lay down general sentencing guidelines (Nicholson, C.H.B., 1992; chapter 10).

Philosophy of Imprisonment in Scotland

It should come as no surprise, therefore, that there is no single, agreed, coherent philosophy of imprisonment in Scotland today. Indeed, apart from the very early days when imprisonment was only used for holding debtors and persons awaiting trial or execution of sentence, there never has been. As a sentence in its own right, imprisonment is of recent origin, a response to the abolition of transportation and one which, for the most part, has not been thought out on any philosophical basis (Cameron, 1983).

It is, of course, possible to link developments in the history of imprisonment to prevailing philosophies of imprisonment in the world at large and to detect the impact of some of these philosophies on particular prisons or through particular people in Scotland. Thus, for example, in the early days the notion of 'lesser eligibility' - the idea that conditions in prison had to be worse than the worst conditions outside - dominated the prisons run by the Burghs. This was perhaps motivated more by parsimony in relation to criminal detainees, for whose upkeep the Burghs themselves were responsible, and by a desire not to throw good money after bad in relation to debtors, who had to be paid for by their creditors, than by any conscious policy developed by the individual Burghs. Once control over prisons was centralised, the absence of any notion of what to do with prisoners became quickly clear and led to the Elgin Committee (1900), the Scottish equivalent of the Gladstone Committee of 1895 in England. Elgin provided a clear agenda for change in Scottish prisons, introducing constructive work and improving material conditions. But that Committee suffered from the limitations which have afflicted and affected every reformer since the start of the century - it had to start with the prisons as they already were and do something with them.

Existing buildings, personnel and prisoners impose severe limitations on what can be envisaged. Buildings designed to maximise security, surveillance or control cannot readily be transformed to perform small group therapeutic functions. Staff recruited for brawn may not be the best at inter-personal skills. Prisoners used to an ordered regime where all that is required of them is obedience might well be suspicious if offered choices. Changing the kind of culture which establishes itself in a prison setting without radically altering these components is virtually an impossible task.

Indeed there have been few opportunities for a fresh start in the history of Scottish prisons. Thus when well motivated individual reformers came along, they too were circumscribed by the history they had inherited. Brebner, Governor of Glasgow Bridewell, made his mark both nationally and internationally and certainly improved the quality of staff in Scottish prisons (Coyle, 1982). He was not, however, able to revolutionise them. Until the 1960s there was little public debate on the issue. Perhaps the interest in prisons reflected the number of people confined in them? This peaked at just over 3,000 in 1910 and did not reach that level again until 1960, by which time the possibility of a new Brebner was buried in bureaucracy and the beginnings of strong political involvement in the penal area were seen.

Borstal, an explicitly therapeutic regime for young offenders, had come to Scotland in 1909 (Prevention of Crime Act 1908). The continued belief that young offenders were somehow more 'saveable' than their older counterparts gave rise to plans to separate them totally and these plans reached fruition with the establishment of detention centres and young offender institutions in the 1960s. The Detention Centre, with its 'short sharp shock' approach, was based on an overtly deterrent philosophy with the idea that young first offenders could be taught some discipline and would thereafter avoid crime. Young Offender Institutions, however, were a junior replica of adult prisons with no clear philosophy of their own. The dominant penal philosophy outside the prisons in the 1960s was clearly rehabilitative, but its actual impact on Scottish Prisons was at best piecemeal. Thus there were some experiments with group work in a variety of establishments, and the famous Barlinnie Special Unit emerged in 1972 as a therapeutic community response to the prisoners identified as the most intractable. The vast majority of prisoners throughout the 1960s and 70s probably never noticed the difference.

The treatment philosophy did spill over into legislation concerning prisoners, but not immediately in connection with prison regimes. The Criminal Justice Act 1967 created the possibility of prisoners serving over 18 months being released on parole if they could satisfy the Executive, through the Parole Board, that their response to imprisonment was such as to justify their early release to 'serve the remainder of their sentence in the community'. The necessity of writing detailed reports on prisoners eligible for consideration for parole sparked a recruitment campaign to bring into the prison service people with greater educational qualifications than had hitherto been required. It also required staff of all kinds in prison to begin to focus attention on factors which might reduce the incidence of reoffending. At the same time, however, a series of spectacular escapes from English prisons, involving the great train robbers and ultimately the spy, George Blake, greatly increased the emphasis placed on security in prisons throughout Britain. Resolving the potential conflicts between security and therapeutic regimes was an issue left to prisons themselves to address.

As Figure 13.1 shows, Scottish prisons had to resolve the issue in the face of a rapid rise in the average daily population between 1963 and 1969. From 3,200 in 1963, the population rose to over 5,000 in 1969, a rise of over 50 per cent. It should not come as a surprise, therefore, that little time was spent in resolving any matters other than the immediate pressure on accommodation. Numbers remained at around 5,000 from 1969 onwards and the Scottish Prison Service became, in effect, a fire fighting organisation, struggling to cope with disturbances, riots, hostage taking and occasional escapes.

Figure 13.1 Average daily population in Scottish prisons

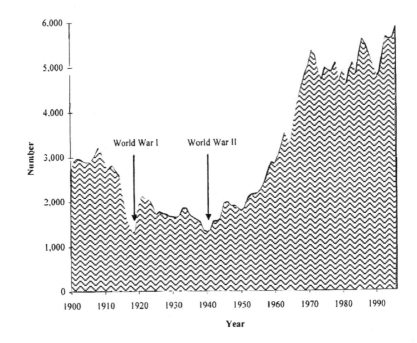

Source: Scottish Office (1997j).

Meanwhile, in a world somewhat apart from Scottish prisons, the 'treatment model' of imprisonment was ousted from its dominant position in the league table of penal philosophies and replaced by the 'justice model' (American Friends Service Committee, 1971). In its most sterile form, the justice model asserted that the only right the State had was to deprive people of their freedom, in proportion to the seriousness of the crime they had committed, lock them up for that period and then let them go. There were, of course, more positive forms which emphasised that, despite being deprived of their liberty, prisoners remained fully human beings, entitled to respect as such. Prisons should thus respect these rights and stop attempting to coerce people to be different. While there are good philosophical arguments for the move from treatment to justice, the fundamental flaw (though some would argue it was a saving grace) of the treatment model in practice was its failure to deliver results - reconviction rates were apparently unaffected by many of the programmes of the 1960s and 70s.

The advance of the justice model was greatly helped by the increasing intervention of courts in ruling on aspects of daily life in prisons. Domestic courts had traditionally been reluctant to become involved in what they saw as internal matters of discipline. Lord Denning summed up their approach beautifully when he stated that:

> if the courts were to entertain actions by disgruntled prisoners the governor's life would be made intolerable. The discipline of the prison would be undermined.[2]

The new approach is best summed up by Lord Wilberforce:

> A convicted prisoner, inspite of his imprisonment, retains all rights not taken away expressly or by necessary implication.[3]

The UK's acceptance of the right of individual petition to the European Court of Human Rights was a crucial factor in altering domestic courts' attitudes and the final result was a manifest about-turn for the UK courts and prison system. Changes were bound to follow (see McManus, 1995).

The courts on their own would have secured some changes in Scotland, but other factors combined to hasten the end of the fire-brigading era. Riots and hostage takings grew in number throughout 1986 and 1987 and it was abundantly clear that there was a need for some new initiative. Those charged with the management of the Scottish Prison Service provided the initiative themselves. There was, at that time, a particularly strong grouping of senior governors who were imbued with both contemporary penological thinking and modern management approaches to running organisations. They proposed a proactive stance in the management of prisons, starting from an understanding of their function and developing a strategic approach to maximising the potential for fulfilling the functions in a cost efficient and professional way.

At each stage of this process, the Scottish Prison Service published 'position papers', clearly setting out the basis of the proposed actions and the plans for implementing the proposals. These papers, which continue to be published in the shape of corporate plans by the Agency which the

Scottish Prison Service has become, started with 'Custody and Care' in 1988, digressed a little in 'Assessment and Control' in 1989 and found their fullest expression in 'Opportunity and Responsibility' in 1990.   The 'Mission Statement' of the Scottish Prison Service (1997) neatly encapsulates this philosophy:

> The aim of the Scottish Prison Service is:
> (i)   to keep in custody those committed by the courts;
> (ii) to maintain good order in each prison;
> (iii) to care for prisoners with humanity; and
> (iv) to provide prisoners with opportunities to exercise personal responsibility and to prepare for release.

Thus the Scottish Prison Service does not hide the fact that its primary task is custodial, but espouses a positive notion of what might be done with the time spent in custody, while stressing that this is ultimately a matter of choice for prisoners.   Implicitly, therefore, it adopts the main tenets of the justice model - and has an explicit commitment to fairness, justice and openness in the process - but accepts responsibility for offering prisoners viable choices to spend their time constructively.

As with all modern management practices, especially in the public sector, mission statement aims and objectives go along with performance measures and accountability.   In developing such measures, the Scottish Prison Service has concentrated on the number of escapes, the cost per prisoner place, the number of assaults within prisons, access to night sanitation for prisoners and the amount of available opportunities for prisoners' self development.   Successes have been recorded in almost every area, but progress on developing programmes for prisoners has not been as speedy as had been anticipated.   It is clear that the major political interest has been in the achievement of the targets relating to escapes and costs, and the success of the Scottish Prison Service in these areas has been notable, but unless significant advances are seen in the areas of quality of life and prisoner programmes there is a danger that the vision contained in 'Opportunity and Responsibility' will be lost.   The increasing tendency for criminal justice in general, and prisons in particular, to be used as a political football, discussed further later in this chapter, has undoubtedly distorted the consistent implementation of the philosophy espoused by the Scottish Prison Service.   It is to be hoped that the organisation's commitment to the full package will be maintained.

Trends in Imprisonment in Scotland

The Scottish Prison Service has thus taken a leading role in developing a coherent philosophy of what imprisonment is for and has made some important advances in implementing its philosophy. Unfortunately, however, it is has had to do much of this work on its own and in isolation from other parts of the criminal justice system in Scotland. Indeed there must be a serious question about whether there is such a thing as a criminal justice *system* in Scotland. The word 'system' implies co-operation and co-ordination between or among component parts, with at least some shared understanding of aims and objectives and a commitment to working together to achieve common goals. There is little evidence of any of this in criminal justice in Scotland. Thus, while the Scottish Prison Service has its own idea of what to do with those for whom it has to provide, it has no say over who is committed to prison and for how long. It cannot therefore predict even the number of people for whom it will have to cater, never mind their characteristics and needs. If inappropriate people, for example the mentally ill, are sent to prison, the Scottish Prison Service has to cater for them at least until, in the best case scenario, it can secure their transfer to a mental hospital. If more people are sent than there are beds available, more beds have to be found. It people are sent for such short periods that no meaningful intervention is possible, the role of the Scottish Prison Service can only be that of custodian. Unless the Scottish Prison Service can begin to influence those who have control over entry to prison, it will always be subject to have its best plans frustrated. There are currently few fora for discussing, never mind resolving, this problem.

We saw above that there was a significant rise in the prison population from the mid 1960s onwards. From 1969 the average daily population has hovered around the 5,000 mark. Since 1992, it has been consistently over 5,000 and reached 5,862 in 1996. As seen in chapter 2, these figures bear no direct relationship to the amount of crime in Scotland. Discerning the true causes of variations in numbers committed to prison over time is virtually impossible; all that can safely be concluded is that imprisonment has become an increasingly popular option for the courts and that this tendency is likely to continue unless some positive steps are taken to alter it.

The average daily population figure is a very general measure of the use of imprisonment. Much more information can be obtained by breaking the figures down and focusing on the number of committals to prison, the reason for them and the average length of stay each year. Thus, the relevant Scottish figures from 1989 to 1996 are contained in Tables 13.1 to 13.4.

There are some significant issues worth drawing out from these figures. First, in 1996, a total of 13,151 people were received on a direct sentence, while 23,976 persons entered prison on remand or in default of payment of a fine. The majority of receptions were thus coming to custody not as a punishment, nor as the first chosen punishment of the court. Most penal philosophy is thus irrelevant to the majority of persons committed to prison in Scotland.

Second, the 23,976 non-direct receptions spent an average of 17.5 days each in custody. It is difficult to imagine what possible benefits accrued to any of them in such a short time. It is much easier to outline the potentially negative effects on their individual lives, and on their families, of the disruption entailed in their imprisonment. In terms of public protection, it might be difficult to persuade the tax payer that the £1,340 which it costs to keep someone in prison for 17.5 days could not be better spent.

Third, while the average sentence imposed on direct receptions into custody has increased each year since 1989, 42 per cent (5,629 out of 13,151) of those directly sentenced to custody in 1996 were sentenced to three months or less. Again, it might be thought that the benefit in terms of increased community safety is very small, the financial cost to the community disproportionately high and the chances of achieving significant change in the prisoner in such a short period virtually non existent.

Table 13.1 Remand receptions

	Numbers	Average Time (Days)
1989	14281	19.7
1990	15168	18.1
1991	13127	21.4
1992	13548	23.7
1993	13412	25.8
1994	14922	24.8
1995	14922	25.6
1996	14997	24.4

Source: Scottish Office (1997j)

Table 13.2   Fine defaulters received into custody

	Numbers	Average Sentence Imposed (Days)
1989	9154	21
1990	6835	23
1991	7909	24
1992	8339	23
1993	9616	13
1994	8875	11
1995	7509	11
1996	8999	11

Source: Scottish Office (1997j)

Table 13.3   Adult direct receptions to penal establishments by length of sentence

	1989	1990	1991	1992	1993	1994	1995	1996
< 30 days	224	243	287	245	310	248	269	394
30 days	885	803	852	793	804	484	559	580
31 to 59 days	61	49	74	68	81	65	61	72
60 days/2 month	1387	1268	1310	1212	1200	1088	1002	1104
61 to 89 days	14	14	21	14	29	19	34	44
90 days/3 month	1826	1822	1886	1995	2304	2203	1966	2127
> 3/< 6 months	875	945	1008	1369	1418	1546	1479	1846
6 months/< 2 yrs	1738	1781	1849	2119	2384	2859	2475	2778
2 years/< 4 yrs	292	308	310	308	453	444	448	559
4 yrs + (not life)	287	293	335	395	428	368	412	496

Source: Scottish Office (1997j)

Table 13.4   Under 21 direct receptions to penal establishments by length and type of sentence 1989-96 Scotland

	1989	1990	1991	1992	1993	1994	1995	1996
< 30 days	49	75	76	52	52	57	63	89
30 days	225	240	175	169	173	112	101	126
31 to 59 days	29	23	25	20	24	24	11	30
60 days/2 month	464	405	298	354	348	253	262	307
61 to 89 days	15	6	12	6	14	6	14	15
90 days/3 month	755	751	581	891	805	712	655	741
> 3/< 6 months	346	353	335	488	463	489	502	538
6 months/< 2 yrs	655	723	706	862	925	957	950	993
2 years/< 4 yrs	77	82	93	115	163	158	116	170
4 yrs + (not life)	29	55	49	72	82	75	86	81

Source: Scottish Office (1997j)

There is a clear need for greater rationality in the use made of imprisonment. It is a financially expensive option. It is also socially expensive. Without clear evidence of benefits to match these costs, it is difficult to make a case for the present level of use in Scotland. For purely practical considerations, it is manifestly unfair on the Scottish Prison Service that there is no limit placed on the number of people it may be required to detain. For deeper moral reasons, much greater consideration requires to be given to the bigger question of what prison can and cannot do and to establishing a mechanism for ensuring that it is only used for appropriate cases. The Scottish Prison Service has taken the lead in proposing a philosophy of imprisonment. The initiative will flounder unless those who decide which persons are sent to prison listen to and learn from those running the prisons. The whole business requires co-ordination so that the component parts of the criminal justice service begin to act like a system.

Parole and Early Release

The recent history of legislation governing the systems of parole and early release in Scotland is an excellent example of many of the problems which affect Scottish prisons. The story shows the lack of a consistent and coherent underlying philosophy, for both early release and imprisonment itself, and the impact of political interest in prison issues which in turn sometimes appears to have no regard to penological thinking, practical issues or, indeed, common sense.

A system of remission of prison sentences was first introduced during the World Wars with the primary intention of freeing prisoners early for service in the Armed Forces. While it was always talked of in Scotland as a privilege, early release soon became in effect a right. Thus by 1952 all determinate sentence prisoners were entitled to unconditional release after having served two thirds of their total sentence, with a minimum sentence of 5 days (Prison (Scotland) Rules 1952, Rule 35). Remission could be forfeited as a punishment for disciplinary offences in prison and indeed its major function had now become that of a mechanism for the maintenance of good order in prisons.

Parole, a system of discretionary release for prisoners serving over 18 months who had served at least one third of their sentence and were judged by the Parole Board to be suitable for conditional early release, was introduced in 1967, at the height of the treatment approach to criminal justice (Criminal Justice Act 1967).

Neither system seems to have provoked much public interest in Scotland at any stage, though there were occasional, minor, concerns expressed when a parolee was convicted of a further serious offence while on parole. It is probably the case that the vast majority of people was not aware of either parole or remission and those who were, were not very concerned about their operation. At the Conservative Party Conference in 1983, this all began to change. The newly appointed Home Secretary, Mr Leon Brittan, used the opportunity to announce that he was introducing a much more restrictive policy in relation to the grant of parole to categories of prisoners serving sentences of over five years. The Scottish Secretary, Mr George Younger, had no such plans at that time, but followed suit some twelve months later despite the fact that there seemed to be little public agitation for change in Scotland.

The introduction of the restrictive policy in Scotland was highlighted by some commentators as a cause of the disturbances experienced in Scottish prisons from 1985 onwards. Whether or not it was a factor, it remains true that prisoners and prison staff alike first heard of the change when it was announced by the media, nobody, including the Parole Board for Scotland, having been consulted in advance of the announcement in Parliament.

Scotland, it seemed, was simply following where England, for the sake of assuaging the Conservative Party Conference by being 'tough on crime', had led. Parole was potentially becoming a party political issue.

Opposition to the new policy continued to be expressed by the Parole Board as well as by voluntary organisations, prison governors and prisoners. Similar opposition was mobilised in England and Wales and the eventual government response was the establishment, in 1987, of a review body in each of the jurisdictions to examine all aspects of early release arrangements. The Scottish Committee, under the Chairmanship of Lord Kincraig, reported in 1989 (Kincraig, 1989) and the majority of its recommendations were implemented in the Prisoners and Criminal Proceedings (Scotland) Act 1993 with effect from November 1993.

The Kincraig Committee had carried out a thorough review of both the theory and the practice of parole and early release. It considered, but rejected, arguments for the total abolition of parole made by adherents of the justice model, though its recommendations did concentrate on giving real effect to the exact sentence of the court ('real time sentencing' in the American jargon) and to improving procedural aspects of the review procedure. Kincraig thought evidence of sufficient change in a prisoner, or in the authorities' knowledge of a prisoner, would require considerable time to accumulate. Parole eligibility, therefore, could only sensibly be assessed after a much longer period than the existing minimum of one year. Kincraig suggested that the doubling of this minimum might be appropriate, that parole should only be available after one half of the sentence had been served, instead of one third under the existing provisions, and accordingly that the minimum sentence which should give rise to parole eligibility should be five years. The 1993 Act reduced this to four years but accepted that the minimum period to be spent in prison should be one half of the total sentence.

Remission on sentences under the existing parole threshold was one third of the total sentence and this remission was also granted to prisoners above the parole threshold who were not granted parole. On release at the two thirds stage, there was no further liability under the original sentence (except for young offenders sentenced to more than six months, who were on licence for six or twelve months, depending on sentence, and subject to recall to custody for three months if they breached their licence). Kincraig suggested that all prisoners serving less than five years should be released after serving one half of their sentence but liable to automatic recall to serve the outstanding portion of their sentence if convicted of an offence punishable by imprisonment before the expiry of the total sentence. The 1993 Act accepted the general proposal, subject to the four year rather than five year maximum, but retained the power of prison governors to add days to a sentence for disciplinary offences in prison and made the recall decision on reconviction subject to the discretion of the judge sentencing for the new offence.

The 1993 Act thus generally followed the philosophy as well as the detailed recommendations of Kincraig and was, if anything, slightly more liberal than Kincraig had been. But the Kincraig remit had excluded examination of sentencing policy and the Committee had been required, therefore, to try to make sense of sentence implementation without being able to look at the motivation behind particular sentences. It chose to concentrate on considerations of public safety and likelihood of reoffending in deciding how long people should serve in prison. There is no way of knowing if these are the factors in the sentencer's mind in the first place (see chapter 10).

It seemed, however, that the provisions of the 1993 Act were not to last very long. A new Secretary of State for Scotland was appointed in 1996 and, despite being of the same government as had introduced the 1993 Act, he quickly decided that fundamental change was required to both parole and remission. A consultation paper was issued in January 1996 inviting views on proposals to abolish the parole system altogether and to reduce the minimum period of early release to one sixth of sentence, which would have to be earned (Scottish Office, 1996i). This was quickly followed by a White Paper confirming the Government's intention to go ahead with the implementation of its proposal (Scottish Office, 1996f). It is thought that almost all respondents to these papers opposed the proposals, on both practical and theoretical grounds, but the proposals were translated into legislation in the Crime and Punishment (Scotland) Act 1997, one of the last measures to pass through Parliament before the General Election of 1997 and whose passage was thus the result of negotiations between the Government and the Opposition.

The relevant part of the 1997 Act (Part III, Chapter 1) has not been implemented and Clause 89 of the recently introduced Crime and Disorder (Scotland) Bill 1997 proposes to repeal the part in its entirety. The provisions of the 1993 Act might thus have the opportunity of coming fully into effect, though political interest seems likely to continue in this area.

Conclusion

Scottish prisons have made some considerable advances since 1988. A spirit of openness and acceptance of accountability pervades the system, in marked contrast to the previous closed world behind the walls. The Prisons and Young Offenders Institutions (Scotland) Rules 1994 give legislative force to many of the promises made in 'Opportunity and Responsibility'. Thus, for example, prisoners are now generally entitled to be given reasons for decisions affecting them in prison and have access to a complaints system which includes, in the Scottish Prisons Complaints Commission, an independent Complaints Commissioner. The Service is striving to introduce a sentence planning programme to enable prisoners to make choices geared to maximising the utility of their time in custody. The new spirit is to encourage and enable, rather than coerce, prisoners to make use of these opportunities. The changes are of course taking some time to implement, but the managerial will is clearly there to complete the process.

But the Scottish Prison Service cannot, on its own, change the face of imprisonment. If only to obtain better value for money from the £164m net current expenditure provision for prisons in 1997-98, there is an urgent need for a review of the use of imprisonment within the criminal justice system. To be effective, any review would need to include all the actors in the criminal justice system and to be able to make recommendations which bind them together, making use of prisons for what prisons are good at and doing something else with the majority of persons currently sent to prison in Scotland.

Notes

1. Smith v McC 1982 S.C.C.R. 115.
2. Becker v Home Office [1972] 2 Q.B. 407.
3. Raymond v Honey [1983] 1 A.C. 1.

14 Preventing Offending by Children and Young People in Scotland

STEWART ASQUITH AND MIKE DOCHERTY

Introduction

Since the Kilbrandon Committee, set up to consider:

> the provisions of the law of Scotland relating to the treatment of juvenile delinquents and juveniles in need of care or protection or beyond parental control and, in particular, the constitution, powers and procedures of the courts dealing with such juveniles

reported in 1964, there have been at least three recurrent themes in the search for appropriate strategies for dealing with children and young people in Scotland who offend. One is the pendulum-like swing between a punitive approach on the one hand and a more welfare based philosophy on the other. The Kilbrandon committee itself had recognised that even though a welfare philosophy could provide the basis for dealing with the majority of young offenders, a number should still be dealt with in court and could rightly be the subject of punitive measures.

The second is the failure, despite the commitment given in the Kilbrandon Report, to implement a truly preventive approach to reducing the numbers of children at risk of becoming offenders later in life. This does not of course apply only to Kilbrandon as the failure to implement recommended preventive strategies has been characteristic of the political response to many reports in the social welfare field generally.

The third is the introduction of measures, policies and practices to deal with those who offend which may owe more to political ideology than to systematic and rigorous research based evidence. The introduction of measures to deal with offenders, and particularly, children and young people who offend, which are not based on substantiated research and other evidence is of course not new. Recently too, Lord McCluskey, in the House of Lords (BBC News February 12th, 1997) criticised the then Secretary of State for Scotland for making radical proposals for change in the judicial, criminal justice and penal systems with no foundation in evaluation or research. However, with specific reference to dealing with young offenders, the danger is that such measures, where they are more punitively oriented, may well conflict with the main philosophy underpinning juvenile justice in Scotland - in this case, the welfare philosophy advocated by Kilbrandon.

In this chapter, we intend to consider the extent to which these three themes are reflected in current developments in juvenile justice and the prevention of delinquency in Scotland. Further, they will be considered in the context of the Children (Scotland) Act 1995, local government reorganisation, devolution in Scotland and the changing political climate generally.

Our argument will be that a number of the more recent proposals for change in how we deal with children who offend are far from evidence based; that the integrity of the Kilbrandon philosophy is threatened; that preventive strategies which seek to reduce the risk of children becoming offenders in later life provide a practical, meaningful and potentially effective response; and that the drive in many parts of Europe to a more preventive approach provides an appropriate basis for future developments in Scottish juvenile justice. Our concern is less with the way in which the system currently operates but addresses broader issues pertinent to the very philosophy on which a truly preventive philosophy might be based.

Much recent literature (see, for example, Asquith *et al.*, 1998) points to the convergence of explanations of offending by children and young people on the nature of their early life experiences. This has a number of implications not only for future developments in juvenile justice but more broadly in terms of the life opportunities, experiences and future development of children. Truly preventive policies have the potential to address those factors experienced by children early in their lives which put them at later risk. The focusing of intervention early in the lives of children and the shift of political will to long term objectives could also substantially reduce the cost borne by society not only financially but in other ways. In many respects, the philosophy of the Scottish Children's Hearings anticipated this convergence of interest in promoting a preventive philosophy.

The Kilbrandon Approach

In 1964, the report of the Kilbrandon Committee was published and although the recommendations contained therein were seen to be radical and controversial at the time, they provided, with some modifications, the philosophical basis of the 1968 Social Work (Scotland) Act and the principles on which juvenile justice in Scotland has been based for almost 30 years.

The Scottish Children's Hearings System was introduced in 1971[1] and since then the general acceptance of the Hearing as an appropriate forum for the making of decisions about children has been reflected in the absence of any vigorous or concerted arguments either in favour of its abolition or in rejection of the philosophy on which it is based. This is despite the fact that it introduced a radical and unique system of justice for children and juveniles, in that the Children's Hearings system is not simply a justice system designed to deal with children who commit offences but is a system of justice for children in which their welfare is the primary concern.

Under the Hearings system, the majority of children who offend will be referred initially to a Reporter whose function is to determine whether the child referred may be in need of compulsory measures of care and consequently whether the child should be referred on to a Children's Hearing. The committal of an offence is in itself not sufficient reason for a child to be referred on to a Hearing since the underlying principle is always whether the child is in need of compulsory measures of care. Children aged up to 16 (or 18 if they are already in the system) may be dealt with in a Children's Hearing.

Though Scotland has had this radical system of justice, based on welfare principles, for over 25 years now, it has to be pointed out that children may still be prosecuted in Scotland though this involves around only 200 children a year. Children may be prosecuted if they have committed a number of stated offences including: technical offences such as road traffic offences; offences committed with an older offender; and serious offences including rape, arson and murder. Although the majority of children are dealt with in the Hearings system, the age of criminal responsibility in Scotland remains at eight.[2]

The Children's Hearings are administrative tribunals and not courts of law. Thus the only decisions that can be made by a Children's Hearing are whether the child is in need of compulsory measures of care and what such measures should be. There is no jurisdiction over the question of guilt or innocence and where facts are disputed, the case must be referred to court. A central feature of the Hearing system is also that the decisions are made by a panel of three lay members of the public, rather than the judiciary, in as informal a setting and procedure as is possible involving the family and child.

What made the recommendations of the Kilbrandon report so controversial was the rejection of a court based system of justice as inappropriate for children. Its unique solution to the basic tension faced by a juvenile court was to recommend the complete separation of responsibility for deciding on guilt or innocence from that of deciding upon appropriate welfare measures. Two main assumptions underpinned the main recommendations of the report:

(i) that there was no essential difference between children who commit offences and children in need of care and protection; and

(ii) that a court-based system of justice is inappropriate for children.

The basic conflict for any system of juvenile justice is how best to reconcile the competing claims of the law, judicial process and punishment with the need to take into consideration the welfare of children. The Kilbrandon committee had argued that delinquency or offence behaviour should be seen as symptomatic of need and that such children should be dealt with in the same way and in the same forum as other children in need of care and protection. It is remarkable just how much this anticipated current developments in prevention and also in explanations of delinquent behaviour which focus on the child's early life experiences in the family and the community.

The Kilbrandon philosophy is one in which justice for children means providing appropriate measures to help children and their families, and the very operation of the system has to be judged on the basis of criteria other than outcomes such as the reduction in offending. Nevertheless, the Children's Hearings system has been in the forefront of juvenile justice systems in promoting a conception of children's rights which include giving children the right to be heard, to be involved in the decision making process, and to be treated with decency and respect in a system that is ultimately concerned with their well-being (Fox, 1991). In that respect, Children's Hearings anticipated many of the conditions laid out in the Convention on the Rights of the Child and adopted by the United Nations in 1989.

To rehearse a number of the points made in the Kilbrandon report:

(i) There is no essential difference between children who commit offences and other children in need;
(ii) delinquency is only one aspect of the life experiences of children;
(iii) punishment is ineffective and inappropriate for the majority of young offenders;
(iv) the delinquent is to be considered in his/her family, community and social context;
(v) parents may need support and help in the parenting process; and
(vi) early preventive measures are important and likely to be effective.

Threats to the Kilbrandon Philosophy

Our concern with current developments is that the integrity of the Kilbrandon philosophy, particularly the commitment to a preventive philosophy as identified in para.178 of the report, is threatened by a number of current proposals which do not rest easily with the Kilbrandon philosophy. These include the following.

Trend Towards Punitive Measures

There has been a general move to more punitive and harsh measures for some offenders.

Emphasis on Protection of Society

There has been an increasing emphasis given to the protection of society. Kilbrandon never denied that social protection was an important element in any system of juvenile justice. What is in question now though is whether the need to protect society might be invoked at a much lower threshold than previously and whether, conversely, the welfare of the child might be given less priority than at present. The Children (Scotland) Act 1995 emphasises the consideration to be given to the welfare of the child at all times. However, that consideration can be over-ruled in circumstances where the protection of the public from serious harm, whether or not physical harm, is considered to be an issue (ss.16(5) and 17(5)). This is indicative of a significant shift from a consideration of the welfare of the child at all times to a qualified approach in which welfare may be over-ruled in favour of other issues. It remains to be seen how this section of the Act is applied, but the implication of using public protection issues to justify measures which are not in the best interests of the child implies that firstly, before such a course of action can be justified and pursued, an assessment of dangerousness must be made. How this is to be done and by what process it is to be reviewed, and how a judgement is to be reached on the seriousness of the offence, is not made clear in the Act.

In the *Crime and Punishment (Scotland)* Bill (Scottish Office, 1996f), the social protection issue was also evident in that it was proposed that the Crown should have the right of appeal to challenge a remit to the Principal Reporter, i.e. where a child or young person has committed an offence or offences, the Crown could challenge the decision not to remit a case to court.

Electronic Tagging

More recently, there has also been the suggestion that electronic tagging could be a useful means of dealing with children who commit offences. However, there is no substantial body of evidence to support its effectiveness for preventing crime.

Identification of Child Offenders

As recently as January 1997, the then Secretary of State for Scotland promoted the idea that children who offended and appeared in court could be identified as a matter of course unless the Sheriff considered it in the public interest not to do so. This of course turns completely on its head the protection afforded by Scots law to children and young people by respecting their right to privacy and *not* to be identified unless it is in the public interest to do so. We can only speculate on the argument underpinning this proposal but it does ignore completely the commitment of the United Kingdom government to the United Nations Convention on the Rights of the Child in which the protection of the privacy of children in the criminal justice is clearly stated in article 40. The whole thrust of the rights legislation and guidelines in the past decade has been to promote the rights of children in criminal justice systems and in particular to recognise the need to protect their identity and privacy.[3]

Age of Criminal Responsibility

What also has to be recognised is that although the Children's Hearings System is based on a welfare commitment and the vast majority of children who commit offences are referred to Hearings, Scotland nevertheless has one of the lowest ages of criminal responsibility in the world at eight years old. One of the direct outcomes of the Bulger and other such cases is that the appropriate age at which a child can be held criminally responsible has once again become a matter for debate and discussion.

Impact of Threats to Kilbrandon

Two further points can be made here. One is that though there is still clearly a commitment to the significance of the Kilbrandon philosophy and to the Children's Hearings, there are nevertheless, as we have outlined above, a number of subtle ways in which the integrity of the Kilbrandon philosophy is being challenged. The danger is of course that these constitute the thin edge of a substantial wedge - the introduction of more punitively oriented measures based on the need for social protection. Such a punitive approach is at odds with the literature and with developments in other European countries including those of Central and Eastern Europe. The other point is that there is considerable evidence available to show that punishment and in particular the use of custodial sentences, although it may fit well with particular ideological leanings, is ineffective and may well be counterproductive.

Evidence Based Preventive Policies

There should be a relationship between explanations of offending by children and young people and policies and practices adopted to prevent this offending. This is the basis of the work of delinquency prevention by Farrington (1994a, p.24) who asserts that:

> methods of preventing delinquency should be grounded in knowledge about the causes of delinquency or at least in knowledge about risk and protective factors that predict delinquency.

In keeping with Farrington's position, strategies to prevent delinquency should be *evidence based*. That is, they should be based on available research, knowledge and information about what we think the causes of delinquency are and on available information on what measures or programmes are the most effective at preventing offending or reoffending. For Kilbrandon, the causes of delinquency could be located in the child's family, community or social background and a truly preventive approach would therefore target those elements in the young offender's life experience.

What is clear from such cases as the Bulger case in England is that responses to offending by children and young people, particularly where they have committed serious offences, are immediate, focused on the short term and are designed as much to assuage public and political opinion as they are to deal with children who offend. Consequently, policies and measures directed at offending by children and young people may bear little relationship to what the causes of the offending behaviour are and indeed may fly in the face of the contribution of research. Detention centres and the value of the 'short, sharp shock', for example, were advocated forcefully by the government in the early 1980s despite the conclusion of a number of research projects pointing to their ineffectiveness and opposition from a number of practitioners. It could also be argued that the advocacy of the introduction of electronic tagging schemes for young offenders, as recently proposed by the then Conservative government, is not supported by research or evidence. It is also the case that the UK government is currently the only European government to be considering the introduction of electronic tagging for children who offend.

What is also clear is that there is available in the criminological literature a substantial body of evidence, mostly research based, on (a) trends in delinquency and (b) explanations of offending by children and young people which illustrate the importance of preventive strategies. There is, then, available information and data on delinquency which would allow policies and practices to be evidence based and relevant to the life experiences of those who offend. As will be discussed later, they also provide further justification for the philosophy of the Kilbrandon Report and on which justice for children in Scotland is based.

Trends in Delinquency

Since the second world war, there are clearly identifiable trends in the European context in offending by children and young people which should inform policy and practice. These can be summarised as:

(i) Until the mid-1980s, there was a general increase in offending behaviour with the increase in offending by children and young people most significant.

(ii) By far the majority of offences committed by children and young people are less serious property offences.

(iii) There has been a reduction in the proportion of less serious offences committed by children and young people.

(iv) There has been an increase in the proportion of more serious offences committed by children and young people, particularly those involving violent behaviour.

(v) In Western Europe there is no discernible increase in the homicides committed by children and young people (Cavadino, 1996; Walgrave, 1995).

(vi) Juvenile delinquency is essentially a male phenomenon and juvenile justice systems deal largely with young boys.

(vii) There has been a small increase in the involvement of girls in offending behaviour with some evidence of girls being more involved in offences of violence.

(viii) Offenders appear to start on an offending career at an earlier age.

(ix) Those children who start offending at a very early age are particularly likely to have an offending career well into their adult lives.

This was also the image of offending behaviour by children and young people presented in the Kilbrandon report.

What is clear is that, horrific though it was, such murders as that of the toddler James Bulger by two young boys occur only rarely. Nevertheless, the Bulger murder, in association with a number of other offences of violence involving children, has been significant in the development of more punitive social and political reactions. It was in direct response to the events surrounding the death of James Bulger that John Major, when Prime

Minister, was to say of young offenders, that 'we should condemn more and understand less', a comment which reflected the growing agenda for a more severe approach to young offenders in England and Wales in the wake of a hardening of attitudes to offenders more generally. More punitive attitudes to children and young people who offend have to be seen in the context of the commitment by Michael Howard, when Home Secretary, to a crackdown on crime, the 'three strikes and you're out policy' and the greater use of imprisonment. The increase by the Home Secretary of the sentence passed on the two boys who killed James Bulger to 15 years, the growth in the number of secure places for young offenders, the possibility that offenders as young as twelve could be the subject of secure training orders, the use of curfew orders and the more recent possibility of electronic tagging, all indicate a substantial swing of the penological pendulum to the right with more punitive and severe responses to young offenders.

The fact that children do appear to start an offending career early in their lives has implications for where we should target preventive strategies as we discuss later. However, it also points to the potential ineffectiveness of measures which are addressed to the adolescent or teenage offender; this may well be too late in their career. The criminological literature has a wealth of information on the life experiences of teenage offenders but rather little on the biographies of very young offenders.

Explanations of Offending by Children and Young People

What is clear from an analysis of the available literature is that offending by children and young people is increasingly attributed to factors in their early life experiences. For delinquency in general, Farrington (1994a; 1994b; 1994c) identifies the significance of the child's experience of poor parenting; family breakdown; a harsh approach to discipline; the unemployment of parental figure; low income; and poverty and its associated variables. There is no suggestion here that any one of these factors will mean that a child will necessarily become an offender. But when children experience one or more of such factors - when they cluster together - they are at greater risk of offending behaviour. What is also clear is that even in relation to those children who commit the most serious offences of violence,[4] including murder, these children are identified as clearly having had negative life experiences. For example, Boswell's (1995) work on 'section 53' offenders (those children and young people convicted of the more serious and violent crimes) in England and Wales manifestly identifies the fact that most of those children who commit serious offences have themselves been the victims of forms of abuse including sexual, physical and emotional abuse.

The further significance of the work of Farrington and Boswell, and also of researchers such as Baillie (1992; 1993) is that it also offers explanations not just of offending behaviour in later life but also of other forms of behavioural problems. In that respect, their work is noted for its relevance to a general enhancing of the life experiences of children. As Farrington (1994a, p.26) states:

> Any measure which reduces crime will probably also reduce alcohol abuse, drink driving, drug abuse, sexual promiscuity, family violence, truancy, school failure, unemployment, marital disharmony and divorce. It is clear that problem children grow up into problem adults.

What the literature now displays is a *convergence of explanations* for the behavioural problems experienced by and posed by children upon the nature of their early life experiences. An *evidence based* approach to the prevention of offending behaviour by children would develop preventive strategies acknowledging the available material on trends in offending and the kinds of explanations offered for their behaviour. A number of implications clearly follow for delinquency prevention which do not fit well with a punitive approach to dealing with children and young people who commit offences. Their relevance for the Scottish context is that they provide an evidence base for the continued adherence to and acceptance of the Kilbrandon philosophy on the one hand and a rejection of threats to that philosophy which have little supporting evidence.

Preventing Offending by Children and Young People

First, prevention will be more effective if the focus of preventive strategies is the causes of offending behaviour. This is the logical imperative of a commitment to the belief that preventive policies must be linked to the ways in which we explain offending behaviour by children and young people.

Second, preventive strategies will be more effective if they are based on a philosophy of early intervention in the lives of those children at risk of becoming offenders in later life. Most of our preventive efforts have been directed at those who are already caught up in offending behaviours and that may well be too late, given the available evidence on the causes of delinquency. Further, the recent White Paper *Crime and Punishment* (Scottish Office, 1996f) focused heavily on what can be referred to as *situational crime prevention* - making targets harder - as well on measures for those already caught up in the formal processes of control. Michael Forsyth, then Secretary of State for Scotland, himself states as an introduction to the White Paper that 'prevention is better than cure'. Whereas we agree with him wholeheartedly on that, we disagree with him on just where the preventive efforts should be concentrated. As was argued in Childhood Matters (1996), the Report of the National Commission of Inquiry into the Prevention of Child Abuse, if prevention is to be long term and reduce the number of those at risk of becoming delinquent, then this demands a shift in political emphasis. It demands a shift of political will to take the long term view and to allocate or redistribute resources to ameliorate the social conditions in which many of our children find themselves.

Thirdly, and closely related, early intervention in the lives of children and young people may not only prevent delinquency but also has the potential to enhance their life experiences generally and may also reduce other behavioural problems and increase their life opportunities. Further, preventive or reductionist strategies have to be based on a view of children or young people in the context of their total life experience. The concern has to be that an approach to dealing with offending behaviour by children and young people which ignores the family, social, and economic context in which they live will inevitably fail. The current emphasis on demonising children, or placing them in the distinct categories of 'demons' or 'threats' on the one hand and 'victims and vulnerable' on the other, has the effect of ignoring the very factors which may well contribute to their behaviour and has the hallmark of what Ryan (1971) referred to some time ago as 'blaming the victim'. What the literature and the international trends in delinquency prevention manifestly show is that there is increasing commitment to an integrated policy approach to enhancing the quality of life of children generally but particularly those at risk. Social policy and crime prevention must inevitably work closely together. This is very much the line of thinking of the UN Convention on the Rights of the Child, which has been accepted in Scotland as the basis for Scottish child care law and policy.

Fourthly, preventive strategies, particularly if they are based on an early intervention philosophy, have to recognise both regional variation in the way services and agencies are involved and the constraints of resource availability. In Scotland there is no one system of juvenile justice. Rather we have a number of regional variations in the way juvenile justice is accomplished in different parts of Scotland influenced by local authority budgets, demographic makeup, the working relationship between different statutory agencies, the role played by voluntary agencies, and the relationship between statutory and voluntary sectors. Local government reorganisation in Scotland may well have seriously affected the ability of local authorities to respond to the needs of our children through increased authorities with smaller budgets. The effect of a shortfall in resources in authorities such as Glasgow will inevitably affect the allocation of resources in a number of policy fields but specifically for our purposes, in the provision of services for children.

Prevention costs money and despite the commitment to prevention in a number of reports over the years, resources committed to long term prevention have been rather small. Our concern with the present political context in Scotland is just how preventive strategies will fare in the wake of local government reorganisation, that is, what impact the budgets of the new unitary authorities will have in developing preventive policies or indeed being able to provide the specialist services in other policy areas. One of the lessons learnt from the Orkney Inquiry was the difficulty faced by smaller authorities in providing specialist services.

Fifth, preventive policies do appear to work best when they are based on a clear philosophy. One of the concerns in the literature is the way in which juvenile justice systems are losing their integrity: that is, they increasingly reflect a mixture of values and assumptions, conflicting aims and objectives. In particular, they reflect attempts to blend in welfare or educative approaches with more punitive or severe approaches to dealing with offending by children or young people.[5] The danger of reaction to such cases as the Bulger case is that delinquency prevention programmes are influenced by concern with the small group of young offenders who commit the more serious offences.

Preventing Delinquency in Scotland

If we are serious about preventing delinquency in Scotland and if we wish to adopt an evidence based approach to the development of preventive strategies, then there are a number of clear implications from the discussion thus far and which will have to be addressed in the context of the changing Scottish political climate, particularly the introduction of a devolved parliament. The fact that we are also bound by the articles of the United Nations Convention on the Rights of the Child has introduced a whole new agenda which will inevitably underpin developments in juvenile justice internationally. The implications of this for Scotland have yet to be fully considered. However, as argued elsewhere (Asquith, 1998), in terms of future developments in juvenile justice, there is a clear convergence of interests between the rights agenda and the promotion of a preventive philosophy. The two are inextricably linked and provide the Kilbrandon philosophy with a further source of legitimation.

Back to the Future: Kilbrandon

The preventive philosophy contained in the Kilbrandon Report is highly relevant in terms of the contemporary commitment to prevention and the recognition of the role of the family and community in preventing delinquent and other behaviours. Similarly, the view, postulated in the Kilbrandon Report, that there is no essential difference between children who commit offences and children in need is strikingly similar to the common currency of current policy debates in Europe on the development of services for children and young people.

As with many social welfare reports, the preventive philosophy which was originally a central element in the Kilbrandon approach has not been realised, largely through a lack of resources but also through the way in which resources to deal with the immediate demands of offending and need are allocated. The significance of a truly preventive philosophy, as postulated in the Kilbrandon Report, should be recognised. This would allow preventive strategies to be accommodated with other elements of the Kilbrandon framework, particularly the Children's Hearing System, and would benefit from current literature and evidence on the merits of particular preventive measures.

The question of resources is of course an issue which may have to be considered by a new government in reference to the new powers of a devolved parliament. The Labour Party is committed to the Kilbrandon philosophy and to the Children's Hearing system but how the new Labour government will make the necessary resources available to implement a truly preventive philosophy is, at this point in time, not yet clear.

What also has to be appreciated though is that there may well be conflict between the Labour Party in Scotland on the one hand, committed to the Kilbrandon philosophy and to the Children's Hearings System,[6] and the philosophy of delinquency prevention developed by the Labour Party in respect of England and Wales. It is not clear at this point in time just how different the Labour Party policies for preventing crime by children and young people will be from those of earlier governments. Though against electronic tagging of children,[7] the Labour government position is clearer on such measures as the use of curfews.

Social Policy and Crime Prevention

Social explanations of offending behaviour which locate the causes of delinquency in the social, family or community background of the young child have become increasingly accepted in the criminological literature. This has clear implications for the involvement of wider social policy initiatives in preventing delinquency. It is no longer the case that juvenile justice or criminal justice systems alone will solve the problem of delinquent behaviour.

The evidence suggests the need for a wider social policy approach in which there is a commitment to enhancing the life experiences of children generally. Increasing numbers of Scottish children and their families experience the effects of poverty with all the associated correlates such as poor health, low educational achievement and behavioural problems. The acknowledged increasing gap between rich and poor may well exacerbate the difficulties encountered by such families and attempts to control delinquent behaviour which ignore the established facts of disadvantage will inevitably fail. One of the distinct advantages of a devolved parliament is that it would have the power to address social policy issues of direct relevance to the Scottish context. Not addressing the socio-economic circumstances - the social, political and economic climate - in which many of our children find themselves would inevitably, from an evidence based perspective, be ineffective.

Early Intervention

What is also clear from the literature is that to be effective a strategy of prevention should target the early life experiences of children and, in particular, pre-school children. There are undoubted long term benefits which could derive from such an investment not just in terms of the reduction of delinquency but in a number of other areas of children's lives. The reduction of delinquency and criminal activity has to be seen in relationship to a general concern for the mental and physical health of children as a means of promoting, in the long term, the mental and physical health of adults. It is for reasons such as these that the National Commission of Inquiry into the Prevention of Child Abuse titled its report 'Childhood Matters', emphasising the long term gains achieved through a refocusing of political will on early preventive measures.

Similarly, and obviously related, the importance of the parenting role in assisting children to healthy emotional and physical development cannot be overstated. No assertion is being made here that parents are to blame for behavioural problems such as delinquency. Rather we suggest that many parents could well benefit from enhanced support and assistance in the parenting role and that this is particularly so where they find themselves in high stress situations, such as poverty, low income, and unemployment. Again, the Kilbrandon argument is highly relevant here in identifying the role to be played by the family and the need to provide families with support. The commitment to pre-school education and parenting programmes, and the recognition of the need for a community based approach, both echo the Kilbrandon philosophy and at the same time find support in the current criminological literature.

In general there is acceptance that programmes which divorce the young offender from his family, social and community environment, with all the support networks he/she may have, will ultimately fail. Conversely, programmes which add resources to the general social environment in which young people find themselves have a greater chance of success and of long term success at that. In addition, to repeat what has been emphasised above, the allocation of resources and political will can be even more effective at the early stages in the lives of children who may be at risk in a number of ways.

Children's Rights

In 1991, the United Kingdom ratified the United Nations Convention on the Rights of the Child since when there have been clear commitments to the importance of basing child care law and child care policy in Scotland on the principles and philosophy of the Convention.[8] The 1995 Children (Scotland) Act is the first piece of legislation to incorporate the principles of the Convention and a commitment to children's rights. The Convention provides a radical statement of the rights of children emphasising their right to be protected from harm, their right to be provided with the necessary conditions to allow for healthy growth and development, and their right to participate in many areas of social life, particularly where decisions may be made affecting their lives.

In terms of the rights of provision, the development of a preventive philosophy is greatly assisted by a commitment to children's rights insofar as both preventive strategies and the UN Convention emphasise the importance of meeting the needs of children to assist in their healthy growth and development. This applies equally to those children who are at risk of later offending as it does to those who are vulnerable and at risk of harm. This reflects the convergence of policies and programmes for children which we referred to above and also the Kilbrandon commitment to the view that there is essentially no difference between children who offend and those in need of care and protection. It also reflects the importance of seeing children at risk of offending as children and not categorising them as 'delinquents', 'evil' or 'demons'. The close association between the rights of children and the development of preventive strategies is reflected in the UN Convention on the Rights of the Child, the Beijing Rules (United Nations, 1985) and the Riyadh guidelines (see Cappelaere, 1993).

Although the Chair of the Scottish All Party Committee on Children has been able to say that she is optimistic about children's rights appearing on the political agenda in the near future, it is still the case that no political party has yet made a clear commitment to treating the rights of children as a central element in a political manifesto. What we do have though is a commitment that there will be a review of just how the Children (Scotland) Act has worked out in practice and whether any amendments may need to be made. In particular, the extent to which the protection of society has been privileged at the cost of the welfare of children and the threat that this, and some of the other developments to which we have referred, pose for the integrity of the Kilbrandon philosophy could well be reviewed.

Concluding Remarks

It might be said that it is utopian to advocate a preventive approach which emphasises a realistic implementation of Kilbrandon: the importance of early life experiences; the need for a wide social policy initiative; the need for a realistic resource base; the significance of structural factors such as poverty and negative life experiences; the refocusing of political will; and the importance of children's rights. Our reply has to be that there is nothing more practical than a good utopia and that rather than make incremental changes in the way we deal with young offenders and thereby introduce conflicting values, aims and objectives, it is time for a new vision of the life experiences we wish to offer our children generally, and those at risk in particular. The critical issue is of course whether the changing political climate in Scotland will allow for such fundamental change.

What is at stake is not simply the most *effective* way of dealing with children and young people who offend but more importantly identifying the most appropriate philosophy on which to base preventive measures. Article 2 of the Riyadh Guidelines on Preventing Juvenile Delinquency illustrates this position succinctly:

> Prevention of juvenile delinquency requires efforts by the entire society to ensure the harmonious development of adolescents, with respect for and promotion of their personality from early childhood.

There is clear evidence from criminological literature, from our knowledge of what is happening elsewhere in Europe and the commitment to the UN Convention on the Rights of the Child, that any attempt to develop measures which ignore the social, economic and political climate in which children find themselves will inevitably fail. Conversely, the literature and current developments provide continued evidence based support for the philosophy on which the system of juvenile justice in Scotland is based. The ultimate concern of any preventive strategy cannot simply be about the reduction of offending and delinquency but must inevitably be about the way in which life experiences are distributed for children and about the kind of society in which they live.[9]

Notes

1. See Martin and Murray (1976); Martin *et al.* (1981) and Scottish Office (1992f) for a fuller description of the Children's Hearings system in theory and in practice.
2. Note that children under 13 may only be prosecuted at the instigation of the Lord Advocate (see chapter 7).
3. See article 8 of the Beijing Rules (United Nations, 1985).
4. We are grateful to Elizabeth Cutting for the discussions we held with her on these topics.
5. It is for this reason that a number of European researchers have developed a new philosophy of juvenile justice based on restorative justice - put rather simply, the idea of repairing damage done (see Walgrave, 1996).
6. Maria Fyfe, in discussion.
7. Although in January 1998, the new Labour government did approve the use of electronic tagging in a pilot scheme for adult offenders in Scotland.
8. See the White Paper *Scotland's Children* (Scottish Office Social Work Services, 1993) and the Clyde Report (Scottish Office, 1992g, recommendation 1 in particular).
9. We are grateful to Maria Fyfe MP for the opportunity to share her views on children and offending.

15 Mental Disorder and Criminal Justice

DEREK CHISWICK

Introduction

Mentally disordered offenders in Scotland form a tiny proportion of the populations passing through the criminal justice and mental health systems. In 1996 there were court proceedings against 175,000 people of whom 153,000 (87 per cent) were found guilty, yet only 121 offenders (less than 0.1 per cent of those convicted) received a psychiatric disposal in court. Similarly, these 121 mentally disordered offenders represent only 0.5 per cent of patients annually admitted to psychiatric hospitals. Although small in number, the identification of these people, their assessment and treatment are complex processes.

There is no agreed definition of the term 'mentally disordered offender'. In practice it is a term applied to those people who have, or appear to have, a psychiatric disorder and who come to the attention of an agency of the criminal justice system. Since psychiatric disorders include a wide range of conditions (see, for example, World Health Organisation, 1992; American Psychiatric Association, 1994), mentally disordered offenders might include not only offenders with severe mental illness such as schizophrenia, but also those with disorders of personality, sexual behaviour, substance misuse, and neurotic conditions such as post traumatic stress disorder. In practice, psychiatric services for offender-patients are principally for people with severe mental illness or a significant learning disability. Thus current use of the term 'mentally disordered offenders' is mainly in relation to offenders with these types of disorder.

Index offences range from breach of the peace to murder but the great majority of mentally disordered offenders commit minor offences and most psychiatric disposals are made under summary procedure. Most of these offenders are known to psychiatric services and are usually, though by no means always, out of touch with services at the time of their offending.

Prosecution provides an opportunity to detain a mentally ill patient in hospital for assessment and treatment (see below); the offence becomes the occasion, rather than the reason, for treatment.

In England since 1994, government policy requires an independent inquiry to be held following a homicide by a psychiatric patient who has had recent contact with psychiatric or social services (NHS Executive, 1994). Many highly publicised reports have drawn attention to failings in the standards of care. The inquiries have in turn been criticised for their unproductive outcomes and for creating a culture of fear, blame and over-reactivity within the relevant agencies (Peay, 1996). Homicides by psychiatric patients occur in Scotland but there is no mandatory requirement for an independent inquiry. Nonetheless concern and sensitivity to criticism has now become part of the working practice of all agencies involved with mentally disordered offenders; these concerns, whether explicit or implicit, have undoubtedly become influential.

Government Policy for Mentally Disordered Offenders

Scotland has no national policy for services for mentally disordered offenders. In England a comprehensive government review of health and social services for mentally disordered offenders (Department of Health and Home Office, 1992), known as the Reed report, made a careful analysis and produced 276 recommendations (Chiswick, 1992). These were based on principles that mentally disordered offenders should receive care of high quality from health and social services. This should be appropriate to their need, at no greater level of security than is justified, with an emphasis on care near to their home area. Further reviews in England have considered the role of the high security hospitals and the treatment of people with psychopathic disorder.

In Scotland a consultation paper (Scottish Office, 1998f) has recently been published which adopts the principles set out in the Reed report. The Government invites comment on 26 proposals for a co-ordinated range of high quality services, including the development of a small number of regional forensic psychiatric units, to meet the needs of mentally disordered offenders. In the absence of additional public spending, which the consultation paper expressly prohibits, it is difficult to see how these services can develop.

The needs of mentally disordered offenders in Scotland are met by a combination of general and specialist forensic psychiatric services. General psychiatric services are in a process of major reconfiguration with reductions in bed numbers, hospital closures and an expansion of community-based services. These factors have implications for the treatment needs of mentally disordered offenders. Specialist forensic services are unevenly developed, often driven by local historical practices, geography, individual enthusiasm and peculiarities of funding. The consequence is that the same type of mentally disordered offender may be dealt with differently depending on the location. In the section that follows there is consideration of the relevant issues concerning mentally disordered offenders at various stages in the criminal justice process, together with a brief review of current facilities.

Arrest, Prosecution and Diversion

Police

The police are commonly the first agency to which mentally disordered offenders present. An American study has described the police as the 'streetcorner psychiatrist' and their mental health resource role as 'pivotal' (Teplin and Pruett, 1992). Section 118 of the Mental Health (Scotland) Act 1984 enables the police to remove a mentally disordered person 'in immediate need of care or control' from a public place to a place of safety where detention for up to 72 hours is permitted. The place of safety should normally be a hospital, though it can be an alternative place, but not a police station except 'by reason of emergency' (section 117). Formal utilisation of section 118 in Scotland is not recorded, there being no statutory documentation, but police procedure in taking mentally disordered people to hospitals is common. In England the equivalent provision of the Mental Health Act 1983 is disproportionately used in London (Cherrett, 1996), and for patients from black ethnic minorities (Dunn and Fahey, 1990). Referrals to hospitals by the police are dealt with by general psychiatric services for emergency referrals. Admission is determined by consideration of clinical need including the appropriateness of compulsory admission. An important consideration today in assessing police referrals is the need to ensure that any assessment is carried out in conditions that preserve the safety of the patient, other patients, members of the public and staff.

The role of the police in relation to mentally ill people in the community was thrown into focus by the tragic events surrounding the killing of a police constable in Glasgow in 1994. The precise circumstances of this incident, in which the police attended at the house of a mentally ill person in response to a general practitioner's request, have not been made public but Philip McFadden was subsequently found insane in bar of trial on a charge of murdering a policeman. An enquiry into the care and treatment of Philip McFadden by the Mental Welfare Commission for Scotland (1995) recommended that guidance be issued by the Secretary of State in relation to the roles of general practitioners and the police in dealing with potentially violent mentally disordered persons; a consultation paper was later issued (Scottish Office, 1997f).

Mentally disordered detainees   No recent figures are available for the frequency of requests for assessment at a police station of a detainee's mental health but such assessments are common. The behaviour of the detainee, nature of the alleged offence or a history of mental disorder are all likely to prompt a request for examination. This may be carried out by a police surgeon or by a psychiatrist. The remit for these assessments and the advice given may both lack definition. The only legitimate task for a psychiatrist is to determine whether or not there is a mental disorder and if so whether immediate admission to hospital is required. However other decisions may also depend on the assessment, for example decisions to question or charge a suspect, or release him from custody. The psychiatric assessment of a detainee's fitness to be interviewed requires a systematic approach (Norfolk, 1997).

The identification by the police of suspected or actual mental disorder in an arrested person is surprisingly reliable (Chiswick *et al.*, 1984). Difficulties may arise in obtaining a psychiatric assessment and in the availability of an appropriate place in hospital if required. The psychiatric assessment of a police detainee is often a difficult clinical task. The location may be less than ideal, there may be limited background information and the clinical picture may be confounded by the effects of alcohol and/or drug intoxication. The task is best performed by a psychiatrist, who has access to psychiatric admission facilities, rather than by a police surgeon. The aspirations of the consultative paper (Scottish Office, 1998f) concerning close liaison between police and multiprofessional assessment teams from health and social care agencies, will not be realised without significant additional resources.

Mentally disordered interviewees and false confessions   A mentally disordered interviewee, whether suspect, victim or witness, may give unreliable answers with the possibility of dire consequences for the interviewee and for the investigation of a crime.   In England unreliable or false confessions have been at the heart of many of the notorious miscarriages of justice that resulted in the Royal Commission on Criminal Justice (*Lancet* Editorial, 1994).   In Scotland, the interviewing of a mentally disordered suspect or witness by the police, in any location, should only take place in the presence of an 'appropriate adult'; that is an adult who is completely independent of the police and the interviewee and who has 'sound understanding of and experience or training in dealing with mentally disordered persons' (Scottish Office, 1998g).   Requirement of an appropriate adult is absolute if the offender is mentally disordered, that is suffering from mental illness or handicap however caused or manifested (section 1 Mental Health (Scotland) Act 1984).   Use of appropriate adults has been patchy and recent draft guidance (Scottish Office, 1998g) recommends that formal appropriate adult schemes be established.   The guidance represents good practice but does not have legal authority.

Three types of false confessions have been described by Gudjonsson (1993).   Firstly, voluntary false confessions where the individual goes voluntarily to the police and confesses to a crime he knows he has not committed, usually to satisfy a pathological need for notoriety.   Secondly, coerced compliant false confessions elicited during persuasive interrogation; they are known to be false by the suspect but are offered for an immediate gain (e.g. a promise of release).   Thirdly, coerced internalised false confessions where either a suspect with amnesia (e.g. alcohol-related) comes to believe he committed a crime he did not commit, or where subtle manipulation by a questioner convinces an innocent suspect that he committed the crime.   The latter is particularly associated with psychiatric factors in the suspect, such as a learning disability or states of anxiety, confusion, guilt or bereavement.

Have there been miscarriages of justice in Scotland arising from false confessions?   A confession to the police is only one source of evidence and it requires corroboration by another independent source of evidence. Griffiths (1992) describes the Scottish courts as paying 'lip-service' to the nature of this corroboration, and warns that the protection of the accused in this matter has been inadequately addressed.

Prosecution

The discretionary role of the Procurator Fiscal in determining prosecution, and the type of proceedings, is a key feature of the prosecution system in Scotland (see chapter 7). The mental health of the accused may be a relevant factor in decisions to prosecute (Chiswick *et al.*, 1984; Duff and Burman, 1994). In the early stages of the process, the Procurator Fiscal is entirely dependent on information contained in the police report. Where it appears that the person may be suffering from mental disorder, the Procurator Fiscal has a duty to bring relevant evidence of the mental condition of the accused to the court (section 52 Criminal Procedure (Scotland) Act 1995). There are two early decisions of a psychiatric nature open to the Procurator Fiscal. Firstly, to discontinue or defer prosecution and divert the case to a psychiatric facility; secondly, to commission a psychiatric report while the accused awaits trial. How are these achieved?

Pretrial psychiatric assessment and diversion Procurators Fiscal have traditionally sought psychiatric reports or advice from their local psychiatric service. As services become more fragmented and with the development of Community Mental Health Teams, it is becoming increasingly difficult for Procurators Fiscal to identify the appropriate psychiatric service or psychiatrist for their needs. There is great advantage in a single point of referral to a psychiatric service that has experience in dealing with requests from the courts and has the capacity for appropriate and, if necessary, urgent response. Diversion, the first option described above, can only occur if the Procurator is satisfied that the person will receive assessment and treatment and not pose an immediate risk to the public or himself. The local psychiatric service may or may not be able to respond with an urgent assessment at the court to determine this matter. In any cases of doubt the most likely action by the fiscal is to continue proceedings with the accused being remanded in custody for a psychiatric report.

Pre-trial diversion from prosecution, and avoidance of custodial remands solely for obtaining a psychiatric report, were key elements in the Reed Report (Department of Health and Home Office, 1992). Court liaison and court diversion schemes, with specific funding, have developed widely in England. Some depend on attendance of a psychiatrist at court at fixed times (Joseph and Potter, 1993), while others involve the sifting of cases held in custody by a Community Psychiatric Nurse (Rowlands *et al.*, 1996).

In Scotland diversion was commended by the Stewart Committee (HMSO, 1983) but there have been only occasional initiatives (Duff and Burman, 1994); most pre-trial diversion takes place on an informal basis and is largely dependent on the relationship between Procurator Fiscal and local psychiatric service. In Glasgow sheriff court a Psychiatric Liaison Service has been established, providing, on request, immediate psychiatric assessments at the court each morning. The principal function is to avoid unnecessary remands of mentally ill people to prison. Outcome of the Glasgow scheme awaits full evaluation. This type of immediate or urgent diversion contrasts with schemes for elective diversion where, following an assessment carried out by arrangement some weeks later, the fiscal then decides whether to prosecute or accept alternatives suggested by social work or health agency.

Services for diversion recently reviewed by McAra and Georghiou (1998) were mostly elective in type, that is not for cases requiring urgent decision-making. Procurators Fiscal have mixed views about the usefulness of diversion schemes, particularly those that do not include a psychiatrist (Cameron and McManus, 1993; Duff and Burman, 1994). A study of 111 minor offenders with psychological difficulties referred electively by fiscals to a psychiatric outpatient clinic in Glasgow was reported by Cooke (1991). A third had no diagnosable disorder and most had combinations of depression, anxiety and substance misuse; only two had schizophrenia. In total, 103 offenders were offered some form of help.

Two matters warrant emphasis. Firstly schemes for urgent diversion require more than simply the presence of a psychiatrist. They need other professionals and administrative support. Court premises should provide decent facilities for examining defendants, availability of other appropriate professional staff, and access to telephone and clerical assistance. Also required are appropriate and sufficient facilities to which accused people may be diverted, and the means of transporting them there from court. Secondly these schemes have developed in England where lengthy periods of custodial remand are much more prevalent than in Scotland with its strictly finite periods of pretrial remand. Whether sophisticated pretrial diversion schemes are required throughout Scotland is uncertain.

Commissioning a pretrial psychiatric report A pretrial psychiatric report may be commissioned by the Procurator Fiscal while the accused is remanded in custody or at liberty in the community. Figures are not available but extrapolation from experience in Lothian would suggest approximately 2,000 per year are commissioned, the majority in summary cases. Most will be prepared by general psychiatrists. Unless the charge is one of murder, where the fiscal automatically requests two psychiatric reports on the accused, the decision to seek a report is entirely discretionary. Factors such as the police report, nature of the charge, behaviour on arrest or while in custody, or an indication of mental disorder are likely to be influential. A common unwritten reason is to gather information in deciding whether or not to oppose an application by the defendant for bail. This is not a psychiatric matter but the contents of the report may be useful.

Remand to hospital Pre-trial psychiatric reports normally address the issues of fitness to plead, mental state at the time of the alleged offence, and recommendations, where appropriate, for disposal; these are all considered later in this chapter. The assessment provides a crucial opportunity to divert an accused from remand in prison to committal to hospital under section 52 of the Criminal Procedure (Scotland) Act 1995; in 1996/97 there were 178 such committals to hospital. Written or oral evidence from one doctor is required and the court must be satisfied that a hospital place is available and suitable for detention of the accused. Section 52 does not contain the word 'assessment' but in practice the committal is often used to assess fitness to plead, the nature of any mental disorder and the appropriateness of recommending a post-conviction psychiatric disposal.

The psychiatric criterion for section 52 is that the person 'appears to the court to be suffering from mental disorder', though once in hospital the responsible medical officer must be satisfied that there is a mental disorder which warrants detention under the Mental Health (Scotland) Act 1984. In summary cases most committals are for two weeks, while on solemn procedure they are normally for the duration of the remand. Committal provides an opportunity for a full psychiatric assessment in a setting that provides care and observation by skilled staff. Section 52 can be terminated by the court if the responsible medical officer reports that mental disorder is not present.

A final opportunity to effect pretrial remand to hospital is by the transfer of an untried prisoner to hospital under section 70 Mental Health (Scotland) Act 1984. There were 38 in 1996/97. This is not a matter for the fiscal or the criminal courts; it requires an application by the Secretary of State, supported by two medical reports, to be approved by a sheriff. Section 70 ceases to have effect when the case is disposed of by the court or if proceedings are dropped.

Trial

Most mentally disordered offenders who receive a psychiatric disposal in the criminal courts, do so after conviction; the sentencer imposes a disposal from the menu of psychiatric alternatives to punishment (see below). In a minority of offenders, mental disorder may affect their capacity to be tried or their responsibility for their crimes. There are three such situations: insanity in bar of trial; insanity at the time of the offence; and diminished responsibility. Each of these will now be discussed in turn.

Insanity in Bar of Trial

It is a principle of law that it would be unfair to try an accused who did not have the mental capacity to mount a proper defence to the charge. Such a person is said to be unfit to plead or insane in bar of trial, and completely new provisions were introduced in the Criminal Justice (Scotland) Act 1995 for dealing with this category of accused together with those acquitted on the grounds of insanity at the time of the act (Scottish Office, 1996g). The new measures swept away the mandatory and indeterminate detention in hospital that previously applied to insane defendants (Chiswick, 1990); there has been no change in the legal criteria for insanity findings. The provisions are contained in sections 54-63 of the Criminal Procedure (Scotland) Act 1995.

Findings of unfitness in Scotland are rare but more frequent than in England (Normand, 1984); in 1996/97 the total number of insanity findings (in bar of trial and by acquittal) was eleven. It has always been available on both summary and solemn procedure in Scotland. Early indications are that the new provisions of 1995 have been followed by significantly increased use of both types of insanity plea. The new procedures for unfitness to plead have three elements: determination of fitness to plead at a mental health proof; for those found unfit to plead, an examination of the facts (EOF); where the facts are found, determination of disposal. Each of these will now be discussed in turn.

Determination of fitness to plead The issue is determined by a judge on the basis of written or oral evidence (almost invariably both) from two doctors, at least one of whom must be approved in terms of section 20 of the Mental Health (Scotland) Act 1984. There is no statutory definition of unfitness to plead; the leading case remains *HMA v Wilson*[1] derived from section 87 of the Lunacy (Scotland) Act 1857. The emphasis is on the ability of the accused to instruct counsel and follow the proceedings in court. The test is different from that of the insanity defence (see below and *Stewart v HMA No 1).*[2] In practice most cases involve severe mental illness of a psychotic nature, or learning disability. The latter can pose particular problems for psychiatrists in determining the required level of understanding of the accused; instructions to examining psychiatrists on this matter by Crown or defence should be explicit as most psychiatrists will have limited knowledge of court proceedings.

Examination of facts (EOF) If the court is satisfied that the accused is insane in bar of trial, it records the finding, discharges the trial diet and orders an examination of the facts. The accused, while awaiting the EOF, may be remanded in custody, on bail or committed to hospital. The functions of an EOF are to determine beyond reasonable doubt whether the accused did the act charged, whether on the balance of probabilities there are grounds for acquittal and, where the facts are found, to determine disposal. An EOF is held in public before a sheriff or judge sitting with no jury; rules of evidence and procedure should be as nearly as possible that of a trial.

Determination of disposal Where the facts are found, and there are no grounds for acquittal, the court must impose one of five non-penal disposals; identical disposals apply to defendants found insane at the time of the act (see below). An exception applies in cases of murder where there is a mandatory disposal by way of hospital and restrictions orders. The disposals are:

(i)   a hospital order;
(ii) a hospital order with a restriction order;
(iii) a guardianship order;
(iv) a supervision and treatment order; and
(v)   discharge with no order.

The first three of these are described in a later section. The supervision and treatment order (which is not available for any other category of mentally disordered offender) is a mechanism 'to secure access to supervision and assistance in the community, including medical treatment' (Scottish Office circular SWSG 4/98 and Schedule 4 Criminal Procedure (Scotland) Act 1995). It requires medical evidence from two or more doctors approved under section 20 of the Mental Health (Scotland) Act 1984. The order requires the person to submit to treatment, comply with instructions, maintain contact with a supervising officer and comply with residential requirements. Procedural matters are complex but the order is not enforceable and gives no authority to administer medical treatment. There are no sanctions in the event of non-compliance. From the psychiatric perspective it is difficult to identify the value of a supervision and treatment order.

Rights of appeal The accused has rights of appeal to the High Court against a finding, or refusal to make a finding, of insanity in bar of trial, against an EOF finding, and against any order made by the court. The Crown has similar rights of appeal but only on a point of law. The Court of Appeal has ruled that following an unsuccessful plea in bar of trial, an accused may again submit a plea in bar of trial at a preliminary diet on a fresh indictment (*Stewart v HMA No 2*).[3]

Insanity at the Time of the Offence

A successful plea of insanity at the time of the offence provides a complete defence and results in acquittal on the ground of insanity. With the exception of murder cases, disposals are flexible and as described above for cases of insanity in bar of trial. The defence is available in both summary and solemn procedure. In contrast with insanity in bar of trial, there are no statutory requirements concerning medical evidence for the insanity defence. Normally written and oral evidence is presented from at least two doctors but there is no requirement that either is approved under section 20 Mental Health (Scotland) Act 1984.

Criteria for the insanity defence derive from the common law and in particular the description by Hume (1844) of an 'absolute alienation of reason' caused by a mental disease (Gordon, 1978b). The leading case is that of *HMA v Kidd*[4] and refers to:

> an alienation of reason in relation to the act committed ... some mental defect ... by which his reason was overpowered.

Self-induced intoxication does not constitute insanity.

Most successful insanity acquittals are in respect of offenders with psychotic mental illnesses such as schizophrenia. The relevant factor is the mental state of the accused at the time of the offence; his condition at the time of trial is irrelevant. There are understandable problems in those rare cases where it is purported that the insanity results from a temporary condition which was only present for the duration of the criminal act.

The law in Scotland in respect of automatic behaviour, where the body is said to act independently of the mind, remains mostly untested. For many years the few such cases were dealt with as insane automatism with mandatory committal to hospital. In *Ross v HMA*[5] the Court of Appeal ruled that the involuntary ingestion of drugs could cause an absence of *mens rea* leading to complete acquittal. The issue has become less acute since the 1995 reforms for disposal of insanity acquitees.

Diminished Responsibility

Insanity in bar of trial and at the time of the offence have important places but in practice, and only for murder, the arcane wrangles associated with insanity can be side stepped by use of the plea of diminished responsibility, a Scottish invention in 1867 (Gordon, 1978b). Figures are not collected but there are probably between five and ten per year in Scotland. Diminished responsibility is a legal concept and therefore it cannot be defined in clinical terms. It has the effect of reducing a charge of murder, with the mandatory life sentence on conviction, to one of culpable homicide for which there is flexible sentencing. When it was introduced in Scotland, and later in England, the mandatory sentence for murder was the death penalty. The leading case for determining diminished responsibility is that of *HMA v Savage*[6] in which it was defined as:

> an aberration or weakness of mind ... bordering on but not amounting to insanity ... a mind so affected that responsibility is diminished from full responsibility to partial ... there must be some form of mental disease.

The importance of regarding the *Savage* definition in its entirety, and the requirement of a mental disease, were re-affirmed in *Connelly v HMA*.[7]

In practice the interpretation of diminished responsibility is narrower in Scotland than in England and Wales. Most cases involve psychiatric disorders such as schizophrenia, depression, brain disease and learning disability. Psychopathic disorder is excluded from its scope (*Carraher v HMA*).[8] Most pleas of diminished responsibility are accepted pre-trial by the Crown depending not only on the medical evidence but on the global nature of the case, thus leading to an uncontested conviction for culpable homicide. Contested cases, where the Crown refuses to accept a plea of guilty to culpable homicide and the matter is put to a jury for decision on a murder charge, are much more likely to result in a conviction for murder than the lesser charge of culpable homicide. Infanticide (killing of a baby under one year by a mentally disturbed mother) has never existed as a separate crime in Scotland and is normally prosecuted as culpable homicide. Most diminished responsibility cases receive a psychiatric disposal; usually a hospital or probation order is imposed (see below). Some offenders receive a determinate prison sentence but occasionally a life sentence is imposed.

Post-Conviction Psychiatric Disposals

The majority of psychiatric disposals by courts are imposed following conviction of the accused. Most psychiatric reports are commissioned by the sentencer through the sheriff clerk or high court clerk; figures are not available but are probably in the region of 2000 per year. A small number are commissioned by defence solicitors. Clinical psychologists may also be asked to provide reports in selected cases. Approximately equal numbers of persons are seen in prisons or while on bail. It is usually preferable if reports are prepared by psychiatrists who have responsibility for providing the local service. Indeed confusion may follow when psychiatrists make recommendations for treatment which they have no responsibility to provide. The number and nature of post-conviction psychiatric disposals has increased over recent years; they are briefly described below.

Informal Treatment

Informal (i.e. non-compulsory) treatment may be offered to a minor offender; strictly speaking this is not a disposal since it cannot be ordered by the court.

Deferred Sentence with Conditions

The wide powers of deferring sentence (section 202 Criminal Procedure (Scotland) Act 1995) may include a condition of psychiatric treatment. This is informal treatment requiring the offender's co-operation and agreement. It is sometimes a useful means of assessing motivation for treatment in, for example, alcohol or substance misusers.

Probation with a Requirement of Treatment

Treatment for a mental condition may be combined with probation under section 230 of the Criminal Procedure (Scotland) Act 1995. There must be evidence from an approved doctor of a mental condition falling short of one that requires compulsory admission. Treatment requires the agreement of the probationer. It may not be for more than twelve months and may be residential or in the community. A named doctor or chartered clinical psychologist must direct the treatment. Successful use of these orders, which are not greatly used, requires collaboration between social work and health care agencies (McAra and Georghiou, 1998).

Remand for Inquiry

In addition to the possibility of remanding an offender in custody or on bail for inquiry into his mental (or physical) condition, the court may also commit him to hospital in terms of section 200 of the Criminal Procedure (Scotland) Act 1995. There were 178 committals in 1996/97. Oral or written evidence from a doctor is required stating that the offender appears to be suffering from a mental disorder and that an appropriate place in hospital is available. Since a psychiatric report will be necessary before making the order, the majority are made after a period of post-conviction remand in custody or on bail often as result of a recommendation in a social inquiry report. No single period of remand may be for more than three weeks; any appeal against committal to hospital must be made within 24 hours. Committal under section 200, like pre-trial committal, gives an opportunity for full psychiatric assessment in a caring environment with 24-hour nursing observation. There is no power to administer any treatment, except under common law in an emergency, to the patient. If there is a mental disorder, the necessary reports can be prepared for recommending a hospital order.

Hospital (and Guardianship) Orders

The corner-stone of psychiatric disposals is the hospital order under section 58 of the Criminal Procedure (Scotland) Act 1995; 93 were made in 1997/98. Evidence is required from two doctors, one of whom must be approved under the 1984 Act, that there is a mental disorder which warrants detention in hospital for treatment. A hospital bed must be available within 28 days of making the order; in most cases the offender goes directly from court to hospital. In hospital the patient has identical rights to those of any other detained patient. The order permits the administration of treatment for mental disorder subject to the consent to treatment provisions of Part X of the 1984 Act. Length of detention is a matter primarily for the responsible medical officer; the court has no further role in the case. Detention requires a review at 28 days and is then renewable six-monthly (twice) and then annually (indefinitely). The patient may appeal for discharge at specified times to a sheriff and at any time to the Mental Welfare Commission for Scotland. Most of these orders are made in respect of offenders with mental illnesses such as schizophrenia, though a few are for offenders with a mental handicap. Detention of offenders with a personality disorder is permissible subject to the requirements of section 17(1) of the 1984 Act; orders in this category are rare. A guardianship order may be made by the court with similar effects as guardianship under the 1984 Act. It is a very rare procedure.

Hospital Order and Restriction Order

Where the court is concerned with protecting the public from serious harm, it can remove the power of discharge from the responsible medical officer and Mental Welfare Commission, by imposing a hospital order with an order restricting discharge (section 59 of the 1995 Act). This places authority for discharge with the Secretary of State in terms of section 62 Mental Health (Scotland) Act 1984. The orders are without limit of time (indefinite) and are thus, in effect, the 'psychiatric life sentence'. There were 17 such orders made in 1996/97. In a review of all restriction orders made in 1989-95, Humphreys and Gray (1996) found the great majority were in respect of men who had committed serious crimes of violence; 38 per cent were for killings. Nearly all were imposed under solemn procedure and 75 per cent resulted in admission to the State Hospital at Carstairs. In assessing protection of the public, the court must have regard to the nature of the crime, the antecedents of the offender and the risk of further offending if the offender is discharged.

Imposition of a restriction order therefore depends on the perceived dangerousness of the offender. By contrast, successful appeal by a restricted patient to a sheriff against detention (section 63-64 Mental Health (Scotland) Act 1984) depends, not on consideration of dangerousness, but on the presence or absence of mental disorder as defined in the 1984 Act. This point is central to a current appeal by a patient with a psychopathic disorder at the State Hospital, in which the Court of Session, in reducing a decision of a sheriff, stated that detention for this type of mental disorder must satisfy the treatability criterion in section 17(1)(a)(i) Mental Health (Scotland) Act 1984 (*R v Secretary of State for Scotland*).[9] An appeal by the Secretary of State against this decision is to be heard in the House of Lords late in 1998. Refusal of the appeal will have wide implications.

State Hospital

Approximately 15 per cent of hospital orders under sections 58 or 59 are for admission to the State Hospital. The court must be satisfied that the offender, 'on account of his dangerous, violent or criminal propensities' requires conditions of special security for his treatment (section 58(5)).

Interim Hospital Order

Where there is doubt about the appropriateness of treatment in the State Hospital under a hospital order, the court may impose an interim hospital order in terms of section 53 Criminal Procedure (Scotland) Act 1995. In 1996/97 there were 29. This allows for a trial period of up to twelve months admission, usually to the State Hospital, after which the offender returns to court for final disposal. The interim hospital order is particularly useful for testing the treatability of offenders with combinations of mental illness and personality disorder.

Hospital Direction ('Hybrid Order')

The clear distinction between disposal to prison or hospital ended with the introduction of the hospital direction, often described as a 'hybrid order', in section 6 Crime and Punishment (Scotland) Act 1997. Under solemn procedure only, and except after conviction for murder, a court may impose a prison sentence which begins with treatment in hospital, followed by either transfer to prison or continued detention in hospital until the sentence is completed. In Scotland the hospital direction applies to all categories of mental disorder, though currently in England it may only be applied in cases of psychopathic disorder. The hybrid order has been criticised as a flawed attempt to combine punishment of mentally disordered offenders with protection for the public (Chiswick, 1996). At the time of writing no hybrid order has yet been made in Scotland or in England.

Psychiatric Aspects of Imprisonment

Mental Illness in Prison Populations

The imprisonment of mentally ill or mentally handicapped people, particularly on remand, has been one of the driving factors in developing better care for mentally disordered offenders (Department of Health and Home Office, 1992). Recent research has identified the nature of the problem. Davidson *et al.* (1995) interviewed a 50 per cent random sample (389 subjects) of all untried prisoners in Scotland. They found only two per cent had major psychiatric disorders, a rate less than would be expected in the general population. However up to 49 per cent of the sample reported symptoms including disrupted sleep, depressed mood, anxiety, poor concentration and tiredness. Up to 75 per cent had life-time histories of illicit drug use and nearly 25 per cent had alcohol-related problems. More than 50 per cent had been in previous contact with psychiatric services; 17 per cent of the females had been inpatients. The rates for major psychiatric disorder are lower than those reported for remand populations in England (Maden *et al.*, 1995). Davidson *et al.* draw attention to factors in Scotland such as short periods of remand, early assessment by psychiatrists with access to beds, and the slower run down of psychiatric hospitals. There has been no psychiatric survey in Scotland of sentenced populations. Evidence from England emphasises the significance of alcohol and drug related conditions together with neurotic and personality disorders (Gunn *et al.*, 1991).

Women in prison show higher rates of neurotic conditions, personality disorder and substance abuse than men (Maden *et al.*, 1990). Prison has become a receptacle for some very disturbed women. Female remanded prisoners have high rates of previous self-mutilation (Wilkins and Coid, 1991). Research at Cornton Vale, the only women's prison in Scotland, has shown that the vast majority of women have used illicit substances, half have serious drug problems, a third have committed acts of self-harm and nearly half have been sexually abused (see chapter 16; Loucks, 1997).

Suicide in Scottish Prisons

The rising rate of suicides in all penal establishments in Britain is evident in Scotland; an annual number of less than ten in the 1980s rose to between ten and 20 by the end of the 1990s. Bogue and Power (1995) report an increase in prison population and receptions of less than two per cent between 1976 and 1993 but an increased suicide rate of 40 per cent over the same period. A spate of suicides at a young offenders institution in Scotland and subsequently at Cornton Vale has led to major reviews (Scottish Home and Health Department, 1985; Scottish Prison Service, 1992; Loucks, 1997).

Bogue and Power (1995) found an excess of suicides in remanded and life sentenced prisoners with the majority occurring within three months of incarceration. Hanging is almost the invariable means of suicide. A previous history of self-harm, substance misuse and contact with mental health services are common. Most reviews agree that prison suicide is a complex phenomenon in which individual vulnerability, stressors outside and within prison, isolation from usual supports, and the particular lethality of hanging as a means of self-harm (compared with, say, an overdose of drugs) all contribute. Screening and rigorous observation procedures and the introduction of ligature-proof cells have made little impact on the overall rate of deaths.

Psychiatric Services in Prison

Depending on perspective the 'need' for psychiatric services should be directed at identifying the two per cent of the prison population who have serious mental illnesses, or at the 50 per cent with mental symptoms. In practice, scarce resources are necessarily targeted at the former, while providing help for some of the latter. Most prisons have the services of a visiting consultant psychiatrist who may or may not be a forensic specialist. For those prisons with a busy remand function, a psychiatrist who has access to inpatient hospital beds is essential. In some prisons there may be designated nurses with a mental health treatment function. No prison in Scotland has a hospital facility suitable for the care of prisoners with any significant degree of mental illness. Mentally disordered convicted prisoners, who meet the criteria, may be transferred to hospital in terms of sections 71 and 72 Mental Health (Scotland) Act 1984. There were 50 in 1996/97.

Parole and Psychiatry

The Parole Board is required to have at least one member who is a psychiatrist (Schedule 2 Prisoners and Criminal Proceedings (Scotland) Act 1993) and psychiatric reports are included in the consideration of all life sentence prisoners and in other selected cases. There is thus psychiatric input concerning decisions to release prisoners under the various types of release licences and their conditions. Psychiatrists have a contribution to make, with other professionals, on risk assessment and management; they have particular skills in those cases where there is a mental disorder. Their particular role is therefore in identifying relevant psychiatric factors in respect of protection of the public, the appropriateness of supervision and any requirement for psychiatric aftercare. Offenders who receive a discretionary life sentence have done so on the basis of perceived dangerousness which may be associated with mental abnormality. Psychiatric and psychological considerations are of particular importance in consideration of release by Discretionary Life Tribunals.

Services for Mentally Disordered Offenders

Mentally disordered offenders may be referred to psychiatric services at any stage of the criminal justice process through police, courts, lawyers, prisons, or from a secure psychiatric hospital. The required combination of general and specialist forensic psychiatric services for these offenders is determined by local factors. A comprehensive service should contain the following elements:

(i) an effective emergency service to deal with police referrals;
(ii) an effective service to local courts, including provision for early diversion;
(iii) accessible outpatient clinics for elective referrals from courts, social work departments, lawyers and other sources;
(iv) liaison with probation agencies and other community based services for offenders;
(v) liaison with medical services in prisons;
(vi) access to a range of inpatient facilities, including open ward, intensive psychiatric care, and medium security for the assessment and treatment of patients before trial and after conviction;

(vii) liaison with the State Hospital for patients returning from, or requiring treatment under, conditions of special security; and

(viii) access to accommodation in the community providing varying levels of support and including appropriate bail hostels.

Mentally disordered offenders may receive treatment in a variety of settings or they may fail to receive treatment at all. There are severe problems in Scotland with no current provision for medium secure facilities and a near absence of residential facilities in the community suitable for mentally disordered offenders who do not require in-patient care. Indeed histories of sexual offending or fire-raising (both common in mentally disordered offenders) may operate as exclusion criteria for certain community placements.

There is an imbalance between provision at the State Hospital and lack of local inpatient secure facilities. A comprehensive survey of State Hospital patients by Thomson *et al.* (1997) found that more than half the patients did not require the level of security provided by the State Hospital, and that for the majority of these patients there was no other facility available. Indeed the survey reported that while half the admissions followed an offence, the other half resulted from disturbed behaviour in prison or hospital. Nearly a quarter were non offender patients transferred from local psychiatric hospitals.

The influence of the Scottish Office consultation paper (1998f) in promoting comprehensive services for mentally disordered offenders awaits testing. Simultaneously perceived as defendants, offenders, prisoners, clients or patients, this is an unpopular group of people with complex needs. These multiple perceptions reflect the importance of a multi-agency approach to developing new services and facilities. In theory this should be feasible in Scotland. But even if local criminal justice, health and local authority agencies begin a dialogue, the issue of funding from diverse and over-stretched budgets is likely to prove insurmountable without a much greater steer from central government than is apparent in the consultation paper.

Notes

1. HMA v Wilson 1942 J.C. 75; 1942 S.L.T. 194.
2. Stewart v HMA No. 1 1997 S.C.C.R. 330.
3. Stewart v HMA No. 2 1997 S.C.C.R. 430.
4. HMA v Kidd 1960 J.C. 61.
5. Ross v HMA 1991 S.L.T. 564.
6. HMA v Savage 1923 J.C. 49; 1923 S.L.T. 659.
7. Connelly v HMA 1990 S.C.C.R. 504.
8. Carraher v HMA 1946 J.C. 108; 1946 S.L.T. 225.
9. R v Secretary of State for Scotland 1998 S.L.T. 162; 1997 S.L.T. 555.

16 Women and the Scottish Criminal Justice System

MICHÈLE BURMAN

Introduction

The past 15 years have seen sporadic attention paid to issues of gender and criminal justice in Scotland. At times the focus has been intense, revealing sources of discrimination, highlighting certain innovations or culminating in significant legal reform but, for the most part, the relationship between women, the law and the institutions of the criminal justice system in Scotland remain relatively unexplored.

This chapter aims to draw together available information about the criminal justice system and women (as offenders, as victims and as legal professionals); to plot key legal reforms and policy and practice developments that have impacted on the way in which women experience the criminal justice system; and to describe the relevant research that has been conducted within the Scottish context.

Women as Offenders

Some information about the position of women as offenders can be gleaned from official statistics. In common with other jurisdictions around the world, considerably less women than men are charged with, and found guilty of, crimes and offences in Scotland. The most recent figures reveal that women comprise just under 14 per cent of those with a charge proved against them in Scotland.[1] From the late 1980s up to 1993, the proportion of women amongst those with a charge proved in Scotland steadily increased, peaking at 16 per cent in 1992.[2] This is despite there being a decrease of over 14 per cent in the overall number of persons with charges proved (from 177,250 in 1988 to 152,087 in 1996) (Scottish Office, 1997h; 1998c). Thus, the increase in the proportion of convicted women to men in the years up until 1993 was inconsistent with the general trend, and ran contrary to charges proved against men, which dropped over the same period.

A closer examination of the figures shows the position of women more clearly. The Scottish Office figures disaggregate charges into crimes and offences, the former generally being considered to be more serious contraventions of the law. Again in the years up to 1993, women increased their proportion within those with charges proved for crimes; although this figure dropped from 15 per cent in 1993 to 13.6 per cent in 1995, increasing again to 14.2 per cent in 1996 (Scottish Office, 1995h; 1997h; 1998). This pattern is repeated in relation to women with charges proved for offences; from 1989 to 1992, there was a rapid increase from 13 per cent to 17 per cent. Yet, in 1993 this dropped to 16 per cent, falling further to 13.8 per cent in 1996. Whilst official figures can be misleading, there was a gradual increase in women's officially documented involvement in the Scottish criminal justice system up until 1993, particularly with regard to less serious offences, although there are signs now that this may be tapering off.

What of the types of crimes and offences that are committed by women? In Scotland, as in other countries, women hardly feature in crimes of violence, but there are four areas in which women make up approximately a third of convicted perpetrators - crimes of indecency (specifically prostitution), crimes of dishonesty (specifically shoplifting and fraud) and non-sexual crimes of violence (which includes physical abuse of children) (Bates, 1995, p.42). In 1996, just under two thirds (65.4 per cent) of charges proven against women were classified as offences; whereas 34.5 per cent were crimes (Scottish Office, 1997h). The ratio is similar for men. However many more males than females had a charge proved against them in 1996 in almost all crime and offence categories. The exception to this is 'other' (that is, miscellaneous) crimes of indecency, where women accounted for 85 per cent of what are mainly offences related to prostitution. A second category where the number of women with a charge proved is only slightly less than men is the 'other' (i.e. general) miscellaneous category - mainly TV licence infractions, but which also includes offences against local legislation, Revenue and Excise Acts, and breaches of probation and community service orders.

Women offenders form a relatively small group, but there have been significant increases in some areas of offending in recent years; for example, the number of women convicted of road traffic offences increased by more than a third from almost 4,500 in 1988 to over 6,100 in 1995 (whereas numbers of males have hardly changed). In 1995, motor vehicle offences accounted for 40 per cent of all offences by women (and 27 per cent of all crimes and offences proved against women). Crimes of dishonesty, for the most part shoplifting, 'other' theft and fraud, accounted for 62 per cent of crimes proved against women in 1995 (and 19 per cent of all crimes and offences by women) (Scottish Office, 1997h).

Age has been found to be a significant factor in patterns of offending. In Scotland, according to official statistics, both male and female offending peaks at age 18. For females aged 18, one in every 100 was convicted in court in 1995; compared to nine out of every 100 males. However the average age of male offenders tends to be older than females, and there is a marked decline in the rate of conviction of both sexes after the age of 20 years. But on the whole, female offenders are comprised of women of all age groups, who are involved in diverse types of offending which is, for the most part, minor.

Gender Differences in Sentencing

Much has been written internationally about gender differences in the way in which male and female offenders are treated by the criminal justice system, particularly in relation to sentencing. No clear picture has yet emerged as such studies tend to be inconclusive, contradictory or methodologically flawed. However, in their analysis of the official statistics relating to young offenders in Scotland, Samuel and Tisdall (1996) did find evidence to suggest that young male and female offenders are dealt with somewhat differently by the criminal justice system. For example, comparing the police response to 15 year old boys' and girls' offending (for shoplifting, petty assault, breach of the peace, and other theft) they found that girls are almost twice as likely to receive a police warning than boys (Samuel and Tisdall, 1996, pp. 112-113); and that, in 1993, young men were more than three times as likely as young women to be given a custodial sentence and half as likely to be cautioned or admonished (Samuel and Tisdall, 1996, p.114). Girls and young women are more likely to receive warnings, admonishments, cautions and discharges than young men, and are less likely to be given a custodial sentence or receive a community service order. These marked differences in sentencing rates lead them to conclude that, at the extreme ends of the sentencing tariff, young women are clearly treated more leniently on aggregate than young men. However, this is not consistent for all types of offences or for all ages of offender. For example, when 15 year old girls commit the stereotypically 'feminine' crimes of shoplifting or fraud, they are treated more harshly than boys of the same age; yet when they are sentenced for the stereotypically 'masculine' offence of serious assault, they are more likely than young men to receive probation (Samuel and Tisdall, 1996, pp.126-127). Whilst recognising the limits of the explanatory power of official figures and the need for more sophisticated statistical data and case information, Samuel and Tisdall nonetheless suggest that young women experience markedly different interactions with the Scottish criminal justice system than do young men.

Women commit less serious crimes than men and have fewer previous convictions, and also receive different types of sentences. Whilst the most common penalty for both females and males is the fine (received by around 70 per cent of both sexes), females are more likely to receive an absolute discharge than males (19 per cent compared with nine per cent in 1995). For all those aged 16 and over, males are almost twice as likely to receive a community service order (four per cent as opposed to two per cent in 1995), but there is little difference between the proportions of males and females given probation orders. Females are much less likely than males to be sentenced to custody (four per cent compared to twelve per cent in 1996) (Scottish Office, 1998c). Whilst these differences owe much to the type of offence which is at issue, and the offending history of the offender, they also reflect the fact that female offenders in Scotland, as in other countries, are mostly involved in minor charges. Yet the small overall percentage of women receiving custodial penalties masks the fact that in recent years there has been a steady increase in the proportion of women given prison sentences in Scotland. The alternative to a custodial sentence would be a Community Service Order. However, there is limited community service work suitable for women; in 1995, just two per cent of women were given a community sentence (as opposed to four per cent of men).

Women in Prison

Currently women constitute around three per cent of the Scottish prison population. However, as John McNeill, the then Chief Executive of the Scottish Association for the Care and Rehabilitation of Offenders (SACRO), pointed out in his introduction to that organisation's 1995 conference report on women offenders, women prisoners are all too easily forgotten in a criminal justice system which is run very largely by men to deal primarily with male offenders (SACRO, 1995).

In 1995, the average daily prison population in Scotland was 5,626 (three per cent of that population was female, although the proportion was slightly greater - five per cent - for those on remand). Of the 2,169 female receptions to prison in that year, 40 per cent (876) were there on remand, rather than as a sentence, and of those 84 per cent (739) were untried and 16 per cent (137) awaiting sentence (Scottish Office, 1996d; see also McManus, chapter 13, who makes the same point about the general prison population). Indeed, the women's prison population in Scotland is dominated by the numbers on remand. Currently, remand receptions represent approximately 25 per cent of the average daily female prison population.

Although the proportion of females to males in the average daily prison population has remained more or less constant over the past decade, this masks an underlying trend - the growth in the numbers of women directly received (i.e. as a sentence) into prison in comparison to the male population. Frizzell (1995, p.19) cites an increase from 3.2 per cent of all direct receptions in 1983 to 5.5 per cent in 1993. Although admittedly the numbers are small, direct receptions of women into custody have risen drastically, from 338 in 1984, peaking at 713 in 1994 (a rise of over 100 per cent), with a fall to 592 in 1995 (Scottish Office, 1996d, p.17). The corresponding figures for men show only a nine per cent increase from 1984 to 1994 (10,731 to 11,491); in 1995 the figures fell to 10,910. In 1995, custodial sentences for women aged under 21 years rose by eleven per cent and for women aged over 20 years, by ten per cent.

Similarly, the number of women received into custody for non-payment of fines has increased by 55 per cent (from 452 in 1984 to 701 in 1995); the figures for men show just a slight increase (Scottish Office, 1996d). In 1995, 54 per cent of female receptions were for fine default as opposed to 38 per cent of male prisoners (Scottish Office, 1995g). Strikingly then, in 1995, more women were sent to prison for fine default (701) than there were direct receptions from the courts (592); and this has been the case for virtually every year since 1984 (Scottish Office, 1996d). This constitutes a major source of concern although (somewhat belatedly) the Government are taking steps which may stem this problem.

In Scotland then, women in prison are there for relatively minor offences and, usually, their sentences tend to be short. In 1995 the average length of prison sentence awarded to those aged 21 or over was five months for women and ten months for men. For adult females, the proportion of the average daily prison population with sentences of three months or less was 17 per cent (compared to five per cent for males). Just under a quarter of women in custody were serving sentences of two years or more (compared to 65 per cent of men). In all crime categories the average sentence length for women is less than that for men (Scottish Office, 1995g). Frizzell (1995) states that, in 1993, of the 678 women directly received into custody, 70 per cent were committed for theft, mainly shoplifting. Almost 80 per cent were sentenced to periods of six months or less (compared to 61 per cent of males) and almost two thirds (62 per cent) for three months or less. Only four per cent of women were sentenced to 18 months or over (Frizzell, 1995, p.21). For the same year, the most common offences for which women were received into custody for fine default were crimes of indecency (mainly prostitution), shoplifting and breach of the peace. Almost two thirds of female fine defaulters serve less than seven days (as opposed to just over half of males) (Frizzell, 1995, pp.21-24).

There is only one female prison in Scotland, HMP Cornton Vale situated outside Stirling.[3] However, women are also housed in Inverness, Aberdeen and Dumfries (male) prisons. Cornton Vale was the subject of a detailed study based on interviews with women prisoners, sentencers, social workers and police officers (Carlen, 1983). In their book on women's imprisonment, Dobash *et al.* (1986) describe the 'therapeutic' regime that characterises Cornton Vale. Both studies emphasise the inappropriateness of prison for the women there, many of whom arrive because it is not known what else to do with them (Carlen, 1983). Women respond to imprisonment in a variety of ways. Very often this involves withdrawing, self-mutilation and sadly, suicide, as the numbers of recent tragic suicides at Cornton Vale show only too vividly.

A more recent study of Cornton Vale by Loucks (1997) focused on the problems affecting prisoners. This study was commissioned following a report published by the Chief Inspector of Prisons for Scotland which expressed deep concern over the 'bleak situation' of the women there, exacerbated by the numbers of drug damaged women and the recent spate of suicides (Loucks, 1997, p.ix). The vast majority of women in Cornton Vale have experience with the use of illicit drugs and 10-15 per cent are addicted to alcohol. A striking 82 per cent of the women had experienced past abuse (either emotional, physical or sexual); for the most part this was from a male partner although sexual abuse was most common in childhood. The report also found bullying to be a hidden, but relatively frequent occurrence within the prison. Over a third of the women had tried to take their own lives at some stage (inside and outside of prison). The experience of prison can intensify existing problems and this study confirms in part findings of the earlier studies, that is, that the majority of women prisoners have histories of victimisation and abuse which, within the context of a prison regime, can compound their vulnerability to depression and self-harm behaviour.

In May 1998, the Scottish Office published a joint review by HM Inspectorate of Prisons for Scotland and HM Inspectorate of Social Work for Scotland on the arrangements for community disposals and the use of custody for female offenders (Social Work Services and Prisons Inspectorate for Scotland, 1998). Prompted by the high number of suicides by women prisoners,[4] the review highlighted the fact that community service is used less frequently for women than for men and stressed the need to reduce the numbers of women sent to prison. It put forward a number of key recommendations. Central among these are: the need for increased provision of bail services (such as bail information, bail supervision and specialist bail accommodation for women) as a means of reducing the remand population; the need fully to investigate the scope for reducing the number of fine defaulters by the possible introduction of unit fines and increased use of Supervised Attendance Orders; and the need to ensure that, by the end of this century, young women under 18 years are not held in prison. Other recommendations highlighted the need to produce accurate and detailed data relating to female offenders, and urged all local authorities to undertake a review of their current arrangements for female offenders and produce a report outlining policy in this area. The aim is to ensure that local authorities take into account the particular issues raised by female offenders and maximise opportunities for dealing with female offenders at the earliest stage of the criminal justice process. The recommendations put forward in the Inspectorate review, taken together, comprise a radical reform package which, if fully adopted and implemented could significantly change the way in which women are punished in Scotland. This would not be before time.

Women as Victims of Crime

Criminal Justice Response to Domestic Violence

It has been well established that the nature of violence committed against women is very different from that of violence against men. Whilst official figures can tell us that almost half of the female victims of homicide recorded in Scotland in 1995 were killed by their male partner, compared to five per cent of male victims, and that 21 per cent of females were killed by a male acquaintance (Scottish Office, 1997h), other, less extreme forms of 'domestic' violence tend to be under-reported. For example, a local survey in Glasgow in 1989 found that 52 per cent of the 1,500 women respondents had experienced some form of abuse by males and that relatively few had ever reported it (Women's Support Project/Evening Times, 1990).

According to the 1993 Scottish Crime Survey, in more than half (55 per cent) of all incidents in which the offender was 'well known' to them, and in 28 per cent of all incidents of violence against women, the offender was either a current or ex-spouse, or boyfriend or partner (Anderson and Leitch, 1998). For male victims the corresponding figures were both less than one per cent. 37 per cent of violent incidents involving women were recorded as domestic violence, compared to three per cent involving men. The SCS also found that, of females aged 16-24 years, 12 per cent had been the victim of a personal crime during 1992; compared with four per cent of all females.[5]

Gendered assumptions are reflected in the way in which the criminal justice system processes women who appear as complainers.[6] Nowhere is this more evident than in respect of women alleging domestic violence and/or sexual assault. In recent years there has been an increased awareness of the need to improve the criminal justice response to domestic violence, in particular the provision of more support for victims and the introduction of pro-arrest policies (see chapter 18). As a result, a number of jurisdictions have introduced a range of innovative responses. In Scotland, these have included developments both in the police response and improved police training in awareness of the issues involved in domestic violence; in some areas, a greater willingness to prosecute; the strengthening of civil interdicts by attaching a power of arrest; and, perhaps most innovative, the introduction of programmes for men who have been convicted of a violent assault on their partner. In 1989, the courts finally revoked a husband's immunity for marital rape, when for the first time, a husband was convicted of the rape of his wife whilst he was living with her.[7]

The different policy developments have met with varying degrees of success. Scottish Office guidance was issued to Chief Constables on the handling of domestic violence in 1990, stressing the need for domestic assault to be treated in the same way as an assault that took place outside the home, the presumption in favour of arrest, and consideration of the safety of the victim and any children.[8] Yet women continue to report that police do not respond actively and, even in cases where women are keen to pursue prosecution, the police are not. Whilst changes in policing policy are desirable, policy change is not, in itself, very useful. It would seem that police discretion in dealing with the abuse of women within the home allows such crimes to be ignored. In some forces, specialist officers deployed in Female and Child Units may also investigate incidents of domestic assault and provide some support for the victim by putting her in touch with other statutory and voluntary agencies such as social work, housing and Women's Aid. However, this is not a standard response across all forces and, for the most part, domestic violence continues to be routinely handled by uniformed officers. A recent study looked at service provision to women experiencing domestic violence in Scotland, and found that just 33 per cent of respondents who contacted the police found their response helpful, whereas 91 per cent of those using Women's Aid and 67 per cent of those using the support of friends, relatives and neighbours found these helpful and supportive (Henderson, 1998). The report recommends a role for central government in raising the profile of domestic violence and in involving all service providers (police, housing organisations, Womens' Aid, Social Work Departments, health services, and so on) in identifying and implementing service changes. It remains to be seen whether these recommendations are taken up.

There are currently two court-based programmes for violent men in operation in Scotland, both of which are closely modelled on American initiatives. CHANGE, established in Stirling in 1989, was the first criminal justice community-based programme for offenders set up in Britain. It operates an intensive three-month group programme for men who are placed on probation by the Scottish courts (Dobash *et al.*, 1996). It also provides community-wide programmes of education and training, raising awareness of domestic violence. The Lothian Domestic Violence Probation Project (LDVPP) was established in 1990 and, unlike CHANGE, is located within a local authority social work department. LDVPP operates in Edinburgh Sheriff Court and offers sentencers the option of placing offenders on probation with a condition that they attend an intensive groupwork programme. Both CHANGE and LDVPP were recently the subject of a detailed longitudinal evaluation which compared the effects of the programmes to the impact of other criminal justice sanctions, such as fines, admonishments, compensation orders, probation and imprisonment (Dobash *et al.*, 1995; 1996). Focusing on the impact on subsequent violent behaviour, this study aimed at ascertaining whether the programmes were more likely than other sanctions to 'inhibit and eliminate violence and enhance the well-being of the women who have been victimised' (Dobash *et al*, 1995, p.368). By considering both men's and women's interpretation of the impact of different sanctions, the study sought to explore if and why men changed. It found strong and significant differences between men who had undergone one of the programmes and those who had received some other criminal justice sanction. The findings indicate that men who have been through one of the programmes were less likely to commit a subsequent violent act and, if they did, then their partners report these were fewer in number. Women whose partners were dealt with by some other means report that their quality of life and their relationship with their partner has either remained the same or worsened.[9]

There is another innovation which deserves mention here. In recent years, the high profile Zero Tolerance campaign has drawn attention to the issue of violence against women in Scotland and has created 'a forum for discussion and debate, and a focus around which initiatives to tackle the problem can coalesce' (Cosgrove, 1996, p.187). This campaign, which is essentially a crime prevention initiative, has been forged within a feminist framework and operates within the context of local authority structures.[10] The message of the campaign is simple - no man has the right to abuse women. This message is conveyed by means of a series of stark, black and white poster and billboard displays situated in prominent locations, which depict women in everyday contexts and with an accompanying text challenging assumptions about male violence. The campaign demonstrates the links between different forms of male violence, encouraging people to view the issue in a wider context. Zero Tolerance has three main objectives: prevention of crimes of violence against women and children; the adequate provision of support and service provisions for abused women and children; and appropriate legal protection by the criminal justice system.

Criminal Justice Response to Rape and Sexual Assault

In the 1980s the publication of two landmark research studies by Chambers and Millar (1983; 1986) drew stark attention to the criminal justice processes which followed women reporting an incident of sexual assault in Edinburgh and Glasgow. The first study focused on police processing of complaints from initial contact with the complainer to sending a report to the procurator fiscal; the second examined the subsequent stages of prosecution and trial up to final outcome. Both studies were highly critical, drawing attention not only to the criminal justice response following an allegation of rape, but also giving voice to women who had experienced the system. Scottish Office guidance concerning the police investigation of sexual assault was issued to Chief Constables in 1985.[11] These guidelines referred explicitly to the first Chambers and Millar study (1983) and took up some of their recommendations. In particular, the guidelines emphasised the need to treat complainers tactfully and sympathetically, that investigative interviews be conducted by trained officers designated for the purpose, that in-depth questioning of a personal nature should be avoided, and that information about the progress of the case should be provided to the complainer. There was also detailed guidance concerning medical examinations, encouraging the services of female doctors.

From the mid-1980s onwards, five of the eight Scottish police forces set up specialist Female and Child Units staffed by teams of (mostly female) officers with a sole remit to assist in the investigation of sexual assault and child abuse. A sixth force deployed individual 'specialist' officers who, in addition to other duties, undertake such investigations.[12] Dedicated facilities - or 'interview suites' as they are known - were set up to provide a 'secure and private environment' for the interviewing of women and children, and many of these incorporate medical examination facilities. Formal training strategies were introduced in all Forces for officers deployed in such units, some of which include input from outside speakers and voluntary agencies, such as Rape Crisis and Victim Support schemes. Although training provision differs substantially in form and content from force to force, in the main it focuses on legal-evidential requirements, interviewing skills, and information on the impact of sexual violence on women including the long-term effects of sexual assault (Burman and Lloyd, 1993).

The changes in policing policy and practice heralded by the introduction of specialist units and officers were the subject of a study which found that whilst it is clearly the case that there has been a change of direction in this area, there is still much room for improvement in the police response to sexual assault (Burman and Lloyd, 1993). The research found that: welfare of complainers is accorded a higher priority; investigations are conducted more swiftly; there is less chance that the woman will have to repeat her allegations to several officers (a key problem documented in the Chambers and Millar study); and there is less preoccupation with the credibility of the complainer and more emphasis placed on her care and support. However, women's experiences may well differ within and between forces, as neither policies nor practices are standardised and individual specialist officers differ markedly in their approach and perspective. Also, the provision of information about the progress of investigation remains patchy (something which the women in the Chambers and Millar studies raised as an important concern).

Burman and Lloyd's study also highlighted the important shift - from rape and sexual assault investigations to a concern with child abuse cases - which occurred in both the workload and the focus of the Units following their inception, and which has important implications for both types of investigation. When first conceptualised, it was envisaged that the work of the Units would lie in the investigation of sexual assault. Since the late 1980s the police in Scotland, as elsewhere in Britain, were faced with increasing demands for a more effective response to child abuse. This demand, coupled with a rise in the numbers of such cases being reported to the police, led to the introduction of joint police/social work investigations in child abuse cases, which far outweighed the number of sexual assault investigations (Lloyd and Burman, 1996). With these developments, the case profile of the Units changed quite drastically. Over a four month period in 1992, specialist officers were involved in a total of 898 cases; 136 (15 per cent) of which were reports of sexual assault and 710 (79 per cent) were child abuse cases.[13]

The Scottish 'Shield' Legislation

In January 1986, legislation came into force which was designed to limit the use of evidence of the victim's previous sexual history in sexual offence trials.[14] Prior to this, Canada, New Zealand, several states in America and in Australia, and England and Wales had introduced 'shield' legislation, and the Scottish reformers were able to draw from the experiences of these other legislatures. Like other jurisdictions, the Scottish legislation does not totally prohibit sexual evidence, but sets out specific conditions and procedures for introducing such evidence if it fulfils certain requirements. However, it also has a number of distinct characteristics. While it excludes sexual evidence concerning the complainer and persons other than the accused, it also - and this is something not found in other jurisdictions - excludes, in the first instance, any evidence of the complainer's past sexual behaviour with the accused.[15]

The Scottish legislation also differs from that passed in other jurisdictions in that it is very broad. It applies not only to rape[16] and rape-related offences, but virtually every offence of a sexual nature: heterosexual as well as homosexual offences; age-defined statutory sexual offences; crimes of indecency; and those where the crime concerns the legal capacity to give consent (that is, offences under the Mental Health (Scotland) Act 1984). Only incest, clandestine injury,[17] and some very rarely used statutory offences were omitted from its gamut.[18]

Unlike England and Wales, where the sexual evidence reform stemmed from a concern with the law of rape, in Scotland, sexual evidence came under scrutiny within the context of a general programme of revision of the law of evidence undertaken by the Scottish Law Commission from 1980 onwards. Consequently, the reform process was guided throughout by issues of principle in relation to the law of evidence. However, there were other events in the early 1980s which drew attention to the handling of sexual assault, such as the case of *Meek and Others v HMA* in which the principle of the 'honest belief' defence was established[19] and the infamous group rape case of 1982[20] which was dropped by the prosecution (without telling the complainer) before it went to court on the basis that she was unfit to endure the trial process (Harper and McWhinnie, 1983; see also chapter 7). In addition, feminist groups in Scotland were campaigning against the criminal justice system's treatment of women alleging rape.[21] Whilst none of these public controversies focused on the issue of sexual evidence, nevertheless they undoubtedly facilitated the Scottish reforms.

Several quite different reasons for restricting the use of evidence concerning a complainer's sexual life were given by the reformers throughout the period of deliberation and drafting of the legislation. In the main these concerned the problematic consequences brought about by the use of sexual evidence. One set of reasons focused on the problems of 'trauma and distress' caused to complainers by 'intimate, or possibly embarrassing questioning' (Scottish Law Commission, 1983). This echoed in many ways feminist concerns about the subjective experience of the complainer in the witness box. The depiction of the trial as a grossly intimidating and humiliating experience was reported by the women interviewed by Chambers and Millar (1986) and has been documented in several other studies (see, for example, Adler, 1987; Temkin, 1987; Lees, 1989). It was also recognised by the reformers that fear of the court room ordeal and a lack of belief in the capacity of the criminal justice system to achieve justice might be contributing to the unwillingness of women to come forward to report sexual assault.

Primarily, however, the legislators were concerned with issues of evidential principle. The focus was on the perceived harmful effects of sexual evidence in terms of its potential for misrepresentation and distortion and, specifically, in its anomalous position in sexual offence trials and in its implications for the questions of credibility and consent. The aim of the reformers in framing the legislation was to achieve a balance between, on the one hand, minimising the use of sexual evidence whilst, on the other, continuing to admit all relevant evidence in order for justice to be done to the accused. These aims are visible in the formulation of the legislation which sets out broad exclusions followed by a series of exceptions. Sexual history and sexual character evidence was to be excluded unless genuinely relevant to key issues in the trial. In order to introduce such evidence the defence has to make an application to the court; the Crown however are exempt from the prohibitions.

Research conducted on the workings of the 'shield' legislation over a three and a half year period found that some success could be claimed for the legislation on the grounds that glaring attacks on the complainer's sexual character were rare when the procedures set down by the new provisions were followed; and that the procedure of making an application to lead sexual evidence provides a forum for the defence to be questioned about their proposed use of evidence and for limits to be placed on that questioning (Brown *et al.*, 1992; 1993). However, the research also indicated that, in practice, the legislation falls some way short of its intentions. Whilst some sexual evidence is effectively excluded, much still persists with the effects that the legislators were trying to prevent. Brown *et al.* (1992; 1993) identify three key problems which hinder the achievement of the aims of the legislation: that the rules are not being followed in all cases; that sexual evidence which is legitimately admitted can be of the type that the legislators wished to exclude; and, despite being recognised problems, the legislation failed to address the issues of innuendo and inference and other more subtle attacks on the credibility of the complainer which throughout the course of the trial can have a cumulative effect prejudicial to the complainer's credibility. Furthermore, the study revealed a number of strategies and tactics used to discredit women, and documented numerous examples of the 'art' of advocates which involved the vilification and harassment of complainers. Thus, despite the good intentions of the legislation, women's experience in rape trials is still governed by what Brown *et al.* (1993) term 'the ordeal of the witness box'. Whilst this study did not explicitly address the effects of the use of sexual evidence on verdicts, it also found that acquittal rates (not guilty and not proven verdicts) in rape trials run very high, at 78 per cent.

Women Working Within the Criminal Justice System

Currently there is only one female judge in the High Court in Scotland. She was appointed (as a temporary judge) in 1992, the first woman ever to sit on the Scottish bench.[22] In 1996, eight per cent of Scottish Sheriffs and 27 per cent of lay justices were female (Scottish Office, 1997i). Of the 380 advocates practising in Scotland, 74 (19 per cent) were female; as were eight (nine per cent) of the 83 Queen's Counsel (Scottish Office, 1997i). As at 31st December 1995, eight per cent of Advocate Deputes, 58 per cent of Procurator Fiscal deputes and Senior Procurator Fiscal deputes, and eleven per cent of Crown Office staff in senior civil service grades were female. The admission of female solicitors steadily increased throughout the late 1980s and early 1990s (from 45 per cent in 1988 to 54 per cent in 1994), but in 1995 this dropped off to 47 per cent. Currently, women solicitors comprise one third of the solicitor's roll.

In 1995, seven per cent of prison officers working in prison halls and ten per cent of those working outwith prison halls and seven per cent of supervisors were women (Scottish Office, 1997i). It is only recently in Scotland that women officers were allowed to work on the halls in male prisons.

The percentage of women officers in the eight Scottish police forces is very low, currently averaging around 10-13 per cent. There has however been a slight increase in the numbers of women recruited into the police in recent years. As at 31st March 1996, 13 per cent (that is, 1,883) of the Scottish police forces were female. The highest rank held by a woman is Chief Superintendent of which, currently, there are two.

Several commentators have pointed to the fact that, within the police, work dealing with women and children is held to be 'women's work' and as such is devalued in relation to other aspects of 'real' policing (Heidensohn, 1992; Young, 1991; Chambers and Millar, 1983). In Scotland, the majority of specialist officers investigating sexual assault are female (indeed in five forces, it is only female officers); and in some forces secondment to a specialist unit is mandatory for all women officers. The significant presence of women officers to do this type of policework reflects gendered assumptions about who is best at carrying out such tasks. This was evident in the highly gendered views of senior (male) officers concerning the suitability of female over male officers to be deployed in specialist units (Burman and Lloyd, 1993, pp.40-1). The assumption that women officers are the 'best for the job' because they are female needs to be challenged, not only because it perpetuates the view of such work as being of low priority and status within police culture, but also because it has implications for women officer's subsequent career paths.

Conclusion

Feminist campaigners in Scotland have, for many years, been extremely vocal about the positions that women occupy in a criminal justice system that is designed primarily with men in mind. It is only in relatively recent years that legislators, policy makers and criminal justice practitioners have begun to turn their attention to some of the issues that affect the way in which women experience the law. Often this comes about as a result of tragic events, as in the Crown's handling of the Glasgow rape case or the more recent Cornton Vale suicides. Whilst there have been several significant and far-reaching reforms, there are still many instances where women (whether as offenders or victims) are seen as pathological or abnormal rather than rational beings, and stereotyped in a way which prevents due consideration of women's gendered circumstances. And so, despite the advances of recent years, there remains a case for vigilant monitoring of the workings of the criminal justice system as it applies to women.

Notes

1. The total number of women with charges proved in 1996 was 21,308 (see Scottish Office, 1998c, p.28).
2. In 1995 it was 14.3 per cent, in 1994 it was 13.6 per cent, in 1993 and 1992 the figure was 16 per cent; and in 1991 it was 15 per cent.
3. This establishment recently began to receive young male offenders.
4. Between June 1995 and December 1997 seven women prisoners committed suicide at HM Cornton Vale, Scotland's only female prison. Their ages

ranged from 17 to 28 years; five were on remand. Over the same period, there were another four attempted suicides.

5. Personal crime, as defined by the SCS, refers to crimes directly targeted against the individual including assault, robbery, theft from the person and other personal theft.

6. 'Complainant' in England and Wales.

7. Stallard v HMA 1989 S.L.T. 469.

8. CC Circular 3/1990: Investigation of Complaints of Domestic Assault, SHHD.

9. For a full account of the evaluation, methodology and findings, see Dobash *et al.* 1995; 1996.

10. Zero Tolerance was launched by Edinburgh District Council's Women's Committee in 1992 and, since then, it has been adopted by a further 13 councils/local authorities and has achieved national and international acclaim (see Cosgrove, 1996, pp. 187-189). Zero Tolerance draws on the approach of the Canadian Government which, in the early 1990s, implemented a multi-million dollar programme to tackle male violence.

11. CC Circular 7/1985: Investigation of Complaints of Sexual Assault, SHHD.

12. The two remaining forces set up specialist units for the investigation of child abuse.

13. The remaining six per cent of cases included the investigation of indecent mail and telephone calls; cot death enquiries; missing person enquiries; and interviewing of abscondees from children's homes.

14. Criminal Procedure (Scotland) Act 1975 ss. 141 and 346, as inserted by the Law Reform (Miscellaneous Provisions) (Scotland) Act 1985 s.36.

15. The English/Welsh legislation, ss. 2 and 3 of the Sexual Offences (Amendment) Act 1976 excludes only the complainer's sexual behaviour with others.

16. The legal definition of rape in Scotland is gender specific, in that it is defined by penile penetration of the vagina to however slight a degree with or without the emission of semen. This is an important difference between Scots and English/Welsh law as, in England and Wales, the Criminal Justice and Public Order Act 1994 extended the definition of rape to include non-consensual buggery of a male. In Scotland, forcible penetration of the vagina by a part of the body other than the penis, or by some object, does not constitute rape, but instead is classified as indecent assault.

17. Sexual intercourse with a sleeping woman.

18. Although incest offences and clandestine injury were later included, following publication of a research study which monitored the use of the legislation (see Brown *et al.*, 1992; 1993).

19. Meek and Others v HMA 1982 S.C.C.R. 6143 and 1983 S.L.T. 280 (Notes). This case involved a girl on her way home from a dance who was raped by a group of boys in a field, some of whom, on appeal, claimed they thought she

was willing as, when they came along, the others were having sex with her. The appeal was rejected but the principle was established that a man had not committed rape if he genuinely believed that the woman was consenting, however unreasonable it might have been to believe that.

20. This was a group rape during which the complainer, known as Carol X, sustained terrible injuries and was left for dead. There was strong evidence of non-consent and she did not know her attackers, yet the prosecution dropped the case on the basis that she was not fit to stand up to the ordeal of the trial. The case was taken up by a local journalist and a lawyer and culminated in Carol X bringing a successful private prosecution against her attackers.

21. s.32 of the Criminal Justice (Scotland) Act 1980 gave power to the Crown in a criminal trial to apply to the court to take evidence 'in commission' from witnesses who were either too infirm to attend or who were abroad. RCCs in Scotland were calling for this to be extended to rape victims.

22. The first female judge in England and Wales was appointed in 1962.

17 Scottish Ethnic Minorities, Crime and the Police

JASON DITTON

Introduction

The most recent and authoritative historical account of Asian migration to Scotland is to be found in Maan (1992), where he traces initial Indian migration to Scotland to as early as 1500. In the post second world war period, migration to Scotland was predominantly from the Indian sub-continent and, in 1950, numbered about 600 persons, increasing to 1,300 in 1955. The flow of migrants to Britain from the Indian subcontinent began to rise sharply over this period, chiefly because of high unemployment in both India and Pakistan. There are over 60,000 persons of ethnic minority origin living in Scotland today.

The Current Ethnic Minority Population

Because the 1991 Census included, for the first time, full questions on ethnic status, profiling the ethnic minority population in Scotland is relatively simple. It is markedly different in both proportionate size and structure from England and Wales. Scotland had, in 1991, 62,634 members of various ethnic minority groups (1.3 per cent of the total population of 4,998,567), and England and Wales had 2,952,416 members of various ethnic minority groups (5.9 per cent of the total population of 49,890,277). Scotland's ethnic minority population is only about one fiftieth the size of that living in England and Wales.

The difference in structure is illustrated in Figure 17.1. Here, it can be seen that Scotland has proportionately far fewer Black ethnic minority members, and proportionately greater numbers of both Asian and, particularly, Chinese residents. Scotland has, for example, proportionately over three times as many Chinese residents as is the case in England and Wales, and proportionately over twice as many Pakistani residents but half as many Indians. Research in England and Wales indicates that Indians typically have socio-economic life chances resembling the white population, whereas both Pakistanis and Bangladeshis typically have socio-economic life chances inferior to Afro-Caribbeans (see FitzGerald, 1993). The Pakistani population in Scotland, however, is noticeably more affluent. Three groups, Pakistanis (34 per cent of all Scottish non-whites), Chinese (17 per cent) and Indians (16 per cent) account for two thirds of all ethnic minorities living in Scotland in 1991.

Figure 17.1   Ethnic Groups, England, Wales and Scotland, 1991 Census

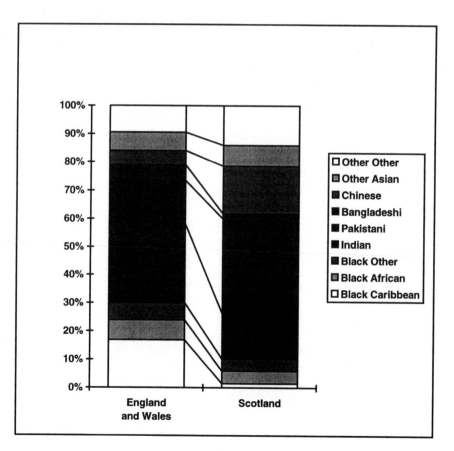

Ethnic Minorities and Crime

Unsurprisingly, given the greater numbers of ethnic minority residents living there, a great deal of research into the participation of members of ethnic minority groups in the criminal justice system has been conducted in England and Wales. This has ranged from seeking evidence of racial bias in offending (*inter alia*, Aye Maung and Mirrlees-Black, 1994; Sibbitt, 1997); in policing (*inter alia*, Jefferson and Walker, 1993; Smith, D., 1991; FitzGerald and Sibbitt, 1997); in sentencing (*inter alia*, Hood, 1992; Walker, 1988; 1989; Jefferson and Walker, 1992; Mair, 1986; McConville and Baldwin, 1982; Crow and Cove, 1984); and more generally (*inter alia*, Gelsthorpe, 1993; FitzGerald, 1995; 1997).

The British Crime Survey (BCS: in truth, now only an English and Welsh one) has become increasingly a source of survey generated information relating to ethnic minority contact with the criminal justice system, although it has to be said that such sources have been criticised as insufficient to inform fully about the nature of, in particular, racial victimisation (Bowling, 1993). In addition to the main sample, the BCS now recruits an ethnic minority 'booster' sample, in order more deeply to probe inter-racial differences (see, *inter alia*, Mayhew, *et al.*, 1989; Aye Maung and Mirrlees-Black, 1994; and Skogan, 1994). The first major report (FitzGerald and Hale, 1996), summarising data from the 1988 and 1992 BCSs combined, concluded that:

(i) Ethnic minority residents are, statistically speaking, more likely than whites to have been crime victims, but that most of the difference can be accounted for by demographic or socio-economic factors.

(ii) Most incidents suffered by ethnic minority respondents were not perceived to be racially motivated, although this was more likely to be the case with threats and with personal (rather than household) victimisations.

(iii) Members of minority groups are more likely to report household offences to the police than were white victims, but were less likely to be satisfied with the police response.

(iv) Members of ethnic minority groups (particularly Asians) are more likely to be fearful of crime.

In sum, and rather summarily, ethnic minorities are more likely to be victimised, and more likely to fear victimisation. The second major report (of the 1996 BCS: Percy, 1998) generally confirmed these earlier conclusions (as have other English studies: for example Walker, 1994) and this is in line with international experience both in Europe (Albrecht, 1991) and in America (Haghigh and Sorensen, 1996; Huang and Vaughn, 1996).

What, though, of the Scottish situation?

Ethnic Minorities and Victimisation in Scotland

The issue has received scant attention in Scotland. Crime featured fleetingly in a major survey conducted in the late 1980s with a large sample of Scottish ethnic minorities and whites, but few victimisation differences were discovered apart from the finding that ethnic minority households were more likely to be victims of vehicle crime than were white households (Smith, P., 1991, p.143). A more recent Scottish office funded research project interviewed Scottish crime victims, and, at one point, compared the experiences of 35 ethnic minority victims with 35 matched white victims. Here, the ethnic minority victims were less satisfied with the action taken by the police than were the white victims, were more likely to think that the police could have done more, and were far less likely to hold favourable attitudes to the police (MacLeod, *et al.*, 1996, pp.88-125). Most recently, the availability of foreign language interpreters in Scottish courts has been examined (MVA Consultancy, 1996).

The Scottish Crime Survey (of which the most recent publication is Anderson and Leitch, 1996) has not, hitherto, added an ethnic minority 'booster' sample to its main sample. In part to pilot this possibility, the opportunity was seized to interview a substantial number of Scottish ethnic minority residents, and subsequently compare their responses to a broadly matched sample of Scottish white residents, as an adjunct to a large, ESRC funded, research project.

Accordingly, in early 1996, 1182 adult residents of the administrative region then known as the Strathclyde Region of Scotland were interviewed face to face in their homes to assess the degree to which they had been victimised the previous year, and to understand more about their general concerns about both crime and the police. Slightly fewer than half (555) of those interviewed were white, and slightly more than half drawn roughly equally from the three most common ordinarily resident non-white Scottish groups: Indians (219), Pakistanis (213) and Chinese (195). This was the first time that a crime survey has been conducted in Scotland to see if there were any ethnic differences in crime victimisation and in perceptions of crime and of the police.

Crime surveys of this sort have various limitations. For example, surveys can only seek information on a restricted range of types of victimisation, and they can only pose questions in the type of language respondents are familiar with. This precludes investigation of, among others, 'white collar' and 'corporate' crimes, and prevents legally precise classification of victimisations. Further, the attitudes and experiences of those aged 15 or younger, or those who live in institutions, are excluded by the nature of the survey design. Finally, the survey instrument was a conventional crime survey one - not one specifically designed to probe the nature of any specifically racially motivated experiences or feelings.

Victimisation and Concern about Victimisation

All respondents were asked a series of questions about crime victimisation that they, or a member of their household, had suffered in the previous calendar year (1995). These questions are taken directly from the Scottish Crime Survey main questionnaire, and are known as the 'screeners'. They were asked in four groups relating to: housebreaking, vehicle crime, assault and vandalism. The survey is reported fully in Ditton, *et al.*, (1998).

Table 17.1 shows that there was very little overall difference between white and ethnic minority victimisation totals, although the rates of white and ethnic minority victimisation for different crimes varied. It is striking that white households were more likely to suffer from housebreaking, and that ethnic minority respondents were more likely to be assaulted. The raw assault victimisation rate is possibly misleading, as the number of ethnic minority assault victims (34) was slightly fewer than the number of white assault victims (37), but each ethnic minority assault victim suffered, on average, about 3.5 victimisations, whereas each white assault victim suffered, on average, only 1.7. Overall, the victimisation rate for respondents in the white sample (59.1 per cent) was remarkably similar to that for respondents in the ethnic minority sample (58.2 per cent).[1]

Table 17.1 Numbers of victimisations and victims**

	White (n=555)		Ethnic Minority (n=627)	
	Victimis'ns* (%n)	Victims (Vn/vm*)	Victimis'ns* (%n)	Victims (Vn/vm*)
House-breaking	94 (16.9%)	53 (1.8)	51 (8.1%)	26 (2.0)
Vehicle crime	135 (40.5%)	79 (1.7)	180 (35.1%)	95 (1.9)
Assault	61 (11.0%)	37 (1.7)	119 (19.0%)	34 (3.5)
Vandalism	38 (6.9%)	26 (1.5)	15 (2.4%)	4 (3.8)
Total	328 (59.1%)	195(1.7)	365 (58.2%)	159(2.3)

* Victimis'ns = Victimisations; Vn/vm = Victimisations per Victim.
** All unweighted data
Because of multiple victimisation (within and between individual categories) number of victims is lower than number of victimisations.
Non-vehicle owning households have been excluded from the 'vehicle crime' row, for which, white n=333, and ethnic minority n=513.

Table 17.2 Percentages of each sample *afraid* of experiencing each of four crime types some/all of the time; and number of victims (expressed as percentages of each sample) *experiencing* each of four crime types*

	1 White	2 Ethnic minority	2.1 Indian	2.2 Pakis- tani	2.3 Chinese
Worry - housebreaking	40	40	31	43	48
Experience-housebreaking	10	4	-	-	-
Worry - vehicle crime	40	36	21	37	50
Experience - vehicle crime	24	19	-	-	-
Worry - assault	25	28	19	34	32
Experience - assault	7	5	-	-	-
Worry - vandalism	30	35	25	37	44
Experience - vandalism	5	1	-	-	-

* Afraid data recoded as 'some of the time' + 'all the time'. 'Don't knows' excluded. Insufficient data to indicate differences between the ethnic minority sub-groups for experiencing each crime type.

Table 17.3 shows how crime victims, of all four crime types, rated their degree of concern about each type. Although it was the case that victims of all four crime categories were more likely than non-victims to say that they worried 'all the time' about their crime type, only between six per cent (assault) and 22 per cent (housebreaking) of victims worried 'all the time' about their crime type.

In addition, between 39 per cent (housebreaking) and 62 per cent (assault) of victims said that they either worried 'not at all' or 'hardly ever' about the crime that they had been a victim of within the previous twelve months.

Table 17.3 Comparative degrees of victimisation concern expressed by victims and (non-victims) in each of four crime types

	House-breaking victims (non-victims)	Vehicle crime victims (non-victims)	Assault victims (non-victims)	Vandalism victims (non-victims)
Not at all	15 (30)	21 (31)	27 (39)	13 (35)
Hardly ever	24 (32)	39 (33)	35 (35)	33 (33)
Some of the time	39 (31)	29 (30)	32 (23)	33 (27)
All the time	22 (8)	10 (7)	6 (3)	20 (5)

Attitudes to Policing in Scotland

Respondents were asked the extent to which they agreed with four statements about attitudes to policing. They were: 'the majority of police in Scotland do a good job'; 'the police try and help the community'; 'there are quite a lot of dishonest police in Scotland'; and 'it is best to avoid the police whenever possible'. Responses from the sample are combined in Table 17.4. The resulting picture is one of little difference between the white and the ethnic minority sample. Members of the Indian sub-group are noticeably more pro-police than both the whites, and the other ethnic minority sub-groups.

Table 17.4 Summary of general attitudes to policing in Scotland*

	1 White	p**	2 Ethnic Minority	2. 1 Indian	2. 2 Pakistani	2. 3 Chinese
Wholly pro-police	22		23	31	25	12
Mixed attitudes	78		75	68	73	88
Wholly anti-police	1		2	2	2	-

* Those defined as 'wholly pro-police' were those who were positive towards the police when answering the four questions; those defined as 'wholly anti-police' were those who were negative towards the police when answering the four questions; those defined as 'mixed attitudes' were those who were positive towards the police in answering some of the four questions, but negative towards the police when answering others of the four.

** There were no statistically significant differences in response.

The sample was also asked about their beliefs relating to police behaviour, firstly by being asked 'when the police are questioning people do you think they ever use threats or unreasonable pressure to get the answers they want?'. Secondly, they were asked 'when the police take written evidence from people do you think what they write down is always a fair and accurate record of what was said?' and thirdly, 'do you think the police in Scotland ever use more violence than necessary?'. Finally, all were asked whether or not they thought that 'the police in Scotland ever make up evidence on people?'.

Attitudes to police behaviour are summarised in Table 17.5. 'Mixed' beliefs again predominate as they did in Table 17.4, although here slightly fewer respondents were wholly pro-police and slightly more of them were wholly anti-police. Overall, there was a very strong relationship between attitudes and beliefs about police, although more than half of those who were pro-police in attitude, had mixed feelings about their behaviour. A small number moved from having mixed beliefs to being anti-police. Respondents

310 Criminal Justice in Scotland

in the white sample were more likely to change their minds than were respondents in the ethnic minority sample.

Table 17.5 Summary of beliefs about police behaviour*

	1 White	p**	2 Ethnic Minority	2. 1 Indian	2. 2 Pakistani	2. 3 Chinese
Wholly pro- police	11		10	14	7	7
Mixed attitudes	77		88	83	91	89
Wholly anti- police	11		3	2	2	4

* Those defined as 'wholly pro-police' were those who were positive towards the police when answering the four questions; those defined as 'wholly anti-police' were those who were negative towards the police when answering the four questions; those defined as 'mixed attitudes' were those who were positive towards the police in answering some of the four questions, but negative towards the police when answering others of the four.

** There were no statistically significant differences in response.

The answers to this set of questions suggest that members of Scottish ethnic minority communities are less likely to be 'anti' police than are white Scottish residents. In part this is confirmed when the answers to two further questions ('do the police offer sufficient protection against crime?' and 'do the police interfere too much in community matters?') are combined, as they are in Table 17.6.

Finally, all respondents were asked what they thought 'of the police presence in this area? Is it about the right amount, or too much, or not enough?'. Their responses are in Table 17.7.

Table 17.6 Summary of attitudes to police involvement*

	1 White	p**	2 Ethnic Minority	2. 1 Indian	2. 2 Pakistani	2. 3 Chinese
Wholly pro- police	18	+++	35	38	38	29
Mixed attitudes	81	++	64	61	61	71
Wholly anti- police	2		1	1	1	1

* Those defined as 'wholly pro-police' were those who were positive towards the police when answering the two questions; those defined as 'wholly anti-police' were those who were negative towards the police when answering the two questions; those defined as 'mixed attitudes' were those who were positive towards the police in answering one of the two questions, but negative towards the police when answering the other.

** P values calculated for each row by non-parametric $\chi2$ test, all 1df. + = p<0.01; ++ = p<0.001; +++ = p<0.0001.

Table 17.7 Police presence in respondent's area. Is it...*

	1 White	p**	2 Ethnic Minority	2. 1 Indian	2. 2 Pakistani	2. 3 Chinese
Not enough	68	+++	35	30	45	29
Don't know	6	+++	24	17	17	39
About right	25	++++	41	52	38	32
Too much	1		-	-	-	-

* 'Don't knows' are included as they constitute a large part of the response.

** P values calculated for each row by non-parametric $\chi2$ test, all 1df. + = p<0.01; ++ = p<0.001; +++ = p<0.0001; ++++ = p<0.00001.

Respondents in the ethnic minority sample (particularly those from the Chinese and Indian sub-groups) were significantly more satisfied than respondents in the white sample with the police presence in their area, even though significantly more respondents in the ethnic minority sample than in the white sample answered 'don't know'.

Table 17.8   A 'mugging': percentages indicating that they would respond in each of five ways*

	1 White	p**	2 Ethnic Minority	2. 1 Indian	2. 2 Pakistani	2. 3 Chinese
'act yourself?'	60	++++	36	28	38	41
'call neighbours?'	76	++++	52	49	54	54
'tell police?'	98	++++	73	71	75	72
'identify people?'	95	++++	67	67	68	65
'give evidence?'	91	++++	53	47	61	49

* 'Act yourself' = 'try to do something about it yourself'; 'call neighbours' = 'go to your neighbours for help'; 'tell police' = 'tell the police what you had seen'; 'identify people' = 'help the police identify the people who had done it'; and 'give evidence' = 'give evidence in court'.

** + = $p<0.01$; ++ = $p<0.001$; +++ = $p<0.0001$; ++++ = $p<0.00001$.   'Don't knows' excluded for simplicity. 'Don't knows' small and roughly equivalent for white and ethnic minority samples except for 'give evidence' where 'don't knows' were 13 per cent for respondents in the white sample and 25 per cent for respondents in the ethnic minority sample. All $\chi2$s more significant with 'don't knows' included.

However, their relatively pro-police sentiments notwithstanding, the ethnic minority sub-groups were seemingly less prepared actually to assist the police if witnessing a criminal act.   To assess preparedness to 'do something' if a witness, all respondents were offered three hypothetical scenarios, and then asked five questions about their response.   The first scenario was 'if you had seen a couple of youths knock down a man and take his wallet' (a 'mugging'). All were asked 'would you do any of the following things'... 'try to do something about it yourself?', 'go to your neighbours for help?', 'tell the police what you had seen?', 'help the police identify the people who had done it?', and 'give evidence in court?'. Responses to the first scenario are in Table 17.8.

Here, the significant differences were between the white and ethnic minority samples taken together. There were no significant differences between the three separate ethnic minority sub-groups. Respondents in the white sample were very significantly more likely to say that they would become involved than were respondents in the ethnic minority sample. The relative apathy expressed by respondents in the ethnic minority sample is interesting given that the direct questions about the police showed that they were relatively more pro-police than the respondents in the white sample. Why this should be so is open to question, but the same relative apathy also typifies responses to the second scenario (what would you do 'if you saw a couple of youths smashing up a bus shelter?'), and, to some extent, the third one (what would you do 'if you saw a traffic accident in which someone had been badly hurt?').

Racially Motivated Victimisation, Harassment and Discrimination

Overall, a fifth of the white respondents and a third of the ethnic minority respondents thought that 'racial prejudice' is a problem in Scotland. However, relatively similar numbers - around two-thirds - did not see it as an issue. The difference is accounted for by the fact that 16 per cent of the white respondents reported that they 'can't say' whether prejudice is a problem, but only six per cent of ethnic minority respondents said this. This is shown in Figure 17.2.

Looking at the different ethnic minority sub-groups in terms of perceptions of 'racial prejudice', the Pakistani and Chinese sub-groups were broadly the same. A third of each sub-group saw 'racial prejudice' as a problem, although respondents in the Pakistani sub-group were slightly more likely to see it as a problem.

Curiously, the respondents in the Indian sub-group were less concerned about 'racial prejudice' even than the white respondents. Only 17 per cent of the respondents in the Indian sub-group, but 21 per cent of the white respondents defined it as serious. Defining 'racial prejudice' as a serious problem increased slightly with age (particularly for ethnic minority respondents), and older ethnic minority females were the group most likely to define it as serious.

Figure 17.2   Degree to which racial prejudice is seen to be a problem

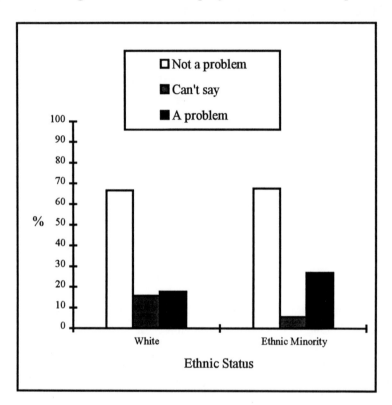

Summary

This was the first crime survey of its kind conducted with large numbers of both white and ethnic minority respondents in Scotland, and the aim of the exercise was simply to provide some robust baseline data on comparative crime concerns, victimisation rates and general attitudes to policing.

One conclusion has to be that this 'experiment' has not been entirely problem free. First, the non-response and refusal rates were anticipated to be higher for members of the ethnic minority communities than for the selected white respondents, but turned out to be even higher than expected (Appendix A of Ditton *et al.*, 1998, has the detail). Second, members of the ethnic minority community were consistently more likely to respond to questions by saying that they 'don't know' or 'can't say'. This may be for cultural reasons, because of language difficulties, or because of a mixture of these, and other unknown reasons. Both these issues need to be addressed and corrected if full confidence in such surveying techniques is to be restored.

A third conclusion is that even though the achieved samples were weighted to represent their communities accurately (see Ditton *et al.*, 1998, Appendix A), the actual communities were still quite different in terms of age, gender and so on. The whites, for example, were older and less likely to be economically active. The ethnic minority sub-samples, on the other hand, were younger and more likely to be in work. Where these demographic differences seemed important, analysis controlled for the variance thus introduced. However, these differences in community demographics differentially expose their members to various crime-related risks and fears, and it is of some value to look briefly at the separate ethnic minority sub-groups which, for most of this chapter, have been aggregated together as the 'ethnic minority sample'.

The Indian Sub-group

Respondents in the Indian sub-group were more likely to live in households with no children than were respondents in the other two ethnic minority groups, were much more likely to be owner occupiers, and this may have affected their overall attitudes to the various problems they were questioned about. They were slightly more satisfied with the area that they lived in than respondents in the other two ethnic minority groups, but had not lived there as long. This sub-group tended to socialise least at night, but were more likely than respondents in the other two ethnic minority groups to say that they stop and chat to people that they meet locally, and that they visit friends locally. When it comes to the seriousness of racial prejudice, the Indian respondents were less likely even than the whites to see it as a problem, and claimed to have experienced fewer abusive comments or obscene gestures than did members of the other two ethnic minority sub-groups.

This relatively relaxed attitude is reflected in the comparatively infrequent degree to which Indian respondents rate various crimes as serious, and by the fact that they were less likely than respondents in the other two ethnic minority groups to say that they would feel unsafe when out walking alone at night. Indian respondents were also significantly less afraid of somebody breaking into their house, of suffering from vehicle crime, of assault and of vandalism.

On a variety of measures, respondents in the Indian sub-group were noticeably more positive about the police in Scotland. This threads their beliefs about police behaviour, and the adequacy of police presence, both generally and in their area. However, they were markedly less likely than respondents in the other two ethnic minority sub-groups to imagine that they would do anything if they had witnessed hypothetical criminal acts. Finally, they were less likely to have contacted the police in the past year, but more likely to have been satisfied with the outcome of that contact if they had.

The Pakistani Sub-group

Respondents in the Pakistani sub-group were more likely to live in households with children than were respondents in the other two ethnic minority sub-groups, and were noticeably less likely to have educational qualifications. They had lived in their area for longer than had members of the Indian sub-group, and were slightly less satisfied with it. Pakistani respondents were more likely to go out at night than members of the other two ethnic minority sub-groups, but less likely to say that they use local amenities than the other ethnic minority respondents. The Pakistani respondents were much more likely to see racial prejudice as a problem than, for example, the Indian respondents. Further, they were more likely to have experienced abusive comments and obscene gestures (which might have had a racial motive) - and to have experienced more of them - than respondents in either of the other two ethnic minority sub-groups.

Pakistani respondents were more likely to view most of a list of crimes as serious than the Indian group, although they were less likely to think of them in this way than the respondents in the Chinese sub-group. Further, they were most likely to claim that they would feel unsafe when out walking alone after dark in their area. They were the most afraid of housebreaking, nearly as worried about vehicle crime as the Chinese respondents, and most afraid of both assault and of vandalism.

Respondents in the Pakistani sub-group were less positive about the police in Scotland than the Indian respondents, and more suspicious of police behaviour. They were also more likely to think that policing resources were, both in general and in their area, inadequate. Nevertheless, they were the sub-group most likely to imagine that they would respond positively if they had witnessed hypothetical criminal acts, although they were more likely than respondents in the other two ethnic minority sub-groups to feel that the police stopped people without reason. They were the sub-group that was most likely to have contacted the police in the past year, but were less satisfied with that contact than respondents in the Indian sub-group.

The Chinese Sub-group

Chinese household structures generally resembled the norm for the ethnic minority sample, although slightly more of them lived as lone adults. Respondents in the Chinese sub-group were much more likely to be in full-time or in part-time work than either Indians or Pakistanis, and this might explain why they tended to have higher incomes and greater access to financial resources. They had lived, on average, longer in the area that they lived in than was the case for the other two ethnic minority sub-groups. Although as satisfied with it as were other ethnic minority members, respondents in the Chinese sub-group were significantly less likely than members of the other two ethnic minority sub-groups to say that it was 'easy to tell a stranger in this area from someone who lives here'. Chinese respondents were much more likely than respondents in the Indian or Pakistani sub-groups to visit pubs or clubs at night, and used local amenities noticeably more often than the Pakistani respondents. Members of the Chinese sub-group were the least likely to have experienced abusive comments and obscene gestures that might have had a racial motive, although they were more likely to define racial prejudice as a problem than respondents in the Indian sub-group.

Chinese respondents were more likely than respondents in the other two ethnic minority sub-groups to rate a list of crimes as serious, were nearly as afraid of housebreaking, assault and vandalism as were the Pakistani respondents, and more afraid of vehicle crime than either of the other two ethnic minority sub-groups.

Attitudes to the police expressed by respondents in the Chinese sub-group were, in general, pitched roughly mid way between the relatively pro-police sentiments of the respondents in the Indian sub-group, and the relatively anti-police sentiments of the respondents in the Pakistani sub-group. The Chinese respondents had had fewer contacts with the police in the past year than had respondents in the other two ethnic minority sub-groups, and were more likely to be dissatisfied with that contact.

Conclusion

Reviewing, at this point, the summary findings derived from various sweeps of the BCS, it seems that the Scottish ethnic minority population presents a radically different picture from that in England. Overall it is the similarities, rather than differences, between respondents in the white sample and respondents in the ethnic minority sample which is the most noticeable finding from this survey. Where differences existed, it was generally the case that respondents in the white sample were more concerned about crime, more victimised, or more critical of the police than were respondents in the ethnic minority sample.[2]

Why this should be so is not clear, although the size of the overall populations, and the size, composition and backgrounds of the ethnic minority groups must clearly be at least part of the answer.

Notes

1. At one point in the survey, 237 of those recording a past year victimisation were asked to comment on various aspects of that experience. 108 of these respondents were drawn from the ethnic minority sub-sample. Of these, only 46 felt that they had been 'targeted' in some way, and only nine cited 'racial' reasons.
2. This is emphatically not to claim that members of ethnic minority groups in Scotland do not experience problems relating to crime, nor that these problems might be different to those experienced by the white population.

18 Victims of Crime

SUE MOODY

Introduction

Consideration of the needs and rights of victims in criminal justice is relatively new in Scotland. Although debates about the place of crime victims in the criminal process have had a major influence in the United States and have begun to impact on the position of the victim in England and Wales (see Zedner, 1997), there has been little sign in this jurisdiction of any significant change. Nevertheless, the last ten years has seen important developments in our knowledge and understanding of the rate of criminal victimisation in Scotland, the effects of crime on victims, their need for support and the difficult position they face in the criminal justice system. This chapter will map out research and policy developments to date, and identify gaps which require further consideration. Before doing so, however, there is an important proviso to be made about the way in which victims of crime are usually defined.

Defining Victims of Crime

The definition of crime victims which is generally used in criminological research and policy statements and which underpins practical intervention is unsatisfactory. It is too narrow in that it concentrates mainly on individual victims of particular types of crime, omitting the impact of crime on families and neighbourhoods, and leaving out those crimes which clearly have a harmful, but a less direct impact on their victims, such as major frauds and environmental pollution. It does not acknowledge the often fluid and sometimes ambiguous nature of the status of victim and of offender and polarises two categories which frequently overlap. The use of the term at the pre-conviction stage is not accurate since verification of criminal victimisation may in many cases depend on a finding of guilt. Finally, the word 'victim' carries unfortunate connotations of powerlessness and vulnerability which may hamper recovery and influence the way 'victims' are viewed by others (Moody, 1997).

319

Criminal Victimisation in Scotland

The study of criminal victimisation did not really begin in Scotland until the early 1980s. Before that time, data on victimisation rates, the impact of crime on victims and the role of victims in Scottish criminal justice was unavailable and little interest was shown in crime victims, either by criminal justice practitioners, policymakers, criminologists or the public. In 1981, a major breakthrough was made with the first British Crime Survey, which was designed to uncover information on levels of victimisation, victims' experiences and reactions to criminal incidents and their evaluation of the performance of criminal justice agencies (Chambers and Tombs, 1984).

Instead of using official criminal statistics, which only noted crimes reported to the police and recorded by them as criminal incidents, it was possible, through interviews with a representative sample of the adult population, to reveal something of the 'dark figure of crime' and also to collect data on a range of other aspects of criminal victimisation. The first British Crime Survey, which included a specific Scottish component, not only demonstrated that the majority of crime was never reported to the police (three times as many incidents occurred as were recorded in Scottish criminal statistics) but also that there were significant differences between Scotland and England and Wales in relation to levels of victimisation. For example, the stereotype of Glasgow as the violent crime capital of the United Kingdom was shown to be a myth and the idea that Scotland had a higher per capita crime rate than England and Wales was also disproved (see chapter 2).

The first British Crime Survey was followed in Scotland by three further surveys, permitting comparisons to be made over the 15 year period between 1981 and 1996 (Payne, 1992; Anderson and Leitch, 1996; MVA Consultancy, 1997). These surveys not only confirmed the differences between victimisation rates in Scotland, as compared with England and Wales, but also demonstrated that the 'avalanche' in crime recorded in criminal statistics was not borne out by the reports from victims themselves. Between 1981 and 1992, recorded crime increased by 52 per cent; over the same period the increase as measured by the three crime surveys was five per cent. Between 1992 and 1995, both officially recorded and Scottish Crime Survey reported crime fell, by 13 per cent and 19 per cent respectively (for further details, see chapters 2 and 3).

These surveys also provided, for the first time, useful data on the characteristics of victims and the impact of crime on victims.[1] They demonstrated the ubiquitous nature of crime in general terms but also the vulnerability of particular groups. Young, single males were most likely to be the victims of assaults and also robberies. There was some association between social class and victimisation, although this was not as strong as the association with age and sex. In addition, crime survey data has graphically illustrated the significant increase in the fear of crime among the public generally, which appears to have had a marked impact on public attitudes to crime and victimisation. According to the 1993 Survey, crime is seen as 'quite' a serious problem or an 'extremely' serious problem by 94 per cent of those interviewed, with only unemployment being regarded as a more serious problem.

International crime surveys have included Scotland as a separate jurisdiction, enabling further comparisons to be drawn. The most recent International Crime Survey, conducted in 1996, suggests that people in Scotland worry particularly about housebreaking and are also concerned about walking alone in their area after dark (Mayhew and van Dijk, 1997). Nevertheless, compared with England and Wales and with the Netherlands, the Scottish population was less likely to suffer criminal victimisation.

The data from national crime surveys has been supplemented by local crime surveys which concentrate on particular geographical areas and may focus on particular groups. The results of these surveys have been to demonstrate very clearly the 'place-specific' nature of victimisation, and to show that national crime survey data may mask considerable differences between levels of victimisation in different geographical areas and in relation to particular groups. For instance, harassment of women was identified as a major problem for young women in the centre of Edinburgh (Carnie, 1994); rates of vandalism varied between nine and 27 per cent on adjacent housing estates in Dundee (Jones *et al.*, 1994); and victimisation rates among young people between eleven and 15 living in Edinburgh were much higher than had been anticipated (Anderson *et al.*, 1994).

The Impact of Crime on Victims

Crime surveys, both local and national, provide a useful way of measuring victimisation and the impact of crime on victims. There are, nevertheless, weaknesses in the crime survey method which limit their usefulness in relation to particular types of offences and specific groups of victims (see chapter 3 for detailed analysis). Fortunately, in Scotland these gaps have been, at least to some extent, filled by other types of research, generally qualitative in nature. In particular, the work of Chambers and Millar in the early 1980s is still regarded as a significant contribution to our understanding of the impact of sexual assault on victims (Chambers and Millar, 1983; 1986). Their study revealed the traumatic effects of such victimisation, as well as providing a damning picture of the reaction of criminal justice agencies to complainers in sexual assault cases.

A study of 255 victims of crime in Dundee, Edinburgh and Glasgow also provides some useful material on the impact of crime on victims (MacLeod *et al.*, 1996). Although a range of responses was obtained, two-thirds of all victims said that they had been affected emotionally by the crime and the researchers were 'struck by the intensity of these effects' (MacLeod *et al.*, 1996, p.44). In addition to the negative effects of criminal victimisation, almost a fifth of responses related to the victims' concerns about the outcome of the criminal case, with some victims feeling let down by the criminal justice system.[2]

Support for Victims of Crime

Research studies of the impact of crime on victims were not alone in identifying that the needs of victims were largely unmet. In the 1970s, Rape Crisis Centres and Women's Aid refuges started to bring to public attention the absence of practical help and emotional support for women who survive sexual assaults and violence in the home (Dobash and Dobash, 1992). By the mid 1980s, it had been acknowledged that crime victims in general needed support. As with Rape Crisis and Women's Aid, however, such help was to come with little assistance from government and through a voluntary organisation, Victim Support, which was mainly staffed by unpaid labour.

Over the last ten years Victim Support has developed right across the United Kingdom. Based on a model of local Victim Support Schemes, run by voluntary management committees, with the day-to-day operation of each scheme in the hands of a co-ordinator, often unpaid, Victim Support has been the fastest growing voluntary organisation of the 1980s. In Scotland, development has been swift, with four schemes in 1985 expanding to 70 by

1992 (Scottish Association of Victim Support Schemes, 1986; Victim Support Scotland, 1993). The focus of victim support work has been on face-to-face contact with victims, who are mainly referred to the service by the police, and who are visited at home by selected and trained volunteers. These volunteers were initially envisaged as offering very limited and short-term emotional support, practical help and information to crime victims, who were mostly victims of housebreaking. It soon became clear, however, that victims of serious crime, particularly involving personal violence and where criminal proceedings were instituted, needed support over a longer period of time, and that volunteers required more extensive training to undertake such work. In addition, particular groups may have specific needs, such as children, those victimised at work and those who experience repeat victimisation.

By 1997, Victim Support Scotland had developed a range of different techniques to address the needs of crime victims, including special projects to assist witnesses giving evidence in court and to help victims seriously affected by crime, training programmes for volunteers helping victims of sexual assault and the families of murder victims, and initiatives involving ethnic minority victims (Victim Support Scotland, 1997). Funding from the Scottish Office increased substantially (from £600 in 1984-5 to £1.28 million in 1996-7) and has enabled local Victim Support Services to employ co-ordinators, and in some cases administrative staff.

Research studies of crime victims' needs, both in Scotland and in England and Wales, have demonstrated that, while most victims do not require the support of professionals, such as psychiatrists or psychologists, to overcome the negative effects of crime, many experience a range of upsetting emotional reactions and value the offer of help from an understanding volunteer (Maguire and Corbett, 1987). In a recent Scottish study (Kerner and Barker, 1998), for instance, victims were overwhelmingly positive about the support offered to them by victim support volunteers. Research in both jurisdictions has also identified the problems of 'secondary victimisation' which may adversely affect victims whose cases come to court (Shapland *et al.*, 1985; Wilson, 1993). Studies of victims of serious violent crime, in particular, reveal the traumatic impact of such crimes as rape (Chambers and Millar, 1983), other crimes of violence against women and children (Burman and Lloyd, 1993) and murder (Brown *et al.*, 1990), and the demands which such cases can place on Victim Support Services (Dobash, 1993).

Work with crime victims has also included involvement in events where whole communities have been traumatised by crime, such as the Lockerbie bombing and the shootings at Dunblane. A great deal more work needs to be done to develop understanding and expertise for professionals and volunteers supporting such victims. Difficulties such as lack of communication between agencies and victims' families and problems arising out of inter-agency co-operation, compounded by intense media coverage, have resulted in a less than satisfactory service in these 'disaster' situations. Sometimes victims' desire for privacy and natural resilience are ignored, and the value of local 'good neighbour' support is not acknowledged by those managing service provision to such victims (*Scotsman*, 27 September 1997).

Other support groups for crime victims have started in Scotland. Their focus is somewhat different from Victim Support in that they are often self-help groups, such as the FoMC (Families of Murdered Children), or groups whose main aim is to push for changes to improve the position of the victim in criminal justice, for example PETAL (People Experiencing Trauma and Loss), whose founders were the parents of a murdered girl and who have campaigned for the abolition of the 'Not Proven' verdict (see Duff, 1996b).

The Victim and Scottish Criminal Justice

Before the establishment of a public prosecution system in Scotland, the person who saw him or herself as a victim of crime was not only the initiator of criminal proceedings but also had primary responsibility for seeing that the case was investigated, the prosecution instituted and the accused brought to trial (Normand, 1938). The prosecution and trial of criminal matters then became the responsibility of the sheriff but by the early nineteenth century the procurator fiscal took virtually every prosecution. The complainer's role was reduced to that of a witness and the complainer no longer had any legal right to waive a prosecution or desert a case once criminal proceedings had been instigated. This contrasted markedly with the situation in England and Wales where private prosecutions were common until the 1960s and a national public prosecution service was not established until 1985 (Fionda, 1995). The only vestige of the complainer's original role could be found in the action for assythment, through which victims of violent crime or the family of a person who had been murdered could claim compensation from the offender (Mackay, 1992).[3]

The move away from private vengeance to a State run prosecution system was a welcome one, removing a heavy burden from victims and making justice more universally accessible in criminal cases. However, it is felt by some that the pendulum may have swung too far the other way, leaving victims of crime, who now have no legal standing except as witnesses, at some disadvantage. Other jurisdictions, for example the United States, have taken steps to rectify this, notably by giving victims of crime, at least on paper, a role in decision-making as a case moves through the criminal justice process. This has, in turn, raised concerns about encroachments on the rights of accused persons and of offenders, and a perception (which seems to be an accurate one) that crime victims are being used as part of law and order rhetoric to secure wider political ends (Elias, 1993).

Nevertheless, the studies already discussed and the personal experience of many crime victims suggest that the Scottish criminal justice system does not sufficiently acknowledge the needs, and some would say the rights, of victims of crime. *The Justice Charter for Scotland* (Scottish Office, 1991f), for instance, while recognising that the public service must provide help and support to crime victims, continued to place the onus on the victim to ask for assistance. The importance of victims for criminal justice generally was first formally noted in the White Paper, *Firm and Fair* (Scottish Office, 1994f). However, the paper underlines the reactive nature of the criminal justice system's responses to victims, although it claims that 'substantial progress has been made' in certain areas, notably the giving of evidence by victims, which is considered further below (Scottish Office, 1994f, para.9.3). In addition, government policy in Scotland has tended to avoid the rhetoric of 'rights' in its consideration of crime victims.[4]

Instead a variety of 'needs' were identified in the White Paper *Crime and Punishment* (Scottish Office, 1996f), including understanding and fairness, information, compensation and taking the victims' interests into account. Four key priorities were identified in that White Paper: the establishment of a Victims Steering Group to advise on policy and good practice; a national strategy for the provision of information to victims; an information leaflet for victims; and a code of practice for statutory and voluntary agencies who routinely deal with victims of crime. Although the Victims Steering Group has been set up and the other proposals are currently being considered by government and criminal justice professionals, little appears to have been achieved in concrete terms. Recent legislation on criminal justice matters, including the Crime and Punishment (Scotland) Act 1997, makes no mention of victims. This contrasts with the position in England and Wales, where the Home Office has produced two Victim's Charters outlining what victims can expect from criminal justice agencies and minimum service standards are in place (Home Office, 1990; 1996). Underlying the difficulties experienced by complainers/victims in Scotland seems to be a lack of awareness of, or sensitivity towards, victims and witnesses generally on the part of criminal justice personnel. Victim awareness training is now being offered in a limited way but this is a very recent development. It should be noted, however, that criminal justice agencies in Scotland have recognised their role in supporting crime victims with, for instance, the Association of Directors of Social Work pledging to include 'the victim perspective' as a core part of social work supervision (Association of Directors of Social Work, 1996).

Victims' main concerns are: the lack of information regarding case progress and outcome; witness support and protection; the impact of the crime and how that is communicated to the court; court accommodation; and compensation. Each of these will now be discussed in turn.

Information on Case Progress and Outcome

There is no legal requirement to keep the complainer informed about the progress of the case after a crime is reported to the police, and no agency charged with the task of providing such information. In addition, up until 1998, no general information was given to complainers in the form, for example, of an explanatory leaflet, unlike the position in England and Wales where since 1991 every complainant has received such a leaflet from the police. A leaflet is now available in Scotland and will be distributed by the police from the Autumn of 1998. At present the degree to which complainers are kept informed depends entirely on the willingness of the police, the prosecution service and the courts to provide an update on developments, the tenacity and determination of the complainer and the existence of an active and well-resourced victim support service.

A research study published in 1995 described the policy and practice of criminal justice agencies in Scotland and the needs of complainers and victims for information (MVA Consultancy, 1995). It appeared that while all police forces had an official policy of keeping victims informed, and adopted a pro-active approach, fiscals and courts had no such policies and only provided information when it was specifically requested by the complainer. Even in the case of the police there were significant differences in the standardisation of procedures, with some forces operating fairly formal arrangements with stated times within which the complainer could expect to be informed, while others adopted a much more informal approach. The majority of the victims surveyed considered that they had not been kept adequately informed about the progress of the case. Most victims wanted to receive information at key stages of the case and felt they had a right to know what was happening. They also expressed a need for more general information about relevant criminal justice procedures.

The main reasons for the failure to provide such information appeared to be resource constraints and lack of victim awareness on the part of criminal justice agencies. The research clearly showed that some complainers and victims felt that they had been insensitively treated, particularly at court, and that this heightened their feelings of dissatisfaction when information was not given to them. Victims were not told and felt they should have been given information on: arrest and charges in connection with the offence; decisions concerning prosecution; granting or refusal of bail (something which is now mandatory in England and Wales); court details and appearances; the case outcome; and the availability of compensation.

Unfortunately, the report concluded that criminal justice agencies were unable to agree as to what specific information should be provided and which agency should provide it. In spite of the fact that the findings of this study were published over two years ago, no significant changes have been made, either in the provision of general or of case-specific information, except in relation to prisoner release. Victims of violent and sexual offences have, since April 1997, been able to choose to receive information about the release date of the offender in their case. A general information leaflet for victims is also now available, although the police are still testing out the best way to distribute it.

Witness Support and Protection

The importance of giving victims (and other witnesses) 'the best opportunity to give their evidence without fear or stress' was noted in *Firm and Fair*

(Scottish Office, 1994f, para.9.3). Steps have been taken to reduce such stress, particularly for child witnesses, by modifying the arrangements for giving evidence. Difficulties faced by complainers in cases of rape and sexual assault have also been taken into account. Special arrangements can now be made for other vulnerable witnesses also. The majority of witnesses, however, do not fall into these categories, and their need for support and information has not been fully addressed. A pilot project, run by Victim Support with funding from The Scottish Office, is currently working with witnesses in three selected sheriff courts. The physical environment of courts has improved significantly over the last five years and the harsh and peremptory wording of the witness citation has been mitigated by a personal letter from the Procurator Fiscal which provides basic information about the location of the courthouse, the practicalities of giving evidence and thanks the witness for his or her assistance. In addition, a joint statement on Crown witnesses, issued by the Crown Office and the Scottish Court Service in 1998, acknowledges shared responsibility for providing a proper and efficient service to such witnesses and giving information about case progress and disposal.

Child witnesses   The position of child witnesses was considered by the Scottish Law Commission in 1989. Its recommendations that children (defined as those aged under 16) should be able to give evidence through a live television link were implemented in 1991 (under section 56 of the Law Reform (Miscellaneous Provisions) (Scotland) Act 1990) and further extended in 1994 to enable children to give their evidence from behind a screen. Under the current provisions, contained in section 271 of the Criminal Procedure (Scotland) Act 1995, children can also give their evidence 'on commission', that is the child is questioned before the trial itself and the videotape of this evidence is played in court. The court must consider the possible effect on the child of giving evidence in the usual way, the benefits to the child of using an alternative method and the child's own views. The judge is expected to take into account the child's age and maturity, the nature of the alleged offence, the nature of the evidence and the relationship between the child and the accused.

The presiding judge can only respond to an application from the prosecution or defence and judges appear to differ in the approach they take to such applications. An evaluation of a child witness support initiative is currently being undertaken in Glasgow Sheriff Court.

Complainers in sexual assault cases For many years Scottish courts have given the complainer in sexual assault cases the benefit of anonymity in the reporting of the proceedings and the trial judge has had the discretion to clear the court (under section 92(3) of the Criminal Procedure (Scotland) Act 1995) when such complainers are giving evidence. However, some women were subjected to cross-examination by the defence which caused them distress (see Chambers and Millar, 1986), particularly when they were questioned about their previous sexual history in order to undermine the credibility of their evidence and suggest that they had in fact consented to the sexual conduct. Under statutory provisions introduced in 1988 the defence were barred from asking questions, either of the complainer or other witnesses, about the sexual character or history of the complainer. This has now been extended to cover virtually all sexual offences, under section 274 of the Criminal Procedure (Scotland) Act 1995, but the provisions permit the trial judge to lift the bar in the interests of justice. A research study of the implementation of this prohibition concluded that the defence was finding ways of circumventing it, either by slipping in evidence which demonstrated that the complainer was sexually active or by obtaining the permission of the judge to introduce such evidence (Brown *et al.*, 1993).

Vulnerable witnesses Giving evidence can be a daunting experience for anyone. The use of technical language, the constraints imposed by evidential and procedural requirements, and the layout of the courtroom makes a criminal courtroom a forbidding and frightening place. Professionals involved in criminal justice can all too easily forget this. The stress may be felt particularly by people who are already coping with other difficulties, such as frailty caused by age and physical or mental ill-health. A recent very welcome move is contained in section 29 of the Crime and Punishment (Scotland) Act which extends the provisions in section 271 of the Criminal Procedure (Scotland) Act 1995 relating to child witnesses to include vulnerable witnesses.

Witness protection More attention is now paid to the needs of certain witnesses for protection. Following several cases at the High Court in Glasgow where witnesses reported that attempts had been made to intimidate them into changing their testimony, efforts were made in 1996 to introduce a Private Member's Bill on the topic, designed to offer anonymity to certain witnesses and to establish a network of support for such witnesses. While the Bill was unsuccessful, witness protection schemes have been established, particularly in Strathclyde. According to Strathclyde police, 30 witnesses have been supported by specially trained officers, in trials ranging from multi-million pound drugs cases to street muggings (*Scotsman*, 31 August 1997).

Information about the Impact of the Crime on the Victim

No agency in Scotland has responsibility for collecting information on the impact of the crime on the victim and at no stage in the criminal justice process is such data-collection a matter of routine. This has important repercussions in both instrumental and symbolic ways. Police officers may not be aware that complainers have concerns for their personal safety and may therefore fail to offer them adequate protection, prosecutors may have no information on which to apply for compensation and judges may pass sentence with no knowledge of the effects of the crime on the victim. For victims this gap in the system may be profound, alienating them from an already strange and sometimes frightening process, encouraging them to feel that the system takes no account of them and reinforcing feelings of secondary victimisation.

The introduction of 'victim statements' as part of the dossier of information which is used in making key decisions in the criminal justice process appears relatively uncontroversial. It is already happening in some cases where the police are including such data in their report. However, the issue has become a matter of controversy largely because the emphasis in other jurisdictions has been on provision of information at the sentencing stage alone and on permitting the victim to play a direct role in determining sentence (Ashworth, 1993). The Scottish courts viewed this trend with some concern in an unprecedented case in which the victim was invited to give her views as to the appropriate sentence. The Crown, when asked to undertake this task, brought a bill of advocation requesting the High Court to set aside this requirement.[5] The High Court held it was entirely wrong for the judge to seek the victim's views, since she had no expertise and could not assist the court in any way.

There have been no recent developments in Scotland, although Victim Support Scotland is keen that consideration be given to the less controversial 'victim statement' which would not involve statements of opinion but would help to inform criminal justice decisions at every stage of the process. In spite of the adoption by government and perhaps by the public of a more retributive stance towards offenders, there has been little support for any major change in criminal procedure allowing the complainer/victim a role in decision-making, particularly in sentencing.

Court Accommodation

A major criticism made by all court users, but one which may impact particularly on complainers, is the accommodation and facilities in courthouses. The majority were built in the last century and are now dealing with much larger numbers of cases, with a significant increase in court staff, prosecutors, agents and witnesses. Two reports by the Scottish Consumer Council were highly critical of court accommodation (Scottish Consumer Council, 1981; 1990). These reports highlighted the spartan nature of many witness rooms; the lack of refreshment, toilet and telephone facilities; the difficulties in access for the disabled; the absence of crèche facilities; and the fact that a substantial minority of courts did not have separate waiting rooms for prosecution and defence witnesses. Poor communication and signing also caused problems for those who were unfamiliar with court layout and procedures. In the High Court, where the most serious cases are dealt with, this problem was particularly acute and could cause considerable distress to complainers who had to sit with defence witnesses, including the accused's family and friends. The Scottish Courts Service has instituted a rolling programme of refurbishment and increasingly Scottish courts are becoming more pleasant places for all court users. 80 per cent of courthouses now meet the standards set out in the Justice Charter (Scottish Courts Service, 1997).

Compensation

Victims of crime may receive compensation in four ways: through a pre-trial reparation and mediation scheme; by means of a compensation order in the criminal courts; through a civil action for damages; and under the Criminal Injuries Compensation Scheme. Each of these will now be discussed in turn.

Reparation and mediation schemes These schemes do enable offenders to compensate their victims, either financially or in kind. Unfortunately their operation is currently limited to certain parts of Scotland only and there are important issues about the kinds of offences which should be dealt with through these schemes. (For further information see Mackay, 1995.)

Compensation orders Under Part IV of the Criminal Justice (Scotland) Act 1980 a court can impose a compensation order as a criminal sentence in its own right or combined with another disposal, except in the case of an absolute discharge or a probation order.[6] However, there are difficulties for the victim in using this avenue to obtain compensation. The victim has no right to apply for a compensation order and is dependent on the prosecutor to make application. Judges vary considerably in their use of these orders and offenders may not have the means to pay. A research study conducted for the Scottish Office looking at compensation orders made between 1989 and 1992 showed that there had been a fall in the number of such orders and that in almost half of such cases the victim was an organisation (such as an electricity supplier) rather than an individual (Hamilton and Wisniewski, 1996). Statistics on proceedings in Scottish courts show that compensation orders were made for 4.7 per cent of all charges proved in 1995 and were particularly likely to be used in cases of vandalism, where compensation would generally be made to a local authority or a business. The High Court has endorsed the value and underlined the restitutory purpose of compensation orders in several recent sentencing appeals.[7]

Civil action for damages Traditionally, as has already been noted, it was the complainer who pursued the case to court. While this has been largely superseded by public prosecution, a complainer can still, nevertheless, bring an action in the civil courts. There has been a small but significant rise in the number of civil actions, mainly for serious assaults, attempted murder and murder.

The Court of Session recently upheld the right of a pursuer to bring such an action, even though the defender had been acquitted on a criminal charge.[8] Some unease was, however, expressed about the use of civil proceedings as a means of alternative punishment rather than compensation.[9] In another case the family of a young woman who had been brutally murdered were awarded £50,000 against the man who had been acquitted of her murder on a Not Proven verdict. This was claimed to be the first case of its kind in Scottish legal history.

Criminal injuries compensation   The Criminal Injuries Compensation Scheme was set up in 1964 to compensate victims of violent crime in Great Britain through the public purse. It was intended that the Board, which administered the Scheme, would award compensation on the same basis as damages recovered following a successful action in the civil courts. Although it was regarded as a major break-through in recognising the State's responsibility to offer redress for crime victims, it was also the subject of criticism because of the restrictions placed on certain classes of claimants, the distinction made between victims of violent and of property crimes, the length of time taken to process applications, and the cost of the Scheme.

A new scheme has now been put in place, which for the first time is based on legislative authority (the Criminal Injuries Compensation Act 1995). The new arrangements, which apply to all applications received on or after 1 April 1996, are very similar to the original ones, with one notable exception. Although compensation is payable as a lump sum, a 'tariff' has been introduced, which fixes a standard award for different types of injury. The scheme now has both a minimum (£1,000) and a maximum award (£500,000) and certain other changes in, for instance, the deductions which will be made from an award, have been made (Duff, 1996c; Brown and Hiram, 1997).

Conclusion

The impact of crime on victims and the need to consider the role of the victim in the criminal process is now acknowledged. Support is offered routinely to victims of recorded crime although the difficulties faced by those who do not report victimisation remain largely unmet. However, it remains the case that victims of crime are not given the consideration and support which they should receive from the Scottish criminal justice system. A more difficult question, and one which has not yet been fully addressed, is what the role of complainers/victims should be in the criminal process and whether their views should not only inform the process but also determine the outcome.

Notes

1. It should be noted that there has been criticism that crime surveys under-report violence against women, particularly violence in the home.
2. Ethnic minority victims were much more likely to express dissatisfaction with the action taken by the police. See chapter 17 for detailed discussion of this issue.
3. This was abolished by section 8 of the Damages (Scotland) Act 1976.
4. This contrasts with the position in England and Wales where the 'rights' discourse has been used by government since 1990 (Victim Support, 1995).
5. HMA v McKenzie 1990 S.L.T. 28.
6. As amended by section 249 of the Criminal Procedure (Scotland) Act 1995.
7. Cameron v Webster 1997 S.C.L.R. 228; Landsborough v McGlennan 1997 S.C.L.R. 464.
8. Mullan v Anderson (No. 2) 1997 S.L.T. 93.
9. Lord Prosser in Mullan v Anderson 1993 S.L.T. 835 at 837.

19 Privatisation, Policing and Crime Control: Tracing the Contours of the Public-Private Divide

NICHOLAS R. FYFE AND JON BANNISTER

Introduction

Ten years ago the inclusion of a chapter on privatisation in a collection of essays on the criminal justice system would probably have been considered 'eccentric' (Johnston, 1996, p.54). Even today, despite 'private' and 'privatisation' being the political buzz-words of the 1980s and 1990s, the use of these terms in the context of policing and crime control might still seem controversial. Such a reaction, however, largely reflects the legacy of the nineteenth century notion that 'the provision of laws, punishment and crime control constitute a unique and privileged realm of activity that should be provided by the State' (Matthews, 1989, p.1). Nevertheless, historically private forms of policing and crime control have existed alongside public forms and, both over space and through time, the distinctions between public and private forms have been continually contested and renegotiated. Indeed, one of the key political lessons of the last ten years in Britain has been to acknowledge that privatisation is a 'catch-all' term referring to a wide variety of different changes in the relationship between the state and market in the provision of goods and services. These include denationalisation (selling ownership of state assets to private agents), commodification (selling state assets to consumers), liberalisation (non-state agencies organising provision but with no change in state ownership) and voluntarism (whereby private citizens take some responsibility for the provision of a public service) (see Saunders and Harris 1990; Johnston, 1992).

Against this background, this chapter maps out some of the different forms of privatisation affecting the criminal justice system in Scotland and in so doing illustrates that the distinctions between 'public' and 'private' are becoming increasingly blurred. The first section considers privatisation and the public police, focusing on the introduction of market disciplines and the promotion of active citizenship. Although both these developments reflect the neoliberal strand of New Right political thinking underpinning much Government policy in the 1980s and 1990s, the movement towards privatisation in the criminal justice system is 'more than just a parochial one based on the shifting political exigencies of Thatcherism' (Reiner and Cross, 1991, p.6), and, one should add, Majorism. As the second section on the private security industry illustrates, there are broader structural forces fuelling the expansion of private sector involvement in policing and crime prevention. These are partly associated with the fiscal crises endemic to capitalist development but also reflect the changing built environment of advanced capitalist societies. One of the key technologies employed by the private security industry is closed circuit television (CCTV) surveillance. Although CCTV cameras have long operated in privately owned and managed spaces of shopping malls and business parks, there has recently been a massive expansion of their use by local authorities in the public spaces of town and city centres. In the final section we consider the implications of these developments in Scotland for what we call the 'privatisation of public space' whereby private interests, whether corporate or individual, increasingly determine the agenda of social control in public spaces.

Market Disciplines and Active Citizens: Privatisation and the Public Police

For Scotland's public police, two forms of privatisation have become increasingly important in the 1990s. First, the police, like other public services, have had to respond to central government's agenda of introducing the 'social market' into the public sector; second, the police, again like other public services, have had to embrace the government's active citizenship strategy which encourages private individuals to take responsibility for certain aspects of service provision. Although rather different in their implications for public policing, these two forms of privatisation share common political-ideological roots. For the last 18 years, law and order policy in Britain has been closely informed by New Right political thinking and, in particular, the two main strands of this doctrine, neo-conservatism and neo-liberalism (see Fyfe, 1995). Neo-conservatism is constructed around the themes of strong government, social authoritarianism and the need for a disciplined society, themes that provided the ideological foundation for several pieces of primarily English legislation aimed at strengthening police powers, including the Police and Criminal Evidence Act 1984, the Public Order Act 1986 and the Criminal Justice and Public Order Act 1994. Neo-liberalism, by contrast, focuses on the themes of minimal government, a market society, the role of the individual and freedom of choice, themes which have underpinned the commitment of successive Conservative governments to various forms of privatisation in the public sector, in particular the introduction of social markets and the promotion of active citizenship.

The Social Market Approach to Policing

The application of the social market approach to public services represents a strategy to 'sharpen management practice, measure levels of performance and provide opportunities for private sector provision' (Loveday, 1995, p.287). A key architect of the social market, Howard Davies (1993), argues its core components include:

(i)   a rational financial framework;
(ii)   clearly defined outputs;
(iii) a purchaser/provider split;
(iv)   market testing and competing providers;
(v)   customer choice;
(vi)   a strong and realistic customer voice;
(vii) comparative data on performance;
(viii) strong lay management; and
(ix)   independent inspection and audit.

These components clearly overlap with what is called the 'new public management' or NPM. Like the social market approach, NPM reflects an ideological belief in the superiority of the market over the state and, more particularly, provides an ideologically acceptable way of managing the public sector by 'reorganising public sector bodies to bring their management, reporting and accounting approaches closer to (a particular perception of) business methods' (Dunleavy and Hood, 1994, p.9).

By the early 1990s, central government's agenda for police reform in Britain was closely informed by the social market approach and the principles of NPM (see chapter 6). For the Scottish police this is apparent in four key areas. First, the introduction of a 'rational financial framework' is evident in the way devolved budgets and cost-centring are replacing unitary central budgets in an attempt to create a more cost-conscious and financially accountable police service. As the Chief Inspector of Constabulary noted in his 1995/6 annual report, most Scottish police forces have now introduced a degree of budget devolution, with divisional and department commanders acting as budget holders. This process has been given added impetus by the reorganisation of local government in 1995. Before reorganisation, financial management of forces was undertaken by regional council officials acting for police authorities. Now, with six forces overseen by joint boards of three or more police authorities, more independent force-centred financial management has been introduced, with decisions on spending within budgets resting ultimately with chief constables served by their own financial mangers. The Inspectorate also noted that with the introduction of compulsory competitive tendering there will be an even greater sense of 'cost-consciousness' among senior police managers (Scottish Office, 1996h, paras. 39-43; see too Leishman *et al.*, 1996, p.22; Savage and Charman, 1996, p.44). This connects with a second important social market development, the increasing civilianization of many tasks previously undertaken by police officers. As Figure 19.1 illustrates, there has been a rapid and dramatic expansion over the last ten years in the number of clerical and technical staff working in Scottish police forces.

From employing just over 2,300 clerical and technical staff in 1985, police forces now have nearly 3,700 such civilians working for them, with an authorised establishment of over 4,000. This represents an increase of 58 per cent in clerical and technical staff in the ten years from 1985, more than six times the increase in the regular force over the same period. From a social market perspective, this increase in civilian staff partly represents a form of market-testing given that it involves deciding what activities can be more efficiently provided by civilians, allowing some regular officers to return to operational duties. However, it also represents an expansion of lay management within the police, given that the civilianization of activities such as finance, personnel, and research and development has involved the appointment of senior professional managers with expertise in these areas as well as lower grade clerical staff.

Figure 19.1   Percentage increases in civilian staff and regular police officers in Scotland 1986 - 1995/6

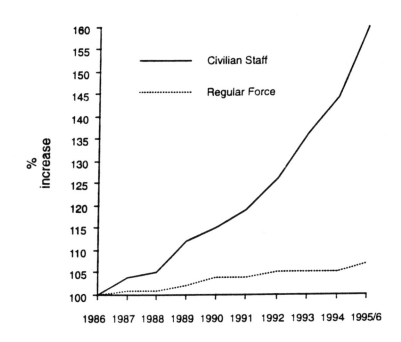

Note: Figures for 1986 set at 100 per cent.

Source: Reports of HM Chief Inspector of Constabulary.

A third key area where the social market and NPM have affected contemporary policing is in developing a performance culture. Described as the 'overarching theme' of NPM, a performance culture focuses on the setting, measuring and evaluation of an organisation's objectives. At a national level, this is reflected in the Scottish Police Matrix of Indicators introduced by the Inspectorate of Constabulary in 1991. Providing performance indicators on matters ranging from deployment, crime statistics, and quality of service, the Matrix has 'actively encouraged and influenced the development of measurable standards' to show variations in individual force performance on an annual basis (Scottish Office, 1996h, para. 19). At a force level too, the performance culture has been embraced in a variety of ways. Lothian and Borders Police, for example, have drawn inspiration from the European Foundation for Quality Management model (a business model originally designed for the private sector but now modified for use in public sector) to create a framework for planning and performance measurement into the next millennium. Known as the 'Forward Planning Guidelines', the key components of this framework are twelve 'Statements of Intent', providing guidance on specific areas of strategic planning, including community safety, community partnership, crime strategy, customer satisfaction and resources. For each Statement of Intent, there is a hierarchy of specific objectives, action plans and tasks which will be measured to provide detailed performance information.

A final theme of the social market approach to have had an important impact on policing relates to strengthening the 'consumer voice'. The main policy initiative here is the *Justice Charter for Scotland* (Scottish Office, 1991f), part of the government's *Citizen's Charter* (HMSO, 1991). Heralded by the then Prime Minister, John Major, as a significant innovation in public policy, the *Citizen's Charter* spells out how people are to be given more power as the consumers of public services (see Fyfe, 1993a). In terms of policing in Scotland, the *Justice Charter* recommends that police forces find out what local people think and take their views into account when setting standards of service and deciding priorities. One consequence of this is that all forces in Scotland have introduced so-called police user surveys, ranging from monthly interviews by officers of people who have had recent contact with the police, to annual postal surveys of public attitudes about crime and policing (see Fyfe, 1994). The findings of these surveys are being used to improve routine, operational aspects of service delivery (for example, by making sure people are kept informed of the progress of a police inquiry) as well as to inform broader strategic decision-making relating to the setting of objectives.

Taken together, these four developments clearly signal that Scotland's police forces are having to adapt to the disciplines of the social market. Nevertheless, it is a process which has sparked off a fierce debate both within and outside the police about the suitability of private sector methods for public sector services. The encouragement of a performance culture focused around performance indicators has, for example, prompted concern that this may distort police activity by concentrating effort on those areas that are easily measurable to the detriment of more qualitative activity (see Butler, 1995). Indeed, as Garland (1996) notes, current performance indicators tend to measure outputs rather than outcomes, measuring what the organisation does (such as response times to emergency calls and the number of hours spent on foot patrol) rather than what it achieves (in terms of, for example, public perceptions of safety and security). Indeed, the Inspectorate of Constabulary recently warned of 'the possibility of real harm being done if performance indicators are ill-designed, mishandled or viewed in isolation without informed interpretation' (Scottish Office, 1996h, para. 19). The *Justice Charter*, too, has its critics. With no sanctions available to the public if the police ignore their wishes or fail to meet performance standards, any claims to empowering consumers are largely illusory. Moreover, the *Charter's* attempt at encouraging local consumerism by giving the public a say via opinion surveys in setting police priorities is also problematic. Allowing individual citizens to act in competitive isolation to influence the delivery of a public good like policing could lead to a 'tyranny of the majority' while weakening the protection of minority interests (Fyfe, 1993b).

The Active Citizenship Strategy

A second form of privatisation affecting policing occurs when private citizens take over some responsibility for public security from police organisations (Johnston, 1992, p.137). Sharing the same neo-liberal ideological origins as the social market approach, this so-called active citizenship (or responsibilization) strategy has a particular resonance in contemporary political discourse about the criminal justice system because it dovetails with attempts by government to qualify its role as the primary provider of security and control. As David Garland (1996) cogently argues, the Conservative governments of the 1980s and 1990s have strongly endorsed those crime prevention strategies which focus not on the responsibilities of the state but on civil society, not on individual offenders but on the conduct of potential victims. Mrs Thatcher declared that 'combating crime is everybody's business. It cannot be left solely to the police anymore than we can leave our health solely to doctors' (quoted in Brake and Hale, 1992, p.10) while a former Tory Home Office minister announced back in 1988 that 'at the very centre of our ideas on how to control crime should be the energy and initiative of the active citizen' (Patten, 1988, pp. v-vi). Indeed, as recent reviews of crime prevention in Scotland point out, the 1980s witnessed the promotion of a crime control model premised on the view that all citizens were responsible for fighting crime and for ensuring that they did not become a victim of crime (Monaghan, 1997; chapter 5).

Active citizenship takes a variety of forms in the criminal justice system but amongst the most significant are Neighbourhood Watch (NW) schemes and the Special Constabulary. NW was introduced into Scotland in 1986 (four years after its introduction into England and Wales), and the number of schemes has grown rapidly. Figure 19.2, for example, shows the exponential increase in the number of schemes in the Strathclyde Police force area.

Figure 19.2   Numbers of Neighbourhood Watch schemes in the Strathclyde Region 1987-1996/7

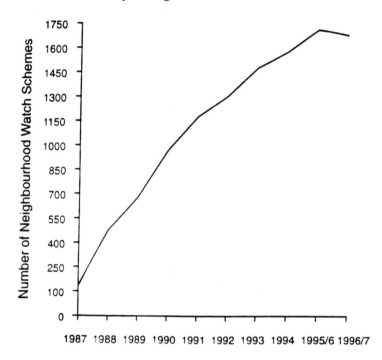

Source: Strathclyde Police Chief Constable's Annual Reports.

Of course, the spread of schemes has not occurred evenly over space. Although the results of the 1988 British Crime Survey in Scotland revealed the early diffusion of NW had resulted in similar proportions of schemes in different neighbourhood types (see Allen and Payne, 1991), viewed over a longer time period the diffusion of NW schemes has revealed substantial over-representation in areas of modern family housing and affluent suburban housing, with under-representation in areas of older housing, multiracial areas and on council estates (Monaghan, 1997). Monaghan suggests two reasons for this. First, owner occupiers are more motivated to protect their property and set up or get involved in a NW scheme. Secondly, many deprived areas suffer from a lack of community cohesion and there may be a reluctance to join a police-led initiative because of apathy and fear of victimisation, with crime just one of several competing concerns for the people that live there.

Whatever the reasons for the uneven geographical distribution of NW schemes, of more immediate significance is explaining continued government encouragement for NW long after its own research reached the unequivocal conclusion that NW has little impact on reducing levels of victimisation (see Bennett, 1992, p.282). As King (1989) argues, such political support should be interpreted less as a stubborn belief in a particular method of crime reduction and more as a commitment to neo-liberal political principles to do with the role and responsibilities of the individual within society. Indeed, this is echoed by Garland (1996, p.453) who observes that:

> the importance of neighbourhood watch and related surveillance schemes - such as 'cab watch' and 'hospital watch' - as examples of the government's project for devolved crime control is demonstrated by the fact that political commitment to these schemes far outruns their level of success in preventing crime.

A second important active citizenship initiative is support for the Special Constabulary. Established in the nineteenth century, membership of the Special Constabulary peaked before the Second World War since when numbers have dramatically declined. In 1961 in Scotland there were 7,312 Specials but by 1996 there were only 1,878, a decline of almost 75 per cent. Nevertheless Conservative Governments in the 1980s and 1990s did encourage police forces to recruit more Specials, partly because the Special Constable, like the member of a NW schemes, is a potent symbol of the active citizen but also because, like NW, the Special Constabulary represent a form of privatised policing that might ease the burden on the regular, public police. As Figure 19.3 illustrates, however, the recruitment drive over the last ten years has met with only limited success.

Figure 19.3   Special police constables in Scotland 1961-1995/6

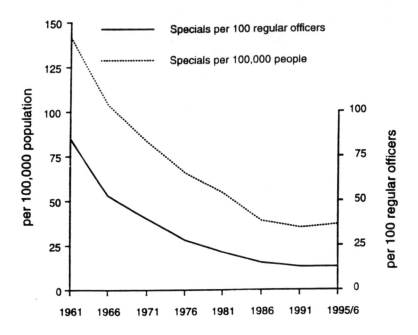

Source: Reports of HM Chief Inspector of Constabulary.

The decline in the numbers of Specials has slowed down in Scotland and in the last five years there has actually been a slight increase in their numbers. But, as Figure 19.4 illustrates, levels of membership vary considerably between forces, with high levels found in forces policing predominantly rural, low crime areas, while lower levels of membership are found in forces dealing with higher levels of crime and more urban based populations. The significance of this pattern is that it suggests that the areas of Scotland in greatest need of the kind of active citizenship associated with Specials are those areas least supportive of such voluntary policing.

Figure 19.4   Special constables per 100,000 population (a) 1986 (b) 1995/6

(a)   (b)

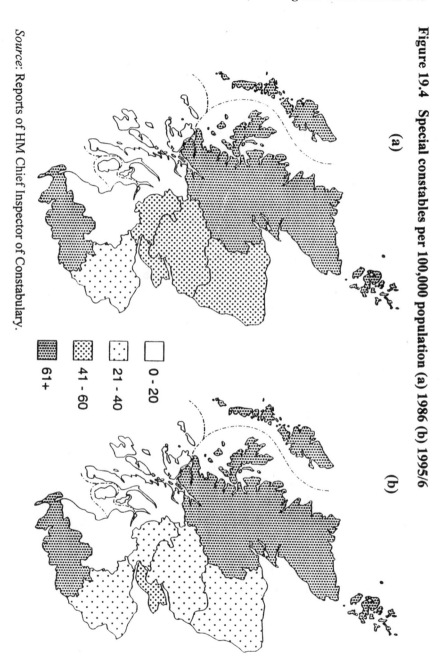

0 - 20

21 - 40

41 - 60

61+

Source: Reports of HM Chief Inspector of Constabulary.

The 'Quiet Revolution': the Rise of the Private Security Industry

The privatisation of the public police intersects with a rather different but increasingly important form of privatisation in the criminal justice system, the growth of the private security industry. Indeed, for many who use Scotland's cities as places to live, work or relax, the presence of private security is now simply part of their taken-for-granted urban experience, whether it is the sight of uniformed guards patrolling shopping malls, hospitals or university campuses; or the video surveillance systems operated by private security firms observing people in shops and banks, on buses and trains, at football matches and in bowling alleys. And it is tempting to account for these developments with reference to the same neo-liberal ideas used in the context of the privatisation of the public police. Both the social market approach, which emphasises consumer choice, and the active citizenship strategy, which focuses on private responsibility for crime control, clearly provide a supportive political climate in which the private security industry can flourish. Nevertheless, it would be misleading to suggest that the recent growth in private security is due simply to neo-liberal political ideology. According to several observers there are two broader structural conditions affecting advanced capitalist societies which have encouraged the development of the private security industry. First, there is the impact of workload and fiscal pressures on the ability of the public police to meet the security needs of corporate capitalism. In Spitzer and Scull's (1977) seminal article, they argue that the rebirth of private policing in the post-war period reflects a growing division between the functions of order maintenance (the concern of the public police) and profit protection (the basis for an expanding private security industry). More specifically, they argue that the growing workload pressures on public police organisations caused by, among other things, changes in the nature of criminal activity from being relatively localised to becoming more geographically dispersed, increasing social problems associated with the widening gap between rich and poor, and the rise in vehicle and traffic-related crime, combined with the increasing fiscal pressures on advanced capitalist states, have all helped create a perception of a 'security vacuum' in which the public police appear to be losing the fight against crime. In such conditions, the growth of private policing is seen as a direct consequence of the inability of the public sector to provide sufficient police resources to meet growing demands. A second, and related, set of developments concerns the enormous post war expansion of mass private property, places like shopping malls, business parks, industrial complexes and university campuses. An important consequence of this is that an increasing amount of economic and social life takes place (quite literally) in areas which are publicly accessible but privately owned and managed. According to Shearing and Stenning (1987), the policing needs of these environments have not been met by the public police for two related reasons. First, the routine patrols of public police are largely confined to publicly owned spaces and officers have only limited legal powers to gain access to private property. Secondly, those who own and manage mass private property have wanted to exercise their right to preserve order on their own property and maintain control over the policing of it.

While both these arguments accounting for the rise of the private security industry are not without their problems (both, for example, suggest a crude functionalism in which it is possible to 'read-off' mechanisms of social control from changing patterns of capitalist development) they do force us to recognise the increasingly important role that private policing plays in contemporary capitalist societies. Indeed, all commentators are agreed that the private security sector has got bigger over the last ten years, although there is far less agreement as to how big it actually is. In part this is because of problems of defining what actually constitutes the private security sector. For example, there is clearly a large contract security industry supplying mechanical devices, such as locks and safes, electronic equipment, such as alarms and closed circuit television, and human resources, in the form of static and patrolling guards. In addition, however, there is 'in-house' security in places like factories and universities as well as the world of private investigators and private security consultants. Other problems of measurement reflect the lack of regulation and licensing and the low visibility of many of its activities. Nevertheless, one possible way of gauging the size of the private security sector is by means of the British Telecom Business Data Base derived from business entries to the Yellow Pages (see Jones and Newburn, 1995). Of course, the number of entries will vary according to how broadly the private security sector is defined. At its broadest such a definition might include 'Burglar alarms and security systems', 'Car alarms and security', 'Closed Circuit Television (installers and manufacturers)', 'Credit investigation services', and 'Security services and equipment'. It is the last of these which is by far the largest single sector and entries under this heading for the Glasgow telephone area are used to illustrate the expansion of private security services in the city over the last 30 years in Figure 19.5.

Figure 19.5 Growth in security services and equipment establishments in Glasgow 1965-1997/8

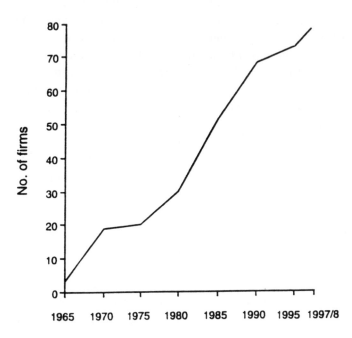

Source: Yellow Pages Telephone Directories.

From just three entries in 1965, the most recent directories list over seventy firms in this sector. Of course, as a data base the Yellow Pages is not without its problems. The listings are for business establishments, not single firms, so it overestimates the total number of firms. Nor does it claim to cover every company because it is only based on business telephone lines and therefore would not include small, home-based investigatory or security services. Nevertheless, the Glasgow data does provide strong evidence of what has been called the 'quiet revolution' (Stenning and Shearing, 1980) referring to the massive expansion in private security activity over the last thirty years such that in many places private police personnel now outnumber their counterparts in public policing (see in particular Shearing and Stenning, 1987; South, 1988; Matthews, 1989; Johnston, 1992).

Despite superficial similarities between the activities of the public and private police, it is important to recognise that private policing is guided by very different objectives. Much of it is about 'policing for profit' (South, 1988), acting in the private interests of clients in order to prevent losses. Indeed, private security police measure their success not in terms of the apprehension of offenders or the clear up of crime, but in terms of the ability to prevent future losses from occurring (Shearing and Stenning, 1983a). This, in turn, has raised important questions concerning the rights of citizens to privacy. As Shearing and Stenning (1983b) argue, in the past notions of private ownership have ensured that when citizens are on private property they have been relatively free from supervision and control. The increasing development of mass private property with their associated systems of private security now means that this traditional assumption is no longer tenable.

The Fortress Impulse and the Cost of Crime: the Privatisation of Public Space?

The growing presence of the private security industry provides support for Christopherson (1994), who suggests that urban space is increasingly tightly controlled and manipulated, creating a 'fortress city': 'the need to manage urban space is a pre-eminent consideration of contemporary urban design' (p.409). Although writing in the context of North America, the fortress impulse is increasingly prominent in British urban management. The private security guards patrolling shopping malls, the remotely operated gates controlling access to apartment complexes, and the increasing deployment of CCTV surveillance systems are all examples of this fortress impulse. Lying behind many of these developments are anxieties about the financial costs of crime. Faced with declining consumer and business confidence in town and city centres, urban managers are increasingly looking to improvements in security as a means of reviving urban economic fortunes. Moreover, in residential areas the costs of crime in terms of maintenance and repairs to the fabric of housing estates is prompting increasing investment in crime prevention techniques (Bannister and Kearns, 1995). Whatever the impact on crime of these developments, they raise important questions about the privatisation of public space as the order maintenance requirements of private interests play an increasingly important role in determining the agenda of social control in public spaces. This section considers these issues by examining the growth in CCTV surveillance in Scottish towns and cities.

Scotland's first town centre CCTV system was established in Airdrie in 1992, comprising 14 cameras covering the main streets and car parks. By the beginning of 1996 there were a further 18 schemes, ranging from quite small scale systems, such as that in Glenrothes with two cameras and Dumfries with six, to more intensive and extensive surveillance systems, like that in Stirling with 49 cameras, Falkirk with 33 and Glasgow with 32 (see Figure 19.6). When later in 1996 the Scottish Office introduced a CCTV-challenge competition to contribute public money towards some of the capital costs of establishing public space CCTV surveillance systems, a further 18 schemes were approved receiving £1.8 million. A similar amount was allocated in a second round of this competition for 1997-8 when 30 more schemes were recommended for approval.

In a period of less than five years, then, the streets and squares of Scottish towns and cities have been transformed by the appearance of CCTV surveillance cameras. Moreover, this appears to have occurred with overwhelming public backing (but see Ditton, 1996). Opinion surveys conducted in areas planning CCTV schemes routinely reveal high levels of support: 95 per cent of those asked in Glasgow said they were in favour of CCTV in the city; in Airdrie 89 per cent said CCTV would reduce their fear of crime; and in Motherwell, 98 per cent of residents in a local housing estate voted to introduce CCTV (Fyfe and Bannister, 1996, p.43; Daniel, 1997, p.23). Against this background, opposition has been relatively muted. The Scottish Council for Civil Liberties (SCCL), for example, has argued that while they are 'in principle opposed to people being spied on in public places' they recognise that 'it can help prevent and detect crime in certain clearly defined circumstances' (Scottish Council for Civil Liberties, 1995, p.5). Their energies have therefore been directed towards devising rules governing the use and operation of CCTV, arguing for a balance between the right to privacy and the right to security, rather than actively opposing CCTV. Moreover, despite SCCL's claim that the link between CCTV and crime reduction is unproven (Scottish Council for Civil Liberties, 1997), the only published independent research to-date on the Airdrie scheme does provide encouraging results.

Figure 19.6 Public space closed circuit television surveillance systems in Scotland

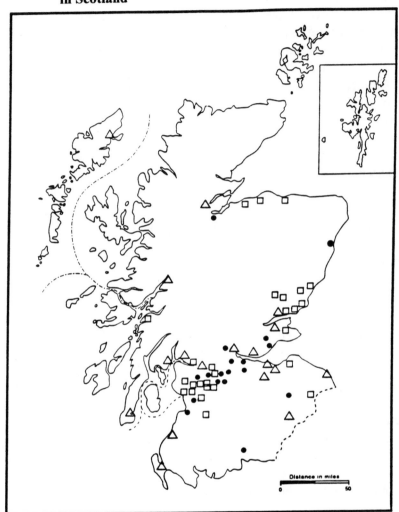

- Schemes under way at 1/1/96

△ CCTV Challenge Competition 1996/7: successful applications

▢ CCTV Challenge Competition 1997-8: Applications recommended for approval

Source: Scottish Office data

It revealed that the police 'cleared-up' (i.e. the offender(s) was apprehended, cited, warned or traced) 16 per cent more crimes and offences in the CCTV area in the two years following the installation of cameras compared to the two years before installation (Short and Ditton, 1996, p.8). In terms of deterrence, the evaluation also yielded encouraging evidence. It showed a 21 per cent fall in the total number of recorded crimes and offences in the CCTV area in the two years after the system was established compared to the two years before its introduction, the greatest reduction occurring in the category of crimes of dishonesty (such as burglary, theft of and from motor vehicles and shoplifting) which fell by almost half in the study period. Such reductions do, of course, beg the question of whether crime has simply been displaced to other areas? In Airdrie, it appeared that 'the crimes prevented in the CCTV area did not, as far as can be ascertained, re-emerge in adjacent or nearby areas' (Short and Ditton, 1996, p.1).

These findings from Airdrie are clearly encouraging from a crime prevention and detection perspective, although whether they would be repeated in other places with CCTV remains an open question at present. The impact of CCTV, however, extends beyond simply its influence on crime. Several studies examining the day-to-day use of city centre CCTV systems have revealed how a substantial proportion of the incidents where CCTV is used to help the police concern drunks, begging, vagrants and 'suspicious youths' (see Graham *et al.*, 1996, p.20; Brown, 1995, p.40). What this evidence suggests is that those perceived not to belong in commercial public spaces of town or city centres now risk being 'monitored and harassed, losing rights as citizens just because they aren't seen to be lucrative enough as consumers' (Graham *et al.*, 1996, p.19). The result is a subtle 'privatisation of public space' as commercial imperatives define acceptable behaviour, excluding those who detract from the consumption experience. As has been noted in relation to the private spaces of the shopping mall (Bianchini, 1990, p.5), this can lead to:

> the virtual disenfranchisement from city life of young people of low spending power and other - generally low income - residents whose appearance and conduct do not conform to the moral codes of well-ordered consumption enforced by shopping centre managers.

Indeed, now that many of the design and management practices associated with privately owned shopping centres, including use of CCTV, have been uncritically adopted in the management of public space, 'the effective implementation of the values of private interest in town centres'

(Reeve, 1996, p.78) is well advanced. Of course this should not come as any great surprise. Given the high costs of establishing and running public space CCTV systems most are funded by both public and private capital. In Glasgow, for example, the private sector contributed £270,000 to the establishment of CityWatch scheme, persuaded by the arguments of the Glasgow Development Agency that by reducing the fear of crime in the city centre, CCTV surveillance would encourage 225,000 more visits to the city a year, creating 1500 new jobs and an additional £40 million of income to city centre businesses (Fyfe and Bannister, 1996). Nevertheless, despite all the claims for the success of CCTV systems, the public-private funding partnerships on which they depend appear quite fragile. Less than 18 months after introducing the cameras in Glasgow, headlines proclaimed 'Crimewatch spy cameras in cash crisis' (*The Glaswegian*, 1996) and 'Spy camera cuts could risk lives' (*The Glasgow Herald*, 1996a). The shortfall in funding for the estimated £200,000 per annum running costs is blamed on non-contributing local businesses. However, defending their decision not to continue funding the system, many businesses argue that as part of the city's public infrastructure street cameras should be funded from business rates, while some retailers, with branches in other towns and cities, point to the ever increasing costs of contributing to several CCTV schemes in different areas (see Bannister *et al.*, 1998).

Whatever the financial future of CCTV systems, the privatisation of public space which their routine use appears to encourage is a matter of wider concern. It lends support to Davis' (1992, p.156) contention that 'the universal consequence of the crusade to secure the city is the destruction of any truly democratic urban space'. Far from the streets being spaces that encourage 'encounters between people of different classes, races, ages, religions, ideologies, cultures, and stances towards life' (*ibid.*, p.484), the potential impact of CCTV is the imposition of 'a middle-class tyranny on the last significant urban realm of refuge for other modes of life' (Boddy, 1992, p.150). Indeed, eager to 'manage out' behaviour which might undermine the economic potential of their area, many local authorities have not only installed CCTV cameras but are introducing bylaws to outlaw 'anti-social behaviour'. In Glasgow, for example, a blanket ban on drinking alcohol in public places was introduced in August 1996 because, as the Chair of the city's licensing board explained, 'the behaviour of some people drinking in the streets and parks is a nuisance to residents and shopkeepers' (*The Glasgow Herald*, 1996b). The effective enforcement of this legislation and the deterrence of proscribed behaviour will clearly be enhanced by the presence of CCTV surveillance.

Concluding Comments

The issues covered in this chapter - of private sector styles of managing the public police, the involvement of private citizens in policing and crime prevention, the growth of the private security industry, and the privatisation of public spaces as a result of crime control - all lead to a reconsideration of what are often taken-for-granted notions about what is 'public' and what is 'private'. As Johnston (1992, p.222) cogently argues:

> Public and private spheres should not be seen as distinct 'places' with inherent characteristics, but rather as strategic arenas where political arguments are deployed and where political conflict takes place.

This is important not least because it suggests that to make sense of the blurring of the public-private divide requires a criminological research agenda with a broader imagination than currently exists. To be sure, evaluations of the impact of private sector styles of management in the public police or the deterrence, detection and displacement of crime by CCTV systems are important. But this narrowly technical perspective fails to engage with some of the wider questions that the developments described in this chapter raise. What changes in urban society have led to the construction of the elaborate public and private policing apparatus which now exists in Scottish cities? To whom are these various public and private policing and crime control agencies accountable? And what are the consequences of these policing and crime control strategies for social and political life in Scotland? The challenge for future criminal justice research, therefore, is not simply to provide ever more rigorous evaluations of innovations in private and public policing and crime control, important though this is. Such research should also inform wider debates in social and political theory about the changing relationship between and meaning of public and private in the criminal justice system.

20 The Politics of Penality: An Overview of the Development of Penal Policy in Scotland

LESLEY MCARA

Introduction

A dominant theme of much contemporary penological literature is that western penal systems are undergoing a profound transformation. As evidence for change, commentators point to: the growth of managerialism within the penal process; the development of new policy objectives such as crime prevention and support for victims; and the trend towards bifurcated penal strategies.[1] The roots of this transformation have been variously attributed to: the decline in faith in rehabilitation and correctional modes of penality; the crisis of penal resources precipitated *inter alia* by overcrowding in prisons during the 1970s and 1980s; and to sociological processes such as the changing nature of social control in late capitalist societies, or the tensions caused by the emergence of an underclass of the most poor and marginalised groups in society (Feeley and Simon, 1994; Bottoms, 1994).

Most of the literature on transformation has focused on the penal systems in the USA or England and Wales (see for example Feeley and Simon, 1994; Simon and Feeley, 1995; Garland, 1996). Indeed, a common feature of this literature is to treat these larger systems as if they were paradigmatic of western systems as a whole. By contrast, developments in the Scottish penal system have rarely featured (if at all). The purpose of this chapter is to begin, in some small way, to remedy this deficiency. It is my intention to demonstrate that rather than being marginal to the field of inquiry, the Scottish case merits close attention for two inter-related reasons.

Firstly, the Scottish penal system appears to have been resistant to a number of the trends outlined above. Within Scotland, welfare strategies have *endured* in the face of both the fiscal crises and the more profound sociological processes which commentators suggest have prompted significant shifts away from the so-called 'solidarity project'[2] in other

355

systems. This is most evident with regard to the role of social work within the penal system and in respect of the juvenile justice system. However it is arguable that welfare strategies have remained an important aspect of policy in other sites within the penal system, particularly with respect to prison policy (as I shall go on to explain later in the chapter).

Secondly, close examination of the substantive differences between Scotland and other systems covered in the literature begins to open to question some of the explanations offered by commentators for penal change. The Scottish case highlights the complex and nuanced character of penality and penal discourse and indicates that the relationship between social and cultural processes and penal change is more unpredictable and contingent than the literature on transformation would suggest.

As my point of departure I am going to outline briefly three different accounts of penal transformation as found in the works of: Feeley and Simon; Garland; and Bottoms. I will then explore the ways in which penal welfarism has continued to dominate official policy discourse within Scotland over the past 25 years, by looking at the role of social work in the penal system, the policy relating to juvenile justice and the prison service. In the final sections of the chapter I will assess critically the explanations of penal change, offered by the literature reviewed, in the light of Scottish developments.

Theorising Transformation

Feeley and Simon

Feeley and Simon (1994) argue that there is a paradigm shift taking place in the penal process from old to new penology. They define old penology as an amalgam of the disparate practices which dominated European and North American penal systems until about the mid 1970s. Old penology is associated *both* with correctional penal-welfare strategies and their concerns to reform and rehabilitate individual offenders *and also* with more punitive strategies which have laid emphasis on just deserts and proportionality of punishment.

By contrast, new penology seeks neither to punish nor rehabilitate individual offenders. It is predominantly 'actuarial', concerned with the identification and management of groups of offenders according to the level of risk or danger which they pose. The primary objective of the new penology is no longer to eradicate crime but to regulate it or manage it at tolerable levels.

Feeley and Simon contend that a number of recent trends provide evidence of the way in which new penology is leading to transformations in the penal process.

Firstly, they argue that the language of actuarial calculation is gradually penetrating penal discourse. This language is constructed around notions of risk and probability and it conceptualises the penal process as a *system* which can be modelled, managed and controlled. Although they acknowledge that this actuarial language has yet to take root within public discourse (by this they would appear to mean both public opinion and official government pronouncements), they consider that it has gained ascendancy within both academic and practitioner discourse.

Secondly, the emergence of new penology has redefined older forms of penal practice. Thus probation and parole, formerly defined as mechanisms for rehabilitating offenders, are now increasingly being used as a cost-effective means of controlling low risk offenders.

Thirdly, they link new penology to the development of new techniques and technologies, for example: the growth of electronic monitoring and surveillance systems; new statistical techniques for assessing risk and predicting dangerousness; and the development of performance indicators and monitoring mechanisms as a means of measuring the efficiency and effectiveness of systemic functioning.

Feeley and Simon's work suggests that the roots of new penology lie in the responses of governments to a number of perceived crises or tensions. They argue that new penology is one response to the perceived failures of correctional penal strategies. Other factors identified include: the pressure on resources within the penal system resulting in demands for more cost-effective accountable procedures (fiscal crisis); and an apparent acceptance on the part of governments of the existence of an underclass of the most poor and most marginalised groups in society. This underclass is considered to be incapable of re-integration into mainstream society and therefore requires to be controlled and managed. In this respect the penal system has a key role to play in the management of social fragmentation and tension.

Garland

While Garland (1996) would accept that the penal system is increasingly being used as a mechanism for managing social tensions, he links recent changes in penality more explicitly to the growing recognition on the part of governments that they have a limited capacity to provide law and order within their territorial boundaries. High crime rates have become an endemic feature of contemporary societies, stemming from social arrangements characterised by 'inflated expectations', deep divisions, weak mechanisms of control and high levels of opportunities for crime. The persistence of high crime rates and the consequent inability of governments to deliver security to their citizens, have undermined one of the State's foundational claims to legitimacy.

According to Garland, the UK government has responded to this predicament (high crime rates and inability to reduce crime) in an ambivalent fashion. On one hand it has become increasingly punitive, implementing policies such as American-style boot camps for juvenile offenders and re-constructing formerly rehabilitative court disposals, such as probation, into community punishments (increased punitiveness being interpreted as symptomatic of weakened authority). On the other hand, it has adopted preventative strategies through which it has sought to devolve responsibility for crime control onto individuals, 'active' communities and private agencies (so-called 'responsibilisation strategies').

These twin strategies are predicated on an official criminological discourse which is becoming increasingly bifurcated. Punitive policies are informed by what Garland terms the 'criminology of the other' (offenders are differentially constituted; they are abnormal or pathological). By contrast, preventative and community strategies are informed by the 'criminology of the self' (offenders are normal, rational, calculating individuals capable of exercising choice).

According to Garland, persistently high crime rates have posed particular dilemmas for agencies working within the criminal justice system such as the police and the courts. Not only are they perceived to have failed in their attempts to control crime but they are faced with increasingly heavy workloads as more and more offenders are processed through the system. Garland identifies two main ways in which this problem has been addressed in penal practice: firstly by 'defining deviance down' - that is by diverting cases out of the system at various stages or by lowering the level of penalty for certain types of offence; and secondly by scaling down expectations through the redefinition of success and failure: the performance of agencies now being measured by the extent to which they have met their own internal goals or targets, rather than whether they have effected broader social goals such as rehabilitation or reductions in crime rates.

Garland claims that the shifts in discourse and changes in penal practice, have led to the eclipse of penal welfarism. Instead of grand proclamations about fighting the war against crime, Government policy documents set out a more modest range of objectives such as risk management, victim support or reducing the fear of crime. The overall aim is now to manage the social divisions which have precipitated the high crime rates rather than to attempt to transform them through programmes for progressive social change.

Bottoms

The final argument I want to review is that developed by Tony Bottoms (1983; 1994). As with the other literature on transformation, Bottoms also aims to link changes in the practice of the criminal justice system to broader social and cultural developments. Although some of his work on penal change would appear to be more narrowly focused than that of the commentators referred to above,[3] his arguments do have wider resonance for the criminal justice system as a whole.

Bottoms claims that penal practice has changed in recent years as a consequence of three key developments: the predominance of just deserts and individual rights in judicial decision-making; increased managerialism within the court process; and a greater emphasis on the concept of community in penal sanctioning (as exemplified by the re-styling of probation and community service as community punishments and in the growth of mediation and reparation schemes). He also identifies a further 'political' factor impacting on sentencing change, namely populist punitiveness.

Drawing on the work of both Garland and Giddens, Bottoms argues that the first three of these developments have been precipitated by a number of deeper historical and sociological processes. Bottoms claims that in the early decades of the century the penal system operated ostensibly as a mechanism for social integration and inclusion. Rather than crushing or breaking the spirit of the offender, the aim of the system was to normalise, to correct or, in cases of incorrigibility, to segregate. In practice, however, the system functioned in an extremely hierarchical and class-based manner. As part of the price for full rights of citizenship, the lower classes were required to uphold the norms of conduct of the 'respectable' middle classes. The principal aim of penal sanctions was, accordingly, to reconstruct the predominantly lower class offender in the image of the middle classes.

As the 20th century progressed, social relationships became less class based and less hierarchical. According to Bottoms, there has been a gradual 'disembedding' of relationships away from intermediate groups such as the family or the local community towards a greater focus on the individual. These processes have been underpinned by changes in the nature and pattern of work (such as have occurred with the erosion of manufacturing industry and increased automation of labour processes); technological developments (such as the growth in techniques of surveillance); and the birth of the consumer culture.

Bottoms argues that the changing pattern of social relations is increasingly reflected within penal imagery: the offender is now regarded as an individual with the right to equal treatment rather than an obedient subject in receipt of expert and indeterminate treatment; rehabilitation has been recast as a means of effecting the responsibilisation of the individual offender; and technological developments have facilitated the shift towards managerialism within the penal system.

According to Bottoms, populist punitiveness (the 'political' factor impacting on change) is less clearly linked to these social processes and, thereby, a less predictable feature of contemporary penal systems. As with Garland, however, Bottoms contends that governments often use punitive policies as a mechanism for addressing the feelings of insecurity and anxiety engendered by persistently high crime levels. These high crime levels are in themselves attributable to the decline in informal mechanisms of social control associated with the disembedding of social relations described above.

Dominant Themes within the Literature on Transformation

It is clear from this brief overview of the literature that there is no settled account as to the character of the changes that have taken place in the penal system nor the particular processes which have precipitated them. Feeley and Simon, for example, highlight risk management as a defining element of contemporary penality whereas for Bottoms and Garland this is one aspect of a more complex set of changes. Nevertheless a number of common themes do emerge and it is these that I now wish to focus on.

To begin with, all commentators are in agreement that the penal welfare programme which has dominated western penal systems for most of the 20th century has been eclipsed, to be replaced by: actuarial justice (Feeley and Simon); punitive and preventative strategies (Garland); or by a penal imagery increasingly informed by the principles of just deserts and individual rights (Bottoms).

Secondly, there is consensus that there has been a growth in managerialism and a shift towards bureaucratic administrative procedures. This has coincided with a shift away from programmes aimed at broader social change (typical of penal welfarism) towards a culture of performance indicators and internalised organisational goals.

Thirdly, commentators agree that penal transformation reflects and is, in part, propelled by, deeper social and cultural processes, for example: the social tensions precipitated by the growth of an underclass (Feeley and Simon); the acceptance of high crime rates as a normal feature of western societies and the resulting crisis of governance (Garland); the changing nature of social relations, shifts in the patterns of work and technological developments typical of late capitalist societies (Bottoms).

The first two of these themes (the eclipse of welfarism and the growth of managerialism) relate to the *characteristics* of the changes which have taken place, the third theme (the relationship between penal forms and social processes) to *explanations* for change. I now want to consider in more detail the relationship between these themes and policy developments within Scotland. In the next section of the chapter I will examine the characteristics of policy development and in the final section I will offer an assessment of the explanations given for change.

Characteristics of Policy Developments in Scotland

Within this section I aim to highlight the ways in which the Scottish penal system has resisted some of the trends identified in the literature on transformation. My argument will be that welfarism continues to play a dominant role within the Scottish penal system and that the recent growth of managerialism, rather than precipitating an eclipse of welfarism, has served instead to facilitate the development and implementation of effective rehabilitative strategies. In order to demonstrate this, I am going to examine the characteristics of policy developments in three pivotal sites in the Scottish penal system: social work criminal justice services; the juvenile justice system; and the Scottish Prison Service (SPS). (For more detailed discussion of each of these areas, see, respectively, chapters 14, 13 and 12).

Social Work and Criminal Justice

The contemporary role of social work in the Scottish penal system was established by the Social Work (Scotland) Act 1968. Under the arrangements introduced by this Act, the functions of the, then, probation service were transferred to the new local authority social work departments and social workers became responsible for the supervision of offenders in the community and the provision of social enquiry and other reports to the criminal justice system. The involvement of social work in criminal justice was underpinned by the 'Kilbrandon Ethos'.[4] This stressed that offending required to be understood in the broader context of the person's social and personal problems and emphasised treatment and rehabilitation: in these respects a classic example of penal welfarism (see chapter 14; Young, 1997; Moore and Wood, 1992).

The role of social work criminal justice services came under increasing scrutiny during the 1980s, culminating in a formal review of services in the latter part of the decade. Research has identified three factors which contributed to this: concern on the part of central government that social work services were ineffective and had lost the confidence of the courts (McAra, 1998); tension between central government and local authority social work departments over the funding of services (in particular the funding of community service, see McIvor, 1992); and a growing crisis within the prison system in the face of overcrowding, riots and industrial unrest (Wozniak, 1994).

At one level these factors mirror aspects of the crises that Bottoms and Feeley and Simon have identified as occurring respectively in England and Wales and the USA: in particular the crisis over penal resources and prison management. However an important difference is that within Scotland concerns about the effectiveness of social work services centred, for the most part, around the *method of delivery* of services rather than a loss of faith in their rehabilitative potential.

During the 1970s and early 1980s social workers were generally organised into generic[5] rather than specialist teams. Research indicates that it was the generic nature of service delivery which led to the loss of confidence on the part of the courts (McAra, 1998). Generic social workers were believed to lack the requisite specialist knowledge, training and skills for dealing with offenders and there was a growing perception that social work supervision of offenders had become increasingly lax or, in extreme cases, non-existent (McAra, 1998). A key aspect of the policy review was therefore to explore ways in which methods of service delivery could enhance the effectiveness of social work and thereby allay the concerns of key criminal justice decision-makers.

The outcome of the review was the introduction of 100 per cent central government funding of certain specified social work criminal justice services[6] (on implementation of the Law Reform Miscellaneous Provisions (Scotland) Act 1990) and the accompanying national objectives and standards (implemented from 1991).

Managerialism In some respects the new funding initiative and national standards represent a significant shift towards managerialism as identified by the literature on transformation. In order to qualify for central government funding, local authorities are required to develop organisational structures directed towards coherent service delivery. They must also develop and review strategic plans for offender services, set out performance targets and institute mechanisms for monitoring and evaluating the achievement of these targets (Social Work Services Group, 1991). However, far from supplanting penal welfarism as Bottoms or Feeley and Simon might suggest, these managerialist initiatives were intended primarily to *facilitate* the development of effective work with offenders. Evidence for this can be found within the national standards document itself which includes a supplement setting out a model of social work practice with offenders (intended as a guide for local authority social work departments). This model is derived from a number of 'meta-analytic' studies, carefully referenced within the supplement, which claim to have identified the characteristics of programmes which are most effective in reducing re-offending risk (see McGuire, 1995; and McIvor, 1990a, for a review of these studies). The meta-analytic literature suggests that programme effectiveness is predicated on the implementation of managerialist techniques[7] and this is reflected within the national standards in the importance accorded to the development of procedures for monitoring and evaluation and to the introduction of strategic planning arrangements.

Risk management Another significant feature of the model of social work practice in the new national standards is the focus on risk management. The model of practice asserts that the most successful programmes are those which are appropriately matched to, or targeted on, the level of risk posed (greater intensity of intervention being warranted only in cases where risk of re-offending is high). According to this model, social work supervision should be aimed at providing the correct balance of control and help (the balance dependent on relative degree of risk), with interventions focused on: the causes and consequences of offending; tackling offenders' underlying problems; and assisting reintegration into the community (Social Work Services Group, 1991). In contrast to policy developments in other jurisdictions,[8] there is an explicit statement within the national standards that punitive approaches are ineffective, particularly in respect of young adult offenders (Social Work Services Group, 1991).

The emphasis on risk could be taken as evidence of a shift towards a more actuarial penal culture (as suggested by Feeley and Simon in particular). However, in contrast to the literature on transformation, risk management has not supplanted rehabilitation as a penal aim, but rather has served to sharpened the focus of intervention aimed primarily at normalisation and behavioural change. Indeed, more generally, the standards are premised on the view that higher risk offenders should be placed back into the community *precisely because* reform and rehabilitation are more likely to be effected within a community based setting (McAra, 1998).

To summarise, the 100 per cent funding initiative and national standards have for the first time introduced an explicit agenda for social work practice. This agenda has served to sharpen the focus of practice around the criminogenic needs of the offenders and has been accompanied by a tightening of control over the management and planning of services. Importantly all of these developments are suggestive of a *continuity* in penal aims rather than a wholesale transformation. At the heart of welfarism is the presumption that offenders can be rehabilitated or changed into law-abiding citizens. The over-riding emphasis of the new policy is on the provision of services geared to achieving this outcome. The managerialist and actuarialist elements of the policy have been constructed as techniques better to effect normalisation. In these respects social work criminal justice policy has constructed a synthetic discourse in which risk management has been conceptualised as a necessary element of the rehabilitative process.

The Juvenile Justice System

The second element of penal policy which I want to focus on is that relating to juvenile justice. Although welfarism has remained a cornerstone of juvenile justice policy in Scotland, I am going to suggest that, within this site in the penal system, debates around the appropriate treatment of child offenders have always been bifurcated between a welfarist perspective (focused on the needs of the *individual* child) and what may be termed a public interest perspective (focused on what are conceived as broader *societal* concerns or the concerns of the *general* public).[9] In contrast to claims in the penological literature that punitive bifurcation is a relatively new and transformative feature of contemporary penality (see Garland, 1996; Bottoms, 1983), within Scotland a bifurcated discourse has shaped debates and institutional responses to children's behaviour at least as far back as the early years of the century, when formal separation of the juvenile and adult criminal justice systems took place. Nonetheless, as I aim to demonstrate, the dominant partner in the welfarist/public interest dyad has generally been the welfarist perspective, in particular with the development of the children's hearings system.

The early years of juvenile justice (1908 - 1968) The early years of the juvenile justice system were underpinned by an ambiguity in penal aims between concerns to 'rescue' and reform children and also to punish them (see Gelsthorpe and Morris, 1994). At that time 'public interest' was strongly associated with the need both to punish and to deter children. The tension between the requirement to look after the needs of the child and also act as a formal court of law within a predominantly public interest perspective, was one of the precipitating factors for the review of juvenile justice conducted by the Kilbrandon committee in the early 1960s. It was this review which laid the groundwork for the new children's hearings system.

Children's hearings system As explained in chapter 14 of this volume, the children's hearings system was set up by the Social Work Scotland (1968) Act. It marked a major watershed in the treatment of juvenile offenders. The children's hearings system is often cited as a paradigm example of a welfare based justice system (Asquith, 1983; McGhee *et al.*, 1996). The Kilbrandon ethos stressed that juvenile offending and other troublesome behaviours should be regarded as manifestations of deeper social and psychological malaise and/or failures in the normal upbringing process (Kilbrandon Committee, 1964). The overall aim of the hearings system was to deal with the needs of the child (whether referred for offending or in need of care and protection) and the best interests of the child were to be paramount in decision-making.

It is important to remember, however, that at the outset the Crown reserved the right to prosecute children who had committed the most serious offences (such as rape, serious assault or homicide) in the adult court system. A number of commentators have argued that although this undermined important aspects of the Kilbrandon ethos,[10] it was a necessary compromise in order to ensure the support of Crown Office, the judiciary and the police for the new hearings system (see Morris and McIsaac, 1978). I would suggest that this compromise is in keeping with the bifurcatory tendencies already inherent within the system. The compromise deals with the tension between welfare and public interest by ensuring that different categories of child offenders are dealt with in different settings: less serious categories in the hearings system, more serious in the adult courts.

Recent policy developments The path of recent policy development has been characterised by a gradual penetration of public interest discourse into the hearings system itself: public interest, however, is now more strongly associated with public protection than with punishment and deterrence. One of the first examples of this relates to the arrangements for secure accommodation introduced by Health and Social Services and Social Security Adjudications Act 1983. As result of this Act, the hearings were enabled to require a child, where he or she was likely 'to injure other persons', to reside in secure accommodation. There is an implicit acceptance in this section of the Act that issues of public safety can take priority over the best interests of the child and, as a consequence, secure care can be used as a mechanism for incapacitation rather than for addressing need.

The penetration of public interest discourse into the hearings system is more explicitly illustrated by a number of the changes introduced by the Children (Scotland) Act 1995. The passage of this Act was the culmination of a major review of the children's hearings system which occurred in the wake of the Orkney and Fife inquiries (prompted by issues of child protection, see Edwards and Griffiths, 1997) and increased concern about persistent offending (McAra and Young, 1997). This Act enabled the hearings system to place the principle of public protection above that of the best interests of the child in cases where the child presented a significant risk to the public. It also empowered sheriffs to substitute their own decision for that of the panel in disputed (and appealed) cases.

What the first of these developments suggests is that the hearings are being *explicitly* directed to work within a bifurcated discursive framework: considering public protection questions in 'high risk' (to the public) cases and the welfare needs of the child in low risk and other child protection cases. As with social work policy, the growing focus on risk and public protection could be taken as evidence of an emerging actuarial penal culture. It is clear however (*contra* Feeley and Simon) that risk management has not, to date, supplanted welfarism as the predominant ethos within the system. The 'best interests of the child' continues to be the key principle informing the system (McAra and Young, 1997) and it remains to be seen how the bifurcated framework, described above, will impact in practice on decisions made by the hearings. Were compulsory measures of care to be used increasingly as a means of incapacitating 'risky' children, then this has the potential to change the character of these interventions (and indeed the ethos of the system) significantly. Much will turn on the numbers of high risk cases processed by the system (which may be small) and how panel members and others working in the system assess risk (for example whether risk is associated with persistence in offending and/or degree of dangerousness).

The second of the developments (the increased powers of the sheriff) indicates a greater concern for due process rights of children and their families as well as the growing importance accorded to a public interest perspective in the hearings (see Cleland, 1995). It could be argued that this development reflects Bottoms' claim, outlined above, that a defining feature of contemporary penality is renewed focus on the rights of individual offenders. However, the extent to which this will have an impact on the underlying rationale of the system will be dependent on how often, and in what ways, sheriffs choose to exercise these powers. In practice the courts will only become involved in cases which are appealed by the child and/or parents. Given the common perception that sheriffs may be more punitive than panel members, it seems unlikely that this provision will be much used (McAra and Young, 1997).

To summarise, a consistent feature of juvenile justice policy has been the manner in which debates have been bifurcated between a welfare perspective and public interest perspective. The trend in recent years has been for the public interest perspective to penetrate more deeply into the aspects of the system which (at least since the instigation of the hearings system) had been the sole preserve of welfarism. While recent developments mirror some of the key themes in the literature reviewed, they have not led to a major transformation in penal aims. Welfarism remains the dominant ethos within the system and is likely to be so for some time to come (see McAra and Young, 1997).

Prisons

The final element of the policy framework which I want to address is prison policy. From around the 1950s until the 1970s, prison policy in Scotland was conceived on rehabilitative and therapeutic lines (Young, 1997). The Prison Rules stated explicitly that the purpose of the prison was to enable prisoners to lead 'good and useful lives' and strands of this approach were evident even as late as the 1980s. (For example, the mission statement issued in 1988 stated that a key aim of imprisonment was to assist prisoners to lead law-abiding and useful lives in custody and after release.) The standard account of developments is that since this period there has been a marked shift in prison policy towards increased managerialism and away from an explicit commitment to rehabilitation (Young, 1997; Wozniak, 1994).

Most commentators agree that the key factor precipitating this shift was the crisis in prisons which occurred in the 1980s (Wozniak, 1994). As was mentioned, overcrowding made prisons extremely difficult to manage, leading to an outbreak of disturbances and riots, including hostage taking. Industrial relations disputes and concerns about increased costs contributed to the sense of crisis, as did concerns about the fundamental purposes of imprisonment which had arisen in the wake of criticisms of the efficacy of rehabilationalism and correctionalism. Prison policy was therefore reviewed in the context of both a philosophical crisis about the purpose of imprisonment and a crisis of penal resources.

The outcome of this review was the implementation of new managerialist initiatives and a recasting of the objectives of imprisonment. Managerialist initiatives have included the Business Plan (Scottish Prison Service, 1989) which set out a number of management tasks, explained the new corporate philosophy of the service and identified priority areas for development. The Scottish Prison Service now produces corporate plans on a regular basis, reviewing progress and setting out key targets to be achieved within the planning cycle.

Shifts in the philosophical underpinnings of prison policy are most evident in the document Opportunity and Responsibility (Scottish Prison Service, 1990). This document states that prisoners should not be regarded as individuals in need of treatment or reform but as individuals who are responsible for their own actions. The role of the prison therefore should be to provide a range of opportunities for the prisoner which will encourage them to accept this responsibility. The facilitation of change - which prisoners have to instigate themselves - now replaces any explicit commitment to providing treatment.

On one level the above changes reflect trends identified in the literature on transformation, in particular: the twin crises over prison overcrowding and the purposes of imprisonment; the instigation of managerialist techniques; and the recasting of rehabilitation in the mould of responsibilisation. However the extent to which these developments have led to a complete eclipse of welfarism and/or rehabilitation is more questionable. There is still a commitment within Opportunity and Responsibility to the provision of prison programmes aimed at tackling offending behaviour and other significant problems such as drug or alcohol abuse.

Key examples of this have been the widespread introduction of cognitive behavioural programmes (in particular those based on the

'Reasoning and Rehabilitation' programmes developed in Canada: see Ross *et al.*, 1988) and in the continuing commitment to the flagship 'STOP' programme at Peterhead (aimed at assisting sex offenders to address their offending behaviour and adjust to law-abiding life). An important aim of the policy is also to minimise the harmful effects of the prisoner's removal from normal life as a means of assisting eventual reintegration into the community. The intention is to improve family contacts through increased opportunities for home leaves and greater access to pay-phones; to develop better pre-release programmes; and to improve conditions within prisons, such as giving every prisoner access to night sanitation or integral cell sanitation (Scottish Prison Service, 1990).

Although prison policy aims to provide choice and emphasises individual responsibility, it is doing so within the context of prison regimes aimed at assisting prisoners to change their behaviour and lifestyles, and to reintegrate into mainstream society. Indeed it is arguable that there are now even greater numbers of rehabilitative programmes being implemented within prisons than during the supposed high point of welfarism between the 1950s and 1970s.

To conclude this section, recent developments in prison policy reflect many of the trends in social work. Prisons have been given a more explicit and sharply focused agenda to work within, based primarily on normalisation and the facilitation of change, and the Scottish Prison Service itself has developed a more coherent approach to the management and planning of services. In many respects these developments do mark a watershed in prison policy. Nevertheless the commitment to programmes based on effective intervention suggests that core aspects of rehabilitation are alive and well within the prison system.

The Crime and Punishment (Scotland) Act 1997

Before I conclude this section on policy development, mention must be made of the White Paper *Crime and Punishment* (Scottish Office, 1996f) and the subsequent Crime and Punishment (Scotland) Act 1997. During the brief tenure of Michael Forsyth as Secretary of State for Scotland (in the last two years of Conservative Government), official pronouncements on penal policy became increasingly punitive, culminating in the publication of the White Paper and the passage of the 1997 Act.

The White Paper included proposals for the abolition of the parole system (to be replaced by a system of remission); for certain community-based disposals to be made tougher and more rigorous; and for the imposition of life sentences for a second serious, sexual or violent offence (the so-called 'two-strikes' policy). These proposals were justified in the White Paper on the grounds that they would enhance the confidence and trust of the public in the criminal justice system and also that the new arrangements would protect the public. If Scotland has ever had a moment of punitive populism then this was it.

Nevertheless the White Paper's proposals both on early release and in respect of prisons still retained a residual commitment to rehabilitative concerns. As a means of ensuring public protection, early release from custody was to be partly contingent on offenders making efforts to address offending behaviour during time spent in custody (thereby demonstrating efforts to effect behavioural change). Prisons were also exhorted to match counselling and educational programmes to the specific needs of their populations. The document also placed concern about crime within a broader crime prevention strategy aimed at supporting families, creating greater employment and training opportunities and better pre-school education. The links to a broader programme for social change indicate that the document Crime and Punishment has the *potential* to be used to promote penal welfare strategies even although the spin placed on the document by the then Conservative Minister of State would have resulted in the partial eclipse of such strategies within the Scottish context.

At the time of writing, the new Labour administration has pledged not to implement many elements of the Crime and Punishment (Scotland) Act, in particular those relating to parole and a number of those relating to sentencing (for example the two-strikes policy). It remains to be seen whether the more punitive edge given to penal policy by the late Conservative administration filters through in any meaningful way to future Labour policy or whether the distinctive penal culture in Scotland will endure (see below).

Policy Developments and Accounts of Transformation

I have now completed the review of policy developments in Scotland. By way of concluding this section I want to reassess briefly these developments in the light of the main themes in the literature on transformation.

Taking Feeley and Simon's work first, while it is clear that risk management and aspects of actuarial justice have penetrated the Scottish penal system (in particular with respect to social work and juvenile justice) these have not become system defining in the manner in which Feeley and Simon would suggest. Within social work, risk management has been conceptualised as a necessary aspect of effective work with offenders; within juvenile justice it is one element of a system based predominantly on a welfarist rationale.

With regard to key themes in Garland's work, there is little evidence that policy in Scotland has become increasingly bifurcated between punitive and preventative strategies, nor between the criminology of 'the self' and of 'the other'. Juvenile justice policy has always been bifurcated between a welfarist and public interest perspective: that is between rehabilitation and (in recent years) protection rather than punishment and prevention. Indeed there is an explicit rejection of punitive approaches in social work policy and the dominant 'criminology' within the policy sites reviewed is one which links offending to certain specified 'criminogenic' needs (for example drug or alcohol problems) and to deeper social and or psychological malaise (as for example in the Kilbrandon ethos).

In respect of the themes in Bottoms' work, while there is some evidence to suggest that rehabilitation has been recast into responsibilisation strategies (particularly in prison policy) and a renewed focus on individual rights (for example in juvenile justice), none of the policy sites reviewed suggest that the penal system has become increasingly focused on just deserts or on proportionality in punishment.

Finally, there is little evidence for the claims made in all of the literature, that penal welfarism has been eclipsed. Within all of the policy sites reviewed, core aspects of rehabilitation remain. This is most notable with regard to the commitment to the provision of programmes which can effect behavioural change and which are aimed at assisting the offender to reintegrate into the community. The main changes that have occurred in Scotland are: firstly a sharpening of focus of penal aims away from broad and often ill-defined notions into a clearly stated and *delimited* set of objectives; and secondly what may be termed a re-professionalisation of penal practice through the adoption of managerialist techniques. Underpinning these changes has been a continued commitment to the values of welfarism.

Explanations for Policy Development

Having examined the ways in which the Scottish penal system has resisted some of the trends identified in the literature on transformation, I now want to assess the explanations for change set out in the literature.

As highlighted above, recent penological theorising links recent changes in policy to deeper social and cultural processes. In this final section of the chapter, I aim to demonstrate that there is no necessary causal connection between these social and cultural processes and the actual *form* which penal policy has taken. In this respect penal development is more contingent and nuanced that the literature would suggest. In order to explore these issues and their implications I will firstly assess Garland's arguments on the relationship between a crisis in legitimation and penal change and secondly Feeley and Simon's and Bottom's arguments regarding the relationship between shifts in social structures and penal forms.

Legitimation Crisis and Penal Change

Garland argues that penal transformation has occurred as a response to a crisis of governance precipitated by the persistence of high crime rates. The Scottish case presents a conundrum for this argument, as Scotland has experienced both high crime rates and a legitimation crisis but neither of these factors has led to an eclipse of welfarism nor indeed to any major penal crisis.

High crime rates High crime rates have become as much a feature of contemporary Scottish society as other western societies. Between 1950 and 1995, for example, there was almost a five-fold increase in recorded crimes and offences in Scotland (from around 40 to 186 per 1,000 of the population: Young, 1997). It is only in recent years that the rate of increase has begun to slow down (see chapter 2 for further discussion).[11] It would be wrong to suggest that concerns about high crime rates have not filtered into the policy making process to some degree. Within juvenile justice for example, high offending rates amongst children and young people was one of the precipitating factors for policy change in the 1990s (see above). However, any shifts in policy attributable to high crime rates, have done little to alter the underlying rationale of the system (as the example of juvenile justice clearly demonstrates). As was said, policy development in Scotland has generally been accomplished by *sharpening the focus* of existing frameworks rather than by a wholesale change of direction. Moreover the link drawn by Garland between high crime rates and a legitimation crisis is fairly tenuous when recent Scottish developments are considered in more detail.

Legitimation crisis During the 1980s and early 1990s central government in Scotland did indeed appear to have a weak claim to legitimacy (see Brown *et al.*, 1996). The sources of this weakness, however, are less linked to high crime rates and more to the growing disjuncture between grassroots politics in Scotland and the right wing policies of the Thatcher/Major governments. According to Brown *et al.*, the ideologies associated with Thatcherism and Majorism cut across the basic consensus that had existed amongst political parties in Scotland, in respect of both economic and social policy (Brown *et al.*, 1996). This is reflected in the fact that skilled working class voters in Scotland did not shift allegiance from traditional (predominantly) Labour party politics to new Conservatism (as happened in England and Wales) and voting patterns during the 1980s and 1990s indicate strong continuity of support for both Labour and increasingly (in the early 1990s) the Scottish National Party (see Brown *et al.*, 1996). In these respects problems of governance in Scotland became increasingly articulated as a *constitutional* rather than penal crisis, with a growing clamour for home rule and increasing resistance to unpopular policies of which the Poll Tax is the most spectacular example (see McCrone, 1996; for further discussion of this).

Paradoxically it may be that (*contra* Garland) this legitimation crisis has served to buttress the penal system against major transformation. To understand why this may be the case requires an explanation of the role of policy networks within the Scottish penal system.

Policy networks Both Young (1997) and Moore and Booth (1989) have highlighted the significance of policy networks for an understanding of the development of policy within a Scottish context. These networks comprise senior civil servants within the Scottish Office and key decision-making elites outwith central government, such as Directors of Social Work, members of the judiciary, Crown Office and the police. Policy networks have grown up and have been sustained by what Young has termed a metaphoric and geographical 'barrier' provided by the constitutional settlement of 1707 (which guaranteed the existence of separate Scottish educational and legal systems and a separate Scottish church) and by administrative arrangements whereby large areas of domestic policy making have been turned over to the Scottish Office. This barrier has enabled these networks to argue for *separate* policies tailored to the distinctive conditions existing in Scotland or to claim that the differences in the Scottish system mean that a special case should be made for *adapting* UK policies in order to ensure effective implementation (Young, 1997; Moore and Booth, 1989). The enduring strength and influence of these networks in the penal realm has been one of the main reasons why the Scottish penal system has been able to sustain a commitment to penal welfare values in the face of a UK national government which was espousing a more punitive approach to penal policy.

The strength and influence of the networks is best exemplified by social work policy in the 1980s and 1990s. The development of the 100 per cent funding initiative and the national objectives and standards (discussed above) was conducted by the Social Work Services Group in consultation with key players in the penal system such as members of the Parole Board for Scotland, the judiciary, the police and local authority social work departments. The aim of this consultation was to facilitate 'common ownership' of the policy (McAra, 1998) and the policy was hammered out amongst these groups behind closed doors. This contrasts with the development of policy relating to community-based disposals in England and Wales at this time. Here 'consultation' took place mainly through a rash of green papers issued by central government (see Mair, 1997a) and the increasingly punitive approach taken to these sanctions by central government (reflected within the Green Papers) served to fragment rather than unite key groups in the system (for discussion of the impact on the probation service, see May and Vass, 1996).

At times when the political arm of central government has a weak claim to legitimacy (as occurred in Scotland during the Thatcher and Major years), the influence of policy networks can arguably increase. Lacking in popular support, government may be *crucially* dependent on the support of key decision-makers at all levels within the system, for effective policy implementation and this can give the voice of policy elites a greater resonance. Nonetheless the balance of power is a delicate matter and, in many respects, is dependent on the political will of the particular Minister involved. During the 1980s and early 1990s, Ministers (such Malcolm Rifkind, the former Secretary of State, and Lord Fraser of Carmylie, the former Minister at the Home Department) were sympathetic to the distinctiveness of the Scottish penal system and were more consensual in their approach to policy development. By contrast the accession of Michael Forsyth as Secretary of State, in the mid 1990s, heralded a more confrontational style of politics and less willingness to negotiate and bargain with key groups in the system. Even still, the main outputs from his era (the *Crime and Punishment* White Paper and subsequent Act, discussed above) retained the imprimatur of a distinctively Scottish commitment to effective practice and to broader social crime prevention strategies, suggestive (although not complete proof) of a continued degree of influence of the policy networks described above.

The implications of this are that the very processes which Garland associates with transformation, may have contributed to continuities within the Scottish system, although further research would be required to provide conclusive evidence. At the very least, however, the Scottish case serves to highlight the contingency inherent within policy development: in particular with regard to the relationship between political exigencies and the relative strengths of elite groups in the penal system at any one time. What this suggests is that: firstly there is no causal relationship between a legitimation crisis, high crime rates and penal transformation; and secondly that any explanation of policy developments requires to examine more carefully than hitherto, the processes through which social, cultural and political processes are mediated within the penal system.

The Relationship between Social Structures and Penal Form

Finally I want to turn to an assessment of the explanations offered by Feeley and Simon and Bottoms for changes in the nature and function of penal forms. Each of these accounts links penal transformation to broader shifts within contemporary social structures. For Feeley and Simon the key change has been the emergence of an underclass of permanently marginalised and thereby potentially threatening groups. For Bottoms key changes include a number of the features of late capitalist societies, in particular the disembedding of social relations, shifts in patterns of work and technological developments.

Again the Scottish case poses a conundrum for these arguments. Most of the changes in social structures identified by the literature are evident within Scotland and yet none would appear to have precipitated an eclipse in welfarism. Indeed technological developments (mentioned by Bottoms) have assisted the development of managerialist techniques aimed at improving the effectiveness of penal practice in achieving essentially welfarist objectives. In these respects the Scottish case can be used to show that there is no causal connection between these social processes and the form which penal policy has taken.

Underclass and the disembedding of social relations Scotland, in common with a number of western societies, has undergone major structural changes over the past 30 years. There has been a massive decline in traditional industries, such as mining and steel making, and a corresponding growth in service industries and part-time, less secure and casual labour (Norris, 1983). This has been accompanied by increased social polarisation, with top income earners becoming even richer and those at the lower of the spectrum becoming poorer.[12] Indeed, research suggests that the number of people living in poverty has risen dramatically in recent years, with one fifth of the Scottish population inhabiting the most deprived post code sectors. Many of those living in poverty are lone parent families and this reflects the growth in divorce and separation rates over the past twenty years (Tennant, 1995).

All of these features suggest that there are growing numbers of marginalised, socially deprived groups within Scotland and that there may have been a gradual disembedding of social relationships away from intermediate groups such as the traditional nuclear family. They also indicate major changes in the pattern of work for large numbers of people, away from the discipline of the factory and the security of long term and skilled employment, to a more shifting, insecure and de-skilled form of labour.

Without further research, the reasons as to why these developments have not been associated with penal transformations in Scotland are difficult to ascertain. A full explanation would be dependent on explaining in greater detail than does the literature reviewed, the *processes* by which social changes impact on, and are mediated by, the penal system. I would suggest however, that part of the answer may lie in the particular nature of Scottish civic culture.

In Scotland, there has been a more democratic tradition within dominant institutions (than for example in England and Wales), particularly with regard to education and the church. This has been accompanied by a strong socialist tradition, especially at local government level, which has gained momentum throughout most of this century. These factors could be said to have contributed to the construction of a civic culture which valorises community, public provision of welfare and mutual support (see Paterson, 1994, for further discussion of such issues), and which intermittently becomes linked to a broader sense of Scottish identity (as occurred increasingly throughout the Thatcher/Major years). It could be argued that this culture shores up and to some extent is reproduced by a penal culture whose predominant rationale is rehabilitative and reintegrative. This civic culture continues to operate on an ideological level in the face of the increased social polarisation, marginalisation and disembedding of social relations described above. In these respects penal change may be averted until the contradictions between culture and structure become too sharp for the culture itself to be sustained.

Conclusion

Within Scotland, penal welfarism endures as the dominant framework within which debates on justice and policy have taken place. Policy developments themselves have been characterised by a gradual sharpening of focus around notions of effectiveness and strategies for balancing care and control, rather than a wholesale change in direction. The sharpening of focus has resulted in greater clarity of purpose and a more explicit agenda for the various interventions reviewed. Even in the Forsyth years, when there was a greater commitment to the values of populist punitiveness, the flagship legislation was underpinned by a commitment to broader social crime prevention strategies and the provision of programmes to effect behavioural change.

In these respects the Scottish case poses a conundrum for the literature on penal transformation. It does so because penal welfarism has endured in the face of social and cultural features which according to the literature should have prompted a significant shift in the nature and function of penality. I have suggested that this is attributable in part to the enduring strength and influence of elite policy networks within Scotland and may be linked to a civic culture which continues to valorise community integration and mutual support in the face of increased polarisation and marginalisation.

What the Scottish case implies is that explanations of penal change need to take more seriously the contingencies inherent within policy development and the processes through which social, cultural and political processes are mediated by the penal system itself. In these respects penological research now requires to develop a political theory of penality.

Notes

1. Bifurcated penal strategies are those in which offenders are divided into two populations: high risk dangerous offenders for whom incapacitation and punishment are seen as appropriate and low risk offenders who can be dealt with safely in a non-custodial setting.
2. The solidarity project is the term used by Garland to describe *inter alia* the penetration of welfare values into the penal system around the turn of the century and the consequent reorientation of penality (for further discussion see Garland, 1985).
3. See, for example, his essay 'The Philosophy and Politics of Punishment and Sentencing' (Bottoms, 1994), which takes as its focus changes in sentencing practice.
4. Named after the chair of the Committee set up in the 1960s to review the then juvenile justice system and the role of social work in the criminal justice system. The committee reported in 1964. Its principal recommendations were put in place by the Social Work (Scotland) Act 1968.
5. Generic social work teams have mixed case loads which include a diverse range of client groups such as children and elderly people, in addition to offender based work. This contrasts with the former probation service which only dealt with offenders
6. Not all social work criminal justice services were included under the scope of the initiative when first implemented. Those included were: throughcare services; social enquiry and other court reports and services; probation

supervision; and community service (which had been the subject of 100 per cent funding and national standards since 1989).

7. This is known within the meta-analytic literature as 'programme integrity', which requires *inter alia*: adequate resources; well trained, highly skilled and motivated staff; and the introduction of mechanisms for monitoring and evaluating performance (see McGuire, 1995).

8. For example penal policy in England and Wales became increasingly punitive during the 1990s, in particular with the Home Secretary's famous dictum in 1993, that 'prison works' (for further discussion of this see Cavadino and Dignan, 1997).

9. Of course there is no necessary nor inevitable tension between a public interest and welfare perspective. For example, it could be seen to be in the public interest that children be dealt with in a welfare based system. However within juvenile justice in Scotland, these perspectives have been consistently juxtaposed.

10. The Kilbrandon ethos would claim that the more serious the deed the greater the welfare needs of the child.

11. This compares with an eight fold increase in notifiable offences in England and Wales from 1950 to 1996, from eleven to 95 per 1000 population (Maguire, 1997). Indeed, Scotland, in common with most western criminal justice systems, has seen a long-term increase in crime rates since the 1930s (Young, 1997). It is only in recent years that crime rates have begun to diverge slightly from those in England and Wales; most notably during the 1980s and early 1990s when the rate of increase in Scotland was slower than that in England and Wales. This is also reflected in crime survey data which suggests that rates of victimisation are now lower in Scotland than in England and Wales (Young, 1997).

12. Figures from research undertaken by Davis *et al.* (quoted in Oppenheim, 1993) indicate that between 1979 and 1992 the richest income earners saw major increases in income (for the top ten per cent of income earners these increases amounted to £87 per week), whereas the lowest income earners saw their share of income decrease (for the poorest groups this amounted to a loss of £1 per week).

21 Bibliography

Adler, A. (1987), *Rape on Trial*, Routledge and Kegan Paul, London.

Adler, M. and Longhurst, B. (1994), *Discourse and Justice: Towards a New Sociology of Imprisonment*, Routledge, London and New York.

Advisory Council on the Penal System (The Wootton Committee) (1970), *Non-Custodial and Semi-Custodial Penalties*, HMSO, London.

Albrecht, H-J. (1991), 'Ethnic Minorities: Crime and Criminal Justice in Europe', in F. Heidensohn and M. Farrell (eds), *Crime in Europe*, Routledge, London, pp. 84-100.

Alison, A.J. (1833), *Practice of the Criminal Law of Scotland*, vol ii, Edinburgh.

Allen, D.M. and Payne, D. (1991), *The Public and the Police in Scotland: Findings from the 1988 British Crime Survey*, Scottish Office Central Research Unit, Edinburgh.

American Friends Service Committee (1971), *Struggle for Justice New York*, Hill and Wong, New York.

American Psychiatric Association (1994), *Diagnostic and Statistical Manual of Mental Disorders*, 4th edition, American Psychiatric Association, Washington.

Anderson, M., den Boer, M., Cullen, P., Gilmore, W.C., Raab, C. and Walker, N. (1995), *Policing the European Union; Theory, Law and Practice*, Oxford University Press, Oxford.

Anderson, S. (1997), *Crime in Rural Scotland*, Scottish Office Central Research Unit, Edinburgh.

Anderson, S. and Leitch, S. (1994), *The Scottish Crime Survey 1993: First Results*, Crime and Criminal Justice Research Findings No. 1, Scottish Office, Edinburgh.

Anderson, S. and Leitch, S. (1996), *Main Findings from the 1993 Scottish Crime Survey*, Scottish Office Central Research Unit, Edinburgh.

Anderson, S., Grove Smith, C., Kinsey, R. and Wood, J. (1990), *The Edinburgh Crime Survey*, Scottish Office Central Research Unit, Edinburgh.

Anderson, S., Kinsey, R., Grove Smith, C. and Wood, J. (1990), *The Edinburgh Crime Survey*, HMSO, Edinburgh.

Anderson, S., Kinsey, R., Loader, I. and Smith, C. (1994), *Cautionary Tales: Young People, Crime and Policing in Edinburgh*, Avebury, Aldershot.

Ashworth, A. (1993), 'Victim Impact Statements and Sentencing', *Criminal Law Review*, pp. 498-509.

Ashworth, A. (1994), *The Criminal Process*, Clarendon, Oxford.

381

Ashworth, A. (1997), 'Sentencing', in M. Maguire, R. Morgan and R. Reiner (eds), *The Oxford Handbook of Criminology*, 2nd edition, Oxford University Press, Oxford, pp. 1095-1135.

Ashworth, A. and Fionda, J. (1994), 'Prosecution, Accountability and the Public Interest', *Criminal Law Review*, pp. 895-904.

Asquith, S. (1983), *Children and Justice: Decision-making in the Children's Hearings and Juvenile Court*, Edinburgh University Press, Edinburgh.

Asquith, S. (1995), *Social Reactions to Juvenile Delinquency*, Directorate of Legal Affairs, Council of Europe.

Asquith, S. (1998, forthcoming), 'Justice for Children Who Commit Offences: Rights Driven Developments', in P. Jaffe (ed), *Implementing the UN Convention on the Rights of the Child*, conference proceedings, University of Geneva, Geneva.

Asquith, S. and Samuel, E. (1994), *A Review of Criminal Justice Related Services for Young Adult Offenders*, HMSO, Edinburgh.

Asquith, S., Buist, M., Loughran, N., McCauley, C. and Montgomery, M. (1998, forthcoming), *Children, Young People and Offending in Scotland*, Scottish Office Central Research Unit, Edinburgh.

Association of Directors of Social Work (1987), *Report of a Working Party on Fines and Fine Default*, Association of Directors of Social Work, Glasgow.

Association of Directors of Social Work (1996), *ADSW Policy on Victims of Crime*, Association of Directors of Social Work, Dundee.

Aye Maung, N. and Mirrlees-Black, C. (1994), *Racially Motived Crime: A British Crime Survey Analysis*, Research and Planning Unit Paper 82, Home Office Research and Statistics Department, London.

Baillie, S. (1992), 'When a Child is a Killer', *Childright*, April, no. 105.

Baillie, S. (1993), 'Fast Forward to Violence', *Criminal Justice Matters*, no. 6.

Baldwin, R. and Kinsey, R. (1982), *Police Powers and Politics*, Quartet, London.

Banister, J. (1991), *The Impact of Environmental Design upon the Incidence and Type of Crime*, Scottish Office Central Research Unit, Edinburgh.

Bankowski, Z.K. (1988), 'The Jury and Reality', in M. Findlay and P. Duff (eds), *The Jury Under Attack*, Butterworths, London, pp. 8-26.

Bankowski, Z.K., Hutton, N.R. and McManus, J.J. (1987), *Lay Justice?*, T&T Clark, Edinburgh.

Bannister, J. and Kearns, A. (1995), *Managing Crime: Findings from a Survey of Scottish Housing Initiatives*, Centres for Housing Research and Urban Studies, Glasgow.

Bannister, J., Fyfe, N.R., and Kearns, A. (1998, in press), 'Close Circuit Television and the City', in C. Norris and G. Armstrong (eds), *CCTV: Surveillance and Social Control*, Gower, Avebury.

Bates, P. (1995), 'What Challenges do Women Offenders Pose for Social Work?', in SACRO Conference Report, *Women Offenders*, March, Edinburgh.

Bayley, D.H. (1985) *Patterns of Policing,* Rutgers University Press, New Brunswick, New Jersey.

Bayley, D.H. (1994), *Police for the Future*, Oxford University Press, New York and Oxford.

Bayley, D.H. and Shearing, C.D. (1996), 'The Future of Policing', *Law and Society Review*, vol. 30, pp. 585-606.

Bennett, T. (1991), 'The Effectiveness of a Police Initiated Fear Reducing Strategy', *British Journal of Criminology*, vol. 31, no. 1, pp. 1-14.

Bennett, T. (1992), 'Themes and Variations in Neighbourhood Watch', in D. Evans, N.R. Fyfe and D.T. Herbert (eds), *Crime, Policing and Place: Essays in Environmental Criminology*, Routledge, London, pp. 272-285.

Berry, G. and Carter, M. (1992), *Assessing Crime Prevention Initiatives: The First Steps*, Home Office, Crime Prevention Unit Paper No. 31, London.

Bianchini, F. (1990), 'The Crisis of Urban Public Social Life in Britain: Origins of the Problem and Possible Responses', *Planning, Policy and Research*, vol. 5, pp. 4-8.

Biderman, A.D. and Reiss, A. J. (1967), 'On Exploring the 'Dark Figure' of Crime', *Annals of the American Academy of Political and Social Science*, vol. 374, pp. 1-15.

Blake-Stevenson Consultants (1993), *Community Involvement in the Castlemilk Partnership*, Castlemilk Partnership, Glasgow.

Bochel, D. (1976), *Probation and After-Care: Its Development in England and Wales*, Scottish Academic Press, Edinburgh.

Boddy, T. (1992), 'Underground and Overhead: Building the Analogous City', in M. Sorkin (ed), *Variations on a Theme Park: The New American City and the End of Public Space*, Hill and Wang, New York, pp. 123-154.

Bogue, J. and Power, K. (1995), 'Suicide in Scottish Prisons, 1976-93', *Journal of Forensic Psychiatry*, 6, pp. 527-540.

Boswell, G. (1995), *Violent Victims: The Prevalence of Abuse and Loss in the Lives of Section 53 Offenders*, The Prince's Trust.

Bottoms, A. (1983), 'Neglected Features of Contemporary Penal Systems', in D. Garland and P. Young (eds), *The Power to Punish: Contemporary Penality and Social Analysis*, Heinenman, London, pp. 166-202.

Bottoms, A. (1994), 'The Philosophy and Politics of Punishment and Sentencing', in C. Clarkson and R. Morgan (eds), *The Politics of Sentencing Reform*, Oxford University Press, Oxford, pp. 17-49.

Bottoms, A.E. and McClean, J.D. (1976), *Defendants in the Criminal Process*, Routledge and Kegan Paul, London.

Bottoms, A.E. and McWilliams, W. (1978), 'A Non-Treatment Paradigm for Probation Practice', *British Journal of Social Work*, vol. 9, no. 2, pp. 159-202.

Bowling, B. (1993), 'Racial Harassment and the Process of Victimisation: Conceptual and Methodological Implications for the Local Crime Survey', *British Journal of Criminology*, vol. 33, no. 2, pp. 231-249.

Bradley, D., Walker, N. and Wilkie, R. (1986), *Managing the Police: Law, Organisation and Democracy,* Harvester Wheatsheaf, Hemel Hempstead.

Brake, M. and Hale, C. (1992), *Public Order and Private Lives: The Politics of Law and Order,* Routledge, London.

Brogden, M. (1982), *The Police: Autonomy and Consent,* Academic Press, London and New York.

Brogden, M. (1991), *On the Mersey Beat: An Oral History of Policing Liverpool Between the Wars,* Oxford University Press, Oxford.

Brogden, M., Jefferson, T. and Walklate, S. (1988), *Introducing Policework,* Unwin, London.

Brown, A., McCrone, D. and Paterson, L. (1996, eds), *Politics and Society in Scotland,* Macmillan, Basingstoke.

Brown, B. (1995), *CCTV in Town Centres: Three Case Studies,* Home Office Police Department, London.

Brown, B., Burman, M. and Jamieson, L. (1992), *Sexual History and Sexual Character Evidence in Scottish Sexual Offence Trials,* Scottish Office Central Research Unit, Edinburgh.

Brown, B., Burman, M. and Jamieson, L. (1993), *Sex Crimes on Trial: the Use of Sexual Evidence in Scottish Courts,* Edinburgh University Press, Edinburgh.

Brown, L. (1992), *Neighbourhood Watch,* Scottish Office Central Research Unit, Edinburgh.

Brown, L. (1994), *A Fine on Time: The Monitoring and Evaluation of the Pilot Supervised Attendance Order Schemes,* Scottish Office Central Research Unit, Edinburgh.

Brown, L., Christie, L. and Morris, D. (1990), *Families of Murder Victims Support Project: Final Report,* Victim Support, London.

Brown, P. and Hiram, H. (1997), *Claiming Criminal Injuries Compensation,* LSA, Glasgow.

Brownlee, I.D. (1995), 'Intensive Probation with Young Adult Offenders: A Short Reconviction Study', *British Journal of Criminology,* vol. 35, no. 4, pp. 599-612.

Burman, M. and Lloyd, S. (1993), *Police Specialist Units for the Investigation of Crimes of Violence against Women and Children in Scotland,* Scottish Office Central Research Unit, Edinburgh.

Burrows, J. (1988), *Retail Crime: Prevention through Crime Analysis,* Home Office, Crime Prevention Unit Paper No. 11, London.

Burrows, J. (1992), *Making Crime Prevention Pay: Initiatives from Business,* Home Office, Crime Prevention Unit Paper No. 27, London.

Butler, A.J.P. (1995), 'A Means to an End? The Future Measurement of Police Performance', *Policing Today,* April, pp. 12-15.

Cain, M. (1973), *Society and the Policeman's Role,* Routledge and Kegan Paul, London.

Cameron, G.D.L. and McManus, J.J. (1993), *Consideration of the Mental State of Accused Persons at the Pre-Trial and Pre-Sentencing Stages*, Scottish Office Central Research Unit, Edinburgh.

Cameron, J. (1983), *Prisons and Punishment in Scotland from the Middle Ages to the Present*, Canongate, Edinburgh.

Cappelaere, G. (1993), *United Nations Guidelines for the Prevention of Juvenile Delinquency: Prevention of Juvenile Delinquency or Promotion of a Society which Respects Children Too?* Proceedings of United Nations World Conference on Human Rights, Vienna, June 14-24.

Carlen, P. (1983), *Women's Imprisonment: A Study in Social Control*, Routledge and Kegan Paul, London.

Carnie, J. (1990), *Sentencers' Perceptions of Community Service by Offenders*, Scottish Office Central Research Unit, Edinburgh.

Carnie, J. (1994), *Evaluation of the Safer Edinburgh Project*, Scottish Office Central Research Unit, Edinburgh.

Carnie, J. (1996), *The Safer Cities Programme in Scotland - Overview Report*, HMSO, Edinburgh.

Carson, W.G. (1984), 'Policing the Periphery: The Development of Scottish Policing 1795-1900: Part I,' *Aust. & NZ. Journal of Criminology*, vol. 17, pp. 207-232.

Carson, W.G. (1985), 'Policing the Periphery: The Development of Scottish Policing 1795-1900: Part II' *Aust. & NZ. Journal of Criminology*, vol. 18, pp. 3-16.

Cavadino, M. and Dignan, J. (1992), *The Penal System: An Introduction*, Sage, London.

Cavadino, M. and Dignan, J. (1997), *The Penal System: An Introduction*, 2nd edition, Sage, London.

Cavadino, P. (1996, ed), *Children Who Kill*, British Juvenile and Family Courts Magistrates Association.

Chambers, G. and Millar, A. (1983), *Investigating Sexual Assault*, Scottish Office Central Research Unit, HMSO, Edinburgh.

Chambers, G. and Millar, A. (1986), *Prosecuting Sexual Assault*, Scottish Office Central Research Unit, HMSO, Edinburgh.

Chambers, G. and Tombs, J. (1984), *The British Crime Survey (Scotland)*, Scottish Office Central Research Unit, HMSO, Edinburgh.

Cherrett, M. (1996), 'Mentally Disordered Offenders and the Police', in *Mental Health Review*, Pavilion, London.

Childhood Matters (1996), Report of the National Commission of Inquiry into the Prevention of Child Abuse, HMSO, Edinburgh.

Chiswick, D. (1990), 'Criminal Responsibility in Scotland', in R. Bluglass and P. Bowden (eds), *Principles and Practice of Forensic Psychiatry*, Churchill Livingstone, Edinburgh, pp. 313-318.

Chiswick, D. (1992), 'Reed Report on Mentally Disordered Offenders', *British Medical Journal*, 305, pp. 1448-1449.

Chiswick, D. (1996), 'Sentencing Mentally Disordered Offenders', *British Medical Journal*, 313, pp. 1497-1498.

Chiswick, D., McIsaac, M.W. and McClintock, F.H. (1984), *Prosecution of the Mentally Disturbed: Dilemmas of Identification and Discretion*, Aberdeen University Press, Aberdeen.

Christie, N. (1986), 'The Ideal Victim', in E. Fattah (ed), *From Crime Policy to Victim Policy*, Macmillan, London, pp. 17-30.

Christie, N. (1993), *Crime Control as Industry*, Routledge, London.

Christopherson, S. (1994), 'The Fortress City: Privatized Spaces, Consumer Citizenship', in A. Amin (ed), *Post-Fordism: A Reader*, Blackwell, Oxford, pp. 409-427.

Clarkson, C. and Morgan, R. (1995, eds), *The Politics of Sentencing Reform*, Clarendon, Oxford.

Cleland, A. (1995), 'Legal Solutions for Children: Comparing Scots Law with Other Jurisdictions', *Scottish Affairs*, no. 10, pp. 6-24.

Cleveland Probation Service (1995), *A Comparative Study of Reconviction Rates in Cleveland*, Cleveland Probation Service, Cleveland.

Cohen, S. (1985), *Visions of Social Control*, Polity Press, Cambridge.

Cohn, E.G. and Farrington, D.P. (1998), 'Changes in the Most Cited Scholars in Major International Journals between 1986-90 and 1991-95', *British Journal of Criminology*, vol. 38, no. 1, pp. 156-170.

Coker, J. (1982), 'Sentenced to Social Work?: An Experiment in Probation Practice', *International Journal of Offender Therapy and Comparative Criminology*, vol. 26, no. 1, pp. 27-31.

Coleman, C. and Moynihan, J. (1996), *Understanding Crime Rates: Haunted by the Dark Figure of Crime*, Open University Press, Milton Keynes.

Cooke, D.J. (1990), *Treatment as an Alternative to Prosecution: Diversion to the Douglas Inch Centre*, Scottish Office Central Research Unit, Edinburgh.

Cooke, D.J. (1991), 'Treatment as an Alternative to Prosecution: Offenders Diverted for Treatment', *British Journal of Psychiatry*, 158, pp. 785-791.

Cosgrove, K. (1996), 'No Man Has The Right', in C. Corrin (ed), *Women in a Violent World*, Edinburgh University Press, Edinburgh.

Coughlan, S.G. (1994), 'The Adversary System: Rhetoric or Reality?', *Canadian Journal of Law and Society*, vol. 8, p. 139.

Coyle, A. (1982), 'The Founding Father of the Scottish Prison Service', *Journal of the Association of Scottish Prison Governors*, vol. 1, pp. 7-14.

Creamer, A. and Williams, B.P. (1996), 'Risk Prediction and Criminal Justice', in G. McIvor (ed), *Working With Offenders*, Research Highlights in Social Work no. 26, Jessica Kingsley, London.

Creamer, A., Ennis, E. and Williams, B. (1994), *The DUNSCORE: A Method for Predicting Risk of Custody within the Scottish Context and its Use in Social*

Enquiry Practice, Department of Social Work, University of Dundee and The Scottish Office, Dundee.

Creamer, A., Hartley, L. and Williams, B.P. (1992a), *The Probation Alternative: A Study of the Impact of Four Enhanced Probation Schemes on Sentencing Outcomes*, Scottish Office Central Research Unit, Edinburgh.

Creamer, A., Hartley, L. and Williams, B.P. (1992b), *The Probation Alternative: Case-Studies in the Establishment of Alternative to Custody Schemes in Scotland*, Scottish Office Central Research Unit, Edinburgh.

Criminal Statistics in Scotland (1904), Cmnd. 1830, Edinburgh.

Criminal Statistics in Scotland (1907), Cmnd. 3829, Edinburgh.

Crow, I. and Cove, J. (1984), 'Ethnic Minorities and the Courts', *Criminal Law Review*, pp. 413-417.

Crown Office and Procurator Fiscal Service (1993-95), *Annual Report*, HMSO, Edinburgh.

Crown Prosecution Service (1994), *Annual Report 1993-1994*, HMSO, London.

Curran, J. and Chambers, G. (1981), *Social Enquiry Reports in Scotland*, HMSO, Edinburgh.

Currie, E. (1996), Is America Really Winning the War on Crime and Should Britain Follow its Example?, *NACRO 30th Anniversary Lecture*, NACRO, London.

Daily Record (1998), 'Nine in ten Scots live in fear', 16 September.

Daly, D. (1991-95a), *Annual Reviews 1991-95*, Safe Greater Easterhouse Project, Glasgow.

Daly, D. (1990-95b), *Crime Profiles 1990-95*, Safe Greater Easterhouse Project, Glasgow.

Damaška, M. (1971), 'Evidentiary Barriers to Conviction and Two Models of Criminal Procedure: A Comparative Study', *University of Pennsylvania Law Review*, vol. 121, pp. 506-520.

Damaška, M. (1975), 'Structures of Authority and Comparative Criminal Procedure', *Yale Law Journal*, vol. 84, p.480.

Damaška, M. (1986), *The Faces of Justice and State Authority: A Comparative Approach to the Legal Process*, Yale University Press, London.

Daniel, C. (1997), 'Not Citizens but Data Subjects', *New Statesman*, 13 June, pp. 23-25.

Davidson, M., Humphreys, M.S., Johnstone, E.C. and Owens, D.G.C. (1995), 'Prevalence of Psychiatric Morbidity among Remand Prisoners in Scotland', *British Journal of Psychiatry*, 167, pp. 545-548.

Davis, H. (1993), *Fighting Leviathan: Building Social Markets that Work*, Social Market Foundation, London.

Davis, M. (1992), 'Fortress Los Angeles: The Militarization of Urban Space', in M. Sorkin (ed), *Variations on a Theme Park: The New American City and the End of Public Space*, Hill and Wang, New York, pp. 154-180.

Day, P. (1981), *Social Work and Social Control*, Tavistock, London.

Dell, S. (1971), *Silent in Court*, Bell, London.

Department of Health and Home Office (1992), *Review of Health and Social Services for Mentally Disordered Offender and Others Requiring Similar Services. Final Summary Report,* Cmnd. 2088, HMSO, London.

Di Federico, G. (1998), 'Prosecutorial Independence and the Democratic Requirement of Accountability in Italy: Analysis of a Deviant Case in a Comparative Perspective', *British Journal of Criminology*, pp. 371-387.

Di Marino, G. (1997), 'L'implantation et les Remises en Cause des Dogmes Accusatoire et Inquisitoire', *Revue Internationale de Droit Pénal*, vol. 17.

Ditton, J. (1990), *Safety in Castlemilk 1990*, Safe Castlemilk, Glasgow.

Ditton, J. (1994), *Safety in Castlemilk 1994*, Safe Castlemilk, Glasgow.

Ditton, J. (1996), 'The Public Acceptability of CCTV', paper presented at the *CCTV: Surveillance and Social Control Conference*, University of Hull.

Ditton, J. and Ford, R. (1994), *The Reality of Probation: A Formal Ethnography of Process and Practice*, Avebury, Aldershot.

Ditton, J., Bannister, J., Farrall, S. and Gilchrist, E. (1998), *Attitudes to Crime and the Police in Scotland: A Comparison of White and Ethnic Minority Views*, Scottish Office Central Research Unit, Edinburgh.

Ditton, J., Nair, G., Phillips, S. and Hunter, G. (1991), *Safe in Greater Easterhouse,* Final Report to the Greater Easterhouse Safety Sub Group, Glasgow.

Ditton, J., Short, E., Phillips, S. and Khan, F. (1994), *Safety in Greater Easterhouse: 1994 Compared to 1991*, Report to Scottish Home and Health Department, Edinburgh.

Dobash, R. (1993), *Supporting Victims of Serious Crime*, Scottish Office Central Research Unit, Edinburgh.

Dobash, R., Dobash, R.E., and Gutteridge, S. (1986), *The Imprisonment of Women*, Basil Blackwell, Oxford.

Dobash, R., Dobash, R.E., Cavanagh, K., and Lewis, R. (1995), 'Evaluating Criminal Justice Programmes for Violent Men', in R.E. Dobash, R. Dobash and L. Noaks (eds), *Gender and Crime*, University of Wales, Cardiff.

Dobash, R., Dobash, R.E., Cavanagh, K. and Lewis, R. (1996), *Research Evaluation of Programmes for Violent Men*, HMSO, Edinburgh.

Dobash, R.E. and Dobash, R. (1980), *Violence Against Wives*, Open Books, London.

Dobash, R.E. and Dobash, R. (1992), *Women, Violence and Social Change*, Routledge, London and New York.

Doob, A. (1990), *Sentencing Aids: Final Report to the Donner Canadian Foundation*, Centre of Criminology, University of Toronto, Toronto.

Doob, A. (1995), 'The United States Sentencing Commission Guidelines: If You Don't Know Where You are Going, You Might not Get There', in C. Clarkson and R. Morgan (eds), *The Politics of Sentencing Reform*, Clarendon, Oxford, pp. 199-251.

Doob, A. and Park, N. (1987), 'Computerised Sentencing Information for Judges: An Aid to the Sentencing Process', *Criminal Law Quarterly*, vol. 30, pp. 54-72.

Duff A. (1995), 'Penal Communications: Recent Work in the Philosophy of Punishment', in M. Tonry (ed), *Crime and Justice: An Annual Review of Research*, vol. 20, University of Chicago Press, Chicago, pp. 1-97.

Duff, A. and Garland, D. (1994), 'Introduction: Thinking about Punishment', in A. Duff and D. Garland (eds), *A Reader on Punishment*, Oxford University Press, Oxford, pp. 1-43.

Duff, P. (1993), 'The Prosecutor Fine and Social Control: The Introduction of the Fiscal Fine to Scotland', *British Journal of Criminology*, vol. 33, pp. 481-503.

Duff, P. (1994), 'The Prosecutor Fine', *Oxford Journal of Legal Studies*, vol. 14, pp. 565-587.

Duff, P. (1996a), 'The Fiscal Fine: How Far can it be Extended?', *Scots Law Times*, pp. 167-171.

Duff, P. (1996b), 'The Not Proven Verdict: Jury Mythology and Moral Panics', *Juridical Review*, vol. 1, pp. 1-12.

Duff, P. (1996c), 'The 1996 Criminal Injuries Compensation Scheme: Part 1', *Scots Law Times*, pp. 221-225.

Duff, P. (1997), 'Diversion from Prosecution into Psychiatric Care: Who Controls the Gates?', *British Journal of Criminology*, vol. 37, pp. 15-34.

Duff, P. and Burman, M. (1994), *Diversion from Prosecution to Psychiatric Care*, Scottish Office Central Research Unit, Edinburgh.

Duff, P. and McCallum, F. (1996), *Grounds of Appeal in Criminal Cases*, HMSO, Edinburgh.

Duff, P., Meechan, K., Christie, M. and Lessels, D. (1996), *Fiscal Fines*, Scottish Office Central Research Unit, Edinburgh.

Duguid, G. (1982), *Community Service in Scotland: The First Two Years*, Scottish Office Central Research Unit, Edinburgh.

Dunleavy, P. and Hood, C. (1994), 'From Old Public Administration to New Public Management', *Public Money and Management*, vol. 14, no. 3, pp. 9-16.

Dunn, J. and Fahy, T.A. (1990), 'Police Admissions to a Psychiatric Hospital; Demographic And Clinical Differences Between Ethnic Groups', *British Journal of Psychiatry*, 156, pp. 373-378.

Edwards, L. and Griffiths, A. (1997), *Family Law,* W. Green/Sweet and Maxwell, Edinburgh.

Elgin Committee (1900), *Report from the Departmental Committee on Scottish Prisons*, Cmnd. 218, HMSO, Edinburgh.

Elias, R. (1993), *Victims Still: The Political Manipulation of Crime Victims*, Sage, London.

Emsley, C. (1983), *Policing and its Context 1750-1870*, Macmillan, London.

Emsley, C. (1991), *The English Police: A Political And Social History*, Harvester Wheatsheaf, Hemel Hempstead.

Emsley, C. (1996), 'The Origins and Development of the Police', in E. McLaughlin, and J. Muncie (eds), *Controlling Crime*, Sage, London, pp. 7-50.

Farrington, D. (1994a), 'Early Developmental Prevention of Juvenile Delinquency', *RSA Journal*, pp. 22-34.

Farrington, D. (1994b), 'Childhood, Adolescent and Adult Features of Males', in L.R. Huessman (ed), *Aggressive Behaviour: Current Perspectives*, Plenum, New York, pp. 215-240.

Farrington, D. (1994c), 'Delinquency Prevention in the First Few Years of Life: Part 1', *Justice of the Peace and Local Government Law*, vol. 158, no. 33, pp. 531-533.

Farrington, D.P. and Langan, P.A. (1992), 'Changes in Crime and Punishment in England and America in the 1980s', *Justice Quarterly*, vol. 9, no. 1, pp. 5-46.

Farrington, D.P. and Wikström, P.-O.H. (1993), Changes in Crime and Punishment in England and Sweden in the 1980s, *Studies on Crime and Crime Prevention*, vol. 2, pp. 142-170.

Farrington, D.P., Langan, P.A. and Wikström, P.-O.H. (1994), 'Changes in Crime and Punishment in America, England and Sweden Between the 1980s and the 1990s', *Studies on Crime and Crime Prevention*, vol. 3, pp. 104-31.

Fassler, L.J. (1990), 'The Italian Penal Procedure Code: an Adversarial System of Criminal Prosecution in Continental Europe', *Columbia Journal of Transnational Law*, vol. 29, pp. 245-260.

Feeley, M. and Simon, J. (1994), 'Actuarial Justice: The Emerging New Criminal Law', in D. Nelken (ed), *The Futures of Criminology*, Sage, London, pp. 173-201.

Ferguson, P.W. (1997), 'Jury Vetting', *Scots Law Times*, vol. 35, pp. 287-291.

Fielding, N. (1984), *Probation Practice: Client Support Under Social Control*, Gower, London.

Findlay, M. and Duff, P. (1988), 'Introduction', in M. Findlay and P. Duff (eds), *The Jury Under Attack*, Butterworths, London, pp. 1-7.

Finnie, W. (1991), 'Public Order Law in Scotland and England 1980-1990,' in W. Finnie, C.M.G. Himsworth, and N. Walker (eds), *Edinburgh Essays in Public Law*, Edinburgh University Press, Edinburgh, pp. 251-277.

Fionda, J. (1995), *Public Prosecutors and Discretion: A Comparative Study*, Clarendon Press, Oxford.

FitzGerald, M. (1993) ''Racism': Establishing the Phemomenon', in D. Cook and B. Hudson (eds), *Racism and Criminology*, Sage, London, pp. 45-63.

FitzGerald, M. (1995), ''Race' and Crime: The Facts?', *Paper delivered to the British Criminology Conference*, Loughborough.

FitzGerald, M. (1997), 'Minorities, Crime, and Criminal Justice in Britain', in I. Marshall (ed), *Minorities, Migrants, and Crime: Diversity and Similarity Across Europe and the United States*, Sage, London, pp. 36-61.

FitzGerald, M. and Hale, C. (1996), *Ethnic Minorities: Victimisation and Racial Harassment - Findings from the 1988 and 1992 British Crime Surveys*, Research Study No. 154, Home Office Research and Statistics Directorate, London.

FitzGerald, M. and Sibbitt, R. (1997), *Ethnic Monitoring in Police Forces: A Beginning*, Research Study no. 173, Home Office Research and Statistics Directorate, London.

Ford, R., Ditton, J. and Laybourn, A. (1992), *Probation in Scotland: Process and Practice*, Scottish Office Central Research Unit, Edinburgh.

Foren, R. and Bailey, R. (1968), *Authority in Social Casework*, Pergamon Press, Oxford.

Foucault, M. (1979), *Discipline and Punish*, Vantage Press, New York.

Foucault, M. (1991), 'Governmentality', in G. Burchell *et al.* (eds), *Michel Foucault: Politics, Philosophy, Culture*, Routledge, London and New York, pp. 242-254.

Fox, S. (1991), *First Kilbrandon Child Care Lecture*, Scottish Office, Edinburgh.

Frase, R.S. (1990), 'Comparative Criminal Justice as a Guide to American Law Reform: How the French Do It, How We Find Out and Why Should We Care?', *California Law Review*, vol. 78, pp. 539-683.

Frase, R.S. (1995), 'Sentencing Guidelines in Minnesota and Other American States: A Progress Report', in C. Clarkson and R. Morgan (eds), *The Politics of Sentencing Reform*, Clarendon, Oxford, pp. 169-198.

Frizzell, E. (1995), 'The Place of Women Prisoners Within the Scottish Prison Service', in SACRO *Conference Report: Women Offenders*, March 1995, Edinburgh.

Fyfe, N.R. (1993a), 'Making Space for the Citizen? The (In)significance of the UK Citizen's Charter', *Urban Geography*, vol. 14, pp. 225-227.

Fyfe, N.R. (1993b), 'Policing Scotland in the 1990s: The Rhetoric and Reality of the Justice Charter for Scotland', in H. Jones (ed), *Crime and the Urban Environment: the Scottish Experience*, Gower, Aldershot, pp. 45-53.

Fyfe, N.R. (1994), *Police User Surveys in Scotland*, Scottish Office Central Research Unit, Edinburgh.

Fyfe, N.R. (1995), 'Law and Order Policy and the Spaces of Citizenship in Contemporary Britain', *Political Geography*, vol. 14, pp. 177-189.

Fyfe, N.R. and Bannister, J. (1996), 'City Watching: Closed Circuit Television Surveillance in Public Spaces', *Area*, vol. 28, pp. 37-46.

Galligan, D. (1987), 'Regulating Pre-Trial Decisions', in I. Dennis (ed), *Criminal Law and Justice*, Sweet and Maxwell, London, pp. 177-202.

Gane, C. and Stoddart, C.N. (1991), *A Casebook on Scottish Criminal Law*, W. Green/Sweet & Maxwell, London.

Gane, C. and Stoddart, C.N. (1994), *Criminal Procedure in Scotland: Cases and Materials,* W. Green, Edinburgh.

Garland, D. (1985), *Punishment and Welfare: A History of Penal Strategies,* Gower, Aldershot.

Garland, D. (1990), *Punishment and Modern Society,* Clarendon, Oxford.

Garland, D. (1995), 'Penal Modernism and Postmodernism', in T. Blomberg and S. Cohen (eds), *Punishment and Social Control,* Aldine de Gruyter Publishing, New York, pp. 181-209.

Garland, D. (1996), 'The Limits of the Sovereign State: Strategies of Crime Control in Contemporary Society', *British Journal of Criminology,* vol. 36, pp. 445-471.

Gelsthorpe, L. (1993, ed), *Minority Ethnic Groups in the Criminal Justice System,* Cropwood Conference Series no. 21, Cambridge.

Gelsthorpe, L. and Morris, A. (1994), 'Juvenile Justice 1954 - 1992', in M. Maguire, R. Morgan and R. Reiner (eds), *The Oxford Handbook of Criminology,* 1st edition, Clarendon, Oxford, pp. 949-996.

Genn, H. (1988), 'Multiple Victimisation', in M. Maguire and J. Pointing (eds), *Victims of Crime: A New Deal?,* Open University Press, Milton Keynes, pp. 90-100.

Giddens, A. (1991), *Modernity and Self-Identity: Self and Society in the Late Modern Age,* Polity Press, Cambridge.

Goldstein, A. and Marcus, M. (1977-78), 'The Myth of Judicial Supervision in Three 'Inquisitorial' Systems: France, Italy and Germany', *Yale Law Journal,* vol. 87, pp. 240-255.

Gordon, G.H. (1978a), 'The Admissibility of Answers to Police Questioning in Scotland', in P Glazebrook (ed), *Reshaping the Criminal Law,* Stevens & Co, London, pp. 317-343.

Gordon, G.H. (1978b), *The Criminal Law of Scotland,* Green, Edinburgh.

Gordon, P. (1980), *Policing Scotland,* SCCL, Glasgow.

Graham, I. and Fehilly, A. (1990-95), *Annual Reports of Safe Castlemilk 1990-95,* Safe Castlemilk, Glasgow.

Graham, J. (1996), 'The Organisation and Functioning of Juvenile Justice in England and Wales', in S. Asquith (ed), *Children and Young People in Conflict with the Law,* Research Highlights in Social Work 30, Jessica Kingsley, London, pp. 73-91.

Graham, J. and Bowling, B. (1995), *Young People and Crime,* Home Office Research Study 145, Home Office, London.

Graham, S., Brooks, J. and Heery, D. (1996), 'Towns on the Television: Closed Circuit TV in British Towns and Cities', *Local Government Studies,* vol. 22, no. 3, pp. 3-27.

Griffiths, D.B. (1992), 'Confessions to the Police in Scottish Criminal Law', *Journal of Forensic Psychiatry,* 3, pp. 215-218.

Gudjonsson, G.H. (1993), *The Psychology of Interrogations, Confessions and Testimony*, Wiley, Chichester.

Gunn, J., Maden, A. and Swinton, M. (1991), 'Treatment Needs of Prisoners with Psychiatric Disorders', *British Medical Journal*, 303, pp. 338-341.

Haghigh, B. and Sorensen, J. (1996), 'America's Fear of Crime', in T. Flanagan and D. Longmire (eds), *Americans View Crime and Justice: A National Public Opinion Survey*, Sage, London, pp. 16-30.

Hall, S., Critcher, C., Jefferson, T., Clarke, J. and Roberts, B. (1978), *Policing the Crisis*, Macmillan, London.

Hamilton, J. and Wisniewski, M. (1996), *The Use of the Compensation Order in Scotland*, Scottish Office Central Research Unit, Edinburgh.

Hardiker, P. (1977), 'Social Work Ideologies in the Probation Service', *British Journal of Social Work*, vol. 7, no. 2, pp. 131-154.

Harper, R. and McWhinnie, A. (1983), *The Glasgow Rape Case*, Hutchinson, London.

Harris, R. (1980), 'A Changing Service: The Case for Separating Care and Control in Probation Practice', *British Journal of Social Work*, vol. 10, no. 2, pp. 163-184.

Harris, R. (1992), *Crime, Criminal Justice and the Probation Service*, Tavistock/ Routledge, London.

Hart, H.L.A. (1968), *Punishment and Responsibility: Essays in the Philosophy of Law*, Clarendon Press, Oxford.

Hart, J. (1981), *The British Police*, Allen & Unwin, London.

Hatchard, J., Huber, B. and Vogler, R. (1996), *Comparative Criminal Procedure* , British Institute of International and Comparative Law, London.

Haw, S. (1989), *The Sentencing of Drug Offenders in Scottish Courts*, Scottish Office Central Research Unit, Edinburgh.

Haxby, D. (1978), *Probation: A Changing Service*, Constable, London.

Heidensohn, F. (1992), *Women in Control? The Role of Women in Law Enforcement*, Clarendon Press, Oxford.

Henderson, S. (1998), *Service Provision to Women Experiencing Domestic Violence in Scotland*, Crime and Criminal Justice Research Findings No. 20, Scottish Office Central Research Unit, Edinburgh.

Her Majesty's Chief Inspector of Constabulary for Scotland (1996), *Annual Report 1995-96*, Cmnd. 3313, HMSO, London.

Hill, D. (1991), *Intensive Probation Practice: An Option for the 1990s*, Probation Monograph no. 109, Social Work Monographs, Norwich.

Hilson, C. (1993), 'Decision to Prosecute and Judicial Review', *Criminal Law Review*, pp. 739-747.

Himsworth, C.M.G. (1996), 'In a State No Longer: The End of Constitutionalism?', *Public Law*, pp. 639-660.

Hindess, B. (1973), *The Use of Official Statistics in Sociology: A Critique of Positivism and Ethnomethodology*, Macmillan, London.

Hine, J. (1993), 'Access for Women: Flexible and Friendly?', in D. Whitfield and D. Scott (eds), *Paying Back: Twenty Years of Community Service*, Waterside Press, Winchester.

HMSO (1983), *Keeping Offenders out of Court: Further Alternatives to Prosecution, (Stewart Committee)*, Cmnd. 8958, HMSO, Edinburgh.

HMSO (1991), *The Citizen's Charter: Raising the Standard*, Cmnd. 1599, HMSO, London.

Hogarth, J. (1988), *Sentencing Database System: User's Guide*, University of British Columbia, Vancouver.

Holdaway, S. (1996), *The Racialisation of British Policing*, Macmillan, London.

Home Office (1990), *The Victim's Charter*, Home Office, London.

Home Office (1993), *Police Reform: A Police Service for the Twenty-First Century*, Cmnd. 2281, HMSO, London.

Home Office (1994), *Criminal Statistics England and Wales 1993*, Cmnd. 2680, HMSO, London.

Home Office (1995), *Information on the Criminal Justice System in England and Wales*, Home Office, London.

Home Office (1996), *The Victim's Charter: A Statement of Service Standards for Victims of Crime*, Home Office Communication Directorate, London.

Home Office (1997), *Criminal Statistics England and Wales 1996*, Cmnd. 3764, HMSO, London.

Honess, T. and Charman, E. (1992), *Closed Circuit Television in Public Places*, Home Office, Crime Prevention Unit Paper No. 35, London.

Hood, R. (1992), *Race and Sentencing: A Study in the Crown Court*, Clarendon, Oxford.

Hough, M. and Mayhew, P. (1983), *The British Crime Survey: First Report*, HMSO, London.

Howard League (Scotland) (1976), *Probation in Scotland: A Programme for Revival*, Howard League, Edinburgh.

Huang, W. and Vaughn, M. (1996), 'Support and Confidence: Public Attitudes Towards the Police', in T. Flanagan and D. Longmire (eds), *Americans View Crime and Justice: A National Public Opinion Survey*, Sage, London, pp. 31-45.

Hüber, B. (1996), 'Criminal Procedure in Germany' in J. Hatchard, B. Hüber and R. Vogler (eds), *Comparative Criminal Procedure*, British Institute of International and Comparative Law, London.

Hudson, B. (1987), *Justice Through Punishment: A Critique of the 'Justice' Model of Corrections*, Macmillan, London.

Hudson, B. (1996), *Understanding Justice*, Open University Press, Buckingham.

Hume, D.H. (1844), *Commentaries on the Law of Scotland Respecting Crimes*, 4th edition, by B.R. Bell, 2 vols, Edinburgh.

Hume, D.H. (1955), *Baron David Hume's Lectures 1786-1882*, Stair Society, Edinburgh.

Humphreys, M.S and Gray, C.M. (1996), 'Restricted Patients in Scotland 1989-1995', *Health Bulletin*, 54, pp. 344-347.

Hutton, N. (1995), 'Sentencing, Rationality and Computer Technology', *Journal of Law and Society*, vol. 22, no. 4, pp. 549-570.

Hutton, N. and Tata, C. (1995), *Patterns of Custodial Sentencing in the Sheriff Court*, Scottish Office Central Research Unit, Edinburgh.

Hutton, N., Paterson, A.A., Tata, C. and Wilson, J. (1996), *A Prototype Sentencing Information System for the High Court of Justiciary: Report of the Study of Feasibility*, Scottish Office Central Research Unit, Edinburgh.

Hutton, N., Tata, C. and Wilson, J. (1995), 'Sentencing and Information Technology: Incidental Reform?', *International Journal of Law and Information Technology*, vol. 2, no. 3, pp. 255-286.

Jefferson, T. and Walker, M. (1992), 'Ethnic Minorities in the Criminal Justice System', *Criminal Law Review*, pp. 83-96.

Jefferson, T. and Walker, M. (1993) 'Attitudes to the Police of Ethnic Minorities in a Provincial City', *British Journal of Criminology*, vol. 33, pp. 251-266.

Johnston, L. (1992), *The Rebirth of Private Policing*, Routledge, London.

Johnston, L. (1996), 'Policing Diversity: the Impact of the Public-Private Complex in Policing', in F. Leishman, B. Loveday and S.P. Savage (eds), *Core Issues in Policing*, Longman, Harlow, pp. 54-70.

Jones, C. and Adler, M. (1990), *Can Anyone Get on These?*, Scottish Consumer Council, Glasgow.

Jones, H., Short, D. and Berry, W. (1991), *Dundee NE Safer Cities Project Household Survey 1991*, Dundee NE Safer Cities Project, Dundee.

Jones, H., Short, D. and Berry, W. (1994), *Dundee NE Safer Cities Project 1994 Household Survey Report*, Scottish Office Central Research Unit, Edinburgh.

Jones, T. and Newburn, T. (1995) 'How Big is the Private Security Sector?', *Policing and Society*, vol. 5, pp. 221-232.

Jones, T.H. (1997), 'Criminal Justice and Devolution', *Juridical Review*, pp. 201-219.

Joseph, P.L. and Potter, M. (1993), 'Diversion from Custody 1: Psychiatric Assessment at the Magistrates Court', *British Journal of Psychiatry*, 162, pp. 325-330

Jung, H. (1997), 'Plea Bargaining and its Repercussions on the Theory of Criminal Procedure', *European Journal of Crime, Criminal Law and Criminal Justice*, vol. 5, pp. 112-122.

Keith, M. (1993), *Race, Riots and Policing: Lore and Disorder in a Multi-racist Society*, UCL Press, London.

Kellas, J. (1989), *The Scottish Political System,* 4th edition, Cambridge University Press, Cambridge.

Kelly, D. (1993), *Criminal Sentences*, T&T Clark, Edinburgh.

Kennedy, R. and McIvor, G. (1992), *Young Offenders in the Children's Hearing and Criminal Justice Systems*, Tayside Social Work Department, Dundee.

Kent Probation Service (1996), *The Kent Reconviction Survey: A Five Year Study of Reconvictions Among Offenders Made Subject to Probation Orders in Kent in 1991*, Kent Probation Service, Maidstone.

Kerner, K. and Barker, C. (1998), *Victim Support Schemes in Scotland*, Scottish Office Central Research Unit, Edinburgh.

Kilbrandon Committee (1964), *Report on Children and Young Persons, Scotland*, HMSO, Edinburgh.

Kincraig (1989), *Parole and Related Issues in Scotland*, Cmnd. 598, HMSO, Edinburgh.

King, J. (1958), *The Probation Service*, National Association of Probation Officers, London.

King, M. (1989), 'Social Crime Prevention à la Thatcher', *Howard Journal*, vol. 28, pp. 291-312

Kinsey, R. (1992), *Policing the City*, Scottish Office, Edinburgh.

Kinsey, R., (1994), *The Second Edinburgh Crime Survey 1994*, (unpublished).

Kinsey, R. and Anderson, S. (1992), *Crime and the Quality of Life: Findings from the 1988 British Crime Survey (Scotland)*, HMSO, Edinburgh.

Kinsey, R., Lea, J. and Young, J. (1986), *Losing the Fight against Crime*, Blackwell, Oxford.

Kitsuse, J. and Cicourel, A. (1963), 'A Note on the Uses of Official Statistics', *Social Problems*, vol. 11, pp. 131-139.

Lancet Editorial (1994), 'Guilty Innocents: The Road to False Confessions', *Lancet*, 344, pp. 1447-1450.

Langbein, J. and Weinreb, L. (1977-78), 'Continental Criminal Procedure: `Myth´ and Reality', *Yale Law Journal*, vol. 87, pp. 1549-1560.

Laurie, P. (1970), *Scotland Yard*, Penguin, Harmondworth.

Lea, J. and Young, J. (1982), 'The Riots in Britain 1981: Urban Violence and Political Marginalisation', in D. Cowell, T. Jones and J. Young (eds), *Policing the Riots,* Junction, London, pp. 5-20.

Lees, S. (1989), 'Trial by Rape', *New Statesman and Society*, 24th November, pp. 10-13.

Leishman, F., Cope, S. and Starrie, P. (1996), 'Reinventing and Restructuring: Towards a 'New Policing Order'', in F. Leishman, B. Loveday and S.P. Savage (eds), *Core Issues in Policing*, Longman, Harlow, pp. 9-25.

Levitt, S.D. (1996), 'The Effect of Prison Population Size on Crime Rates: Evidence from Prison Overcrowding Litigation', *The Quarterly Journal of Economics*, May, pp. 319-351.

Lloyd, S. and Burman, M. (1996), 'Specialist Police Units and the Joint Investigation of Child Abuse', *Child Abuse Review*, vol. 5, pp. 4-17.

Loader, I. (1996), *Youth, Policing and Democracy,* Macmillan, London.

Loader, I. (1997a), 'Policing and the Social: Questions of Symbolic Power', *British Journal of Sociology*, vol. 48, pp. 1-18.

Loader, I. (1997b), 'Private Security and the Demand for Protection in Contemporary Britain', *Policing and Society*, vol. 7, pp. 143-162.

Lothian, A. (1991), 'A Prescription for the Sick Man of the System', *The Glasgow Herald*, 9 January.

Loucks, N. (1997), *HMPI Cornton Vale: Research into Drugs and Alcohol, Violence and Bullying, Suicides and Self-Injury, and Backgrounds of Abuse*, Scottish Prison Service Occasional Papers Report No. 1/98, Edinburgh.

Loveday, B. (1991), 'The New Police Authorities in the Metropolitan Counties', *Policing and Society*, vol. 1, pp. 193-212.

Loveday, B. (1995), 'Contemporary Challenges to Police Management in England and Wales: Developing Strategies for Effective Service Delivery', *Policing and Society*, vol. 5, pp. 281-302.

Lustgarten, L. and Leigh, I. (1994), *In From the Cold? National Security and Democratic Politics*, Oxford University Press, Oxford.

Maan, B. (1992), *The New Scots: The Story of Asians in Scotland*, John Donald, Edinburgh.

Mackay, R. (1992), 'The Resuscitation of Assythment? Reparation and the Scottish Criminal Law', *Juridical Review*, pp. 242-255.

Mackay, R. (1995), 'Alternative Dispute Resolution and Scottish Criminal Justice', in S. Moody and R. Mackay (eds), *Alternative Dispute Resolution in Scotland*, W. Greens, Edinburgh, pp. 16-35.

Mackenzie, G. (1678), *The Laws and Customs of Scotland in Matters Criminal*, James Glen, Edinburgh.

MacLeod, M., Prescott, R. and Carson, L. (1996), *Listening to Victims of Crime: Victimisation Episodes and the Criminal Justice System in Scotland*, Scottish Office Central Research Unit, Edinburgh.

Maden, A., Swinton, M. and Gunn, J. (1990), 'Women in Prisons and the Use of Illicit Drugs before Arrest', *British Medical Journal*, 301, p.1133.

Maden, A., Taylor, C., Brooke, D. and Gunn, J. (1995), *Mental Disorder in Remand Prisoners*, Home Office Research and Planning Unit, London.

Maguire, M. (1991), 'The Needs and Rights of Victims of Crime', in M. Tonry (ed), *Crime and Justice: A Review of Research, Vol. 14*, University of Chicago Press, pp. 363-433.

Maguire, M. (1997), 'Crime Statistics, Patterns and Trends: Changing Perceptions and their Implications' in M. Maguire, R. Morgan and R. Reiner (eds), *The Oxford Handbook of Criminology*, 2nd edition, Clarendon, Oxford, pp. 135-188.

Maguire, M. and Corbett, C. (1987), *The Effects of Crime and the Work of Victim Support Schemes*, Gower, Aldershot.

Maher, G. (1988), 'The Verdict of the Jury', in M. Findlay and P. Duff (eds), *The Jury Under Attack*, Butterworths, London, pp. 40-55.

Mair, C. and Wilkie, R. (1997), 'Policing Scotland: Past, Present and Future', *Policing Today*, vol. 3.

Mair, G. (1986) 'Ethnic Minorities, Probation and the Magistrates' Courts', *British Journal of Criminology*, vol. 26, pp. 147-155.

Mair, G. (1996), 'Intensive Probation', in G. McIvor (ed), *Working With Offenders*, Research Highlights in Social Work no. 26, Jessica Kingsley, London, pp. 120-132.

Mair, G. (1997a), 'Community Penalties and the Probation Service', in M. Maguire, R. Morgan and R. Reiner (eds), *The Oxford Handbook of Criminology*, second edition, Clarendon, Oxford, pp. 1195-1232.

Mair, G. (1997b, ed), *Evaluating the Effectiveness of Community Penalties*, Avebury, Aldershot.

Mair, G. and Brockington, N. (1988), 'Female Offenders and the Probation Service', *The Howard Journal*, vol. 27, no. 2, pp. 117-126.

Mair, G., Lloyd, C. and Hough, M. (1997), 'The Limitations of Reconviction Rates', in G. Mair (ed), *Evaluating the Effectiveness of Community Penalties*, Avebury, Aldershot, pp. 34-46.

Manning, P. (1977), *Policework: The Social Organisation of Policing*, MIT Press, Cambridge, Mass.

Marenin, O. (1982), 'Parking Tickets and Class Repression: The Concept of Policing in Critical Theories of Criminal Justice', *Contemporary Crises*, vol. 6, pp. 241-266.

Marenin, O. (1996a), 'Changing Police: Policing Change', in O. Marenin (ed), *Policing Change, Changing Police: International Perspectives*, Garland, New York and London.

Marenin, O. (1996b, ed), *Policing Change, Changing Police: International Perspectives*, Garland, New York and London.

Marshall, G. (1978), 'Police Accountability Revisited', in D. Butler and A.H. Halsey (eds), *Policy and Politics*, Macmillan, London, pp. 51-65.

Marsland, M. (1977), 'The Decline of Probation in Scotland' , *Social Work Today*, vol. 8 no. 23, pp. 17-18.

Martin, F. and Murray, K. (1976), *Children's Hearings*, Scottish Academic Press, Edinburgh.

Martin, F., Fox, S. and Murray, K. (1981), *Children out of Court*, Scottish Academic Press, Edinburgh.

Matthews, R. (1989), 'Privatisation in Perspective', in R. Matthews (ed), *Privatising Criminal Justice*, Sage, London, pp.1-23.

Matza, D. (1964), *Delinquency and Drift*, John Wiley, New York.

Mawby, R.I. (1991), *Comparative Policing Issues: The British and American System in International Perspective*, Allen & Unwin, London.

May, T. and Vass, A.A. (1996), 'Introduction: The Shifting Sands of Working with Offenders', in T. May and A.A. Vass (eds), *Working with Offenders: Issues, Contexts and Outcomes*, Sage, London.

Mayhew, P. and Smith, L. J. F. (1985), Crime in England and Wales and Scotland: A British Crime Survey Comparison, *British Journal of Criminology*, vol. 25, pp. 148-159.

Mayhew, P. and van Dijk, J. (1997), *Criminal Victimisation in Eleven Industrialised Countries: Key Findings from the 1996 International Crime Victimisation Surveys*, Home Office Research and Statistics Directorate, London.

Mayhew, P., Dowds, L. and Elliott, D. (1989), *The 1988 British Crime Survey*, Home Office Research Study no. 111, Home Office Research and Statistics Directorate.

Mayhew, P., Maung, N.A. and Mirrlees-Black, C. (1993), *The 1992 British Crime Survey*, Home Office Research Study no. 111, HMSO, London.

McAllister, D., Leitch, S. and Payne, D., (1993), *Crime Prevention and Housebreaking in Scotland*, Scottish Office Central Research Unit, Edinburgh.

McAra, L. (1998), *Social Work and Criminal Justice Volume 2: Early Arrangements*, The Stationary Office, Edinburgh.

McAra, L. and Georghiou, N. (1998), *A Review of the Literature on Community Services for Mentally Disordered Offenders*, Scottish Office Central Research Unit, Edinburgh.

McAra, L. and Young, P. (1997), 'Juvenile Justice in Scotland', *Criminal Justice*, vol. 15, no. 3, pp. 8-10.

McCluskey, Lord (1992), *Criminal Appeals,* Butterworths, Edinburgh.

McCluskey, Lord (1997), *Hansard (Lords),* 11th February, cols. 216-219.

McConville, M. and Baldwin, J. (1982), 'The Influence of Race on Sentencing', *Criminal Law Review*, pp. 652-658.

McConville, M., Hodgson, J., Bridges, L. and Pavlovic, A. (1994), *Standing Accused*, Clarendon, Oxford.

McConville, M., Sanders, A. and Leng, R. (1991), *The Case for the Prosecution*, Routledge, London.

McCrone, D. (1991), 'Excessive and Unreasonable: the Politics of the Poll Tax in Scotland', *International Journal of Urban and Regional Research*, pp. 443-452.

McDonald, D.C. (1986), *Punishment Without Walls: Community Service Sentences in New York City*, Rutgers University Press, New Brunswick.

McGhee, J., Waterhouse, L. and Whyte, B. (1996), 'Children's Hearings and Children in Trouble', in S. Asquith (ed), *Children and Young People in Conflict with the Law*, Jessica Kingsley, London, pp. 56-72.

McGowan, J. and Slater, J. (1988-94a), *Crime Profiles 1988-94*, Safer Edinburgh Project, Edinburgh.

McGowan, J. and Slater, J. (1988-94b), *Safer Edinburgh Project Papers 1988-94* Safer Edinburgh Project, Edinburgh.

McGuire, J. (1995, ed), *What Works: Reducing Reoffending - Guidelines from Research and Practice*, Wiley, Chichester.

McIvor, G. (1990a), *Sanctions for Serious and Persistent Offenders: A Review of the Literature*, University of Stirling Social Work Research Centre, Stirling.

McIvor, G. (1990b), *Community Service by Offenders: Assessing the Benefit to the Community*, Social Work Research Centre, University of Stirling, Stirling.

McIvor, G. (1992), *Sentenced to Serve: The Operation and Impact of Community Service by Offenders*, Avebury, Aldershot.

McIvor, G. (1997), 'Gender Differences in Probation Practice', research paper presented at *British Criminology Conference*, Belfast, July 1997, unpublished.

McIvor, G. (forthcoming), 'Jobs for the Boys?: Gender Differences in Referral to Community Service', *The Howard Journal of Criminal Justice*.

McIvor, G. and Barry, M. (1996), *The Process and Outcomes of Probation Supervision* (Research Report to The Scottish Office Home Department), Social Work Research Centre, University of Stirling, Stirling.

McIvor, G. and Tulle-Winton, E. (1993), *The Use of Community Service by Scottish Courts*, Social Work Research Centre, University of Stirling, Stirling.

McLaughlin, E. (1996), 'Police, Policing and Policework', in E. McLaughlin and J. Muncie (eds), *Controlling Crime*, Sage, London, pp. 51-106.

McManus, J.J. (1995), *Prisons, Prisoners and the Law*, W. Green, Edinburgh.

McManus, J.J. and Greenhalgh, J. (1988), *Selection and Training of LayJustices: The Perth Experiment*, Scottish Office Central Research Unit, Edinburgh.

Melvin, M. and Didcott, P. (1976), *Pre-Trial Bail and Custody in the Scottish Courts*, Scottish Office Central Research Unit, Edinburgh.

Mental Welfare Commission for Scotland (1995), *Report into the Enquiry into the Care and Treatment of Philip McFadden*, Mental Welfare Commission for Scotland, Edinburgh.

Midwinter, A., Keating, M. and Mitchell, J. (1991), *Politics and Public Policy in Scotland*, Mainstream, Edinburgh.

Millar, A.R. (1993), *Appeals in the Scottish Criminal Courts*, Scottish Office Central Research Unit, Edinburgh.

Mirrlees-Black, C., Mayhew, P., and Percy, A. (1996), *Home Office Statistical Bulletin: The 1996 British Crime Survey England and Wales*, Issue 19/96, Home Office, London.

Monaghan, B. (1997), 'Crime Prevention in Scotland', *International Journal of the Sociology of Law*, vol. 25, pp. 21-44.

Monger, M. (1964), *Casework in Probation*, Butterworth, London.

Moody, S. (1997), 'Victims and Scottish Criminal Justice', *Juridical Review*, vol. 42, pp. 1-11.

Moody, S. and Tombs, J. (1982), *Prosecution in the Public Interest*, Scottish Academic Press, Edinburgh.

Moody, S. and Tombs, J. (1983), 'Plea Negotiation in Scotland', *Criminal Law Review*, pp. 297-306.

Moore, C. and Booth, S. (1989), *Managing Competition: Meso-corporatism, Pluralism and the Negotiated Order in Scotland,* Oxford University Press, Oxford.

Moore, G. (1978), 'Crisis in Scotland', *Howard Journal*, vol. 17, no. 1, pp. 32-40.

Moore, G. (1980), 'Social Work Reports and Recommendations', *Journal of the Law Society of Scotland,* July, pp. 271-273.

Moore, G. and Wood, C. (1981), *Social Work and Criminal Law in Scotland,* Aberdeen University Press, Aberdeen.

Moore, G. and Wood, C. (1992), *Social Work and the Criminal Law in Scotland,* Mercat Press, Edinburgh.

Morgan, P.M. (1992), *Offending While on Bail: A Survey of Recent Studies,* Home Office Research and Planning Unit, Paper 65, HMSO, London.

Morgan, R. and Newburn, T. (1997), *The Future of Policing,* Oxford University Press, Oxford.

Morris, A. and McIsaac, M. (1978), *Juvenile Justice? The Practice of Social Welfare,* Cambridge Studies in Criminology, Heinemann, Cambridge.

Morris, N. (1953), 'Sentencing Convicted Criminals', *Australian Law Journal,* vol. 27, pp. 186-200.

Muncie, J. and Fitzgerald, E. (1996, eds), *The Problem of Crime,* Open University Press, Milton Keynes.

Mungham, G. and Bankowski, Z. (1976), ' The Jury in the Legal System', in P. Carlen (ed), *The Sociology of Law,* University of Keele, Keele, pp. 202-225.

Murdoch, J. (1995), 'Police', in *Stair Memorial Encyclopaedia of Scots Law,* vol. 16, Butterworths, Edinburgh, pp. 234-352.

Murphy, J. (1992), *British Social Services: The Scottish Dimension,* Scottish Academic Press, Edinburgh.

MVA Consultancy (1995), *Information Needs of Victims,* Scottish Office Central Research Unit, Edinburgh.

MVA Consultancy (1996), *Foreign Language Interpreters in the Scottish*

MVA Consultancy (1997), *The 1996 Scottish Crime Survey: First Results,* Crime and Criminal Justice Research Findings no. 16, Scottish Office Central Research Unit, Edinburgh.

Nagel, I. and Johnson, B. (1994), 'The Role of Gender in a Structured Sentencing System: Equal Treatment, Policy Choices and the Sentencing of Female Offenders under the United States Sentencing Guidelines', *Journal of Criminal Law and Criminology,* vol. 85, no. 1, pp. 181-221.

Nagin, D.S. (1998), 'Criminal Deterrence Research at the Outset of the Twenty-first Century', in M. Tonry (ed), *Crime and Justice,* vol. 23, University of Chicago Press, Chicago.

Nairn, T. (1997), 'Sovereignty after the Election', *New Left Review,* no. 224, pp. 3-18.

National Audit Office (1989), *Prosecution of Crime in Scotland: Review of the Procurator Fiscal Service,* HMSO, London.

Nelson, S. (1977), 'Why Scotland's After-Care is Lagging', *Community Care*, vol. 14, no. 12, p. 87.

NHS Executive (1994), *Guidance on the Discharge of Mentally Disordered People From Hospital and their Continuing Care in the Community*, HSG(94)27, Department of Health, London.

Nicholson, C.G.B. (1981), *The Law and Practice of Sentencing in Scotland*, W. Green & Son, Edinburgh.

Nicholson, C.G.B. (1992), *Sentencing: Law and Practice in Scotland*, 2nd edition, W Green/Sweet & Maxwell, Edinburgh.

Nicholson, L. (1992), *The Deferred Sentence in Scotland*, Scottish Office Central Research Unit, Edinburgh.

Nicholson, L. (1994), *Monetary Penalties in Scotland: A Research Based Review*, HMSO, Edinburgh.

Norfolk, G.A. (1997), 'Fitness to be Interviewed - A Proposed Definition and Scheme of Examination', *Medicine Science and the Law*, 37, pp. 228-234.

Normand, A.C. (1984), 'Unfitness for Trial in Scotland: Proposed Adjudication of the Facts and the Right to Re-Prosecute', *International Journal of Law and Psychiatry*, 7, pp. 415-435.

Normand, W.G. (1938), 'The Public Prosecutor in Scotland', *Law Quarterly Review*, pp. 345-350.

Norris, G.M. (1983), 'Poverty in Scotland', in G. Brown and R. Cooke (eds), *Poverty and Deprivation in Scotland*, Mainstream Publishing Company, Edinburgh.

O'Malley, P. and Palmer, D. (1996), 'Post-Keynesian Policing', *Economy and Society*, vol. 25, pp. 137-155.

Oliver, I. (1987), *Police, Government and Accountability*, Macmillan, London.

Oliver, I. (1997), *Police, Government and Accountability*, 2nd edition, Macmillan, London.

Oppenheim, C. (1993), *Poverty: The Facts*, Child Poverty Action Group.

Osner, N., Quinn, A. and Crown, G. (1993, eds), *Criminal Justice Systems in Other Jurisdictions*, HMSO, London.

Paddison, R. (1997), 'The Restructuring of Local Government in Scotland', in J, Bradbury and J. Mawson (eds), *British Regionalism and Devolution: The Challenges of State Reform and European Integration*, Kingsley, London, pp. 99-117.

Paterson, A.A. and Bates, T.S.J.N. (1993), *The Legal System of Scotland: Cases and Materials*, W. Green/Sweet & Maxwell, Edinburgh.

Paterson, F. (1993), 'Bail Decisions: Risk, Uncertainty, Choice', in M. Adler, A. Millar and S. Morris (eds), *Socio-Legal Research in the Scottish Courts*, Scottish Office Central Research Unit, Edinburgh, pp. 60-65.

Paterson, F. (1996, ed), *Understanding Bail in Britain*, HMSO, Edinburgh.

Paterson, F. and Whittaker, C. (1994), *Operating Bail: Decision Making under the Bail etc. (Scotland) Act 1980*, HMSO, Edinburgh.

Paterson, L. (1994), *The Autonomy of Modern Scotland*, Edinburgh University Press, Edinburgh.

Patten, J. (1988), 'Foreword', in T. Hope and M. Shaw (eds), *Communities and Crime Reduction*, HMSO, London, pp. v-vi.

Payne, D. (1992), *Crime in Scotland: Findings from the British Crime Survey*, Scottish Office Central Research Unit, Edinburgh.

Pearce, F. (1976), *Crimes of the Powerful*, Pluto Press, London.

Pease, K., Durkin, P., Earnshaw, I., Payne, D. and Thorpe, J. (1975), *Community Service Orders*, Home Office Research Study, no. 29, HMSO, London.

Peay, J. (1996, ed), *Inquiries After Homicide*, Duckworth, London.

Percy, A. (1998), *Ethnicity and Victimisation: Findings from the 1996 British Crime Survey*, Home Office Statistical Bulletin, 6/98, London.

Phipps, A. (1988), 'Radical Criminology and Criminal Victimisation: Proposals for Development', in M. Maguire and J. Pointing (eds) *Victims of Crime: A New Deal?*, Open University Press, Milton Keynes, pp. 177-186.

Pizzi, W. (1993), 'Understanding Prosecutorial Discretion in the United States: The Limits of Comparative Criminal Procedure as an Instrument of Reform', *Ohio State Law Journal*, vol. 54, pp. 1325-1373.

Poole, Sheriff I. (1991), 'Comments on the Papers by Bryan Williams and Gill McIvor and Jim Cairnie', in M. Adler and A. Millar (eds), *Socio-Legal Research in the Scottish Courts*, vol. 2, Scottish Office Central Research Unit, Edinburgh.

Raynor, P. (1985), *Social Work, Justice and Control*, Basil Blackwell, Oxford.

Raynor, P. (1996), 'Effectiveness Now: A Personal and Selective Overview', in G. McIvor (ed), *Working With Offenders*, Research Highlights in Social Work no. 26, Jessica Kingsley, London, pp. 182-193.

Reeve, A. (1996), 'The Private Realm of the Managed Town Centre', *Urban Design International*, vol. 1, pp. 61-80.

Reiner, R. (1992), *The Politics of the Police*, 2nd edition, Harvester Wheatsheaf, Hemel Hempstead.

Reiner, R. (1993), 'Police Accountability: Principles, Patterns and Practices', in R. Reiner and S. Spencer (eds), *Accountable Policing: Effectiveness, Empowerment and Equity*, Institute for Public Policy Research, London, pp. 1-23.

Reiner, R. (1995), 'From Sacred to Profane: The Thirty Years' War of the British Police', *Policing and Society*, vol. 5, pp. 121-128.

Reiner, R. (1997), 'Policing and the Police', in M. Maguire, R. Morgan and R. Reiner (eds), *The Oxford Handbook of Criminology*, 2nd edition, Oxford University Press, Oxford, pp. 997-1049.

Reiner, R. and Cross, M. (1991), 'Introduction: Beyond Law and Order - Crime and Criminology into the 1990s', in R. Reiner and M. Cross (eds), *Beyond Law and Order*, Macmillan, London, pp. 1-17.

Remington, F. (1993), 'The Decision to Charge, the Decision to Convict on a Plea of Guilty, and the Impact of Sentence Structures on Prosecution Practices', in L. Ohlin and F. Remington (eds), *Discretion in Criminal Justice,* State University of New York Press, pp. 73-133.

Renton, R.H. and Brown, H.H. (1996), *Criminal Procedure,* 6th edition, W. Green, Edinburgh.

Report of the Departmental Committee on the Probation Service (Morison Committee) (1963) Cmnd. 1650, HMSO, London.

Rifkind, M. (1989), 'Penal Policy: the Way Ahead', *The Howard Journal,* vol. 28, pp. 81-90.

Roberts, R. (1973), *The Classic Slum,* Penguin, London.

Rokkan, S. and Urwin, D. (1982, eds), *The Politics of Territorial Identity: Studies in European Regionalism,* Sage, London.

Ross, R.R., Fabiano, E.A. and Ewles, C.D. (1988), 'Reasoning and Rehabilitation', *International Journal of Offender Therapy and Comparative Criminology,* vol. 32, no. 1, pp. 29-35.

Rowlands, R., Inch, H., Rodger, W. and Soliman, A. (1996), 'Diverted to Where? What Happens to the Diverted Mentally Disordered Offender', *Journal of Forensic Psychiatry,* 7, pp. 284-296.

Royal Commission on the Police (1962), *Final Report,* Cmnd. 1728, HMSO, London.

Ryan, W. (1971), *Blaming the Victim,* Orbach and Chambers, London.

SACRO (1995), *Conference Report - Women Offenders,* March 1995, Edinburgh.

Samuel, E. and Tisdall, K. (1996), 'Female Offenders in Scotland: Implications for Theory', in S. Asquith (ed), *Children and Young People in Conflict with the Law,* Jessica Kingsley, London, pp. 102-130.

Sanders, A. and Young, R. (1994), *Criminal Justice,* Butterworths, London.

Saunders, P. and Harris, C. (1990), 'Privatization and the Consumer', *Sociology,* vol. 24, pp. 57-75.

Savage, S.P. and Charman, S. (1996), 'Managing Change', in F. Leishman, B. Loveday and S.P. Savage (eds), *Core Issues in Policing,* Longman, Harlow, pp. 39-53.

Schmatt, E. (1996), 'Judicial Information Research System (JIRS): A new and integrated approach to the provision of electronic information services for the judiciary', *Judicial Officers Bulletin,* vol. 8, no. 7, Judicial Commission of New South Wales.

Scottish Association of Victim Support Schemes (1986), *SAVSS Annual Report 1985-6,* Scottish Association of Victim Support Schemes, Edinburgh.

Scottish Consumer Council (1981), *Waiting for Justice: An SCC Survey of Facilities in Scotland's Sheriff Courts: Results and Recommendations,* SCC, Glasgow.

Scottish Consumer Council (1990), *Court Reports: A Review of Facilities in Scotland's District Courts,* SCC, Glasgow.

Scottish Council for Civil Liberties (1995), *Rules for the Operation and Use of Closed Circuit Television (CCTV) in Public Places*, Scottish Council for Civil Liberties, Glasgow.

Scottish Council for Civil Liberties (1997), *Monitor: Newsletter of the Scottish Council for Civil Liberties*, January 1997.

Scottish Courts Service (1997), *Scottish Courts Service Annual Report and Accounts 1996-7*, The Stationery Office, Edinburgh.

Scottish Home and Health Department (1985), *Report of the Review of Suicide Precautions at HM Detention Centre and HM Young Offender Institution, Glenochil*, HMSO, Edinburgh.

Scottish Law Commission (1983), *Evidence: Report on Evidence in Cases of Rape and Other Sexual Offences*, Scottish Law Commission, Edinburgh.

Scottish Law Commission (1993), *Responses to the 1993 Review of Criminal Evidence and Criminal Procedure, Programming of Business in the Sheriff Courts*, Scottish Law Commission, Edinburgh.

Scottish Legal Aid Board (1992-1997), *Annual Report*, Scottish Legal Aid Board, Edinburgh.

Scottish Office (1951a - 1982a), *Criminal Statistics Scotland.*, Cmnd. papers, Scottish Office Home and Health Department, Edinburgh.

Scottish Office (1983b - 1996b), *Statistical Bulletin: Recorded Crime in Scotland*, Scottish Office Central Statistical Unit, Edinburgh.

Scottish Office (1987c - 1998c), *Statistical Bulletin: Criminal Proceedings in Scottish Courts*, Scottish Office Central Statistical Unit, Edinburgh.

Scottish Office (1993d - 1996d), *Statistical Bulletin: Prison Statistics Scotland*, Scottish Office Central Statistical Unit, Edinburgh.

Scottish Office (1995e - 1997e), *Statistical Bulletin: Homicide in Scotland*, Scottish Office Central Statistical Unit, Edinburgh.

Scottish Office (1987f), *Government to Provide Total Funding for Community Service Schemes*, Scottish Information Office, Edinburgh.

Scottish Office (1991f), *The Justice Charter for Scotland*, Scottish Office, Edinburgh.

Scottish Office (1992f), *21 Years of Children's Hearings*, Scottish Office, Edinburgh.

Scottish Office (1992g), *Report of the Inquiry into the Removal of Children from Orkney* (The Clyde Report), Scottish Office, Edinburgh.

Scottish Office (1993f), *Criminal Legal Aid Review*, HMSO, Edinburgh.

Scottish Office (1993g), *1993 Review of Criminal Evidence and Criminal Procedure*, HMSO, Edinburgh.

Scottish Office (1994f), *Firm and Fair, Improving the Delivery of Justice in Scotland*, Cmnd. 2600, HMSO, Edinburgh.

Scottish Office (1994g), *Juries and Verdicts*, HMSO, Edinburgh.

Scottish Office (1994h), *Sentencing and Appeals*, HMSO, Edinburgh.

Scottish Office (1995f), *Statistical Bulletin: Community Service by Offenders in 1992 and 1993*, Scottish Office Central Statistical Unit, Edinburgh.

Scottish Office (1995g), *Gender, Race and the Criminal Justice System*, Scottish Office, Edinburgh.

Scottish Office (1995h), *Statistical Bulletin*, CrJ/1995/7, HMSO, Edinburgh.

Scottish Office (1996f), *Crime and Punishment*, Cmnd. 3302, HMSO, Edinburgh.

Scottish Office (1996g), *Criminal Procedure (Scotland) Act 1995 Sections Relating to Mental Disorder*, Circular HD 6/1996, Home Department, Edinburgh.

Scottish Office (1996h), *Her Majesty's Chief Inspector of Constabulary for Scotland: Report for Year end 31 March 1996*, Scottish Office, Edinburgh.

Scottish Office (1996i), *Making the Punishment Fit the Crime*, HMSO, Edinburgh.

Scottish Office (1997f), *Roles and Responsibilities of General Practitioners and Police in Dealing with Potentially Violent Mentally Disordered Persons in the Community*, Consultation paper, Department of Health, Edinburgh.

Scottish Office (1997g), *Scotland's Parliament*, Cmnd. 3658 HMSO, Edinburgh and London.

Scottish Office (1997h), *Statistical Bulletin*, CrJ/1997/2, HMSO, Edinburgh.

Scottish Office (1997i), *Gender, Race and the Criminal Justice System*, Scottish Office, Edinburgh.

Scottish Office (1997j), *Statistical Bulletin*, CrJ/1997/8, HMSO, Edinburgh.

Scottish Office (1997k), *Recording of Offending While on Bail*, Statistical Bulletin CrJ/1997/1, Scottish Office, Edinburgh.

Scottish Office (1998f), *Health and Social Work and Related Services for Mentally Disordered Offenders in Scotland*, Consultation document, Department of Health, Edinburgh.

Scottish Office (1998g), *Interviewing People who are Mentally Disordered: 'Appropriate Adult' Schemes*, Consultation document, Home Department, Edinburgh.

Scottish Office Social Work Services, (1993), *Scotland's Children: Proposal for Child Care Policy and Law*, Cmnd. 2286, Scottish Office, HMSO, Edinburgh.

Scottish Prison Service (1989), *Business Plan*, Scottish Office, Edinburgh.

Scottish Prison Service (1990), *Opportunity and Responsibility*, HMSO, Edinburgh.

Scottish Prison Service (1992), *Suicide Prevention Strategy*, Scottish Prison Service, Edinburgh.

Scottish Prison Service (1997), *Business Plan*, Scottish Office, Edinburgh.

Senior, P. (1984), 'The Probation Order: Vehicle of Social Work or Social Control?' *Probation Journal*, vol. 31, no. 2, pp. 64-70.

Shapland, J. (1988), 'Fiefs and Peasants; Accomplishing Change for Victims in the Criminal Justice System', in M.Maguire and J. Pointing (eds), *Victims of Crime - A New Deal?*, Open University Press, Milton Keynes, pp. 187-194.

Shapland, J., Wilmore, J. and Duff, P. (1985), *Victims in the Criminal Justice System*, Gower, Aldershot.

Shearing, C.D. and Stenning, P.C. (1983a), 'Private Security - Implications for Social Control', *Social Problems*, vol. 30, pp. 493-506.

Shearing, C.D. and Stenning, P.C. (1983b), *Private Security and Private Justice*, Institute for Research in Public Policy, Montreal.

Shearing, C.D. and Stenning, P.C. (1987, eds), *Private Policing*, Sage, California.

Sheehan, A. (1990), *Criminal Procedure*, Butterworths, Edinburgh.

Sheehy Inquiry into Police Responsibilities and Rewards (1993) Report, Cmnd. 2280, HMSO, London.

Short, E. and Ditton, J. (1996), *Does Closed Circuit Television Prevent Crime?*, Scottish Office Central Research Unit, Edinburgh.

Sibbitt, R. (1997), *The Perpetrators of Racial Harassment and Racial Violence*, Research Study no. 176, Home Office Research and Statistics Directorate, London.

Simmel, G. (1978), *The Philosophy of Money*, Routledge and Kegan Paul, London.

Simon, J. and Feeley, M. (1995), 'True Crime: The New Penology and Public Discourse on Crime', in T. Blomberg and S. Cohen (eds), *Punishment and Social Control*, Aldine de Gruyter Publishing, New York, pp. 147-180.

Skogan, W. (1986), 'Methodological Issues in the Study of Victimisation', in E. Fattah (ed), *From Crime Policy to Victim Policy*, Macmillan, London, pp. 80-116.

Skogan, W. (1994), *Contacts Between Police and Public: Findings from the 1992 British Crime Survey*, Home Office Research Study, London.

Smith, D. J. (1991), 'The Origins of Black Hostility to the Police', *Policing and Society*, vol. 2, pp. 1-15.

Smith, D.J. (1995), 'Youth Crime and Conduct Disorders: Trends, Patterns, and Causal Explanations', in M. Rutter and D. J. Smith (eds), *Psychosocial Disorders in Young People: Time Trends and their Causes*, Wiley, Chichester, pp. 389-489.

Smith, D.J. (1996), 'Explaining Crime Trends', in W. Saulsbury, J. Mott and T. Newburn (eds), *Themes in Contemporary Policing*, Independent Committee of Inquiry into the Role and Responsibilities of the Police, London.

Smith, L.J.F. (1983), *Criminal Justice Comparisons: The Case of Scotland and England and Wales*, Research and Planning Unit Paper 17, Home Office, London.

Smith, P. (1991), *Ethnic Minorities in Scotland*, Scottish Office Central Research Unit, Edinburgh.

Smout, T.C. (1970), *A History of the Scottish People 1560-1830*, Collins, Glasgow.

Social Work Services and Prisons Inspectorate for Scotland (1998), *Women Offenders - A Safer Way: A Review of Community Disposals and the Use of Custody for Women Offenders in Scotland*, HMSO, Edinburgh.

Social Work Services Group (1989), *National Standards and Objectives for the Operation of Community Service by Offenders Schemes in Scotland*, Scottish Office, Edinburgh.

Social Work Services Group (1991), *National Objectives and Standards for Social Work Services in the Criminal Justice System*, Scottish Office, Edinburgh.

Social Work Services Group (1996a), *Revised National Objectives and Standards for Community Service*, The Scottish Office, Edinburgh.

Social Work Services Group (1996b), *Community Service by Offenders: Public Awareness, Environmental Work and Hours*, SWSG Circular 12/96, The Scottish Office, Edinburgh.

Social Work Services Inspectorate (1996), *Realistic and Rigorous: The Report of an Inspection of Discipline and Enforcement of Community Service Orders in Two Local Authority Areas*, Scottish Office, Edinburgh.

South, N. (1988), *Policing for Profit*, Sage, London.

Sparks, R., Genn, H. and Dodd, D. (1977), *Surveying Victims*, Wiley, Chichester.

Spitzer, S and Scull, A. (1977), 'Privatization and Capitalist Development: The Case of the Private Police', *Social Problems*, vol. 25, pp. 18-29.

Stedward, G. and Millar, A. (1989), *Diversion from Prosecution: Diversion to Social Work*, Scottish Office Central Research Unit, Edinburgh.

Stenning, P.C. and Shearing, C.D. (1980), 'The Quiet Revolution: The Nature, Development and General Legal Implications of Private Security in Canada', *Criminal Law Quarterly*, vol. 22, pp. 220-248

Stewart, A.L. (1997), *The Scottish Criminal Courts in Action*, Butterworths, Edinburgh.

Stewart Committee (1980), *The Motorist and Fixed Penalties*, Cmnd. 8027, HMSO, Edinburgh.

Stewart Committee (1983), *Keeping Offenders Out of Court: Further Alternatives to Prosecution*, Cmnd. 8958, HMSO, Edinburgh.

Storch, R. (1975), 'The Plague of Blue Locusts: Police Reform and Popular Resistance in Northern England 1840-57', *International Review of Social History*, vol. 20, pp. 61-90.

Stott, G. (1995), *Judge's Diary,* Mercat Press, Edinburgh.

Strathclyde Police (1998), 'Fear of Crime falling in Strathclyde', Strathclyde Police Press Release, Glasgow, 26/1/98.

Sykes, G. (1958), *The Society of Captives*, Princeton University Press, Princeton.

Tata, C. (1997), 'Conceptions and Representations of the Sentencing Decision Process', *Journal of Law and Society*, vol. 24, no. 3, pp. 395-420.

Tata, C., Hutton, N., Wilson, J., Paterson, A.A. and Hughson, I. (1997), *A Sentencing Information System for the High Court of Justiciary of Scotland: Report of the Study of the First Phase of Implementation and Enhancement*, Scottish Office, Edinburgh.

Taylor, I., Walton, P. and Young, J. (1973), *The New Criminology*, Routledge and Kegan Paul, London.

Temkin, J. (1987), *Rape and the Legal Process*, Sweet and Maxwell, London.

Tennant, R. (1995), *Child and Family Poverty in Scotland: The Facts*, Save the Children and Glasgow Caledonian University, Glasgow.

Teplin, L.A. and Pruett, N.S. (1992), 'Police as Streetcorner Psychiatrist: Managing the Mentally Ill', *International Journal of Law and Psychiatry*, 15, pp. 139-156.

The Daily Mail (1998), 'Scared off the streets', 16 September.

The Glasgow Herald (1996a), 'Spy camera cuts 'could risk lives'', May 29, p.8.

The Glasgow Herald (1996b), 'Drinking outside the law', August 16, p.9.

The Glaswegian (1996), 'Crimewatch spy cameras in cash crisis', 22 February, p.1.

The Herald (1998), 'Scotland turns into a crime-fearing nation', 16 September.

The Portman Group (1993), *Keeping the Peace: A Guide to the Prevention of Alcohol-Related Disorder*, Portman Group, London.

The Scotsman, 31 August 1997; 27 September 1997.

Thomas, D.A. (1979), *Principles of Sentencing: The Sentencing Policy of the Court of Appeal Criminal Division*, 2nd edition, Heinemann, London.

Thomas, D.A. (1995), 'Sentencing Reform: England and Wales', in C. Clarkson and R. Morgan (eds), *The Politics of Sentencing Reform*, Clarendon, Oxford, pp. 125-148.

Thomson, A., Horne, D. and Jarret, A. (1989-94), *Crime Profiles 1989-94*, Dundee NE Safer Cities Project, Dundee.

Thomson, A., Horne, D. and Jarret, A. (1991-95), *Dundee NE Safer Cities Annual Reports 1991-95*, Dundee NE Safer Cities Project, Dundee.

Thomson, L., Bogue, J., Humphreys, M., Owens, D. and Johnstone, E. (1997), 'The State Hospital Survey: A Description of Psychiatric Patients in Conditions of Special Security in Scotland', *Journal of Forensic Psychiatry*, 8, pp. 263-284.

Tilley, N. (1992), *Safer Cities and Community Safety Strategies*, Home Office, Crime Prevention Unit Paper No. 38, London.

Tilley, N. (1993), 'Crime Prevention and the Safer Cities Story', *The Howard Journal*, vol. 32, pp. 40-57.

Tombs, J. and Moody, S. (1993), 'Alternatives to Prosecution: The Public Interest Re-defined', *Criminal Law Review*, pp. 357-365.

Uglow, S. and Telford, V. (1997), *The Police Act 1997*, Jordans, Bristol.

Uildriks, N. and Mastrigt, H. van (1991), *Policing Police Violence,* Aberdeen University Press, Aberdeen.

United Nations (1985), *United Nations Minimum Guidelines on Juvenile Justice* (Beijing Rules), United Nations Department of Social Affairs, New York.

Van den Wyngaert, C., Gane, C., Kühne, H.H. and McAuley, F. (1993), *Criminal Procedure Systems in the European Community*, Butterworth, London.

Vass, A. (1984), *Sentenced to Labour: Close Encounters with a Prison Substitute*, Venus Academica, St Ives.

Victim Support (1995), *The Rights of Victims of Crime*, Victim Support, London.

Victim Support Scotland (1993), *Victim Support Scotland Annual Report 1992-3*, VSS, Edinburgh.

Victim Support Scotland (1997), *Victim Support Scotland Annual Report 1996-7*, VSS, Edinburgh.

Vogler, R. (1996), 'Criminal Procedure in France', in J. Hatchard, B. Hüber and R. Vogler (eds), *Comparative Criminal Procedure* , British Institute of International and Comparative Law, London.

von Hirsch, A. (1976), *Doing Justice: The Choice of Punishments*, Hill and Wang, New York.

von Hirsch, A., Bottoms, A.E. and Wikström, P.-O. H. (forthcoming), *Criminal Deterrence: A Review of Recent Literature*.

Walgrave, L. (1995), Juvenile Justice in Belgium, unpublished conference paper.

Walgrave, L. (1996), 'Restorative Juvenile Justice: A Way to Restore Justice in Western European Systems?', in S. Asquith (ed), *Children and Young People in Conflict with the Law*, Research Highlights in Social Work 30, Jessica Kingsley, London, pp. 169-199.

Walker, M. (1988), 'The Court Disposal of Young Males, by Race, in London in 1983', *British Journal of Criminology*, vol. 28, pp. 441-460.

Walker, M. (1989), 'The Court Disposal and Remands of White, Afro-Caribbean, and Asian men (London, 1983)', *British Journal of Criminology*, vol. 29, pp. 353-367.

Walker, M. (1994), 'Measuring Concern About Crime: Some Inter-racial Comparisons', *British Journal of Criminology*, vol. 34, pp. 366-78.

Walker, N. (1983), 'The Effectiveness of Probation', *Probation Journal,* vol. 30, no. 3, pp. 99-103.

Walker, N. (1993), 'The International Dimension', in R. Reiner and S. Spencer (eds), *Accountable Policing: Effectiveness, Empowerment and Equity*, IPPR, London, pp. 113-171.

Walker, N. (1994), 'Care and Control in the Police Organisation', in M. Stephens and S. Becker (eds), *Police Force, Police Service: Care and Control in Britain,* Macmillan, London , pp. 33-66.

Walker, N. (1995), 'Police and Government in Scotland', *Scots Law Times*, 22, pp. 199-204.

Walker, N. (1996), 'Defining Core Police Tasks: The Neglect of the Symbolic Dimension?', *Policing and Society*, vol. 10, pp. 53-71.

Walker, N. (1998a), 'Justice and Home Affairs', *International and Comparative Law Quarterly*, vol. 47, pp. 231-238.

Walker, N. (1998b), 'Constitutional Change in a Cold Climate: Reflections on the White Paper and Referendum on a Scottish Parliament', in A. Tomkins (ed), *Scottish and Welsh Self-Government: The Challenge*, Key Haven, London.

West, J. (1978), 'Community Service for Fine Defaulters', *Justice of the Peace*, vol. 142, pp. 425-8.

White, R.M. (1998), 'Disciplining Chief Constables', *Scots Law Times*, 11, pp. 77-80.

Wilkins, J. and Coid, J. (1991), 'Self-mutilation in Female Remanded Prisoners: 1. An Indication of Severe Psychopathology', *Criminal Behaviour and Mental Health*, 1, pp. 247-267.

Williams, B.P. and Creamer, A. (1989), *Social Enquiry Within a Changing Sentencing Context*, Scottish Office Central Research Unit, Edinburgh.

Williams, B.P. and Creamer, A. (1997), 'Evaluating Scottish Special Probation Schemes', in G. Mair (ed), *Evaluating the Effectiveness of Community Penalties*, Avebury, Aldershot.

Williams, B.P., Creamer, A. and Hartley, L. (1988), *The Second Chance: Scottish Probation Orders in the Late 1980s*, (Interim and second research reports to the Scottish Office Social Work Services Group), Social Work Research Unit, University of Dundee, Dundee.

Williams, B.P., Creamer, A. and Hartley, L. (1991), 'Probation as an Alternative to Custody', in M. Adler and A. Millar (eds), *Socio-Legal Research in the Scottish Courts*, vol. 2, Scottish Office Central Research Unit, Edinburgh, pp. 23-29.

Williams, P. and Dickson, J. (1993), 'Fear of Crime: Read All About It? The Relationship between Newspaper Crime Reporting and Fear of Crime', *British Journal of Criminology*, vol. 33, no. 1, pp. 33-56.

Willock, I. (1993), 'The Verdict Muddle: A Way Out', *SCOLAG*, vol. 196, p.5.

Willock, I. (1996), *The Jury in Scotland*, Stair Society, Edinburgh.

Wilson, C. (1997), *An Exploratory Study of the Impact of Intensive Probation on the Lives of Young Offenders*, unpublished MSW dissertation, University of Dundee.

Wilson, J.Q. and Kelling, G.L. (1982), 'Broken Windows: The Police and Neighbourhood Safety', *Atlantic Monthly*, pp. 29-38.

Wilson, R. (1993), *Supporting Victims in the Criminal Justice System*, Scottish Office Central Research Unit, Edinburgh.

Women's Support Project/Evening Times (1990), *Violence Against Women Survey*, March.

World Health Organisation (1992), *The ICD-10 Classification of Mental and Behavioural Disorders*, World Health Organisation, Geneva.

Worrall, A. (1995), 'Gender, Criminal Justice and Probation', in G. McIvor (ed), *Working With Offenders: Research Highlights in Social Work 26*, Jessica Kingsley, London, pp. 68-83.

Wozniak, E. (1994), 'A Customer Focused Prison Service in Scotland' in A. Duff, R. Marshall, R. Dobash and R.E. Dobash (eds), *Penal Theory and Practice: Tradition and Innovation in Criminal Justice*, Manchester University Press, Manchester, in association with the Fulbright Commission, London.

Wozniak, E. Scrimgeour, P. and Nicholson, L. (1988), *Custodial Remands in Scotland*, The Scottish Office Central Research Unit/SOHHD Criminal Statistics Unit, Edinburgh.

Youell, J. (1991), *Assessment and Monitoring of Safer Cities Schemes: A Guidance Manual for Co-ordinators*, Home Office, London.

Young, M. (1991), *An Inside Job? Policing and Police Culture in Britain*, Clarendon Press, Oxford.

Young, P. (1987), *Punishment, Money and Legal Order*, unpublished PhD thesis, University of Edinburgh.

Young, P. (1989), 'Punishment, Money and a Sense of Justice', in Carlen, P. and Cook, D. (eds), *Paying for Crime*, Open University Press, Milton Keynes, pp. 46-65.

Young, P. (1997), *Crime and Criminal Justice in Scotland*, The Stationery Office, Edinburgh.

Zappala, E. (1997), 'Le procès pénal italien entre système inquisitoire et système accusatoire', *Revue Internationale de Droit Pénal*, vol. 17, pp. 111-120.

Zedner, L. (1994), 'Victims' in M. Maguire, R. Morgan and R. Reiner, *The Oxford Handbook of Criminology*, Clarendon, Oxford, pp. 1207-1240.

Zedner, L. (1997), 'Victims', in M. Maguire, R. Morgan and R. Reiner (eds), *The Oxford Handbook of Criminology*, 2nd edition, Clarendon, Oxford, pp. 577-612.